"Debate about the dating of *Beowulf*] years, and it shows no sign of abating.] control, commitment, and clarity, is tha that can be read as allegories or reflexes of the period beginning with the Viking raids on England in the late tenth century, leading to the Danish conquest in 1016, and, following Cnut's death in 1035, to the emergence of Queen Emma in a role that animates the joint and separate reigns of Harald Harefoot and Harthacnut. To say any more would be to spoil the ride. . . "

Simon Keynes, Elrington and Bosworth Professor of Anglo-Saxon,
University of Cambridge

"Damico makes an elegant and thought-provoking case for *Beowulf* as a political allegory of late Anglo-Saxon England. She weaves a subtle argument for her provocative thesis, and in doing so she illuminates not only the poem but the eleventh-century world of Cnut, Emma, and their offspring, the original audience for *Beowulf* and perhaps its hidden subject."

R. M. Liuzza, University of Toronto

"Although paleographers have always included the early eleventh century in dating the script of the *Beowulf* manuscript, historians and literary scholars have studiously neglected this period in their otherwise wide-ranging theories on the composition of *Beowulf*. Now Helen Damico has bravely ventured forth with the first book-length study of how the historical context of the manuscript might have influenced the making of the epic poem. Thoroughly researched and cogently argued, Damico's revolutionary thesis and supporting documents demand the attention of all serious students of *Beowulf*."

Kevin Kiernan, author of *Beowulf and the Beowulf Manuscript*,
The Thorkelin Transcripts of Beowulf, Electronic Beowulf and Professor
Emeritus, University of Kentucky

"Damico demonstrates that historical allegory need not be a passively reflexive or coyly cryptic mode of poetic invention, but can also serve as an imaginative technique of active political thought and critical analysis."

Craig R. Davis, Professor of English Language & Literature and
Comparative Literature, Smith College

Beowulf
AND THE
GRENDEL-KIN

MEDIEVAL EUROPEAN STUDIES XVI
Patrick W. Conner, Series Editor

OTHER TITLES IN THE SERIES:

Beowulf

and the Grendel-kín

Politics & Poetry in Eleventh-Century England

HELEN DAMICO

MORGANTOWN 2015
WEST VIRGINIA UNIVERSITY PRESS

First edition published 2015 by West Virginia University Press

21 20 19 18 17 16 15   1 2 3 4 5 6 7 8 9

PB   978-1-938228-71-1

EPUB   978-1-938228-72-8

PDF   978-1-938228-73-5

Library of Congress Cataloging-in-Publication Data

Damico, Helen.

  Beowulf and the Grendel-Kin : politics and poetry in eleventh-
    century England / Helen Damico.

      pages cm

  Includes bibliographical references and index.

  ISBN 978-1-938228-71-1 (pbk. : alk. paper) -- ISBN 1-938228-71-5
    (pbk. : alk. paper) -- ISBN 978-1-938228-72-8 (epub) -- ISBN
    1-938228-72-3 (epub) -- ISBN 978-1-938228-73-5 (pdf) -- ISBN
    1-938228-73-1 (pdf)

  1. Beowulf--Criticism, Textual. 2. Politics and literature--
    England--History--To 1500. 3. English poetry--Old English, ca.
    450-1100--History and criticism. 4. Epic poetry, English (Old)--
    History and criticism. 5. Anglo-Saxons--Intellectual life. I. Title.

  PR1586.D36 2014

  829'.3--dc23

                              2014029377

Book and cover design by Than Saffel.

The cover image is a composite assembled from images in the public
domain. The sky was sourced from "The Fens near Ely," by Alan
Parkinson.

Calvin B. Kendall, Catherine E. Karkov, and Linda Ehrsam Voigts

Contents

Preface

Beowulf and the Grendel-kin: Politics and Poetry in Eleventh-Century England
is a literary-textual study of the first two-thirds of *Beowulf* in the political and cultural context of Anglo-Saxon England at mid-eleventh century. I limit the inquiry to that portion of the poem that is the work
of Scribe A, whose hand has the scribal characteristics of the eleventh
century, although the time-range has yet to be determined. To this end,
I examine the major historical events of the first half of the eleventh
century and contend that key Beowulfian passages and characters hold
striking parallels to events and personages represented in the *Anglo-
Saxon Chronicle* and the *Encomium Emmae Reginae* (two of several historical documents discussed) and conclude that an intertextuality may
exist between the Old English vernacular epic extant in Cotton Vitellius
A.xv, the *Chronicle*, and the political history in Latin rhyming prose. I
argue that the *Beowulf*-poet imaginatively reconfigured contemporary
events and political figures into his fictionalized North Germanic imperial world, creating a type of historical allegory, an interplay between
historical reality and the poem's imaginative present, whereby the
events and characters (and at times, setting) of the surface narrative
were so constructed as to contain two levels of meaning, the literal sense
represented in the surface story and a concurrent sense found in the
historical account. As is apparent, my underlying premise rests on the
supposition that vernacular poetic epic rises up from and interacts with
a contemporaneous culture, a supposition held by a number of critics.
My points of argument throughout indicate that an eleventh-century
composition date may be likely for the extant *Beowulf* in British Library,
Cotton Vitellius A.xv.

Although the arguments presented here would be of primary interest to students and scholars of Anglo-Saxon literature, especially of *Beowulf* and heroic poetry, as their focus is riveted on the poem and its composition, they might also pique the interest of scholars and students of Old Norse literature not only because of the similarities in compositional modes inherent in the two literary cultures but because of what must have been a continuous political, economic, and cultural interaction among the medieval states of the northern world. Nor would historians of the early medieval period find the discussion presented herein uninteresting, for my argument throughout the work is founded on the presupposition that in large measure it is facts of history that serve as inspiration for epic invention. Finally, those engaged in the study of powerful and exceptional political women of the early period would find, I think, few more rewarding subjects to ruminate upon than the representations of Ælfgifu of Northampton and Emma of Normandy in history and poetic epic.

Acknowledgments

Portions of the monograph have been presented at a number of scholarly venues, among which have been The Medieval Academy of America; The International Medieval Congress at Kalamazoo; Center for Medieval Studies at the University of Minnesota; Center for Medieval Studies at York, England; The Manchester Center for Anglo-Saxon Studies; The Haskins Society Conference; IAUPE Triennial Conference, Malta; Georgetown University; Fordham University; and a conference at Harvard on The Dating of *Beowulf: A Reassessment*. A portion of Chapter 4 as "*Beowulf*'s Foreign Queen and the Politics of Eleventh-Century England," first appeared in *Intertexts: Studies in Anglo-Saxon Culture Presented to Paul E. Szarmach*, ed. Virginia Blanton and Helene Scheck (ACMRS and Brepols, 2008), and a section of Chapter 2 as "Grendel's Reign of Terror" may be found in *Myths, Legends, and Heroes: Essays on Old Norse and Old English Literature in Honor of John McKinnell*, ed. Daniel Anlezark (Toronto: University of Toronto Press, 2011).

Many voices have gone into the making of this book during the lengthy process of bringing it to its conclusion. My thanks to Theodore M. Andersson, Calvin B. Kendall, Jay Rubenstein, and Craig R. Davis for their comments on portions of the manuscript in its early stages; Kaaren Grimstad, for her review of the Old Norse materials, and John McKinnell, for his incisive comments, especially on Symeon of Durham; Robert L. Schichler for his generosity in sharing his work with me; Michelle Brown and Timothy C. Graham for their guidance in manuscript readings; Leslie A. Donovan for her keen observations and technological expertise; Gary Kuris for his valuable commentary as a non-Anglo-Saxonist; Paul E. Szarmach for including me in the NEH

Seminar on Manuscripts, which permitted my visits to major research libraries in England; and finally to Catherine E. Karkov and Linda Ehrsam Voigts for their unrelenting encouragement.

Others who have my unreserved thanks are Susan Tarcov, for her assistance in editing; Donald Fennema for his assistance in proofing; Susan Ray and Adam Oberlin for their assistance in translating. Finally, I continue to be grateful for the generosity of Elizabeth M. Wertheim and Robert Wertheim (now deceased) for their confidence in my work by twice awarding me the Elizabeth M. Wertheim Endowed Lectureship in English.

In addition, I am indebted to a number of institutions with which I interacted during the time I have been working on this monograph, in particular to the British Library, especially its manuscript division and Angela Clark for enabling me to view Ms. Harley 603; the Parker Library of Corpus Christi College Cambridge and Gill Cannell for her guidance; the Cambridge University Library; the Museé de la Tapisserie de Bayeux, Cité de Bayeux; and the Institute for Historical Research in whose reading rooms I first entertained the possibility of an interrelationship between the events of eleventh-century Anglo-Saxon culture and those in *Beowulf*. At the University of New Mexico, my unceasing thanks go to Randy Morehead and his ILL staff at Zimmerman Library and to Ann Massmann at Special Collections. Others at the University of New Mexico to whom I wish to extend my gratitude are members of the staff of the Department of English for being extraordinarily merciful to an Anglo-Saxonist in their midst. Finally at West Virginia University Press, I extend my thanks to Carrie Mullen, Hilary Attfield, Than Saffel, Jason Gosnell, and Patrick W. Conner for the attention they have given to the publication of this monograph.

INTRODUCTION

From History to Vernacular Epic

This monograph contends with the interplay between history and vernacular epic as it is manifested in *Beowulf*, in particular as it appears in the first two-thirds of the 3,182-line poem that dramatize Beowulf's youthful exploits in Denmark. In this regard, it is a limited examination of the poem, and thus it should be understood that its conclusions, apparent as they may seem, are meant to be provisional as they relate to the entire poem. In the limitations of its inquiry, then, it complements Christine Rauer's recent work on the Beowulfian dragon fight in the last third of the poem and its relation with literary hagiographical sources and analogues.[1] That the *Beowulf*-poet worked in a relational manner, that he freely appropriated legendary, folklorish, mythological, classical, biblical, and now hagiographical materials in the construction of his narrative, is one of his identifying characteristics.[2] The discussion contained in this brief monograph on the first two-thirds of *Beowulf* is directly related to the artful appropriation and adaptation of materials, but the materials in this case are factual sociopolitical events of the poet's time. I propose that in addition to his adroitly extracting stories about the sixth-century Scyldings from a variety of received sources and

---

1. Christine Rauer, *Beowulf and the Dragon: Parallels and Analogues* (Cambridge, UK: D. S. Brewer, 2000).

2. Andy Orchard, *A Critical Companion to Beowulf* (Cambridge, UK: D. S. Brewer, 2003), esp. chaps. 4 and 5.

artfully incorporating them into his epic poem, he also seized upon major historical events that were contemporary within his own culture. The incorporation of timely historical events into the construction of secular vernacular epic reflects the compositional methods practiced by medieval poets of secular vernacular epics in general.[3] In line with his eclectic and allusive style, which one may call his trademark, he used the tools of his trade—compression, substitution, skillful encoding of character—and imaginatively reinterpreted and transformed grave sociopolitical "facts" of history concerning the fall of the Anglo-Danish kingdom of the eleventh century into a sublime ahistorical vernacular epic about the fall of the greatest of the Scandinavian hero-kings.

My argument revolves around several narrative passages that seem to have been arbitrarily inserted into the narrative and that have vexed students of the poem for many years, such as the Cain motif; the *gifstōl* passage, together with its theme of apostasy; the Æschere beheading sequence; Grendel's mere; the fantastic narrative that surrounds Grendel's attacks; Grendel's questionable paternity; the uncanny representation of the shadow-queen, Grendel's mother; and the issues of female sovereignty and legitimacy exemplified in the person of Heorot's illustrious reigning queen, Wealhtheow. Given the skill of the poet and the care he expends on other narrative units, as, for example, his marked orderliness in introducing new characters or thematic set-pieces,[4] it would be somewhat inadvisable to conclude

---

3. Joseph J. Duggan, "Medieval Epic as Popular Historiography: Appropriation of Historical Knowledge in the Vernacular Epic," in *La Littérature historiographique des origines à 1500, Grundriss der romanischen Literaturen des Mittelalters*, ed. Hans Ulrich Gumbrecht et al., vol. 11.1 (Heidelberg: C. Winter, 1986), 285–311; Suzanne Fleischman, "On the Representation of History and Fiction in the Middle Ages," *History and Theory* 23 (1983): 278–310, esp. 281, 291–94, as one of several works on the literary appropriations of historical materials.

4. Orchard, *Companion to Beowulf*, chap. 2 passim; *Klaeber's Beowulf and the Fight at Finnsburg*, ed. R. D. Fulk, Robert E. Bjork, and John D. Niles, with a Foreword by Helen Damico, 4th ed. (Toronto: University of Toronto Press, 2008), lxxix–lxxxvi; hereafter cited as Klaeber, 4th ed.

that these eight segments were inserted without narrative design. For although they might appear arbitrary and disconnected at first, on closer inspection one sees that they all touch upon the struggle for the Scylding throne and the avaricious desire of the Grendel-kin to wrest control of Heorot from its legitimate rulers. The poem is indeed about dynastic succession, about ancestral inheritance. But the poem touches upon more vexing issues than just the struggle for the throne of the sixth-century legendary Scyldings. I propose rather that it may very well concern issues of dynastic inheritance that plagued the Scyldings of the eleventh century as well, if Cnut and his sons were so regarded,[5] issues that would bear immediate relevance to the poet and, possibly, to his select audience.[6]

My examination of these units primarily in the context of two major eleventh-century documents, the *Anglo-Saxon Chronicle* and the *Encomium Emmae Reginae*, has led me to discover interactive resonances between the Beowulfian material and public events and personages that pertain to Cnut's court and that of his sons, thus placing *Beowulf* in the context of eleventh-century Anglo-Danish political history. I posit that entries in English, continental, and Scandinavian historical texts, primarily of the eleventh, twelfth, and thirteenth centuries, recount events that serve as parallels to Beowulfian events and constitute a logical Beowulfian metatext that intertwines with the poem's existing sixth-century historio-legendary narrative. *Beowulf* contains a number of distinctive features in the ordering of events, in images, in location, and in character that suggest that the narrative

---

5. On the designation of Scylding as a dynastic title applied to Cnut, see Roberta Frank, "Skaldic Verse and the Date of *Beowulf*," in *The Dating of Beowulf*, ed. Colin Chase (1981; Toronto: University of Toronto Press, 1997), 123–39, esp. 126–30, often reprinted.

6. No extant evidence specifically points to the poem's circulation orally or in written form; nonetheless, the first and last pages of *Beowulf* in the manuscript show signs of excessive handling as reported by Humfrey Wanley (1705) that would suggest the poem may have been circulated separately from the Nowell codex itself; see Kevin S. Kiernan, "The Legacy of Wiglaf: Saving a Wounded *Beowulf*," in *Beowulf: Basic Readings*, ed. Peter S. Baker (New York: Garland Publishing Inc., 1995), 195–218, esp. 208–9, 217nn55, 56.

core of the first two-thirds of the poem, extant in London, British Library, Cotton Vitellius A.xv, may be a poetic treatment of early- and mid-eleventh-century English political events that plagued the West-Saxon royal court; as such, the first two-thirds of *Beowulf* may be, in large measure, a type of historical allegory in which events and personages allusively resonate in a literary work.

The political events that form the focus of my discussion occur roughly between 1035 and 1041, although I refer to historical events and figures in earlier decades to which they are inextricably tied and which offer causation and clarification of the argument. From the mid-1030s to the accession of Edward the Confessor in 1042, Anglo-Saxon England was politically vulnerable and in turmoil. The event that precipitated the national emergency and polarized the political factions was Cnut's death on 12 November 1035, although pressing issues concerning succession existed prior to that date. The political chaos that ensued culminated in the assassination of the atheling Alfred in 1036 on the orders of his stepbrother, the usurper King Harold Harefoot, and Harold's subsequent decapitation in 1040 as an act of revenge by the legitimate heir, King Harthacnut, upon the latter's accession to the throne. These two events and their cause and consequences, I suggest, may be seen as forming a veiled narrative core that informs the first two-thirds of *Beowulf*. To my knowledge, this discussion represents the first attempt to examine events and characters in *Beowulf* in the context of eleventh-century Anglo-Danish politics, and in so discussing them, I have taken as my guides several invaluable studies that have been produced over the past twenty years, in particular the work of Roberta Frank, Margaret Gelling, Simon Keynes, Andy Orchard, Pauline Stafford, Elizabeth M. Tyler, Elisabeth M. C. van Houts, Ann Williams, and the combined controversial studies on the dating of the poem by David N. Dumville and Kevin S. Kiernan, all of which, at various points of my inquiry, exerted a directive force upon my examination and impelled it forward.

The primary issue that has hindered scholars from investigating what, if any, contemporary political analogues may exist in *Beowulf*, or even from entering into a discussion of the poem as a possible

4   Introduction

eleventh-century document, is, of course, the poem's dating. One of the most recent discussions is that of Michael Lapidge, who argues on paleographic grounds for an archetypal *Beowulf* in set minuscule existing in the "first half of the eighth century."[7] The eleventh-century historical events that I will be discussing as parallels to the extant *Beowulf* of Cotton Vitellius A.xv are far removed from the Lapidge "pre-750" archetypal version of *Beowulf*,[8] or from Robert D. Fulk's version based on a strict metrical and linguistic argument for a composition of not later than around 725 (if the text be Mercian) or after around 825 (if Northumbrian) that itself has not gone unchallenged,[9] or from those of any number of scholars applying a

---

7. Michael Lapidge, "The Archetype of *Beowulf*," *ASE* 29 (2000): 5–41, quote at 35. Lapidge bases his conclusion on the inaccurate transmission of five individual letter pairs by both scribes, which is illustrative of their unfamiliarity with a system of script that had been replaced by Anglo-Saxon Square minuscule at the very beginning of the tenth century (29, 34–36). To explain the early and late West Saxon scribal features found in Cotton Vitellius A.xv, Lapidge posits "at least three stages of transmission" of the archetype (36), to which we have no access– "the early eighth-century archetype; a recopying during the late ninth or early tenth century . . . and the final act of copying which produced Cotton Vitellius A.xv." For objections to Lapidge's argument on the faulty transmission of the letter pairs, see E. G. Stanley, "Paleographical and Textual Deep Waters: <a> for <u> and <u> for <a>, <d> for <ð> and <ð> for <d> in Old English," *ANQ* 15, no. 2 (Spring 2002): 64–72; for both adherents of and dissenters from Lapidge's hypothesis, see most recently Roberta Frank, "A Scandal in Toronto: The Dating of '*Beowulf*' a Quarter Century On," *Speculum* 82 (October 2007): 843–64, esp. 850–54.
8. Lapidge, "Archetype of *Beowulf*," quote at 34.
9. Fulk's arguments for his proposed version of *Beowulf* are primarily found in R. D. Fulk, *A History of Old English Meter* (Philadelphia: University of Pennsylvania Press, 1992), esp. 164–68, 381–92; his "Contraction as a Criterion for Dating Old English Verse," *Journal of English and Germanic Philology* 89 (1990): 1–16 (hereafter *JEGP*); see also his "Dating *Beowulf* to the Viking Age," *Philological Quarterly* 16 (1982): 354–55; and his "On Argumentation in Old English Philology, with Particular Reference to the Editing and Dating of *Beowulf*," *ASE* 32 (2003): 1–26, esp. 9–25. For discussions on linguistic tests as providing inconclusive evidence for dating manuscripts, see Ashley Crandall Amos, *Linguistic Means of Determining the Dates of Old English Literary Texts* (Cambridge, MA: Medieval Academy of America, 1981); Angus F. Cameron, Ashley Crandall Amos, and Gregory Waite et al., "A Reconsideration of the

variety of approaches to a poem that may have been quite different from that which appears in Cotton Vitellius A.xv.[10] The dates of the historical events to be discussed postdate even the late scribal dating of Cotton Vitellius A.xv, proposed by Dumville (on paleographic grounds) as falling between AD 997 and AD 1013 and by Kiernan (on paleographic and codicological grounds) as post-AD 1016.[11] It was thus with some hesitation that I undertook to air my findings. Yet the

---

Language of *Beowulf*," in *Dating of Beowulf*, ed. Chase, 33–75. Voicing strong caution against using metrics as the sole argument for dating a poem found in a unique manuscript is Roy Michael Liuzza, "On the Dating of *Beowulf*," in *Beowulf: Basic Readings*, ed. Baker, 281–302, who offers significant statistical variances on poems for which more than one surviving manuscript exists to support his conclusion. Dissenting from Fulk's adherence to Kaluza's law is B. R. Hutcheson, *Old English Poetic Metre* (Woodbridge, UK: D. S. Brewer, 1995), 90n75, 92–94; and his "Kaluza's Law, the Dating of *Beowulf*, and the Old English Poetic Tradition," *JEGP* 103 (2004): 297–322; Frank, "Scandal in Toronto," 850, 855–58.

10. For other notable arguments voiced on various disciplinary approaches for dates of composition ranging from the eighth to the eleventh centuries, see *Dating of Beowulf*, ed. Chase, passim, and Robert E. Bjork and Anita Obermeier, "Date, Provenance, Author, Audiences," in *A Beowulf Handbook*, ed. Robert E. Bjork and John D. Niles (Lincoln, NE: University of Nebraska Press, 1997), 13–34.

11. David N. Dumville, "*Beowulf* Come Lately: Some Notes on the Paleography of the Nowell Codex," *Archiv für das Studium der neueren Sprachen und Literaturen* 225 (1988): 49–63, esp. 50 and 63, repr. as chap. 7 in his *Britons and Anglo-Saxons in the Early Middle Ages* (Brookfield, VT: Variorum, 1992); and his "The *Beowulf*-Manuscript and How Not to Date It," *Medieval English Studies Newsletter* 39 (December 1998): 21–27, esp. 22; Kevin S. Kiernan, *Beowulf and the Beowulf Manuscript* (New Brunswick, NJ: Rutgers University Press, 1981; rev. ed. Ann Arbor, MI: University of Michigan Press, 1996), xv–xxviii, passim. Kiernan's discussion on the dating goes beyond paleographic and codicological issues to include historical and linguistic arguments; see also his "The Eleventh-Century Origin of *Beowulf* and the *Beowulf* Manuscript," in *Dating of Beowulf*, ed. Chase, 9–21, repr. in *Anglo-Saxon Manuscripts: Basic Readings*, ed. Mary P. Richards (New York: Garland Publishing Inc., 1994), 277–99; and "Legacy of Wiglaf: Saving a Wounded *Beowulf*," in *Beowulf: Basic Readings*, ed. Baker, 195–218. Both Dumville and Kiernan adhere to Neil Ker's dating of the manuscript (975 to 1025), which Kiernan characterizes as a conservative interpretation of his dating notation; for a summary of their positions, see Orchard, *Companion to Beowulf*, 19–22.

historical parallels that are the concern of this monograph seemed too compelling to dismiss, even in face of the equally compelling paleographic and linguistic arguments around which there has been continuous debate[12] and aspects of which will continue to engage discussion. For even within Dumville's and Kiernan's larger disagreements concerning concurrent scribal stints or the exact meaning of Neil Ker's dating formulation "s.X/XI," there are points of agreement that do not negate my thesis—that the hands of Scribe A and Scribe B are "disharmonious" (Dumville's phrase), that the manuscript was produced in a lesser scriptorium, and that the hand of Scribe A is clearly eleventh-century Anglo-Carolingian and later than that of Scribe B,[13] although the date-range within the century has not been established. The Beowulfian units I will be discussing—for example, the beheading sequence (1232-1650) which is central to my argument and the subject of chapter 1—lie solidly within the province of Scribe A's stint (lines 1-1939).[14] This observation, of course, does not minimize the paleographic or metrical complexities of dating *Beowulf*; it does, however, make it possible to place both the political events

12. Precise dating of Anglo-Saxon scribal hands in the first half of the eleventh century is one such possibly unresolvable problematic area. Ker speaks to the "impossibility" of dating OE scribal hands from "990 to 1040" because of the extreme variety and differences in imitative hands using the emerging Carolingian script; cited in *The Will of Æthelgifu: A Tenth-Century Anglo-Saxon Manuscript*, trans. Dorothy Whitelock (Oxford: Oxford University Press, 1968), 45–46 (first noted and discussed by Kiernan, *Beowulf and the Beowulf Manuscript*, rev. ed., "Re-Visions," xix); see Helen McKee, "Script, Anglo-Saxon," in *The Blackwell Encyclopaedia of Anglo-Saxon England*, ed. Michael Lapidge, John Blair, Simon Keynes, and Donald Scragg (Oxford: Blackwell, 2001), 409–10, for comments on the rise of the Anglo-Saxon Carolingian script from 960 onward, especially in lesser scriptoria wherein both the square minuscule and the newer Anglo-Carolingian script were being used and where there would be limited access to manuscripts used as scribal guides. Apparently, there are no examples in tenth-century manuscripts of the Caroline minuscule characteristics found in Scribe A's hand.

13. Dumville, "*Beowulf* Come Lately," 55–56; Kiernan, *Beowulf and the Beowulf Manuscript*, rev. ed., "Re-Visions," esp. xvii–xxi.

14. I am grateful to Professor Dumville for discussing the dating complexities with me and directing my attention to this point.

under discussion and Scribe A of *Beowulf* within a reasonable his-torical proximity, and thus offers an opportunity to discuss a literary, textual argument for an eleventh-century *Beowulf*.

From a literary-cultural perspective, an eleventh-century context is not incompatible with a syncretic and hegemonic poem like *Beowulf*, whose narrative reflects a shared Anglo-Danish cultural and literary tradition that exudes values consonant with Germanic and Christian idealism, in a society that for some nineteen years had been under the rule of a Danish king. Roberta Frank and Matthew Townend have already provided such a societal framework, although neither critic locates the poem in Cnut's reign or that of his sons.[15] What they do lay out is an eleventh-century cultural and literary milieu in which a poem like the *Beowulf* recorded in BL, Cotton Vitellius A.xv could have been composed as an appropriate presentation for an eleventh-century audience. Frank and Townend focus on a sig-nificant group of extant skaldic verse, which Townend collects under the name *Knútsdrápur* and which, Frank observes, shows the "casual use" of "Old English words, idioms and syntax, as if the skalds were composing for a Norse-speaking community enisled in a sea of Anglophones."[16] In essence the *Knútsdrápur* are political poems (as is most skaldic verse), extolling the battle prowess and the rise to imperial status of Cnut. Except for two early poems whose geo-graphical center is London (1016–23), the majority of the verse was composed between 1026 and 1029[17] and performed for a mixed court

---

15. Roberta Frank, "King Cnut in the Verse of His Skalds," in *The Reign of Cnut: King of England, Denmark and Norway*, ed. Alexander R. Rumble, Studies in the Early History of Britain (London and New York: Leicester University Press, 1994), 106–24; Matthew Townend, "Contextualizing the *Knútsdrápur*: Skaldic Praise-Poetry at the Court of Cnut," *ASE* 30 (2001): 145–79; on Frank's arguments, see further note 20 below.

16. Frank, "King Cnut in the Verse of His Skalds," 108, cites linguistic evidence ("Anglicisms" in skaldic verse) collected by Dietrich Hofmann in *Nordisch-englische Lehnbeziehungen der Wikingerzeit*, Bibliotheca Arnamagnæana 14 (Copenhagen: E. Munksgaard, 1955), 59–101.

17. Dating skaldic verse is a slippery and complex matter, and Townend metic-ulously argues for the individual dating of the poems, which I follow here;

audience of politically minded Anglo-Danish earls and ecclesiastics.[18] Townend further argues for Winchester as the precise location, which by 1030 had become a multilingual imperial capital accommodating the needs and aspirations of Danish and Anglo-Saxon aristocratic interests.[19] Although Townend's study centers specifically on skaldic poetry and does not address *Beowulf* or its composition directly, he provides a cultural landscape that would have been compatible with the values expressed in the poem.

From a literary perspective, Frank cleared the path for a consideration of *Beowulf* in a contemporary multilingual cultural context over twenty years ago with a pair of essays—"Skaldic Verse and the Date of *Beowulf*" and "The *Beowulf* Poet's Sense of History"[20]—that poised the poem's *terminus a quo* at mid-to-late tenth century but did not argue for the poem's *terminus ad quem*, except by noting the conventional century mark of the manuscript.[21] Yet, it seems to me that Frank's aim in these and subsequent essays has been to argue incisively for compatibility among the compositional techniques employed by the poet and the skalds, the poem's cultural syncretism, and the multilingual Anglo-Danish society that produced it. In "Skaldic Verse and

---

"Contextualizing the *Knútsdrápur*," 151–62, and his citations therein.

18. Frank, "King Cnut in the Verse of His Skalds," 107–10; Townend, "Contextualizing the *Knútsdrápur*," 164–68; Simon Keynes, "Cnut's Earls," in *Reign of Cnut*, ed. Rumble, 43–88, discusses thirteen Danish and nine English earls.

19. Townend, "Contextualizing the *Knútsdrápur*," 167–73, 175. To this equation might be added the need to satisfy Queen Emma's Norman interests. See also Townend's "Viking Age England as a Bilingual Society," in *Cultures in Contact: Scandinavian Settlement in England in the Ninth and Tenth Centuries*, ed. D. M. Hadley and J. D. Richards, Studies in the Early Middle Ages 2 (Turnhout: Brepols, 2000), 89–105.

20. Roberta Frank, "The *Beowulf* Poet's Sense of History," in *The Wisdom of Poetry: Essays in Early English Literature in Honor of Morton W. Bloomfield*, ed. Larry D. Benson and Siegfried Wenzel (Kalamazoo, MI: Medieval Institute Publications, 1982), 53–65; Frank, "Skaldic Verse and the Date of *Beowulf*, " 123–39; the composition of skaldic verse apparently began around the early tenth century.

21. Frank, "Skaldic Verse and the Date of *Beowulf*," 123.

the Date of *Beowulf*," Frank offered countless examples of a "casual use" of Norse terms, word order and verse patterns, narrative motifs, and generic conventions by the *Beowulf*-poet that bore close similarities to the compositional process and "Anglicisms" employed by eleventh-century skalds noted in her recent essay, a considerable number of whom worked between 1026 and 1029 and in Cnut's court.[22] The argument of these early essays, then, stabilized the composition of the poem's *terminus a quo* as far forward as the latter part of the tenth century, after the ages of Bede, Aldhelm, Alcuin, and Alfred, whose societal structures and literary compositional strategies failed to reflect the Anglo-Danish hybridity in ecclesiastical, governmental, and literary matters that would be compatible with the poem's syncretism. For Frank, such a societal construct could not have occurred before the second half of the tenth century after Æthelstan's reign:[23] by then, Danes and Anglo-Saxons pointed to a common ancestral line, the *Scaldingi* (ON *Skjǫldingar*, OE *Scyldinga*), the Beowulfian Scyldings; second- and third-generation Danes were established in ecclesiastic and political offices, suggesting that the reconciliation of Danish and English interests was in place; and the secular heroic epic, in the context of continental literatures, was gaining prominence.[24] In the context of Dumville's and Kiernan's discussions, which in the

---

22. Frank, "Skaldic Verse and the Date of *Beowulf*," 124–37; quotes are from her "King Cnut in the Verse of His Skalds," 108.

23. But see Craig R. Davis "An Ethnic Dating of *Beowulf*," *ASE* 35 (2006): 111–29, who argues for an Alfredian-age *Beowulf*, ca. 890, after the settlement of the Danelaw, when the roots of a cultural hybridity were being established and celebrated in the West Saxon court of King Alfred based on Alfred's lineage with the Geats through his mother.

24. Frank, "*Beowulf* Poet's Sense of History," 57–58, 60–61, 63–64; esp. 60, where she compares the compositional process of the secular heroic epic of Widukind, monk of Corvey and historian of the continental Saxons, in the writing of his secular heroic epic (ca. 967), with that of the *Beowulf*-poet. For a discussion on the compositional styles of Widukind and Dudo, see Lars Boje Mortensen, "Stylistic Choice in a Reborn Genre: The National Histories of Widukind of Corvey and Dudo of St. Quentin," *Dudone di San Quintino*, ed. Paolo Gatti (Trento: Università degli studi di Trento, 1995), 77–102, as for one example, on narrative technique as a series of episodes (89–90).

course of two decades have brought the manuscript dating forward into the eleventh century, it might be profitable to look again at those early studies and revisit Frank's particular arguments for a shared literary compositional tradition between the Nordic and Anglo-Saxon poetry, which, it seems to me, allow for positing an eleventh-century contextualization of the composition of *Beowulf*, especially in light of Townend's and her recent work on skaldic poetry discussed above.

In "Skaldic Verse and the Date of *Beowulf*," Frank not only addressed cultural issues that had been viewed as stumbling blocks to what she considered a late dating of the poem (that is post-Bedean, post-eighth century),[25] but also cited examples of comparable compositional techniques used by the *Beowulf*-poet and the skalds. She pointed to formulaic verbal similarities between *Beowulf* and the first and second Helgi poems, for instance, which deal with the affairs of the Scylding kings, the first of which is dated provisionally between 1020 and 1046.[26] In addition, she found numerous instances of technical

---

25. She offers evidence, for example, that the Geats (ON *Gautar*) were referred to as a people into the eleventh century (126), and a chronological history of the term *Scylding* (ON *Skjǫldung*), which in the eleventh century was associated with Cnut in a "precise way"; Frank, "Skaldic Verse and the Date of *Beowulf*," 125–29.

26. Dating the Helgi poems is a difficult task. In any event, there are similarities in the rhetorical framework and formulaic verse patterns between the speeches of Sigrún in *Helgakviða Hundingsbana I* (provisionally dated between 1020 and 1046, and conjecturally attributed to a royal skald) and those of Wealhtheow in *Beowulf*, with identical terminology in one instance (e.g., *HHI* 55.1, 56.3; *Bwf* 1217, 1225; *HHI* 55.1, 55.2, 56.3; *Bwf* 1216, 1217, 1218), in addition to the paired *glaðir Ylfingar/glæde Scyldingas* (*HHI* 49; *Bwf* 58); the formulaic construction likewise appears twice as *niðr Ylfinga* in *Helgakviða Hundingsbana II* (8, 48). *HHII* (which antedates *HHI*, with no agreed-upon precise dating) holds an additional pair of appellatives with *Beowulf*: *dís Skjǫldunga/ides Scyldinga* (*HHII* 51; *Bwf* 1168; see also *Brot af Sigurðarkviðu*, 14); Frank, "Skaldic Verse and the Date of *Beowulf*," esp. 124n7, 132; for dating of the Helgi poems, see Joseph Harris, "Eddic Poetry as Oral Poetry: The Evidence of Parallel Passages in the Helgi Poems for Questions of Composition and Performance," in *Edda: A Collection of Essays*, ed. Robert J. Glendinning and Haraldur Bessason, Icelandic Studies 4 (Winnipeg: University of Manitoba Press, 1983), 210–42; his essay "Eddic Poetry," in *Old Norse-Icelandic Literature: A Critical Guide*, ed. Carol J. Clover and

vocabulary, idioms, and terms appearing in *Beowulf* that held a particular Norse meaning.[27] Frank's argument extended to include Beowulfian imitations of Old Norse word order and verse patterns, and refashionings of mythological motifs and genres.[28] Finally, the *Beowulf*-poet's mode of thought, she suggested, his rhetorical style and metaphorical allusions, and his attention to court etiquette

John Lindow (Ithaca, NY: Cornell University Press, 1985), 68–156, esp. 77–78, 123–24; and his entry in the *Dictionary of the Middle Ages*, ed. Joseph Strayer, vol. 4 (New York: Scribner, 1984), 385–392; Jan de Vries's discussion in *Altnordische Literaturgeschichte* in Hermann Paul's *Grundriss der germanischen Philologie*, vol. 15.1 (Berlin: Walter de Gruyter & Co., 1941–42), 303–17, esp. 304, 309; Sophus Bugge, *Helge-Digtene I den Ælder Edda, Deres Hjem og Forbindelser*, translated into English by W. H. Schofield as *The Home of the Eddic Poems: with especial reference to the Helgi-Lays* (London: D. Nutt, 1899), esp. 2, 6–8, 48, 202, 205; and Helen Damico, *Beowulf's Wealhtheow and the Valkyrie Tradition* (Madison, WI: University of Wisconsin Press, 1984), esp. 87–98, 217–18 nn. 1–7.

27. In particular, *lofgeornost* (ON *lofgjarn*), "most eager for fame," appears only in *Beowulf* with the ON meaning; OE *missan*, "to miss the mark" (ON *missa*), unique to *Beowulf* in OE; *þeodcyning* (ON *þjóðkonungr*), a poetic term in OE and reserved only for Hrothgar, Ongentheow, and Beowulf, first appears in ON in *Ynglingasaga* (ca. 900) and "does not occur again" until the skaldic poems produced between 1014 and 1040, referring to Cnut, Olaf, and Magnus; and the idiom *hafelan hýdan*, "to hide one's head," with the sense of to "bury one's head," has its counterpart in ON *hylja hǫfuð*, from a mid-eleventh-century skaldic poem on the death of King Magnus the Good; for these and other terms, see Frank, "Skaldic Verse and the Date of *Beowulf*," 130, 132, 135, 136; for a recent discussion of Old English poetic terms and their Norse counterparts, see her "Terminally Hip and Incredibly Cool: Carol, Vikings, and Anglo-Scandinavian England," *Remakes: A Symposium in Honor of Carol J. Clover, Representations* 100 (Fall 2007): 23–33, esp. 26, 28–30.

28. Frank ("Skaldic Verse and the Date of *Beowulf*") speaks particularly of recasting Beowulf as an "anti-Odinic, anti-Volsung" hero and of incorporating the Baldr myth into the fratricide at Hrethel's court (131–32); of corresponding verse patterns and diction between the Helgi poems of the Edda (132) and *Beowulf*; of the manipulation of the Old Norse flyting, with word-for-word parallels with the first Helgi poem (133); and cites similarities between skaldic memorial poems, *erfidrápur* (composed between 900 and 1076), and the last forty-six lines of *Beowulf*, where the "combination of personal lament, public eulogy, and prophecy of impending catastrophe joined with praise of a hero's deeds and goodness" is a "pattern of consolation . . . not easily paralleled" (134).

and protocol resembled those found in Old Norse skaldic poetry, pointing to Sighvatr Þórðarson's praise poems as an example.[29] The *Beowulf*-poet's Nordic stylistic appropriations were such that Frank concluded:

> When the Old English poet inverts the character of a traditional Norse hero, changes the outcome of traditional Norse incidents, and modifies the ending of a traditional Norse memorial genre, all the while garnishing his epic with Norse names, colour, and decorative motifs, it is easy to imagine that he was composing not long after, or far from the Danish skalds he was outdoing.[30]

Sighvatr Þórðarson was an Icelandic poet of the eleventh century, born around its beginning and dying around 1043. Court poet to Saint Óláfr, Cnut's great rival, Sighvatr was a habitual traveler who recorded his journeys in his poems. In one of these, *Vestrfararvísur* (Western Journeys), Sighvatr describes a diplomatic mission to Cnut's court, a moment of which is translated by Frank as an example of one of several parallel attitudes regarding court protocol between skaldic verse and *Beowulf*—"I had to inquire outside the door of the hall before I could get a word with the lord of the Jutes; I saw the house barred before me"—verses that are reminiscent of Beowulf's exchange with Wulfgar upon his arrival at Heorot (*Bwf* 331ᵇ–47).[31] For Frank, the type of societal syncretism that marked the poem would also mark the culture that produced it.

The compositional method described by Frank and used by the *Beowulf*-poet is reflective of venerable rhetorical techniques used by poets in reconstructing materials from myth, legend, or history into new works, oral or written, that hold contemporary meaning. The

---

29. Frank, "Skaldic Verse," 136–37.

30. Frank, "Skaldic Verse," 138.

31. Frank, "Skaldic Verse," 136–37, quote at 137; for a summary of Sighvatr's life and career, see Russell Poole's entry on the skald in *Medieval Scandinavia: An Encyclopedia*, ed. Phillip Pulsiano, Kirsten Wolf, Paul Acker, Donald K. Fry (New York: Garland Publishing Inc., 1993), 580, which dates *Vestrfararvísur* ca. 1025–26; and Townend, "Contextualizing the *Knútsdrápur*," 173, who cites this verse in his discussion of Sighvatr's visit to Cnut's court about 1027.

prime function of a secular vernacular epic is to commemorate and celebrate the ancestral past and to glorify it by dramatizing those values that exemplify the race in concrete examples for the edification of the present. Commemorative, celebratory, and propagandistic, *Beowulf*, as well as the Old English secular heroic poems *The Battle of Brunanburh* and *The Battle of Maldon*, is exemplary of that function. It was the *Beowulf*-poet's masterful ahistoricity in reconstructing the legendary Danish golden age, so remarkably vivid and "internally consistent," that pointedly distanced the past from the poet's present and led to the "illusion of historical truth . . . being taken for the reality."[32] The poet, Frank concludes, used the tales of the sixth-century ancestral Scyldings as a backdrop to discuss contemporary concerns, a construction of poetic narrative similar to that of Virgil's *Aeneid*.[33] Like Virgil before him, who began with his Augustan "symbol complex" into which he appropriated Odyssean and Iliadic themes,[34] in distancing himself, the *Beowulf*-poet projected "onto the distant past features of the society of [his] own day, consciously and deliberately in order to provide a sense of continuity."[35] Both poets were thus engaged in a type of polysemous narrative whereby the past and the present were meant to be seen as coexistent, leading Frank to conclude: "Virgil's Rome is grounded in an earlier Rome; the *Beowulf*-poet anchors the West Saxon *imperium* in a brilliant North Germanic antiquity."[36]

---

32. Frank, "*Beowulf* Poet's Sense of History," 54.

33. Frank, "*Beowulf* Poet's Sense of History," 64.

34. For a discussion of Virgil's methodology in assimilating old material into the creation of a fresh contemporary work, see Brooks Otis, "The Odyssean Aeneid and the Illiadic Aeneid," in *Virgil: A Collection of Critical Essays*, ed. Steele Commager (Englewood Cliffs, NJ: Prentice-Hall, 1966), 89–106; repr. from the author's *Virgil: A Study in Civilized Poetry* (Oxford: Clarendon Press, 1964).

35. Frank, "*Beowulf* Poet's Sense of History," 64.

36. Frank, "*Beowulf* Poet's Sense of History," 64. The first study on Virgilian influences on *Beowulf* was Klaeber's ("*Aeneis* und *Beowulf*," *Archiv* 126 [1911]: 40–48, 339–59), in part adapted by Tom Burns Haber, *A Comparative Study of the Beowulf and the Aeneid* (1931; New York: Phaeton Press, 1968). Two of several studies of narrative affinities between the *Aeneid* and *Beowulf* are by Theodore M. Andersson, *Early Epic Scenery: Homer, Virgil, and the Medieval Legacy* (Ithaca,

The essays of Frank and Townend complement the critical perspective inherent in my argument in which I posit that events and personages in contemporary culture, woven into and in a sense camouflaged by a narrative of the legendary past, inspired the composition of the first two-thirds of *Beowulf*. If we accept the *Beowulf*-poet's stylistic affinities with the practicing skalds, then the poet's present would fall within historical proximity of the end of Cnut's reign. Both the fictive and the contemporary landscapes appeal to and reflect the traditions and values of a pan-Nordic world that includes the nations of the Scandinavian peninsula and the northern continental borderland. Frank's discussion of the age of the skalds in the early articles, it seems to me, could apply equally and perhaps more directly to the latter part of Cnut's reign and that of his sons; for at last for a significant space of time, some twenty-five years, Danes refrained from invading England, burning and desecrating its land, and mutilating its people. Toward the end of Cnut's reign, there seems to have been a sense of a unification of peoples (if not entirely voluntary) within the compass of the northern world. By 1030, the Danish Cnut, and hence the English, ruled Norway, Denmark, and lower Sweden (the ancestral home of the Geats), with an Anglo-Danish England being the center of their hegemony, a geographical and political spread that calls to mind the compass-point description of the Beowulfian Danes.[37] By 1035, Cnut's sudden death brought the nation at home into turmoil, which would

---

NY: Cornell University Press, 1976), who, after examining the scenic articulation of Beowulf's voyage to Denmark and to Grendel's mere, finds a similar "scenic consciousness" between the two poets that cannot be readily dismissed (quote at 182), and by Alastair Campbell, "The Use in *Beowulf* of Earlier Heroic Verse," in *England before the Conquest: Studies in Primary Sources Presented to Dorothy Whitelock*, ed. Peter Clemoes and Kathleen Hughes (Cambridge, UK: Cambridge University Press, 1971), 283–92, esp. 284–85, who holds that the use in *Beowulf* of the device of the inserted narrative as originally practiced by Homer and Virgil is almost unique; see further Andersson's "Sources and Analogues," in *Beowulf Handbook*, ed. Bjork and Niles, 125–48, esp. 138–41.

37.   On the *Beowulf*-poet's use of the compass-point designations, see Francis P. Magoun, Jr., "Danes, North, South, East, and West, in *Beowulf*," in *Philologica: The Malone Anniversary Studies*, ed. Thomas A. Kirby and Henry Bosley Woolf (Baltimore, MD: Johns Hopkins Press, 1949), 20–24.

suggest that Cnut's reign had not been entirely void of factionalism and political conflict.[38] It is conceivable that an Anglo-Saxon poet might have associated Cnut's empire with the glories of the Danish legendary past, for Cnut's reign, despite its internal conflicts, more than any other cultural period, answers to the poem's "brilliant North Germanic antiquity" and its subsequent fall.

Thus, it seems to me that in addition to the paleographic ambiguities in the manuscript dating of scribal hand A, the poem's social syncretism and its affinity to a skaldic compositional and stylistic mode solicit, rather than dismiss, further discussion of the date of its composition. I thus set aside a pre-AD 1016 date for *Beowulf* in the interest of exploring the possibility that the events noted above might have informed the composition of the extant *Beowulf* of Cotton Vitellius A.xv and that they might reveal a narrative that is contemporary and political, veiled though it may be, and, hence, establish a cultural grounding for the poem's material, opening another avenue for a consideration of the poem's eleventh-century political context.

As dictated by the nature of my argument (at its base comparative), my rhetorical strategy is analogic and falls within the purview of the study of parallels and analogues. There is a speculative element inherent in the study of parallels to literary works, for in the rhetorical reconstitution of a narrative there are a number of allowable substitutions (in the number, status, or fusion of *dramatis personae*, for example, or in the transposition, fragmentation, or compression of scenes).[39] If this methodology seem lax, in the comparative process, nonetheless, it does present an invaluable tool in understanding the

---

38. For a discussion of the fragility of Cnut's reign and its underlying "cultural trauma" as can be discerned from an examination of manuscripts containing homilies and documentary prose of the period, see Elaine Treharne, *Living Through Conquest: The Politics of Early English 1020–1220* (Oxford: Oxford University Press, 2012), esp. chaps. 1–4.

39. See Thomas D. Hill, Introduction, in *Sources of Anglo-Saxon Literary Culture: Volume One*, ed. Frederick M. Biggs, Thomas D. Hill, Paul E. Szarmach, and E. Gordon Whatley (Kalamazoo, MI: Medieval Institute Publications, 2001), xvi–xviii; and Rauer, *Beowulf and the Dragon*, esp. chap. 1, for her definitions of the terms analogue, source, and parallel.

compositional artistry of a poet. The suppression of the licentious Scylding sea-king Helgi, a major figure in the legendary materials, to a single mention in the genealogical passage; the relegation of his son Hrólfr, the greatest of the Scandinavian hero kings, to the status of a bit player; the corresponding heightening of Hroar, a sickly, shadowy figure, slain early in all versions of the legendary materials, into the revered patriarchal figure of Hrothgar, graced with past victory at war and fame in peace; and the creation of Beowulf, the supreme Nordic hero-king, entirely absent from the legendary parallels, are but some of the examples of the poet's compositional manipulation of the Scylding material so that he might bring it into harmony with his metatextual tale of a contemporary people in political turmoil, fighting for survival.[40] Moreover, a characteristic of the *Beowulf*-poet, as Andy Orchard has recently concluded, is his skill in bringing together "disparate traditions" from a variety of mythological, legendary, religious, and secular materials and recasting them into an original work.[41] That a poet of his sensitivity and skill would be affected by and moved to comment upon contemporary political events is not an unreasonable assumption.

My argument that the *Beowulf*-poet reconfigures contemporary factual events and figures into his "North Germanic" world to create a politically potent work does not counter but is illustrative of the poet's compositional process: he breaks apart principles of chronology and place; reshapes character relationships; introduces fictive figures; and encodes character identity. These devices, as Joseph Duggan has demonstrated in his typological study of poetic appropriations of historical elements in the Romance vernacular epic, are time-honored rhetorical alterations by which history was reconstituted as vernacular epic, which he characterizes as "popular historiography."[42] Artful manipulation of historical materials in the

---

40.   For a further discussion of the changes wrought by the *Beowulf*-poet, see Orchard, *Companion to Beowulf*, 105–14.

41.   Orchard, *Companion to Beowulf*, esp. chaps. 4 and 5, quote at 168.

42.   See Duggan, "Medieval Epic as Popular Historiography," 285–311, where he treats the issue of the basic historicity of medieval vernacular epic; see also

composition of narrative is not restricted to the making of vernacular poetic epic.[43] Diana Whaley's discussion of Snorri Sturluson's artistry in restructuring received materials in the Kings' Sagas collected in *Heimskringla* demonstrates the illusory aspect of Snorri's historical works, producing a hybrid form which she aptly characterizes as "imaginative historiography," a form that blends fact (reality) and fiction (myth).[44] Snorri's remolding of factual events into moments in historical narrative is at base the same process used by secular epic poets. Each creates the historical narrative anew. For Whaley, the act of composition itself undermines factual accuracy in that the historian, because he is presenting an individual interpretation of a complex series of historical issues and events, must reconfigure them arbitrarily into a narrative line, employing principles of unity, causality, and embellishment, principles inherent in the creation of imaginative literature.[45] The essential fictionality of an eleventh-century political history is also at the center of two studies by Elizabeth M. Tyler on the *Encomium Emmae Reginae*, a text that is central to my discussion of the intertextuality between contemporary history and *Beowulf*. In her discussion of the relationships among historiography, poetry, and history in eleventh-century England, Tyler demonstrates the Encomiast's (the term by which the author is traditionally

---

Fleischman, "On the Representation of History and Fiction in the Middle Ages," 278–310, esp. 281, 291–94.

43. For arguments on the inherent fictive nature of historical writing, in that it employs rhetorical devices and principles of construction essential to the construction of literature, see Hayden White's collection *Tropics of Discourse: Essays in Cultural Criticism* (Baltimore, MD: Johns Hopkins University Press, 1978), esp. "Interpretation in History," "The Historical Text as Literary Artifact," "Historicism, History, and the Figurative Imagination," and "The Fictions of Factual Representation"; and his Introduction, "The Poetics of History," in his *Metahistory: The Historical Imagination in Nineteenth-Century Europe* (Baltimore, MD: Johns Hopkins University Press, 1973).

44. Diana Whaley, *Heimskringla: An Introduction*, Viking Society for Northern Research 8 (London: University College, 1991), esp. chaps. 5, "Style and Structure," and 6, "From History to Literature?," 83–143, quote at 113.

45. Whaley, *Heimskringla: An Introduction*, 127–29.

identified) appropriation of the *Aeneid* narrative in refashioning his contemporary history and isolates what she characterizes as "markers of fictionality" that come close to moving historical text into the realm of fiction.[46]

Artful manipulation of historical or legendary materials to create a new imaginative work is pointedly illustrated by the *Beowulf*-poet himself when he describes Hrothgar's scop forging a figural relationship between a hero from the legendary past and one from the poem's present as he creates Beowulf's panegyric:

> Hwīlum cyninges þegn,
> guma gilphlæden, gidda gemyndig,
> sē ðe ealfela ealdgesegena
> worn gemunde, word ōþer fand
> sōðe gebunden; secg eft ongan
> sīð Bēowulfes snyttrum styrian,
> ond on spēd wrecan spel gerāde
> wordum wrixlan; wēlhwylc gecwæð,
> þæt hē fram Sigemunde[s] secgan hȳrde
> ellendǣdum, uncūþes fela,
> Wælsinges gewin.
> (*Bwf* 867ᵇ-77ᵃ)[47]

---

46. See Elizabeth M. Tyler, "Fictions of Family: The *Encomium Emmae Reginae* and Virgil's *Aeneid*," *Viator* 36 (2005): 149–79, esp. 155–58, 165; see also her "Talking about History in Eleventh-Century England: The *Encomium Emmae Reginae* and the Court of Harthacnut," *Early Medieval Europe* 13 (2005): 359–83; and her "'The Eyes of the Beholder Were Dazzled': Treasure and Artifice in *Encomium Emmae Reginae*," *Early Medieval Europe* 8 (1999): 247–70, where she comments on the similarities between the *Encomium* and *Beowulf* in the authors' lavish treatments of treasure.

47. Textual reference to and quotations from *Beowulf* are to *Beowulf and the Fight at Finnsburg*, ed. Fr. Klaeber, 3rd ed. (Lexington, MA: D. C. Heath & Co., 1950); hereafter Klaeber, 3rd ed. Unless otherwise noted, all textual references to and quotations from other works in the Anglo-Saxon poetic corpus will rely on the collective edition, *The Anglo-Saxon Poetic Records*, ed. George Philip Krapp and Elliott Van Kirk Dobbie, 6 vols. (New York: Columbia University Press, 1931–53), hereafter cited as *ASPR*.

[At times, a thane of the king, a man laden with speeches, bearing songs in his mind, who could call to mind many, a great many, of the old sagas, devised new words, artfully joined; in turn, the man began to recite [a song about] Beowulf's adventure, and successfully declaim, to interexchange with words, the appropriate tale; he related everything he had heard about Sigemund's valorous deeds, many an unknown struggle of the Wælsing.]

Beowulf's superhuman act of purging Heorot of Grendel's tyranny served as inspiration for the scop's adaptation and elaborate composition of a fresh narrative, in which he conflated Beowulf's heroic acts in present time and space with those of the legendary Sigemund, who likewise battled monstrous beings,[48] and though the plot was not original, it nonetheless served as the vehicle by which Beowulf not only was raised to but surpassed the level of the most striking hero of the Germanic legendary past.

Ideally, of course, not only should an analogic argument present a number of striking similarities in theme and verbal resonances that would identify a text as a reasonable parallel, analogue, or source (and by "text" I also mean historical events and places), but, in addition, there should be a "plausible literary and historical context" shared by the given texts, as I have suggested might exist between the political events to be discussed and Scribe A's portion of *Beowulf*.[49] Finally, and most particularly, the underlying intent of any analogic argument is to demonstrate that the shared narrative provides a coherent explication of the target text[50] that will inform it with new cultural or symbolic significance. My argument is thus text-centered

---

48. See Klaeber, 3rd ed., 159–61, notes to lines 875–900.
49. The phrase is Rauer's, *Beowulf and the Dragon*; see esp. 3–22. For her delineation of terms and workable distinctions between the study of sources, analogues, and parallels (the difference between the last two being a matter of degree), see 3–10, esp. 10.
50. The phrase is Katherine O'Brien O'Keeffe's, in "Source, Method, Theory, Practice: Reading Two Old English Verse Texts," *Bulletin of the John Rylands University Library of Manchester* 76 (1994): 51–73, at 58, cited in Rauer, *Beowulf and the Dragon*, 9.

and conservative: it offers cumulative distinctive features in theme, landscape, character, cultural setting, narrative pattern, and word choice that form correspondences between the contemporary eleventh-century political events of national importance as presented in historical documents and the poetic dramatization and ennoblement of them in *Beowulf*, producing what may be characterized as a type of historical allegory, whereby two parallel narratives, one literal and another veiled, are operative.

Allegory, a "highly oblique and allusive" rhetorical strategy, was a literary phenomenon not uncommonly practiced by Old English authors from Bede to Wulfstan, in genres that ranged from homilies to biblical epics, as Malcolm Godden has discussed.[51] As a compositional vehicle it was fostered by Christian and pagan authors—Augustine, Boethius, and Virgil—whereby parallel narratives, one literal, the other (or others) hidden, were simultaneously present in a work producing multilayered meaning.[52] For Christian authors, it

---

51. Malcolm Godden, "Biblical Literature: The Old Testament," in *The Cambridge Companion to Old English Literature*, ed. Malcolm Godden and Michael Lapidge (Cambridge, UK: Cambridge University Press, 1991), 206–26; see also Michael W. Twomey, "Allegory and Related Symbolism," in *Medieval England: An Encyclopedia*, ed. Paul E. Szarmach, M. Teresa Tavormina, and Joel T. Rosenthal (New York: Garland Publishing Inc., 1998), 22–26; and Alvin A. Lee, "Symbolism and Allegory," in *Beowulf Handbook*, ed. Bjork and Niles, 233–54, who argues for "allegorical tendencies" in the poem (233).

52. For a discussion of works within the allegorical interpretative and compositional tradition, see Jon Whitman, *Allegory: The Dynamics of an Ancient and Medieval Technique* (Oxford: Clarendon Press, 1987), esp. chaps. 1, "The Allegorical Problem," on the tension between obliquity and directness, and 4, "Ages of Renewal: The Early Medieval Period"; for a discussion of key political events in late medieval England and their allegorical treatment in the works of Langland, Gower, Chaucer, Malory, and the *Gawain*-poet, see Ann W. Astell, *Political Allegory in Late Medieval England* (Ithaca, NY: Cornell University Press, 1999). Chap. 1, "The Materia of Allegorical Invention" (23–43), discusses the process of allegorical invention as expressed in the works of classical authors like Augustine, Boethius, and Cicero and later medieval writers. For a discussion of allegory as a figure or trope of poetic expansion and amplification and as characteristically Cynewulfian in its understanding by his audience, see Martin Irvine, "Cynewulf's Use of Psychomachia Allegory: The Latin Sources

was a rhetorical means by which their readers might make "imaginative parallels between moral truths and physical actuality, or between spiritual experience and historical events."[53] Godden speaks of this "multi-valency" as being basic to the Old English *Exodus* poem, as one of many examples in his discussion, whereby the literal narrative—the Hebrews traversing the desert and crossing the Red Sea, for the promised land—is meant to be interpreted on a multiplicity of levels.[54] For Godden, one meaning symbolizes the Christian *viator* myth, the passage through life into the heavenly realm by means of baptism. For Nicholas Howe, the literal narrative has national significance, for it functions as a parallel narrative to the Anglo-Saxon migration, allegorizing and interlocking the Hebraic foundation myth with that of the Anglo-Saxons.[55] Most often associated with Ælfric's and Wulfstan's homilies, historical allegory presupposes a multi-tiered narrative that is reflective of political or historical awareness, the main thrust of Howe's discussion. Ælfric's adaptations of the "historical" texts of the Old Testament, as for example Judith and Maccabees, relate the suffering of the Jews within the context of the political and military turmoil of the early eleventh century, when the recurrent Danish incursions into Anglo-Saxon England laid bare the country and mutilated its people, in a sense effecting an intertextuality between literature and history, between the biblical past and the immediate historical present.[56]

---

of Some 'Interpolated' Passages," in *Allegory, Myth, and Symbol*, ed. Morton W. Bloomfield, Harvard English Studies 9 (Cambridge, MA: Harvard University Press, 1981), 39–62.

53. Godden, "Biblical Literature," 208.

54. Godden, "Biblical Literature," 217–18.

55. Nicholas Howe, *Migration and Mythmaking in Anglo-Saxon England* (New Haven, CT: Yale University Press, 1989), 77–107. Howe discusses the pervasiveness of the biblical tradition in Old English literature, a pervasiveness that is equally evident in *Beowulf*.

56. Godden, "Biblical Literature," 219–25; for a deeper analysis of Ælfric's assimilation of Biblical material with contemporary historical events, see Godden's "Apocalypse and Invasion in Late Anglo-Saxon England," in *From Anglo-Saxon to Early Middle English: Studies Presented to E. G. Stanley*, ed. Malcolm Godden, Douglas Gray, and Terry Hoad (Oxford: Oxford University Press, 1994), 130–62.

In the homilies of Ælfric and Wulfstan, although the figurative relationship was sustained throughout the work, its allegorical meaning was revealed at closure, pointing to the mode of communication by which the author instructed and persuaded his audience to moral action.

But despite its didactic function, historical allegory based on contemporaneous events often does not reveal its hidden meaning, and it is left to the audience to piece together the author's intention in composing the work and to absorb simultaneously the literal and the unstated meanings. The term allegory itself assumes a type of "guarded language" by which ideas were expressed through indirection rather than openly,[57] either because allegory was the author's mode of thought, as in the multilayered *Exodus* narrative referred to above, or because these ideas were dissident and politically sensitive, with a topical social relevance that might lead to severe admonition or censure, both of which, I suspect, being applicable to the *Beowulf*-poet's compositional choices. An illustration of oblique and guarded language in a political arena that is relevant to my argument in the following pages has been put forth by Mary Clayton in her recent analysis of Ælfric's adaptation of the biblical *Esther* into his *Homily on Esther*, dated between 1002 and 1005.[58] As an example of the prevalence of the interplay between history and literature in Anglo-Saxon England, Clayton reads Ælfric's homily as a *speculum reginae*

---

57. See Whitman, *Allegory*, appendix 1, "On the History of the Term 'Allegory,'" 263–68; Astell, *Political Allegory*, 8; and Angus Fletcher, Introduction, *Allegory: The Theory of a Symbolic Mode* (Ithaca, NY: Cornell University Press, 1964); the classic definition ("allegory says one thing and means another") is on 2; see also his discussion of allegory and its relationship to genre, esp. 121–22, 348–59 ("allegory is only a mode of symbolizing," at 358); and Twomey, "Allegory and Related Symbolism," in *Medieval Scandinavia*, ed. Szarmach et al., 22.

58. Mary Clayton, "Ælfric's *Esther*: A *Speculum Reginae*?" in *Text and Gloss: Studies in Insular Language and Literature*, ed. Helen Conrad-O'Brian, Anne-Marie D'Arcy, and John Scattergood (Blackrock, Co. Dublin: Four Courts Press, 1999), 89–101; Clayton follows Peter Clemoes's dating of Ælfric's works in "The Chronology of Ælfric's Works," in *The Anglo-Saxons: Studies in Some Aspects of Their History and Culture Presented to Bruce Dickins*, ed. Peter A. M. Clemoes (London: Bowes & Bowes, 1959), 212–47, esp. 244.

for Queen Emma, Æthelred's newly wed Danish-Norman queen, whereby Ælfric deliberately referenced the queen in "resonances evident to the queen and court."[59] Ælfric omits characters, rearranges and suppresses events, and selects as his narrative focus the Jewish Esther's becoming Ahasuerus's new foreign queen and her counseling the king to refrain from massacring the Jews. Clayton argues convincingly that Ælfric's narrative strategy was allegorical and that the homily carried political resonances that drew correspondences between the Old Testament story of the deliverance of the Jews and the St. Brice's Day massacre of a large number of the Danes in the Danelaw on 13 November 1002, the same year in which a young Emma of Normandy, of Danish-Norman heritage, became Æthelred's queen. In Clayton's view, Ælfric would have been repulsed by such an order exterminating a large mass of people indiscriminately with no apparent provocation, and he would have articulated his disapproval indirectly as he had on previous occasions.[60] Political pressure would have necessitated such indirection. *The Homily on Esther*, she argues, is a veiled condemnation of Æthelred's order and a "mirror" of exemplary queenly behavior for his new queen. Clayton's view presupposes Ælfric's audience, inclusive of the queen herself, to comprise individuals who would be expected to recognize his veiled interplay between the immediate tangible events and his narrative of a heroic Jewish queen, reigning over a foreign court.

Another allegorical treatment of Queen Emma in ancient guise, one that points up her distinctively sensitive and unprecedented powerful role in the issue of succession, occurred at the beginning of Cnut's reign, when her actions became of extreme concern to the Norman duchy and, one would imagine, to the West Saxons;[61] in

---

59. Clayton, "Ælfric's *Esther*," 99.
60. Clayton, "Ælfric's *Esther*," 99. For Ælfric's treatment of Old Testament queens as a means to discuss sociopolitical issues of contemporary queenly authority, see Stacy S. Klein, *Ruling Women: Queenship and Gender in Anglo-Saxon Literature* (South Bend, IN: University of Notre Dame Press, 2006), esp. chaps. 4 and 5.
61. For the less than amiable relations between the Norman ducal house and

consenting to become Cnut's queen, Emma in essence had jeopardized the rights of succession of the Anglo-Norman athelings Edward and Alfred, her offspring by Æthelred. For not only was there the possibility that she would give birth to a new heir sired by Cnut, but Cnut's illegitimate sons with his consort Ælfgifu of Northampton had a right to the throne, even though the Mercian noblewoman continued to be spurned by the Church for what it considered her promiscuous conduct. Thus, soon after being crowned as Cnut's queen, Emma became the target of a barbed admonition in the second of two anonymous Norman Latin allegorical political satires, the first mocking the nature of the relations between Cnut and his unofficial consort.

Described by Elisabeth van Houts as the "queens poems," and more recently entitled by Andrew Galloway the "Rouen Cnut Satires,"[62] the poems were first discussed by Peter Dronke who titled them *Jezabel* and *Semiramis* after their major characters.[63] The poems appear consecutively in a unique manuscript of the late eleventh century, separated only by a scribal rubric, *Explicit liber primus. Incipit secundus* (Here ends the first book. Here begins the second), indicating that they were to be seen as a pair, a supposition which Dronke rejects. For despite their "superficial" resemblance in theme (sexual perversion), form (dialogue), and use of leonine hexameters, *Jezabel*, in Dronke's view, is much inferior to *Semiramis*, and is rather one of the

---

Anglo-Saxon England, see Simon Keynes, "The Æthelings in Normandy," *Anglo-Norman Studies* 13 (1991): 173–205, esp. 175–77, 181–96, and more particularly 185–86, 193–95 (on the possible plan of Duke Robert to invade England on the athelings' behalf).

62.   Elisabeth M.C. van Houts, "A Note on *Jezebel* and *Semiramis*, Two Latin Norman Poems from the Early Eleventh Century," *The Journal of Medieval Latin* 2 (1992): 18–24, at 24; Andrew Galloway, "Word-Play and Political Satire: Solving the Riddle of the Text of *Jezebel*," *Medium Ævum*, 68, no. 2 (1999): 189–208, at 204; Galloway was the first to suggest Jezebel as the allegorized Ælfgifu of Northampton.

63.   Peter Dronke, *Poetic Individuality in the Middle Ages: New Departures in Poetry, 1000-1150*, 2nd ed. (London: University of London, 1986), chap. 3, "Semiramis: The Recreation of Myth," 66–113; line numbers given in the text refer to Dronke's edition contained in this chapter.

"more primitive and monotonous" of misogynistic dialogue poems of the period, a characterization heartily rejected by *Jezebel*'s editor, Jan M. Ziolkowski, as well as by Galloway and van Houts.[64]

For one, the resemblances that do exist between the poems, Ziolkowski extensively argues, are not "merely superficial."[65] Both poems have as their central figures two of the most notorious female monarchs of antiquity, known in the medieval period as idolatrous and sexually wanton, whose powers were such that they reigned as rulers or co-rulers, initiating and executing policy on their own authority. Yet both characters are purposefully delineated to depart from their exegetic and mythographic persona: Jezebel is a more visibly tantalizing sexually depraved figure rather than the tyrannical stock figure found in exegetical writings; Semiramis veers from a historical figure to one that takes on the mythological proportions of Europa.[66]

---

64. Fols. 28r to 32v, in Paris, Bibliothèque Nationale, lat. 8121A; Dronke, *Poetic Individuality*, on the manuscript, 76–78; against coupling the poems and discussion of *Jezabel*, 77–80, esp. 80; on the dating, esp. 83–84; and Jan M. Ziolkowski, ed. *Jezebel: A Norman Latin Poem of the Early Eleventh Century* (New York: P. Lang, 1989), on coupling the poems, 33–37; on the dating, 37–47; van Houts, "*Jezebel* and *Semiramis*," 18–19; Galloway, "Word-Play and Political Satire," esp. 189, 197.

65. Ziolkowski, *Jezebel*, at 33–36, at 34.

66. Other similarities arise, among which are in the poems' use of onomastics; their allusions to classical myth (*Jezebel* 50, *Semiramis* 163) and to classical authors (e.g., Horace, Virgil); and their singular organization, uncommonly found in dialogues, in that both contain brief prologues spoken by male characters with religious associations: in *Semiramis*, a "nineteen-line tirade," excoriating the whore (*meretrix*) Semiramis for succumbing to the advances of a bull and in *Jezebel*, a seven-line affirmation of the rights of the poet to use poetic license, which allows him to create a "horned she-bear . . . through the tongue of poets" (*sub uatum lingua cornuta creabitur ursa*, 7). Ziolkowski further remarks on the likenesses of the poems' male characters: both interlocutors have religious associations (in *Jezebel*, he is an anonymous Christian; in *Semiramis*, he is Tolumpnus, the augur and brother of the lascivious queen), and guard their reputation, while the lustful queens disdain it (*Jezebel*, 52; *Semiramis*, 106, 111), consumed as they are by desire (*Semiramis*, 5, 10; *Jezebel*, 24–26), that of Jezebel being more extreme as she equates her desire to that of animals (*Jezebel*, 72–73, 132, 141). See Ziolkowski, *Jezebel*, chap. 1, "The Figure of Jezebel in the Middle

As do Dronke, van Houts, and Galloway, Ziolkowski agrees that the allegorical "queen" satires probably were written in the first quarter of the eleventh century for a mixed audience of nobility and ecclesiastics in Rouen during the reign of Emma's brother Duke Richard II (996–1026), for two political satires by Warner of Rouen that precede the "queens poems" in the manuscript—the first on *Moriuht* and the second on a runaway monk Franbaldus from Mont St. Michel—are dedicated to Archbishop Robert of Rouen, brother of Duke Richard II and Emma of Normandy, and their mother, the Duchess Gunnor.[67] Further, both *Jezebel* and *Semiramis* resemble *Moriuht* in theme (sexual perversion and bestiality) and in language and style (sexual terminology and onomastic play), as well as in the topicality of their classical and pagan allusion, which would suggest that the "queens poems" and Warner's political satire were composed within the same literary school of dialogue poems.[68] That such a literary tradition may have been active in England as well has been asserted by Michael Lapidge in his examination of Warner's satires and the *Altercatio magistri et discipuli*, a poem in the tradition of medieval dialogic and debate poetry, written and circulated in Æthelwold's school in Winchester.[69] Lapidge finds the similarities

---

Ages," 5–23, esp. 23, 25–26, 34–36, also 66, 80; on Jezebel, Ziolkowski (176n20) cites Louis Ginzberg, *The Legends of the Jews*, trans. Henrietta Szold (Philadelphia: Jewish Publication Society of America, 1937–1966), 4:189, 6:313n51; Dronke, 100–109, esp. 107; on Semiramis, see Irene Samuel, "Semiramis in the Middle Ages: The History of a Legend," *Mediaevalia et Humanistica* 2 (1944): 32–44.

67.   Neither poem is titled in the manuscript, although modern editors refer to Warner's first satire as *Moriuht*. Christopher J. McDonough, ed. *Warner of Rouen, Moriuht: A Norman Latin Poem from the Early Eleventh Century*, Studies and Texts 121 (Toronto: Pontifical Institute of Mediaeval Studies, 1995); description of the manuscript, at 63–65. On the relationship to *Jezebel* and *Semiramis*, and dedication to the archbishop and duchess; McDonough, *Moriuht*, at 66–68, 106–107; Dronke, *Poetic Individuality*, 81–83; van Houts, "Note on *Jezebel* and *Semiramis*," 18–20; Ziolkowski, *Jezebel*, 30–33.

68.   Dronke, *Poetic Individuality*, 81–87 (resemblances between *Semiramis* and *Moriuht* on the themes of sexual perverson and bestiality, 83–84); Ziolkowski, *Jezebel*, 30–33; van Houts, "Note on *Jezebel* and *Semiramis*," 19.

69.   Michael Lapidge, "Three Latin Poems from Æthelwold's School in

among the poems to be "too close to be coincidental," but because they lack "direct and unmistakable verbal reminiscences," he cannot point to the actual nature of the relationship between them, although he affirms the vitality of the tradition in England.[70]

In 1991 and 1992, Elisabeth van Houts approached the "queens poems" from a historian's perspective that shed further light on Dronke's and Ziolkowski's literary analyses of the enigmatic and misogynistic pair of dialogues concerning the sexual proclivities of two ancient queens. In *Jezebel*, Jezebel's outrageous responses to issues of marital duties, as one example, could be understood and appreciated by an audience only if both poet and audience were aware of the wide ideological differences between the Christian precepts on marriage and "pagan and profane" marital customs still in existence in eleventh-century Normandy.[71] Moreover, if the dialogues were meant to be performed, about which van Houts is in agreement with Dronke, they would have more dramatic potency if they were a satiric commentary on contemporary personages and events,[72] rather than imagined occurrences in the lives of ancient queens. Keeping in mind the interrelated sociopolitical mix of Anglo-Saxon, Scandinavian, and Norman cultures that existed in eleventh-century Rouen and the less than amiable relations between the Norman ducal house and Anglo-Saxon England as explicated by Simon Keynes,[73] van Houts

---

Winchester," *ASE* 1 (1972): 85–137. The *Altercatio* is one of three Anglo-Latin poems he edits from MS Cambridge University Library Kk. 5. 34, 71r–80r; on the resemblances between the *Altercatio* and Warner's satires, 101–2.

70. Lapidge, "Three Latin Poems," 102. For interrelated political and cultural interests between Anglo-Saxon England and Normandy, see Lucien Musset, "Rouen et l'Angleterre vers l'an mil: du nouveau sur le satiriste Garnier et l'école littéraire de Rouen au temps de Richard II," *Annales de Normandie* 24 (1974): 287–90; also, Keynes, "Æthelings in Normandy," above n. 61; van Houts, "Note on *Jezebel* and *Semiramis*," 20–23.

71. Elisabeth M. C. van Houts, "A Review of *Jezebel. A Norman Latin Poem of the Early Eleventh Century*, ed. Jan M. Ziolkowski," in *Journal of Medieval Latin* 1 (1991): 204–6, at 205.

72. van Houts, "Note on *Jezebel* and *Semiramis*," 19.

73. Keynes, "Æthelings in Normandy," 173–205, esp. 175–77, 181–96, and more particularly 185–86, 193–95.

posits *Semiramis* as a contemporary satire commenting upon Emma of Normandy's abduction by and subsequent marriage to the Danish Cnut, conqueror and emergent king of England (to be discussed in chapter 4), whom the poem refers to as a "bull" and "horned adulterer" (the reference being to his irregular alliance with Ælfgifu of Northampton), and to whose advances she succumbs.[74] Ziolkowski likewise points to the idiosyncratic phrasal and word choice in *Jezebel* and *Semiramis* in the use of the

> adjective *cornutus,-a, -um*: compare "Sub uatum lingua cornuta creabitur ursa" (*Jezebel* 7 "a horned she-bear will be created through the power of poets") with "cornutus adulter" (*Semiramis* 102 "a horned adulterer") and "Cum fabricaretur cornutus de bove moechus" (*Semiramis* 107 "when out of a bull a horned adulterer was made").[75]

One might say that these were less than salutary allusions either to Cnut, his illegitimate consort, or his newly consecrated queen.

Van Houts's argument is based on several resemblances she finds between circumstances in the dialogue and historical fact: the "horned adulterer" refers to Cnut's existent irregular alliance with the pagan Ælfgifu of Northampton, despite his marriage to the Anglo-Norman queen; Semiramis's death alludes to Emma's symbolic death to the court of Rouen, as a result of her having abandoned her children—the heirs to the throne of England and the nephews of the Rouen royal house—for the embraces of Cnut. Markedly, van Houts finds parallels between the sites of the queens' submissions, associating London with Babylon,[76] and between Cnut and the image of an

---

74. *Semiramis*, line 1: *Fama puellaris tauri corrumpitur extis* (A woman's honour was stained by the loins of a bull [Dronke, *Poetic Individuality*, 66, 71]), and elsewhere; *cornuto, cornutus* adulter, *Cum fabricaretur cornutus de bove moechus* (when out of a bull a horned adulterer was made [*Semiramis*, lines 99, 102, at 107, etc.; Dronke, *Poetic Individuality*, 68, 69, 73, 74]).

75. Ziolkowski, *Jezebel*, 35; see also Galloway, "Word Play and Political Satire," 203.

76. *Prodiit a Babilon talis confusio stupri* (such lewd disorder spread from Babylon, [*Semiramis*, line 11; Dronke, 66, 71]); *Femina que Babilon cepit se sub bove*

aroused bull and Jupiter, the first instance of a comparison that, van Houts argues, may have been taken up some twenty years later by the Encomiast[77] in his description of Cnut's invasion of England:

> Nam quis contrariorum leones auri fulgore terribiles, quis metallinos homines aureo fronte minaces, quis dracones obrizo ardentes, quis tauros radiantibus auro cornibus necem intentantes in puppibus aspiceret, et nullo metu regem tantae copiae formidaret?[78]

> [For who could look upon the lions of the foe, terrible with the brightness of gold, who upon the men of metal, menacing with golden face, who upon the dragons burning with pure gold, who upon the bulls on the ships threatening death, their horns shining with gold, without feeling any fear of the king of such a force?]

Later, once Cnut was an *"imperator"* in control of five kingdoms in the North (England, Wales, Scotland, Norway, and Denmark), and once he had fashioned himself as a preeminent Christian ruler, the Encomiast compares him to Caesar and Jupiter by quoting a pseudo-Virgilian phrase: *"Nocte pluit tota, redeunt spectacular ma(ne); / Diuisum imperium cum Ioue Cesar habes"* (It rains all night, but the public games duly take place in the morning; / You, Caesar, hold divided empire with Jove (*EER* iii.10).[79] These and other similarities between the sociopolitical events of the day and the fictional adaptation of them by the poet lead van Houts to propose *Semiramis* "as a contemporary satire ridiculing Emma's relation with King Cnut" in the politically

---

stravit (the woman who took Babylon has submitted to the bull [*Semiramis*, line 16; Dronke, 66, 71]).

77. van Houts, "Note on *Jezebel* and *Semiramis*," 20–22.

78. *Encomium Emmae Reginae*, ed. and trans. Alistair Campbell, with a supplementary introduction by Simon Keynes, Camden Classical Reprints 4 (Cambridge, UK: Cambridge University Press, 1998), 20–21; hereafter cited as *EER*, ii.11. Van Houts likewise points to the metalic animals that decorate Sveinn's ships in his prior invasion (*EER*, i.5, pp. 12–13): . . .*atque illinc tauros erectis sursum collis protensisque cruribus mugitus cursusque uiuentium simulantes* (there bulls with necks raised high and legs outstretched were fashioned leaping and roaring like live ones).

79. van Houts, "Note on *Jezebel* and *Semiramis*," 22.

troubled final years of the second decade of the eleventh century.[80] As does Ziolkowski, then, Van Houts sees the "queens poems" as closely related satires, but unlike him (and Dronke, in this matter), she claims that the "queens poems" have as their source the actions of contemporary women, although she has been unable to discover a Norman noblewoman who would answer to and be the butt of the audacious irreverent tart represented in *Jezebel*.[81]

In agreement with van Houts that allegorical satire must be placed within a contemporary social context to achieve its desired end of making laughable the defects of the personages being represented, in 1999, Andrew Galloway put forth a dense literary argument upholding van Houts's position that *Semiramis* was a political allegory satirically commenting upon Emma's union with Cnut by positing a thematic unity between the queens poems: both poems, he argued, were to be viewed as a unified "mordant political satire"[82] concerning the "wives" of Cnut. Thus, as Part I, the poem *Jezebel* is an allegorical rendering of the character and acts of Cnut's impenitent pagan and sexually perverse concubine, Ælfgifu of Northampton. In essence, Galloway's argument rests (1) on his conjectural emendations of the last three lines in *Jezebel*'s seven-line prologue which differ from the emendations offered by Ziolkowski but which produce a telling unity between the two poems and (2) on his identifying the hermeneutic pattern of the prologue as that of the "graphic riddles" which are meant "to scrutinize language for the secret additional meanings that its separate parts might yield" (190, 195). It is a pattern Galloway sees operative in Warner of Rouen's onomastic riddling in *Moriuht* to introduce his central character in the first of two political satires that precede *Jezebel* in the manuscript (196). This predilection for name-play, for uncovering what hidden information the name might yield, likewise appears in *Semiramis*, especially in the reference to Cnut as a *cornutus adulter* (a horned adulterer). Galloway finds the same

---

80. van Houts, "Note on *Jezebel* and *Semiramis*," 20, 23.
81. van Houts, "Note on *Jezebel* and *Semiramis*," 23–24.
82. Galloway, "Word-Play and Political Satire," 190.

type of onomastic word-play being employed by the *Jezebel* poet in two particular instances: in his interpretation of Jezebel's name in the opening line of the prologue as embodying Jezebel's luxuriant display of unrepentant promiscuity throughout the poem, and in his conjectural emendation of lines five through seven of the prologue where, he argues, by means of logographic and multilingual punning on Cnut's name, the newly crowned Danish king is unveiled as he who has horned the two queens[83]:

> Laus est < *Cnutoni* > sub mobilitate trochei:
> Pi<c>torum digiti cornu fecere rudenti.
> Sub surmise lingua cornuta creabitur ursa.
> (Acclamation is Cnut's—subject to the transformation of a tro-
>   chee: / the painter's
> fingers have made a horn [*cornu*] for a rope [i.e. a knot, ON,
>   *knútr*] / Under the
> tongue of poets a she bear will be made horned [Cnuted]. (*Jeze-*
>   *bel* 203)

Suspecting that *cornu* and *cornuta* may be playing on a link with a form of Cnut's name that would "metrically fit" and rhyme in the "leonine manner" with a trochee, Galloway surveys all the possible attested forms of the name in Latin, Danish, Old Norse, Norman, and Old English, arriving at a "dative of possession of 'Cnuto,'" Cnutoni. The "acclamation" that is Cnut's, Galloway argues, is a further pun on Cnut's having been "*coronatus*, crowned, as new king of England," and the means by which he gained his accession to the throne, first by means of the Mercian concubine and second by the Anglo-Norman queen, both of whom were essential to his political hold over England.

An issue as crucial as a contested national succession would necessarily be of intense interest to the cosmopolitan political and ecclesiastical courts of Rouen and one might venture to say to those of

---

83. Galloway, "Word-Play and Political Satire," 198–203.

Introduction

England as well, which would not have looked kindly on having a Norman-Danish king on the English throne instead of the descendants of Cerdic and Alfred. Still, there is no evidence that the "queens poems" circulated in the courts of England at the end of the second quarter of the eleventh century, even though Lapidge's studies affirm the vitality of the literary tradition in England as well as Normandy. It would not be unreasonable to surmise, however, that the cosmopolitan sociopolitical and multilingual culture existing in England discussed above by Frank and Townend, like that of Rouen, would be capable of understanding the obscure word-play and allusions found in political allegorical satires—especially those related to contemporary events of national importance—as well as they could comprehend allegorical treatments of momentous biblical events.

There is critical consensus that the *Beowulf*-poet episodically uses allegorical strategy throughout the narrative, especially in his rendering of Grendel, who symbolizes the primeval demon in strife with God and who typifies the fratricidal Cain. In the early 1970s, however, Margaret E. Goldsmith argued for a pervasive view of *Beowulf* as a Christian allegory, a work entirely informed by theological and doctrinal ideology. Viewed from Goldsmith's vantage point, the *Beowulf*-poet becomes a type of moralist-seer in his presentation of "a microcosm of the story of carnal man," with Beowulf as the exemplification of the sinner, a conclusion not wholly justifiable textually.[84] Some ten years later, as a response to Goldsmith, David Williams's *Cain and Beowulf: A Study in Secular Allegory* likewise found the poet working allegorically, but not within the strict doctrinal and theological tradition Goldsmith proposed. Although agreeing with Goldsmith that the poet's intent was ideological and didactic, Williams argued that

---

84. Margaret E. Goldsmith, *The Mode and Meaning of 'Beowulf'* (London: Athlone, 1970), 245–68, passim; despite the narrowness of its approach that is contrary to the text and its apparent disregard of the poem as imaginative literature driven by narrative exigencies, Goldsmith's work still holds much value in presenting an abundance of theological and patristic material as part of the intellectual background to *Beowulf*, an approach that continues to be important to the study of the poem.

his rhetorical strategy was rather closer to the typical two-type literary adaptation favored by medieval authors who worked within the literal and symbolic dimensions.[85] Using the exegetical and biblical tradition of Cain as revealed in medieval thought, Williams argued for the Cain metaphor as controlling the entire poem inclusive of the dragon episode, even though he pointedly refrained from addressing the fact that explicit references to Cain are character-specific to Grendel and his mother and end abruptly with the *healðegn*'s (hall-thane) decapitation (*Bwf* 1599). For Williams, an allegorical key to Christian exegesis drives the narrative; thus, his work did not wholly serve as a corrective to Goldsmith, as was his intention. For both Goldsmith and Williams, the foundation of the poem was its ideological stance, doctrinal and exegetical religiosity, a view that, it seems to me, jars not only with the poem's genre as a vernacular heroic epic but with its inherent theatricality, its unnerving discontinuous and deflective narrative, and its blatant secular and martial concerns. Even such elements as its gnomic passages, Hrothgar's "sermon," Beowulf's alleged "confessional" ruminations on his life, and the messenger's doom-laden final address betray a consonance with artistic idioms of performance; and although their concerns offer glimpses of Christian morality, their narrative function is grounded not in ideology or doctrine, but in the palpable reality of human actions. Grendel, Williams's central concern, is unavoidably human despite his titles that bear a metaphorical relationship to demons, ogres, and the devil. He is as much a part of the natural world of human time and space as are his antagonists Hrothgar and Beowulf, and like them, as Tolkien noted long ago, he is "conceived as having a spirit," punishable and unredeemable.[86]

I suggest an alternative contemporary, political significance for the

---

85. David Williams, *Cain and Beowulf: A Study in Secular Allegory* (Toronto: University of Toronto Press, 1982), esp. 4–5.

86. The central importance of the poet's fabulous rendering of Grendel is a major element in J. R. R. Tolkien's argument in *Beowulf: The Monsters and the Critics*, repr. of 1936 *Proceedings of the British Academy* (Oxford: Oxford University Press, 1958), appendix A.

Introduction

poet's polysemous and allusive narrative of the *fēond on helle* (enemy from hell) and his *mōdor* (mother), the *brimwylf* (sea-wolf), for no human character in the poem is disturbed by or questions the identification of these *mearcstapan* (striders of the boundary wastelands) as monstrous carnivores. Rather, these destructive hybridic creatures—monsters in male and female form, both genealogically linked to the fratricidal Cain who aim to wrest Heorot from its legitimate rulers—are "guarded" reflexes, albeit in fabulous guise, of contemporary figures whose greed for the throne of England is so unrelenting that they are shown to engage in the most extreme form of violence against the ruling house of Heorot, expressed as cannibalism in the poem. The *Beowulf*-poet's allegorical mode closely aligns his fictive and historical narratives in time (the poem's contemporary present), in space (the environs of Heorot/England, whose fame spreads throughout the world), and in action (who rules Heorot/England), manipulating reality and fantasy to accommodate his secular historical narrative.[87] The allegorical line of the Beowulfian narrative, it seems to me, is driven not by doctrine or ideology but rather by a poetic response

---

87. For a study of the uses of fantasy in the mimetic appropriation of reality, see Kathryn Hume, *Fantasy and Mimesis: Responses to Reality in Western Literature* (New York: Methuen, 1984), esp. chap. 1, "Critical Approaches to Fantasy," wherein she presents diagrammatic models of literature and definitions of modes of fantasy. In this work, which offers examples from classical to medieval to postmodern literature, Hume does not discuss the *Beowulf*-poet's manipulation of reality into a fantastic mode but rather concentrates on John Gardner's appropriation of the Beowulfian Grendel narrative in his *Grendel* (1971; New York: Knopf, 1979), esp. 83, 89, 169–70. Hume's own definition of fantasy ("Fantasy is any departure from consensus reality") is inclusive and based on the assumption that literature is the "product of both mimesis and fantasy" (Hume, 21). For a definition and examples of the ubiquitous use of fantasy in literature, see also J. R. R. Tolkien, "On Fairy-stories," in *The Tolkien Reader* (New York: Ballantine Books, 1966), 3–84; on fairy stories and "faërie," 10–33; on fantasy, 46–55; for a study of the fantastic in literature as a genre, see Tzvetan Todorov, *The Fantastic: A Structural Approach to a Literary Genre*, trans. Richard Howard (Cleveland, OH: Press of Western Reserve University, 1973), esp. 63–64, 76–77, 84–90; for distinctions between the fantastic and fantasy, see also Eric S. Rabkin, *The Fantastic in Literature* (Princeton, NJ: Princeton University Press, 1976), esp. 4, 27–29, 38, and 118 on Todorov's view of fantasy.

to and rendering of a tangible contemporaneous reality, in particular the events and personages of the 1035 succession crisis, whereby the monstrous in Grendel and in his mother is symbolic of the diseased and avaricious inner spirit of contemporary beings.

There is consensus that the *Beowulf* in Cotton Vitellius A.xv is not an "original" work, no more than was the scop's panegyric to Grendel's *bana* (slayer), or Ælfric's rendering of the biblical Esther, or one might say the biblical book of Esther itself, or the satirically biting "queens poems." If not original, it is, nonetheless, invention, a poetic fabrication of something new out of a number of previous constructions—some biblical, some classical, some legendary, some fabulous, some contemporaneous—constructions the poet would have ruminated about and finally brought together as a fresh work.[88] That he included more than one narrative line in his text, each with its own relational systems, is likewise generally held and, to an extent, is self-evident from the poem's digressionary structure that artfully erodes temporal and geographical boundaries. Like Hrothgar's scop, Ælfric, or the anonymous poet of the "queens poems," he would have some expectation that a portion of his audience would be familiar with the ancient material he chose to bring to the forefront of their minds in relating his new tale with its particular relevance to their joint experience in the time and space of their immediate reality. Like Virgil, who occluded the sociopolitical issues of Augustus's imperial vision by crafting a secular historical epic of Aeneas's founding of Rome, the *Beowulf*-poet calls up past legendary history in order to contemplate and dramatize the grave succession crisis that arose at the death of Cnut in 1035 and that plagued the Anglo-Saxon court. The *Beowulf*-poet's invocation at the poem's opening articulates his presupposition of a literary and sociopolitical experience shared with his audience—*Hwæt wē Gār-dena in geārdagum, / þēodcyninga þrym gefrūnon* (Listen, we have heard of the power/glory of the Spear-Danes, of the kings of nations of years gone by). By his use of the more "inclusive,

---

88. The process is captured by Tolkien in his striking image of an author's Cauldron of Story; Tolkien, "On Fairy-stories," in *The Tolkien Reader*, esp. 26–33.

emphatic" pronoun *wē*, the only instance of its appearance in the *gefrūnon* formula,[89] the poet presupposes that there is a type of interactive communication between himself and his audience and that his audience, or a portion of it, would be capable of recognizing the shifts from classical allusion to biblical paraphrase, from Germanic legend to the contemporary succession struggle that had begun with Cnut's crowning as king of England, his subsequent marriage to Emma of Normandy, and his continuing concupiscent relationship with Ælfgifu of Northampton.

My argument centers on the anomalous eight narrative units announced at the start of this Introduction that are contrived to signify at the same time a literal and an allegorical meaning to the narrative. The discussion is incremental, augmenting and enlarging upon implications that arise from the accumulated points discussed. As will be readily apparent, the disposition of the argument into four chapters follows the aesthetic dictates of the poem's definable treatment of time. The matter of chapter 1—the beheading sequence, the Cain allusion, and the mere—and chapter 4—the elevation of the hero's status—is concerned with the poem's immediate narrative in present time. The matter of chapter 2—Grendel's attacks and the *gifstōl* (throne, gift-seat)—and chapter 3—Grendel's mother and the paternity controversy—deals with events that are subject to the poet's manipulation of present and past time and to his pointed direction that the audience look upon events of the present as subject to and informed by those engendered in the past.

Chapter 1, "The Severed Head: Poetic Image and Historical Text," lays the political groundwork for the poet's relational system by examining three of the poem's narrative anomalies—the beheading of Æschere and Grendel, the mere, and the Cain allusion—as epic appropriations of historical facts. Its argument is structured in two parts: the first reexamines the nearly universally accepted (prior to 1981) literary analogue to the beheading sequence (a folkloric episode found in *Grettis saga Ásmundarsonar*) in order to heighten its

---

89. See Klaeber, 4th ed., nn. 1–3, who notes this.

unacceptability in the face of the Beowulfian sequence's unique political, military, and historical tone, what Edward Irving described as its "all-important context of both epic dignity and expansiveness."[90] In addition, the discussion underscores the primacy of an East Anglian setting for the mythic mere inhabited by the Grendel-kin and offers a historical place, key to the political narrative, as its possible "source." The second part addresses the Cain allusion in the context of the Beowulfian sequence and the contemporary political events leading to the assassination of Alfred atheling, an heir to the English throne, by his rival stepbrother, Harold Harefoot in 1036, which I then conclude may be considered as having been poetically reconstituted into the poem's fabulous monster narrative, a type of subversion of political reality.

Chapter 2, "The *Gifstōl* and the Grendel-kin," builds upon the implications that have arisen from the analysis of the beheading sequence as a poetic reflex of tragic political events in mid-eleventh-century England and moves retrospectively to the first two decades of the eleventh century, when England was steeped in military and political turmoil. Its argument proposes that the external military and internal political conflicts of these decades led inescapably to the events of 1036, clarifies ambiguities in the poem on such pressing issues as Grendel's stranglehold on Heorot by his concentrated onslaughts, and offers a mid-eleventh-century political parallel for the *gifstōl* passage.

The discussion of Chapter 3, "*Álfífa in ríka* and the Beowulfian *Konungamóðir*," continues the retrospective engagement with the past, addressing contemporary events and figures as they appear in English and Scandinavian sources. It sheds light on Grendel's mother, the poem's *broga* (terror) in the likeness of an *ides onlícness* (noblewoman): it views her parodic reign over the underwater *nīðsele* (battle-hall) and Grendel's questionable paternity as aspects of episodes in the lives of the historical figures Harold Harefoot and his mother,

---

90. Edward B. Irving, *A Reading of Beowulf* (New Haven, CT: Yale University Press, 1969), 84–85.

the noblewoman Ælfgifu of Northampton, a member of one of the most powerful Mercian noble families, granddaughter of Wulfrun, founder of Wolverhampton, niece of Wilfric Spot, and daughter of Ælfhelm, earl of Northampton and Northumbria. Finally, Chapter 3 sees the antithetical pairing of the accursed Beowulfian *brimwylf* (sea-wolf) and Heorot's *beaghroden cwēn* (ring-adorned queen) as the poetic rendering of the pairing of the historical figures of Ælfgifu of Northampton, or *Álfífa in ríka* (Álfífa the powerful), who was Cnut's concubine and regent in Norway, and Emma of Normandy, Cnut's legitimate queen and queen mother to Harthacnut. Upon Cnut's untimely death, these two politically powerful women were principal antagonists in the dynastic struggle to secure the throne of England for their respective sons, a struggle that first culminated in the assassination of Alfred atheling in 1036 and came to an end with the beheading of Harold Harefoot in the reign of Harthacnut.

Chapter 4, "Emma and Wealhtheow: Female Sovereignty and Poetic Discourse," further augments and examines the implication that major political figures have been allusively rendered as key Beowulfian characters, by focusing on Heorot's foreign and imposing Queen Wealhtheow as a unique poetic dramatization of the eleventh-century female sovereign Emma of Normandy. The argument details correspondences that are particular to Wealhtheow and Emma of Normandy: their singular circumstances as foreign queens and queen mothers, their authority and power to act in the governance of the court, and their overriding concerns with the legalities of inheritance and the orderly disposition of the kingdom within the kin group. I argue that Wealhtheow's name may serve as a key to an event in the historical queen's life, and that her speeches hold verbal resonances with the treatment of Emma of Normandy found in the *Encomium Emmae Reginae*, an eleventh-century political history in Latin rhyming prose, commissioned by Queen Emma herself. These resonances point to a textual interrelationship between the eleventh-century historical work and *Beowulf* and lead to the strong consideration that *Beowulf* could very well be regarded as a document of the mid-eleventh century.

To avoid any possible confusion as to my objective in presenting this material, I should perhaps state again that the discussion is not meant to nor can it offer a final definitive reading of *Beowulf* as a mid-eleventh-century composition. The argument articulated here is limited in its scope, being concerned only with units that are the work of Scribe A, found in the first two-thirds of *Beowulf*; as such, it must be viewed only as a first step, though a compelling one, I suggest, toward a reevaluation of the poem as an eleventh-century sociopolitical document, a thesis that is certain to be continually challenged. Yet it is an argument that needs to be made, given the evidence that I have accrued.

The Severed Head: Poetic Image and Historical Text

"Ne sorga, snotor guma! Sēlre biŏ ǣghwǣm,
þæt hē his frēond wrece, þonne hē fela murne." (*Bwf* 1384–85)

["Wise man, do not grieve! It will be better for each of
us to avenge his kinsman than to mourn overmuch."]

The poetic image of the title refers to a pair of severed heads—that of
Æschere, "the most exemplary atheling" (*[æþeling] ǣrgōd*, 1329ᵃ), and
that of Grendel, the "notorious stalker (or strider) of the boundary
(or borderland)" (*mǣre mearcstapa*, 103ᵃ) and ruler of the fen. The
beheading sequence in which these two events occur occupies over
four hundred lines of the poem's center (1232–1650) and contains
the beginning and end of a feud narrative. It begins with the poet's
encomium to the sleeping warrior band and the surprise night attack
of Grendel's mother, progresses to the subsequent decapitation of
Æschere, and ends with the decapitation of Grendel's corpse and
the display of his head, Beowulf's "sea-booty" (*sǣlāc*, 1624ᵇ, 1652ᵃ),
before Hrothgar's court. First identified as a feud narrative by the
poet at the close of Grendel's mother's attack— *"Ne wæs þæt gewrixle
til, / þæt hīe on bā healfa bicgan scoldon / frēonda fēorum!"* (That was not
good bartering, that both sides should forfeit the lives of kinsmen!
Bwf 1304ᵇ–6ᵃ)—this characterization of the dramatic action is rein-
forced four times within the space of some eighty lines; the action

is so defined by Hrothgar (*Bwf* 1333[b], 1340[b], 1380[a]),[1] and finally by Beowulf in the lines quoted in the epigraph. Beowulf's speech (*Bwf* 1384–96) functions as a turning point in the sequence, for it is here that he accepts the role of the avenger and calms Hrothgar's savage spirit (*þā wæs frōd cyning . . . on hrēon mōde* "then was the wise king . . . savage in his mind," *Bwf* 1307[b]–8).[2] Hrothgar's reaction to the abduction of Æschere is uncharacteristic; earlier when faced with the near destruction of his hall-troops, he was not so moved. Rather, the old king sat "joyless" (*unblīðe*, 130[b]) in patient "suffering" (*þolode*, 131[a]), "enduring the loss of his thanes" (*þegnsorge drēah*, 131[b]). Here, upon hearing of Æschere's abduction, he is propelled into action, demanding vengeance. The poet's observation (repeated by Beowulf) that Hrothgar's loss is that borne by a kinsman explains the king's passionate response, which matches that of Grendel's mother, faced with the loss of Grendel.[3]

---

1. "*Hēo þā fæhðe wræc / þē þū gystran niht Grendel cwealdest*" (She avenged the feud in which you killed Grendel last night, *Bwf* 1333[b]–34); "*gē feor hafað fæhðe gestǣled*" (You have further avenged the feud, *Bwf* 1340); "*Ic þē þā fæhðe fēo lēanige*" (I will recompense you the feud with riches, *Bwf* 1380) .

2. Although Klaeber glosses *hrēon* as "troubled" here, the term most often has a more intense meaning. See *Bwf* 1564, where it describes Beowulf's emotional state as he is about to kill Grendel's mother, or *Bwf* 2581[b] where it describes the Dragon's state of mind after he has received the sword stroke (*æfter heaðu-swenge on hrēoum mōde*, "[he was] after the battle-stroke savage in mind"); see also *Bwf* 548, 2131–32, 2180, and 2296.

3. Elsewhere, I have suggested that the key to understanding Hrothgar's reaction lies in translating "*frēond*" as "kinsman," which accurately describes Grendel and his relationship to his mother, to whom he is "*mǣg*" (kinsman, 1339[b]), and is a response, in accord with the feud structure, of outrage (the mutilation and murder of Æschere) and revenge (the decapitation of Grendel's corpse). For a discussion of the alternative readings of *frēond* in *Beowulf*, see Damico, *Beowulf's Wealhtheow and the Valkyrie Tradition*, 162–64; for instances elsewhere in Old English literature in which "*frēond*" carries the meaning of "kinsman," see ibid., 235–36n21. See also Howell D. Chickering's translation (*Beowulf: A Dual-Language Edition* [Garden City, NY: Anchor Books, 1977]), where he uses both senses: "kinsmen and friends" (1306[a]).

Underlying the feud narrative—and anticipating the diptych of severed heads—is a complex network of cranial imagery that repeatedly points to and encompasses both literal and metaphorical meanings of heads: the warrior bands' setting their shields above their heads, the atheling's towering helm, the hart's refusal to save his head by diving into the mere, Æschere's severed head on the mere's edge, Beowulf's glistening helmet, Grendel's head being dragged along Heorot's floor—these are but some examples of the image pattern that permeates the passage. As James L. Rosier and Stanley B. Greenfield argued some years ago, this associative cluster of images—*hēafod* (head), *hafela* (head), *helm* (as protection and ruler)—carries a physical and metapolitical resonance, especially in the context of the poet's emblematic use of other body parts that allude to Æschere's martial importance to Hrothgar.[4] Thus, in image pattern and in feud structure, the twin beheadings are causally linked: it is the abduction and beheading of Æschere (a person of some political importance if we accept the

---

4. James L. Rosier, "*Heafod* and *Helm*: Contextual Composition in *Beowulf*," *Medium Ævum* 37 (1968): 137–41; Stanley B. Greenfield, "The Extremities of the *Beowulf*ian Body Politic," in *Saints, Scholars, and Heroes: The Anglo-Saxon Heritage*, vol. 1, ed. Margot H. King and Wesley M. Stevens (Collegeville, MN: Hill Monastic Manuscript Library, 1979), 1–14, where he associates heads, hands, and hearts with the political aspects of the lord-and-thane relationship. Emblematic imaging of body parts has been the subject of several essays: see, e. g., Rosier's "The Uses of Association of Hands and Feasts in *Beowulf*," *PMLA* 78 (1963): 8–14, where he discusses the frequency of hand imagery in *Beowulf* ; Greenfield's "Three *Beowulf* Notes: Lines 736[b] ff., 1331[b] ff., 1341–44," in *Medieval Studies in Honor of Lillian Herlands Hornstein*, ed. Jess B. Bessinger, Jr. and Robert Raymo (New York: New York University Press, 1976), 169–72, where he emblematically associates Hrothgar's renewed impotence to act as king with the loss of Æschere's hand (ll. 1341-44); Alfred Bammesberger, "Old English *cuðe folme* in *Beowulf*, Line 1303A," *Neophilologus* 89, no. 4 (2005): 625–27, who identifies the "famous hand" as a metaphor for Hrothgar's right-hand man Æschere; L. Whitbread, "The Hand of Æschere: A Note on *Beowulf* 1343," *Review of English Studies* 25 (1949): 339–42; and Chickering, *Beowulf: A Dual-Language Edition*, esp. 334–37. My thanks to Craig R. Davis for referring me to the Bammesberger article.

symbolic significance of the cranial imagery) that throws the Danish court into a renewed state of feud with the Grendel-kin (1338-42, 1381-82) and culminates in Grendel's decapitation (1590).

Typically, however, the spectacle of Æschere's bloodied head and Grendel's waterlogged cranium has taken second billing to what has been judged as the main event, the wrestling match with Grendel's mother, where Beowulf annihilates the savage and corrupt *merewīf* (sea-wife, 1519).[5] In this context, Grendel's beheading may be mistakenly seen as an anticlimax, so violently does Grendel's mother attack the prince as she pins him to the ground, her knife held in readiness to kill him. Yet in the context of the feud structure, Beowulf's destruction of Grendel's mother functions as narrative retardation, a repetition and reversal of Beowulf's earlier fight with Grendel (as noted by J. R. R. Tolkien and, more recently, by Andy Orchard), and is the first step toward his final act of revenge.[6] For it is not until Beowulf has tracked down Grendel (whom he has previously mortally wounded and whom he indeed finds dead in the underwater *nīðsele* (battle-hall, 1513[a]) and beheaded his corpse, an action that takes place a line away from the exact center of the poem, that he achieves satisfaction, so profound is his need to make full restitution for Æschere.

Within Beowulfian scholarship, moreover, Beowulf's retaliatory decapitation of Grendel has been viewed as a refashioning of folktale

---

5. See Alexandra Hennessey Olsen's summary of the literature on Grendel's mother, in her chapter "Gender Roles," in *Beowulf Handbook*, ed. Bjork and Niles, 311–24, esp. 319–20. The classic article on Grendel's mother is Jane Chance's "The Structural Unity in *Beowulf*: The Problem of Grendel's Mother," *Texas Studies in Language and Literature* 22 (1980): 287–303, reprinted in *New Readings on Women in Old English*, ed. Helen Damico and Alexandra Hennessey Olsen (Bloomington, IN: Indiana University Press, 1990), 248–61; and elsewhere often reprinted.

6. See Andy Orchard, *Pride and Prodigies: Studies in the Monsters of the Beowulf Manuscript* (Toronto: University of Toronto Press, 1995), 142–43, who interprets both fights as a structural continuum. J. R. R. Tolkien's earlier perception of Grendel's mother as a doublet of Grendel provokes a view of the fight as narrative repetition of Beowulf's earlier fight with Grendel; see *Beowulf: The Monsters and the Critics*, 39.

figures, with parallels that describe heroes battling and overcoming ghoulish beings, an association that further obscures the essential feud structure of the sequence. However, these folkloric units are usually isolated cameo events depicting supernatural conflicts with no particular consequence in narrative structure. Their objective lies solely in illustrating the physical strength of the hero. The beheading sequence, on the other hand, functions as the climax of the monstrous Grendel's repeated nocturnal onslaughts on Heorot and his systematic feasting on its hall-troops.[7] Beowulf's decapitation of Grendel brings to closure the main narrative of the first two-thirds of the poem, the unsuccessful struggle to possess Hrothgar's kingdom by the Grendel-kin, for the motif of the night attack on a hall is absent from the rhetorical design of the rest of the poem.[8] Thus, the folkloric elements in *Beowulf* function as counterpoints to the underlying feud narrative essential to the Beowulfian sequence and its unique political, martial, and regal tone and concerns.

The historical text of my title refers to two political events that took place in Anglo-Danish England in 1036 and 1040 and are recorded in a number of Anglo-Saxon and Norman texts from the mid-eleventh and twelfth centuries. These, I argue, have been appropriated and allusively fictionalized into the Beowulfian beheading sequence, providing an allegorical dimension to the poem's narrative structure similar to that found in Bede, the biblical epic *Exodus*, and Ælfric's saints' lives, as discussed in the Introduction (above, 21–24). Even though the dates of the events postdate even Kiernan and Dumville's late scribal datings of the manuscript,[9] the historical parallels discussed

---

7. Heorot's ravaging begins with Grendel's first attack (115–20, where he is called an *wiht unhælo* "evil/unholy creature," 120[b]) and slaughters thirty thegns (*þritig þegna*, 123[a]), fifteen of whom he feasts on; the second dramatized attack (702[b]–836) contains his devouring of Hondscio in Beowulf's presence.

8. I am excluding the night-burnings of the *eald uht-sceaða* (old dawn-ravager), which I see as a repetition in fantastic guise of the attacks of the Grendel-kin in the first two-thirds of the poem.

9. See above, Introduction, 6–7.

below are too compelling to dismiss, especially since the beheading sequence (*Bwf* 1232–1650) lies solidly within the province of Scribe A (*Bwf* 1–1939), the date-range of whose hand has yet to be established.[10] My discussion is structured in two parts: the first re-examines the medieval Icelandic literary analogue to the beheading sequence (a folkloric episode found in *Grettis saga Ásmundarsonar*) in order to demonstrate how distant it is in narrative texture from the Beowulfian beheading sequence. I then address (and examine in the context of the Beowulfian sequence) the contemporary events recounted in the historical texts, which I conclude may have been poetically reconstituted into the poem's fantastical monster narrative; thus, the prototypical folktale motif may have been used to encrypt political reality, producing the multitiered narrative of historical allegory.

Folkloric Parallels and the Mere

The nearly universally accepted analogue to the Beowulfian beheading sequence comes from fifteenth-century Icelandic manuscripts, the

---

10. See above, Introduction, 7. On the question of the feasibility of the scribal span of the "earlier" hand of the Beowulfian Scribe B beyond 1010, there is an interesting instance of a scribal hand spanning some forty years in CCCC MS 270 (The "Missal" of St. Augustine's Abbey) and CCCC MS 286 (The Gospels of St. Augustine of Canterbury). On the end leaves at the back of MS 286 are some twelfth- and thirteenth-century records "relating to the abbey (fols.i^{r-v} and ii^{v}–iii^{r})" dated 1146, but that "record transactions respectively datable to 1110," and "inscribed probably by a known master scribe at the abbey in the Post-Conquest period. Datable to 1110 (*in illa Quadragesima in qua rex Henricus dedit filiam suam imperatori*), the transaction was probably entered by the scribe of the original portions of the so-called 'Missal' of St. Augustine's Abbey" (MS 270); Mildred Budny, *Insular, Anglo-Saxon, and Early Anglo-Norman Manuscript Art at Corpus Christi College, Cambridge: An Illustrated Catalogue*, Vol. 1 of 2 (Kalamazoo, MI: Medieval Institute Publications, 1997), quote at 8; see further on the scribal hand of the "original portions" of MS 270, "made or completed after 1091 and perhaps after 1100" (at 694). My thanks to Timothy C. Graham for referring me to these manuscripts; and to Gill Cannell at the Parker Library for her help in accessing them.

Sandhaugar incident in *Grettis saga Ásmundarsonar* (chaps. 63–67), in which Grettir chops off the arm of a she-troll in the course of their wrestling and then swims to the bottom of a pool and behind a waterfall to do battle with a *draugr* (giant spirit), a living dead, seated by a fire, whom he decapitates.[11] The argument rests on some compelling details found in both sequences—the light in the underwater cave, the sword on the wall, the rune staff retrieved as booty, the decapitation of the *draugr*, the blood on the water seen by an accomplice—and on a similarity they both share with a basic folktale plot, the "Bear's Son

---

11. *Grettis saga Ásmundarsonar*, ed. Guðni Jónsson, in *Íslenzk Fornrit*, vol. 7 (Reykjavík, 1936), hereafter cited as *Grettis saga*. The composition of *Grettis saga* dates ca. 1310–20. See Robert Cook, "Grettis Saga," in *Medieval Scandinavia*, ed. Pulsiano et al., 241–43. See also the translation in G. N. Garmonsway and Jacqueline Simpson, *Beowulf and Its Analogues, including Archaeology and Beowulf* by Hilda Ellis Davidson (New York: E. P. Dutton, 1971), 312–16; and in R. W. Chambers, *Beowulf: An Introduction to the Study of the Poem with a Discussion of the Stories of Offa and Finn*, 3rd ed., supplement by C. L. Wrenn (Cambridge, UK: The University Press, 1967), 156–63, 175–82; Klaeber, 3rd ed., xiv–xvii. Other parallels cited for Beowulf's underwater struggle with Grendel's mother come from *Samsons saga fagra* (ca. 1300, chaps. 3, 78), and *Orms þáttr Stórólfssonar* (ca. 1300, chaps. 6–9). *Samsons saga*, first proposed as a parallel by William Witherle Lawrence ("*Beowulf* and the Saga of Samson the Fair," in *Studies in English Philology: A Miscellany in Honor of Frederick Klaeber*, ed. Kemp Malone and Martin B. Ruud [Minneapolis, MN: University of Minnesota Press, 1929], 172–81, and in his *Beowulf and Epic Tradition* [1928; repr. New York: Hafner Publishing, 1963], 188–91), lacks the beheading motif, as does *Orms þáttr*, and thus will not be considered here; see *Beowulf and Its Analogues*, 316–20, 322–24; Klaeber, 3rd ed., xiv–xviii; Chambers, *Beowulf: An Introduction*, 53–54, 186–92, 454–58, 502–03. R. W. McConchie contributed another episode in *Grettis saga* as an analogue to the Beowulfian sequence, Grettir's struggle with the *draugr* Kárr, but this episode also lacks specific details so that again the relationship is weak; R. W. McConchie, "Grettir Ásmundarson's Fight with Kárr the Old: A Neglected *Beowulf* Analogue," *English Studies* 63 (1982): 481–86; Orchard, *Pride and Prodigies*, 140–68. For a survey of the sources of and analogues to *Beowulf*, see Theodore M. Andersson, "Sources and Analogues," in *Beowulf Handbook*, ed. Bjork and Niles, 125–48; see also n. 16 below.

The Severed Head: Poetic Image and Historical Text

Tale," first discussed in Friedrich Panzer's 1910 study of Germanic narrative, volume 1 of which was devoted to *Beowulf*.[12] Panzer's theory—which posits *Grettis saga* and *Beowulf* as two independent versions of a folktale of some two hundred variants—was and continues to be accepted in part or in whole,[13] for as one of its early adherents, W. W. Lawrence, wrote, it provides "something tangible upon which to base conclusions as to the history of the materials in *Beowulf*."[14]

---

12. Friedrich Panzer, *Studien zur germanischen Sagengeschichte*, vol. 1: *Beowulf* (Munich: C. H. Beck, 1910). For thorough discussions of Panzer's theory and the relationship of the Bear's Son Tale to *Grettis saga* and *Beowulf*, see Lawrence, *Beowulf and Epic Tradition*, 165–87; Chambers, *Beowulf: An Introduction*, 365–81; and, more recently, J. Michael Stitt, *Beowulf and the Bear's Son: Epic, Saga, and Fairytale in Northern Germanic Tradition* (New York: Garland Publishing Inc., 1992); and Magnús Fjalldal, *The Long Arm of Coincidence: The Frustrated Connection between Beowulf and Grettis saga* (Toronto: University of Toronto Press, 1998), esp. chap. 7. Fjalldal's monograph is the most recent discussion and summary of critical work (from 1881 to the close of the twentieth century) on the relationship between *Beowulf* and *Grettis saga* (chap. 1); see also Peter A. Jorgensen, "The Two-Troll Variant of the Bear's Son Folktale in *Hálfdanar saga Brönufóstra* and *Gríms saga loðinkinna*," *Arv* 31 (1975): 35–43; and Anatoly Liberman's comprehensive examination of the issue of "common source" in "Beowulf-Grettir," in *Germanic Dialects: Linguistic and Philological Investigations*, ed. Bela Brogyanyi and Thomas Krömmelbein (Amsterdam: J. Benjamins, 1986), 353–401.

13. Panzer, *Studien . . . Beowulf*, 1: 319. A concise summary of the points of similarity between the folktale, epic, and saga, Panzer's theory, and the ensuing critical response is found in Fjalldal, *Long Arm of Coincidence*, 88–95. The main criticisms against Panzer's theory were aimed at his use of modern versions to reconstruct the medieval materials and his reduction of the different versions to make a composite plot; see Fjalldal, *Long Arm of Coincidence*, 93–94, where he puts forth Carl W. von Sydow's argument (in "Beowulf och Bjarke," in *Studier i nordisk filologi* 14, no. 3 [*Skrifter utgivna av svenska litteratursällskapet i Finland*, 170, 1923], 25–26, 34) against a relationship between *Beowulf* and *Grettis saga* based on the *märchen* theory. See also Tolkien's earlier comments against a folktale structure as the poem's dominant structural element (*Monsters and the Critics*, 11–15).

14. Lawrence, *Beowulf and Epic Tradition*, 165.

What appealed to Lawrence (and in part to R. W. Chambers, who, though approving of a popular tale as a source for *Beowulf*, nonetheless argued for the differences between the folktale and the Beowulfian sequence, to be noted below) must have been the relative indestructibility of the folktale plot, what Lawrence called the "popular" essence of the plot, around which all the other narrative elements were arranged.[15] That a basic folktale pattern exists in the Beowulfian narrative may be taken as a given, as has been shown in the works of Thomas A. Shippey, Richard L. Harris, and others;[16] yet it is a critical commonplace that the *Beowulf*-poet demonstrates sophisticated skill in layering his narrative, in weaving together folkloric and mythological elements and events from the distant and historio-legendary Scandinavian past with contemporary Anglo-Danish

---

15. Lawrence, *Beowulf and Epic Tradition*, 166–75; after his discussion of Panzer's theory, Chambers concludes that although there is a "likeness" to a "large number of recorded folk-tales [the versions of the *Bear's Son Tale*]," the Beowulfian plot "at most . . . is a version of a portion of them" and an "epic glorification of a folk-tale motif," *Beowulf: An Introduction*, 380, 381. See Klaeber, 3rd ed., cxv, however, who rejects the theory that the poem's genesis lay in a popular tale; see also Fjalldal, *Long Arm of Coincidence*.

16. Thomas A. Shippey, "The Fairy-Tale Structure of *Beowulf*," *Notes and Queries*, n.s. 16, no. 1 (January 1969): 2–11; Richard L. Harris, "The Deaths of Grettir and Grendel: A New Parallel," *Scripta Islandica* 24 (1973): 25–53. Although Harris agrees that versions of the Bear's Son Tale lie behind *Grettis saga* and *Beowulf*, his article is more concerned with illustrating the Icelandic author's masterly use of a core narrative unit in *Grettis saga*; on this point, see Andy Orchard's elaborate analysis in his *Pride and Prodigies*, chap. 6, 140–68, in particular his handling of the Sandhaugar incident, which he presents as a continuation of the earlier Glámr episode; Orchard sees the five monster episodes in *Grettis saga* as a movement toward the human hero's emergence as a monster. See also Fjalldal, *Long Arm of Coincidence*, 127–28, and also 119–29, where he negates a direct link between *Beowulf* and *Grettis saga* and instead demonstrates the creative appropriation by the author of *Grettis saga* of episodes and brief details from other sagas (especially from *Hávarðar saga*); see also note 6, above; and Andersson, "Sources and Analogues," 125–48.

concerns.[17] None of these has been, or would be, understood as the determinate core that drives the poem's narrative. Thus, it is difficult to accept the folkloric pattern as the distinguishing characteristic of the poem, the "tangible" presence that Lawrence seeks. The formulaic plot pattern common to the epic, the saga, and the folktale is so "universal" that it loses its specific relevance to the plot, as Theodore M. Andersson noted in his recent survey of the analogues for *Beowulf*,[18] and as exhaustively demonstrated by Magnús Fjalldal in his recent monograph, and by Anatoly Liberman in his survey of the scholarship dealing with the relationship of *Grettis saga* and *Beowulf*.[19] It is possible the poet appropriated the folktale element and imaginatively refashioned it as a patterned counterpoint for his contemporary political narrative.

Separate from his argument for the individual debt that the beheading sequences in *Beowulf* and the *Grettis saga* Sandhaugar incident owed to the tested and useful folktale structure, Lawrence also strove to link the topographical features in the two narratives; the

---

17. For recent discussions, see especially Frank, "*Beowulf* Poet's Sense of History," and her "Old Norse Memorial Eulogies and the Ending of *Beowulf*," *The Early Middle Ages, Acta* 6 (1982): 1–19. See also (as a brief selection) Robert E. Bjork, "Digressions and Episodes," in *Beowulf Handbook*, ed. Bjork and Niles; John D. Niles, "Myth and History," *Beowulf Handbook*, 213–32, and, generally, his *Beowulf: The Poem and Its Tradition* (Cambridge, MA: Harvard University Press, 1983); Joseph Harris, "A Nativist Approach to *Beowulf*: The Case of Germanic Elegy," in *Companion to Old English Poetry*, ed. Henk Aertson and Rolf H. Bremmer, Jr. (Amsterdam: VU University Press, 1994), 45–62, which examines the Lament of the Old Father (*Bwf* 2444-62) as an analogue to *Sonatorrek* in *Egils saga* in the context of Baldr's death; see also Helen Damico, "*Sörlaþáttr* and the Hama Episode in *Beowulf*," *Scandinavian Studies* 55 (1983): 222–35, and "*Þrymskviða* and the Second Fight in *Beowulf*: The Dressing of the Hero in Parody," *Scandinavian Studies* 58, no. 4 (1986): 407–28.

18. Andersson, "Sources and Analogues," esp. 133.

19. Liberman, "Beowulf-Grettir," 353–401; Liberman, however, offers a linguistic argument for the *hæftmēce/heptisax* connection (367–91); but see Orchard, *Pride and Prodigies*, 151, 162. See also Fjalldal, *Long Arm of Coincidence*, ix, and his discussion on 27–30, 46–53, 126–29, and passim.

stark Icelandic landscape of the Sandhaugar episode, with its inland pool and waterfall, he argued, was similar to the misty marshland of Beowulf's second adventure.[20] Lawrence's Icelandic landscape thesis produced a number of critical responses, the fullest of which were the correctives by W. S. Mackie and Kemp Malone.[21] Instead of Lawrence's murky "inland pool" surrounded by cliffs and a waterfall, both scholars, through lexical studies of the Beowulfian passage, concluded that the "mere" was in reality a "sea" or a "land-locked arm of the sea,"[22] some aspect of a large expanse of water, which in fact is one description of the realm of the Grendel-kin (*flōda begong*, "the expanse of sea," 1497).[23] Augmenting their argument in part, some years later Roberta Frank stressed the critical uncertainty that surrounds the meaning of *mere*. In poetic usage, she notes, the simplex *mere* (ON *marr*, "the sea") does carry the meaning of an expanse of water, with a connotative force associated with sea and salt water as, for example, in the Finn episode;[24] in prose, however, where one might encounter the term in charters or in homilies, *mere* signifies either local inland landmarks of enclosed bodies of water (perhaps similar to Lawrence's pool) or the confined and emblematic stagnant pools associated with hell. The *Beowulf*-poet merged the two *meres*, a stylistic characteristic, Frank suggests, that reflects

---

20.   Lawrence first discussed his landscape theory in "The Haunted Mere in *Beowulf*," *PMLA* 27 (1912): 208–45, and again in his *Beowulf and Epic Tradition*; see also his "Grendel's Lair" *JEGP* 38 (1939): 477–80.

21.   W. S. Mackie, "The Demons' Home in *Beowulf*," *JEGP* 37 (1938): 455–61; Kemp Malone, "Grendel and His Abode," in *Studia Philologica et Litteraturia in Honorem L. Spitzer*, ed. A. G. Hatcher and K. L. Selig (Bern: Francke, 1958), 297–308; see also Malone's "Review of *Beowulf: An Introduction to the Study of the Poem with a Discussion of the Stories of Offa and Finn* by R. W. Chambers," *English Studies* 14 (1932): 190–93; Fjalldal, *Long Arm of Coincidence*, ix, and his discussion on 27–30, 46–53, 126–29, and passim; Andersson, "Sources and Analogues," 125–48.

22.   Mackie, "Demons' Home in *Beowulf*," 458.

23.   Malone, "Grendel and His Abode," 303–4.

24.   *eard gemunde, / þēah þe ne meahte on mere drīfan / hringedstefnan* (*Bwf* 1129[b]–31[a]).

"his sophisticated balancing of the roles and registers of Christian homilist and northern scop."[25]

Mackie and Malone took issue with other topographical features that Lawrence claimed were characteristic of the saga episode and the Beowulfian sequence. Lawrence's waterfall, Mackie argued, the *fyrgenstrēam*—literally translated by Lawrence as "mountain stream"— was inconsistent with the use of the word in other Old English poetic works (*Andreas* 390; *Riddle* 10, 2; *Maxims* II, 47), where the term invariably means "sea" or "flowing sea."[26] Malone expanded the argument: based on his survey of all the sea terms in their simplex and compound forms, he argued that the *fyrgenstrēam* should be understood metaphorically as a "stream that is a mountain (of intensity)," the first element functioning here as an intensifier, as it does in *fyrgenbēam*, "mountain tree, or a tree that is a mountain in size, gigantic tree," and in *fyrgenholt*, "a conflated term for *fyrgenbēamholt* 'a grove of giant trees.'"[27]

Still other terms describing Grendel's domain evoke topographical features more common to marshy floodplains, separating it further from Lawrence's inland Icelandic landscape and aligning it closer to a southeastern English cultural setting. Margaret Gelling's studies of settlement place-names in Anglo-Saxon England, which define a settlement by reference to its chief topographical feature, for example, reveal that the landscape features describing Grendel's habitat are consistent with settlement place-names in southeastern

---

25. Roberta Frank, "'Mere' and 'Sund': Two Sea-Changes in *Beowulf*," in *Modes of Interpretation in Old English Literature: Essays in Honour of Stanley B. Greenfield*, ed. Phyllis Rugg Brown, Georgia Ronan Crampton, and Fred C. Robinson (Toronto: University of Toronto Press, 1986), 153–72, at 158.

26. *swa ðu hyldo wið me / ofer firigendstream freode gecyðdest* (*And* 389–90), in *ASPR* 2; *ond ic neoþan wætre, / flode underflowan, firgenstreamum* (Exeter *Rid* 10, 2), in *ASPR* 3; *ymb ealra landa gehwylc, / flowan firgenstreamas* (Cotton *Max II*, 47), in *ASPR* 6. See Mackie, "Demons Home in *Beowulf*," 457.

27. Malone, "Grendel and His Abode," 298, expands on G. Sarrazin's argument that *fyrgenstrēam* "was an epithet or kenning for the ocean"; see also 300–301, 304.

England, conveying images of wetness and of boggish wasteland (e.g., OE *fen*, *mōr*, *mersc*, *næs*).[28] In topographical place-names, OE *næs*, for instance, which Klaeber glosses as "headland, bluff" and characterizes as *neowle* (precipitous), evokes an image of a high projecting coastal promontory. In OE settlement place-names, a *næs* is indeed a coastal feature, but what distinguishes it is not so much its height as its peninsular shape. In southeastern England, in East Anglia, for example, *næs* most often describes a "flat, murky" promontory or peninsula projecting into a lake or marsh. Peterborough (*Medeshamstede*), as one example, stood on a *næs*, a flat promontory of "dry ground jutting out into the fen."[29] The *næs* onto which a Geatish man (or prince) deposits the slain *wundorlīc wǣgbora* (wondrous wave traveler, *Bwf* 1440[a]) dragged out of the *mere* harmonizes with a description of a flat, raised peninsula jutting out into the water. Further, with Gelling's topographical feature in mind, the *neowle nǣssas* (dangerous promontories) that Beowulf and Hrothgar pass on the *uncūð gelād* (translated by Gelling and Dennis Cronan as "perilous water crossing") to Grendel's habitat (*Bwf* 1410-11) likewise could be seen as elongated banks of dry ground that project into the East Anglian marshland, these being anywhere from three (March) to eight (Thorney) to twelve (Soham and Wicken) to twenty

---

28. See Margaret Gelling, *Place-Names in the Landscape* (London: J. M. Dent & Sons, 1984), esp. 62–73, 172–73. See also her "The Landscape of *Beowulf*," *ASE* 31 (2002): 7–11, in which Gelling discusses *hlið*, *hop*, and *gelad*: *hlið* (when a second element in compounds) means "concave hill slope" or "hill with a hollow" (a specialized meaning found in place-names of southern England and the West Midlands), an appropriate hiding place for the Grendel-kin (8–9); *hop* (again the second element in the hapax terms *fenhopu* and *morhopu*) carries the basic sense of "a piece of enclosed ground in marsh . . . a remote, secret place" (9–10). See also Margaret Gelling and Ann Cole, *The Landscape of Place-Names* (Stamford, UK: Shaun Tyas, 2000), which elaborates on some of the topographical settlement names.

29. Gelling, *Place-Names in the Landscape*, 172–73. Settlement place-names that refer to *næs* as a flat, coastal promontory are found in Cambridgeshire, Lincoln, and Essex. See also ON *nes*.

(Littleport) meters in height.[30] The danger connected with the *næssas*, then, would have to do with their murkiness, the precarious nature of their surface, and the difficulty of the water crossing. In settlement place-names, *gelād* signifies "water crossing," a structure akin to a causeway, a topographical feature especially found in the eastern fenlands and in the southern half of England. Thus, when Beowulf sets out on the *uncūð gelād* to avenge Æschere (*Bwf* 1410), he traverses, Gelling suggests, a "difficult water crossing liable to be rendered impossible by flooding."[31] The narrow and hazardous water crossing that *gelād* signifies in *Beowulf* is, as Dennis Cronan has argued, consistent with its use elsewhere in Old English poetry.[32]

Thus, Lawrence's second argument—that the Sandhaugar episode in *Grettis saga* and Beowulf's second fight take place on similar terrain —when examined proves to be somewhat untenable, for what emerges from the comparison is a striking difference in the geographical space. The examination by Mackie, Malone, Frank, Gelling, and Cronan of the terms used to describe Grendel's dominion distances its horrific space from the setting of the Sandhaugar episode. Rather, what is evoked is a vast expanse of marshland, where, to use Malone's phrase, "earth and water are mysteriously mingled," and whose waters

---

30. See David Hall, *Fenland Landscapes and Settlement between Peterborough and March*, East Anglian Archaeology Report no. 35 (Cambridge, UK, 1987), 38 (March), 48 (Wittlesey), 55 (Thorney). March Island, for instance, has a "bed of clay . . . with some gravelly admixture [known as March Gravels]" (38), which might result in a precarious surface. See also his *The Fenland Project*, Number 10: *Cambridgeshire Survey, the Isle of Ely and Wisbech*, East Anglian Archaeology Report no. 79 (Cambridge, UK, 1996), 19 (Littleport) and 72 (Soham and Wicken). Both these reports deal with the fen islands associated with Ely.

31. Gelling, "Landscape of *Beowulf*," 10–11; see also her discussion in *Place-Names in the Landscape*, 23–25, 73–76. Gelling refers to Seamus Heaney's translation of *frecne fengelad* as "treacherous keshes," keshes being an Irish word meaning "wicker road across a bog," which calls up both the wetlands and the danger of the passage way.

32. Dennis Cronan, "Old English *gelād* 'Passage across Water,'" *Neophilologus* 71 (1987): 316–19.

are peopled with serpent-like aquatic creatures, a physical setting that is unlike the stark landscape of the farmstead at Sandhaugar.

The final argument against a connection between the Sandhaugar episode and *Beowulf* was put forth by Chambers. Chambers saw in the Beowulfian episode certain characteristics that were incompatible with the saga's folkloric narrative. In particular, he noted the heroic and courtly setting absent from the Icelandic work, but so prominent in *Beowulf*, and the theme of vengeance, an essential element in Icelandic sagas, present in *Beowulf* but curiously missing from the Sandhaugar episode. Even Chambers, who was a supporter of Lawrence's theory and who saw *Beowulf* as an interweaving of popular tale and historical matter, was nonetheless highly ambivalent about connecting the two sequences.[33]

There is justification to Chambers's objection, for the *Beowulf*-poet's execution of the folktale sequences was highly nuanced. Except for the folkloric motif of heroes battling and overcoming supernatural, ghoulish beings, the Sandhaugar/*Beowulf* analogue contains few features to support an argument that the dominant narrative core of the Beowulfian sequence is folkloric. Distinctive features in the sequence's courtly and martial environment, its aquatic setting, and its narrative pattern argue for a dissonance between the texts. In *Grettis saga*, the Sandhaugar encounter is episodic and functions as one of a series of steps in the strongman Grettir's attainment of monsterhood, as Orchard has argued (see above, n. 16). Grendel's beheading, on the other hand, functions as final revenge for outrages committed against Hrothgar's hall; the focus is not on Beowulf's physical strength but rather on his generosity, bravery, and faithfulness, which imbue the poem with cultural and symbolic significance. Instead of countering the poem's narrative, the historical events I turn to next accord with a narrative line that condemns treachery and praises virtue. They contain particular details in theme, landscape,

---

33. R. W. Chambers, "Beowulf's Fight with Grendel and Its Scandinavian Parallels," *English Studies* 11 (1929): 81–100, esp. 84–95. Chambers accepts other correspondences between the two works.

character, cultural setting, and organizational pattern that harmonize with the poem's revenge narrative and suggest that the *Beowulf*-poet utilized the folktale narrative as an extended metaphor, a dissonant complement to the revenge narrative of the beheading sequence, within which he might carefully reconstruct contemporary political figures and events through indirection and in guarded language.

I begin with particularized features in the Beowulfian sequence: its courtly and martial setting noted by Chambers; its funereal journey to the mere; its fishing motif and the display of the corpse of the giant *wundorlīc wǣgbora* (wondrous wave traveler) to the gaze of the soldiers; its display of Grendel's head to the Danish court as *wergild*; its allusion to Cain that accompanies the introduction of Grendel's mother; and finally Æschere's execution and the surprise night attack on his troops. All these have compelling correspondences in the historical narrative to suggest that the poem's "tangible" center should be sought not within a folkloric topos but within the poet's own political milieu, for although the deeds of ancestors were the poet's putative subject, he was also engaged in a type of polysemous narrative whereby the ancestral world of the poem was meant to be seen as co-existent with the political turmoil of the poet's present.[34] I now turn my attention to that present: to the West Saxon royal court that at its height (1027-30) ruled Denmark, Norway, southern Sweden, and England, and to the events that led to its downfall.

Eleventh-Century Political Parallels for the Beheading Sequence

The historical events I offer as parallels evoke the Beowulfian elements outlined above and center on political issues related to the poem's main concern of dynastic succession. The first parallel is close, but the second is frighteningly direct. The events in question are the execution of Alfred atheling and his warrior-band in 1036 on the supposed orders of King Harold Harefoot, his stepbrother,

---

34. See Frank's argument in "*Beowulf* Poet's Sense of History," 53–65, esp. 64.

and the subsequent decapitation of Harold Harefoot's corpse on the orders of King Harthacnut, Alfred's half-brother, in 1040 as an act of vengeance. I will discuss them in order of chronological occurrence.

The Assassination of Alfred ætheling

Nine documents discuss the mutilation and consequent murder of Alfred atheling and his comrades, five from the eleventh century and four from the twelfth; doubtless there are others.[35] The political background runs as follows: in the aftermath of Cnut's death

35. The eleventh-century texts are *The Anglo-Saxon Chronicle: Two of the Saxon Chronicles Parallel, with Supplementary Extracts from the Others*, ed. Charles Plummer, on the basis of an edition by John Earle, 2 vols. (Oxford: Clarendon, 1892–99), hereafter cited as *ASC*; *EER*, ed. Campbell; *The Gesta Normannorum Ducum of William of Jumièges, Orderic Vitalis and Robert of Torigni*, ed. Elisabeth M. C. van Houts, 2 vols., vol. 1: introduction and books I-IV; vol. 2: books V-VIII (Oxford: Clarendon Press, 1992–95), hereafter cited as *WJGND*; William of Poitiers, *The Gesta Guillelmi of William of Poitiers*, ed. and trans. R. H. C. Davis† and Marjorie Chibnall (Oxford: Clarendon Press, 1998), hereafter cited as *WPGG*; *Vita Ædwardi Regis: The Life of King Edward Who Rests at Westminster, Attributed to a Monk of St Bertin*, ed. and trans. Frank Barlow (New York: T. Nelson, 1962; repr. New York: AMS Press Inc., 1984), hereafter cited as *VÆdr*. The twelfth-century texts are *Liber Eliensis*, ed. E. O. Blake, Camden 3rd ser. 92 (London: Royal Historical Society, 1962), hereafter cited as *LE*, ed. Blake; see also *Liber Eliensis: A History of the Isle of Ely from the Seventh Century to the Twelfth*, trans. Janet Fairweather (Woodbridge, UK: The Boydell Press, 2005), hereafter cited as *LE*, trans. Fairweather; *The Chronicle of John of Worcester*, vol. 2: *The Annals from 450 to 1066*, ed. R. R. Darlington and P. McGurk, trans. Jennifer Bray† and P. McGurk (Oxford: Clarendon Press, 1995), hereafter cited as *JWChron*; Henry, Archdeacon of Huntingdon, *Historia Anglorum: The History of the English Peoples*, ed. and trans. Diana Greenway (Oxford: Clarendon Press, 1996), hereafter cited as *HHHA*; William of Malmesbury, *Gesta Regum Anglorum: The History of the English Kings*, ed. and trans. R. A. B. Mynors†, completed by R. M. Thomson and M. Winterbottom, 2 vols. (Oxford: Clarendon Press, 1998), hereafter cited as *WMGRA*. Unless otherwise noted, all references to and quotations from these works will be to these editions.

in November 1035, England fell into a dynastic crisis; the succession dispute dominated and ripped apart the political factions. It was a time, as Simon Keynes describes it, "full of incident, subterfuge, treachery, and murder."[36] There were four potential heirs to the throne—Harthacnut, Emma and Cnut's son (who was reigning in Denmark at the time of Cnut's death); Edward and Alfred, Emma's sons by Æthelred (at Cnut's accession to the throne in 1016, they had been sent to their uncle at the Norman court for safekeeping); and Harold Harefoot, Cnut's alleged son by Ælfgifu of Northampton, of Mercian nobility and Cnut's illegitimate consort, although the *Anglo-Saxon Chronicle* texts C, D, and E as well as later documents disclaim him as Cnut's son.[37] Harthacnut was the legitimate heir, the result of a possible marital agreement between Emma and Cnut at the time of their marriage, that only their joint son would ascend the throne,[38] and because Cnut had acknowledged Harthacnut as a rightful heir by appointing him king of Denmark. At Cnut's death, because of the political factionalism between the Mercian and West Saxon *witan* (councilors), doubtless exacerbated because

---

36. Keynes's 1998 introduction to *EER* [lxii]; Keynes, "Æthelings in Normandy," 195–96. See also his "Cnut's Earls," 43–48; "The Declining Reputation of King Æthelred the Unready," in *Ethelred the Unready: Papers from the Millenary Conference*, ed. David Hill, British Archaeological Reports, British Series 59 (Oxford: BAR, 1978), 227–53; and "Ely Abbey 672–1109," in *A History of Ely Cathedral*, ed. Peter Meadows and Nigel Ramsay (Woodbridge, UK: The Boydell Press, 2003), 3–58. This monograph is indebted to Professor Keynes's studies on Cnut's reign and its aftermath.

37. The paternity controversy as reported in eleventh- and twelfth-century sources is examined below in chap. 2 (141–49). See also M. K. Lawson, *Cnut: The Danes in England in the Early Eleventh Century* (London & New York: Longman, 1993), 131–32, where he cites Cnut's law (II Cnut 54.1), and Pauline Stafford's discussion in her *Queen Emma and Queen Edith: Queenship and Women's Power in Eleventh-Century England* (Oxford: Blackwell, 1997), 233–34, 236–37.

38. *EER* ii.16, 32–33; *VÆdr* i.1, 7–8, reports a similar contract and oath concerning Edward.

of Harthacnut's absence in Denmark at war with Norway, Harold Harefoot and his mother emerged from the shadows, moving swiftly among the Oxford *witenagemōt* (synod; meeting of the councilors) to claim the throne. There is a letter sent by a certain Immo, priest in the court of Conrad II, to Azeko, bishop of Worms, quoting messages from England that had been brought to Gunnhild, Harthacnut's sister and Emma's daughter, describing the political maneuvers of Cnut's pseudo-queen, Ælfgifu of Northampton, and her son.[39] In the end, the pair succeeded with the support of Leofric, earl of Mercia (perhaps Ælfgifu of Northampton's kin),[40] the *liðsmen* (shipmen) at London, and powerful men north of the Thames—that is to say, of "all the specially Danish part of the people."[41] In this struggle for the throne, they vied against Queen Emma, who fought, with the aid of Godwine, the earl of Wessex, and the chief men of Wessex, to retain the throne for Harthacnut. The outcome of a meeting at Oxford among the chief counselors of both sides was a compromise of a double rule that lasted until about 1037: Emma from Winchester ruled for Harthacnut, the legitimate successor to Cnut, with the help of Godwine as Harthacnut's minister; Harold Harefoot ruled in all the lands north of the Thames with Leofric as counselor.[42]

---

39. See below, chap. 3 (173–74) where the letter is discussed.

40. Pauline Stafford, *Unification and Conquest: A Political and Social History of England in the Tenth and Eleventh Centuries* (London: Hodder Arnold, 1989), 77; Ann Williams, "Leofric," in *Blackwell Encyclopaedia*, ed. Lapidge et al., 282; Keynes, "Cnut's Earls," 74–75, 77–78; P. H. Sawyer, ed. *The Charters of Burton Abbey*, Anglo-Saxon Charters 2 (Oxford: Oxford University Press, 1979), xiii–xlix, esp. xxii, xliii. The prestige and sizable political power held by Ælfgifu of Northampton's Mercian kin are discussed below in chap. 3.

41. *ASC* E-text, s.a. 1036 [1035]; for *liðsmen* referring to the Danes, see *The Battle of Maldon* (ll. 96–99), ed. D. G. Scragg (Manchester, UK: Manchester University Press, 1981), where *liðsmen* appears in apposition to the Viking *werod* (host); *Dictionary of National Biography*, ed. Sir Leslie Stephen and Sir Sidney Lee, vol. 8 (Oxford: Oxford University Press, 1917), 1301; see also *ASC* 2:209–10.

42. *ASC* C-, D-texts (s.a. 1036) E-, F-texts [1035]; see also *ASC* 2:208–10; Edward A. Freeman, *The History of the Norman Conquest of England: Its*

In 1036, Queen Emma's two sons by Æthelred, the athelings Edward and Alfred, who, upon Cnut's accession to the throne in 1016, had been sent to the Norman court for safekeeping, returned to England. Their return, some suggest, was at the queen's request; others say that it was in response to a forged letter of invitation in her name by their stepbrother Harold Harefoot; and still others that it was at their own instigation to claim the throne.[43] The athelings took different routes, with Edward returning swiftly to Normandy after an abortive landing at Southampton. Alfred, taking a more circuitous route through Flanders and crossing the Channel at Wissant to Dover with a "few men of Boulogne,"[44] was intercepted by Godwine, who by late 1036 had defected to the Harold Harefoot camp, and was sent by him to Harold in chains. Thereupon, as William of Poitiers relates,

Gauisus Heraldus in uinculis conspecto Aluerado, satellites eius quam optimos coram eo iussit decapitari, ipsum orbari lumini-bus, dein equestrem nuditate turpatum ad mare deduci sub equo pedibus colligatis, ut in Elga insula exilio cruciaretur et egestate.

Causes and Its Results, vol. 1: *The Preliminary History of the Election of Edward the Confessor*, 3rd ed. rev. (Oxford: Oxford University Press, 1867), 1:482, 775–78.

43. The narrative concerning the ill-fated journeys to England is variously reported in *ASC* C-, D-texts (s.a. 1036); *EER* iii.2–4; *WJGND* vii.6(9); *WPGG* i.1–3; *JWChron* (s.a. 1036). *VÆdr* i.2, 20–21, suggests they came to claim the throne; the twelfth-century *HHHA* vi.20 places Alfred's return after the deaths of Harold Harefoot and Harthacnut; and *WMGRA* ii.188.6, between Harold's death and Harthacnut's return. Alfred's narrative in *LE* ii.90 is derived from *WPGG* and *JWChron*. For a discussion of slight variances in the sources, see Keynes's introduction in *EER* [xxix] and [lvii–lxxi]; Keynes, "Æthelings in Normandy," 195–96; *ASC* 2:212–13. For a pro-Godwinian summary, see Freeman, *History of the Norman Conquest*, 1:489, 779–87.

44. See Keynes, 1998 introduction, *EER* [xxxi]; *EER* iii.4; the number of men accompanying Alfred varies (see *WJGND* vii.5(8)–6(9), who describes Alfred's companions as "a considerable military force"). Alfred may have chosen his itinerary through Flanders as Godgifu, Edward and Alfred's sister and Emma's daughter, had married Eustace, count of Boulogne (her second marriage). See summary in *ASC* 2:212–15.

Delectabat ipsum uita inimici grauior morte. . . . Ita deperiit formosissimus inuuenis, laudatissimus bonitate, regis proles et regum nepos, nec superuiuere potuit diu: cui dum oculi effoderentur cultro, cerebrum uiolauit mucro.[45]

[King Harold rejoiced and ordered that the best of his companions be beheaded in his presence, and that Alfred's eyes be put out. Harold then put him in shameful nakedness on a horse, and had him led to the marshes with his feet tied beneath his horse, so that he could be tortured in exile and starvation on the isle of Ely. . . . Thus [continued William with characteristic flourish] perished the most beautiful youth, worthy of the highest praise for his goodness, offspring of a king, descendant of kings; for he could not survive long since while they were putting out his eyes with a knife the point damaged his brain.]

The other two eleventh-century Norman sources—the anonymous *Vita Ædwardi Regis* and William of Jumièges's *Gesta Normanorum Ducum*—as well as the twelfth-century chronicles of John of Worcester and the *Liber Eliensis*, relate the same tale. All grieve for the "most noble" Alfred, unjustly butchered and worthy of the highest praise.[46] The narrative of the murdered prince survives in a thirteenth-century manuscript of Ailred of Rievaulx's *Life of St. Edward the Confessor*, which in addition contains illustrations rendering the sequence of events (fig. 1).

The mutilation and subsequent murder of Alfred and the massacre of his comrades are fully rendered in two English eleventh-century documents; both reflect a more heightened awareness of the injuries inflicted on the atheling and his troops. These, the closest in time to the event, are the renderings in the C-text (and with minor variations, the D-text) of the *Anglo-Saxon Chronicle*[47]—where Alfred's execution

---

45. *WPGG* i.3.
46. Quote from *WJGND* vii.6(9); *LE* ii.90; *JWChron* (s.a. 1036).
47. The *Chronicle* E-text is silent on this event, apparently because of its

is the subject of one of six major poems[48]—and the *Encomium Emmae Reginae*, a political history concerning the rise of the Anglo-Danish realm written by a monk of Saint-Bertin around 1041 at the request of Queen Emma.[49]

The *C-Chronicle* poem particularizes and sharpens the barbarity of the crimes committed against Alfred and his comrades. Although the Chronicler is partisan, he is restrained in his condemnation of Godwine's and the other noble's defection to Harold's camp; nonetheless, his tone, further heightened by rhymed alliteration, conveys outrage in the course of the enumeration of the crimes, which Katherine O'Brien O'Keeffe has argued were ironically legal punishments for offenses in Cnut's and Æthelred's laws.[50]

Godwinian leanings. Plummer holds the C-text to be more original (*ASC* 2:212) as do O'Brien O'Keeffe and Conner. See Campbell's 1949 introduction to *EER* [cxlv–cxlvii], for variations on reporting of the event. See further Katherine O'Brien O'Keeffe's introduction in her edition of *The Anglo-Saxon Chronicle: A Collaborative Edition, MS. C*, vol. 5 (Cambridge, UK: D. S. Brewer, 2001), esp. xx–xxiv, lxiv–lxxxix, and that of Patrick W. Conner in *The Anglo-Saxon Chronicle: A Collaborative Edition, The Abingdon Chronicle A.D. 956–1066 (MS. C, with Reference to BDE)*, vol. 10 (Cambridge, UK: D. S. Brewer, 1996), esp. xxxiv–lx.

48. All six of the poems appear in the C-Text, and are traditionally identified as *The Battle of Brunanburh* (937, in versions ABCD of *ASC*), *The Capture of the Five Boroughs* (942, in versions A-, B-, C-, and D-texts), *The Coronation of Edgar* (973, in A-, B-, C-texts), *The Death of Edgar* (975, A-, B-, C-texts), *The Death of Alfred* (1036, C-, D-texts), *The Death of Edward* (1065, C-, D-texts). See Thomas A. Bredehoft, *Textual Histories: Readings in the Anglo-Saxon Chronicle* (Toronto: University of Toronto Press, 2001), esp. chap. 4, for a discussion of these and the additional *Chronicle* entries that Plummer printed as verse; Bredehoft identifies thirty-six poetic passages inclusive in seventeen different poems (78–79).

49. See Keynes's 1998 introduction, *EER* [xiv–xv], and Campbell's 1949 introduction, *EER* [cii–cv], for discussions of the genre; for the argument that *EER* is political propaganda on the part of Emma, see Sten Körner, *The Battle of Hastings: England and Europe 1035-1066* (Lund: C. W. K. Gleerup, 1964); and see further below, chap. 4 (230–31, 230n62).

50. In a recent article that examines the relationship between the

1036. Her com Ælfred, se unsceððiga æþeling, Æþelrædes sunu cinges, hider inn and wolde to his meder, þe on Wincestre sæt, ac hit ne geþafode Godwine eorl, ne ec oþre men þe mycel mihton wealdan, forðan hit hleoðrode þa swiðe toward Haraldes, þeh hit unriht wære.

Ac Godwine hine þa gelette and hine on hæft sette;
and his geferan he todraf, and sume mislice ofsloh;
sume hi man wið feo sealde, sume hreowlice acwealde,
sume hi man bende, sume hi man blende,
sume hamelode, sume hættode.
Ne wearð dreorlicre dæd gedon on þison earde,
syþþan Dene comon and her frið namon.
Nu is to gelyfenne to ðan leofan gode,
þæt hi blission bliðe mid Criste
þe wæron butan scylde swa earmlice acwealde.
Se æþeling lyfode þa gyt; ælc yfel man him gehet,
oððæt man gerædde þæt man hine lædde
to Eligbyrig swa gebundenne.
Sona swa he lende, on scype man hine blende
and hine swa blindne, brohte to ðam munecon,
and he þar wunode ða hwile þe he lyfode.
Syþþan hine man byrigde, swa him wel gebyrede,
[þæt wæs] ful wurðlice, swa he wyrðe wæs,

---

physical body and its use in juridical discourse, Katherine O'Brien O'Keeffe comments on the significance of the "repeated protestations of innocence" in the poem as signs that these outrages on the body depicted in the C-text must be read in light of the law codes enacted by Alfred's two fathers—Æthelred, his natural father, and Cnut, his stepfather—which detail the mutilation of specific bodily parts as legal satisfaction for crimes committed. O'Keeffe suggests that the chronicler's tone of outrage rests more on the violation of innocence than on the barbarity of the acts; "Body and Law in Late Anglo-Saxon England," *ASE* 27 (1998): 209–32, esp. 214–15. See also *ASC* 2:215.

æt ðam westende, þam styple ful gehende,
on þam suðportice; seo saul is mid Criste.[51]

[1036. In this year Alfred, the innocent atheling, son of king
Æthelred, came hither; he wanted to visit his mother who was
in Winchester; but earl Godwine would not permit him to, nor
would other men who wielded great power, because the cry was
greatly in favour of Harold, although it was wrong.

But then Godwine prevented him, and placed him in fetters,
Drove away his comrades, and slew some in various ways;
Some were sold as slaves, some savagely murdered,
Some were put in chains, and some were blinded,
Some were hamstrung, and some scalped.
No bloodier deed was done in this land
Since the Danes came, and seized peace here.
Now it is for us to trust in the beloved God
That they will rejoice blissfully with Christ,
Those who without guilt were so miserably killed.
The atheling still lived. He was threatened with every evil,
Until it was counseled that he would be led
To the city of Ely, fettered as he was.
As soon as he arrived, his eyes were put out on board ship,
And thus blinded he was brought to the monks.
And he remained there as long as he lived.
Later he was buried, as it was befitting,
With great splendor, as he was of high rank,
At the west end of the church, very near to the steeple,
In the south aisle. His soul is with Christ.]

The innocence of the loyal war band, their surprise seizure in the night,
the sudden terror that sweeps in upon them, and the barbarous acts

---

51. *The Anglo-Saxon Minor Poems*, ed. E. V. K. Dobbie, *ASPR* 6 (New York:
Columbia University Press, 1942), 24–25; [*þæt wæs*] supplied by Plummer
from the D-text; *ASC* 1:160; O'Brien O'Keeffe, *MS.C*, 105–06.

make the scene strikingly moving, despite the fact that the warriors being lamented by the Anglo-Saxon Chronicler are Normans. The Chronicler is anti-Godwine and decries the faction's switched loyalties to Harold. His restrained anger and pain at the atrocities perpetrated on the son of the late king Æthelred, the "innocent atheling," and his comrades are heightened when he links their present betrayal, their tortures and mutilations with the horrors inflicted upon England in the early years of the eleventh century; then marauding Danes (from 1003 to 1016) butchered the bodies of those whom they did not kill as they ravaged and burned the English countryside, receiving tribute for peace but never holding to it, employing a type of martial tactics that recall those of Grendel in the poem (*Bwf* 154^{b}-58).[52] Scalping and blinding were then the order of the day. These present heinous acts—committed at the command of Harold Harefoot and executed by Godwine—become less of a personal offense against the innocent atheling and his comrades and more of a treasonous offense against the English people. The Chronicler's sense of powerlessness in relating Alfred's fate—to be conveyed to Ely in bonds and blinded there on the shore of the "vast solitary marshland"[53]—was mitigated by the splendor of the prince's burial and the knowledge that his soul dwelt with Christ.[54]

---

52. *sibbe ne wolde / wið manna hwone mægenes Deniga / fearhbealo feorran, fea þingian, / nē þær nænig witena wēnan þorfte / beorhte bōte tō banan folmum* (he [Grendel] desired no peace-pact with any man of the Danish military force, no termination to the deadly evil; [nor did he desire] to settle on a tribute; none of the counselors there had need to expect bright compensation at the hands of the killer).

53. See Charles William Stubbs, *Historical Memorials of Ely Cathedral* (New York: Charles Scribners' Sons; London: J. M. Dent & Co., 1897), for descriptions of the Ely marshland before and after the drainage, esp. 4–10. H. C. Darby, *The Medieval Fenland*, 2nd ed. (Newton Abbot, UK: David & Charles, 1974), 1–21, 44–45, 74–75, 106–13; and his *The Draining of the Fens* (Cambridge, UK: University Press, 1940); see also Hall, *Fenland Project*, esp. 30–40.

54. See O'Brien O'Keeffe's discussion of the need to emphasize the innocence of the victims in the context of their bodies' displaying criminal

"The Death of Alfred" contains the generic characteristics found in the other canonical *Chronicle* poems, which Thomas Bredehoft has argued are concerned with the genealogy (and dynastic succession) of West-Saxon kings.[55] Alfred atheling is in the direct line of Cerdic and Alfred, while the usurper Harold not only is of questionable parentage but is equated to and is the embodiment of those Danes who razed, burned, and ravaged Æthelred's England, even penetrating and laying bare the wild fenland for years.[56] Other *Chronicle* poems back-reference the founding of the West-Saxon dynasty; "The Death of Alfred" is emblematic of its destruction.[57]

The second eleventh-century English historical account, that of the *Encomium Emmae Reginae*, fills in the particulars absent in the C-text, recording the setting and circumstances of the savagery perpetrated on Alfred and his comrades more fully and in a less restrained tone.

> Uerum ubi iam erat proximus, illi comes Goduinus est obuius factus, et eum in sua suscepit fide, eiusque fit mox miles cum sacramenti affirmatione. Et deuians eum a Londonia induxit eum in uilla [Geldefordia] nuncupata, inibique milites eius uicenos et duodenos

---

actions and the effort to make a martyr of Alfred; "Body and Law in Late Anglo-Saxon England," 228–29.

55. Bredehoft, *Textual Histories*, 35–38, 70–71, 100–13, and passim; see, as examples, the entries for 937, 942, 959, 973, 975, and 1036 that identify the English kings as descendants of Cerdic and Alfred. In essence, all the canonical poems evoke and codify a historical or genealogical origin, their purpose being to give permanence to events that rise above the transience of history. See also Janet Thormann, "The *Anglo-Saxon Chronicle Poems* and the Making of the English Nation," in *Anglo-Saxonism and the Construction of Social Identity*, ed. Allen J. Frantzen and John D. Niles (Gainesville, FL: University of Florida Press, 1997), 60–85, who posits a "national ideology" to the *Chronicle* poems.

56. *ASC* E-text, s.a. 1004, 1006, 1010. The 1036 diaspora motif (ll. 6-10) also appears in the entry for 1075 (E-, D-texts) in the context of treason against William the Conqueror.

57. *The Battle of Brunanburh* (937) and *The Death of Edward the Martyr* (979) back-reference to the Saxon invasion and the founding of the West-Saxon line.

decenosque singula duxit per hospicia, paucis relictis cum iuuene, qui eius seruitio deberent insistere. Et largitus est eis habundanter cibaria et pocula, et ipse ad sua recessit hospicia, mane rediturus, ut domino suo seruiret cum debita honorificentia [*EER* iii.4].⁵⁸

[But when he [Alfred] was already near his goal [to visit Queen Emma], Earl Godwine met him and took him under his protection, and forthwith became his soldier by averment under oath. Diverting him from London he led him into the town called Guildford, and lodged his soldiers there in separate billets by twenties, twelves and tens, leaving a few with the young man, whose duty was to be in attendance upon him. And he gave them food and drink in plenty, and withdrew personally to his own lodging, until he should return in the morning to wait upon his lord with due honour.]

In the *Encomium* description, the details of the surprise night attack on the warrior-band alluded to in the *Chronicle* poem are graphically outlined. Godwine's betrayal is made more heinous because he violated his oath (recorded in other accounts as well).⁵⁹ The Encomiast makes more specific the lodging of the soldiers, noting especially Godwine's cunning separation of the prince from his men by placing them in separate billets (thus making them more vulnerable to attack) and his personal withdrawal to his own lodgings after he has lavished food and drink upon them. The evocation of the ensuing attack, in graphic particulars, follows:

Sed postquam manducauerant et biberant, et lectos, utpote fessi, libenter ascenderant, ecce complices Haroldi infandissimi tiranni adsunt, et singula hospicia inuadunt, arma innocentum uirorum furtim tollunt et eos manicis ferreis et compedibus artant, et ut crucientur in crastinum seruant. Mane autem facto adducuntur insontes in medio et non auditi dampnantur scelerose. Nam

---

58. *EER* 42–43, ed. Campbell.
59. *WPGG* 1.4; *WJGND* vii.6(9); *JWChron* (s.a. 1036); *WMGRA* ii.188.6; *HHHA* vi.20.

omnium exarmatis uinctisque post tergum manibus atrocissimis
traditi sunt carnificibus, quibus etiam iussum est, (ut nemini) par-
cerent nisi quem sors decima offerret. . . . Unde huius <s> cemodi
tortores canibus deteriores digne omnia dicunt secula, qui non
miliciae uiolentia sed fraudium suarum insidiis tot militum hone-
sta dampnauerunt corpora. Quosdam ut dictum est perimebant,
quosdam uero suae seruituti mancipabant; alios ceca cupidine
capti uendebant, nonnullos autem artatos uinculis maiori inri-
sioni reseruabant. Sed diuina miseratio non defuit innocentibus
in tanto discrimine consistentibus, quia multos ipsi uidimus quos
ex illa derisione eripuit caelitus sine amminiculo hominis ruptis
manicarum compedumque obicibus. (*EER* iii.5)[60]

[But after they had eaten and drunk, and being weary, had gladly
ascended their couches, behold, men leagued with the most abomi-
nable tyrant Haraldr appeared, entered the various billets, secretly
removed the arms of the innocent men, confined them with iron
manacles and fetters, and kept them till the morrow to be tortured.
But when it was morning, the innocent men were led out, and were
iniquitously condemned without a hearing. For they were all dis-
armed and delivered with their hands bound behind their backs
to most vicious executioners who were ordered, furthermore, to
spare no man until the tenth lot should reprise him. . . . Hence
all ages will justly call such torturers worse than dogs, since they
brought to condemnation the worthy persons of so many soldiers
not by soldierly force but by their treacherous snares. Some, as has
been said, they slew, some they placed in slavery to themselves;
others they sold, for they were in the grip of blind greed, but they
kept a few loaded with bonds to be subjected to greater mockery.
But the divine pity did not fail the innocent men who stood in
such peril, for I myself have seen many whom it snatched from
that derision, acting from heaven without the help of man, so that
the impediments of manacles and fetters were shattered.]

---

60. *EER* 42–45, ed. Campbell.

Chapter One

The soldiers, their fighting spirit weakened after having been feasted by Godwine, ascend to their resting places, unaware of the terror that is to come, when Harold's men break into the hall. Charged and without legal recourse, the men are stripped of their arms and manacled; some are slain, some sold into slavery, some endure further indignities, the crimes recalling the outrages enumerated in the *Chronicle* poem, which O'Brien O'Keeffe perceives visibly embody the law: "To view those eyeless, noseless faces, those scalpless heads, arms without hands, legs without feet is to read upon their bodies the legal enactment of punishment for crimes."[61]

The Encomiast then continues his narration by pointedly detailing the barbarities inflicted on the prince:

Captus est igitur regius iuuenis clam suo in hospicio, eductusque in insula Heli dicta a milite primum inrisus est iniquissimo. Deinde contemptibiliores eliguntur, ut horum ab insania flendus iuuenis diiudicetur. Qui iudices constituti decreuerunt, illi debere oculi utrique ad contemptum primum erui. Quod postqu[am] parant perficere, duo illi super brachia ponunter, qui interim tenerent illa, et unus super pectus unusque super crura, ut sic facilius illi inferretur paena. Quid hoc in dolore detineor? Mihi ipsi scribenti tremit calamus, dum horreo quae iuuensis passus est beatissimus. Euadam ergo breuius tantae calamitatis miseriam, finemque huius martyrii fine tenus perstringam. Namque est ab inpiis tentus, effossis etiam luminibus inpiissime est occisus. Qua nece perfecta relinqu[u]nt corpus exanime, quod fideles Christi, monachi scilicet eiusdem insulae Haeli, rapientes sepelierunt honorifice. In loco autem sepulcri eius multa fiunt miracula, ut quidam aiunt,

---

61. O'Brien O'Keeffe sees the enumeration of the mutilations to be more significant in the *Chronicle* text because of the relationship to the early English law codes; see her elaboration on the early English law codes dealing with specific offenses in the context of the mutilations endured by the warrior band ("Body and Law in Late Anglo-Saxon England," 214–17, quote on 214–15).

qui etiam se haec uidisse saepissime dicunt. Et merito: innocen-
ter enim fuit martyrizatus, ideoque dignum est ut per eum inno-
cencium exerceatur uirtus. Gaudeat igitur Emma regina de tanto
intercessore, quia (quem) quondam in terris habuit filium nunc
habet in caelis patronum. (*EER* iii.6)[62]

[The royal youth, then, was captured secretly in his lodging, and
having been taken to the island called Ely, was first of all mocked
by the most wicked soldiery. Then still more contemptible persons were selected, that the lamented youth might be condemned
by them in their madness. When these men had been set up as
judges, they decreed that first of all both his eyes should be put
out as a sign of contempt. After they prepared to carry this out,
two men were placed on his arms to hold them meanwhile, one on
his breast, and one on his legs, in order that the punishment might
be more easily inflicted on him. Why do I linger over this sorrow?
As I write my pen trembles, and I am horror-stricken at what the
most blessed youth suffered. Therefore I will the sooner turn away
from the misery of so great a disaster, and touch upon the conclusion of this martyrdom as far as its consummation. For he was held
fast, and after his eyes had been put out was most wickedly slain.
When this murder had been performed, they left his lifeless body,
which the servants of Christ, the monks, I mean, of the same Isle
of Ely, took up and honourably interred. However, many miracles
occur where his tomb is, as people report who even declare most
repeatedly that they have seen them. And it is justly so: for he was
martyred in his innocence, and therefore it is fitting that the might
of the innocent should be exercised through him.]

Here the Encomiast explicitly choreographs the tortures inflicted
upon Alfred alluded to in the Chronicle poem. Facing a bizarre kan-
garoo court and condemned, the atheling is pinned to the ground
by four men, his arms, chest, and legs entirely restrained. Thus held,

---

62. *EER* 44–47, ed. Campbell.

the prince, blinded and maimed by the knife's point,[63] is left to die in the remote marshlands of *insulae Haeli*, the isle of Ely. The Encomiast raises the stakes for Alfred's martyrdom and the establishment of his cult, alluded to in the Chronicle entry, by citing the miraculous healings that have taken place at his tomb.

Such, then, is the material recorded for the first historical event under consideration. The distinctive features that ideally should harmonize with the Beowulfian sequence are: (1) the surprise night attack on a loyal warrior-band and their atheling; (2) their subsequent mutilation on the orders of the atheling's stepbrother, Harold Harefoot, a fratricidal act analogous to that of Cain; and (3) the final outrage—the atheling's mutilation and eventual murder take place on the shore of a vast solitary marshland where he has been taken by Harold's men, his torturers. Additional details in the *Encomium* entry to be kept in mind as elements that might be alluded to in another guise in the beheading sequence are: the sequestering of the men from their prince; their abandonment by their host; and the pinning down of the prince threatened at knifepoint. Though, as I have noted in the Introduction, an analogic critical strategy may be subject to individual judgment, my argument below adheres to conservative criteria: demonstration of similarities of theme, setting, character, narrative pattern, action, and a reasonable similarity in cultural and historical context.

The Beowulfian Sequence

The first Beowulfian passage is a panegyric on the nobility, courage, and loyalty of the warrior band. Lines 1232–50, which form the prelude to the surprise night attack of Grendel's mother, reverberate with martial tones as they set the scene for the massacre of Æschere. After having feasted the men, Hrothgar departs to his chambers, leaving the warriors alone in the hall. The troop's war gear fills the hall—battle shields, bright wooden boards, are set above the warrior

---

63. The use of a knife, explicit in *WPGG* i.3, is implicit here.

band's heads; the atheling's towering battle helmet, his magnificent forged spear are spotlighted—all in battle readiness.

> Þǣr wæs symbla cyst,
> druncon wīn weras. Wyrd ne cūþon,
> geōsceaft grim*m*e, swā hit āgangen wearð
> eorla manegum, syþðan ǣfen cwōm,
> ond him Hrōþgār gewāt tō hofe sīnum,
> rīce tō ræste. Reced weardode
> unrīm eorla, swā hīe oft ǣr dydon.
> Bencþelu beredon; hit geondbrǣded wearð
> beddum ond bolstrum. Bēorscealca sum
> fūs ond fǣge fletræste gebēag.
> Setton him tō hēafdon hilderandas,
> bordwudu beorhtan; þǣr on bence wæs
> ofer æþelinge ȳþgesēne
> heaþostēapa helm, hringed byrne,
> þrecwudu þrymlīc. Wæs þēaw hyra,
> þæt hīe oft wǣron an wīg gearwe,
> gē æt hām gē on herge, gē gehwæþer þāra
> efne swylce mǣla, swylce hira mandryhtne
> þearf gesǣlde; wæs sēo þēod tilu.

(*Bwf* 1232^b-50)

[The most excellent of banquets took place there; the warriors drank wine. They could not know the grim fate, determined destiny of old, as it was to come to pass for many of the noblemen, after evening came and Hrothgar departed to his dwelling, the chieftain to his resting place. A countless number of nobles guarded the building, as often they had done before. They cleared away the benchplanks. It became covered with bedding and bolsters. One of the beer-feasters, ready and fated for death, bent toward his hall-resting place. They placed battle shields over their heads, bright wood-boards; there on the bench above the atheling, easily visible, was the towering battle-helmet, a ringed byrnie, a magnificent forged spear. Such was their custom so that they might often be prepared for combat both at home and on raids, and each of them perform at such times as need befell their liege lord. That was a good nation.]

I find it difficult to read the passage—which concludes with the panegyrical statement "that was a good nation [or a good race]"—as anything other than an encomium to the warrior band. Except for lines 1240^b–41^b and lines 1243^b–46, when the reader's focus is directed to the doomed atheling (whom I take to be Æschere, here and in the subsequent references, until he is named in line 1323), the passage creates a portrait of the ideal warrior band accompanying their leader, ignorant of the grim fate that was to befall them. The departure of the host, the comfort of the bedding, the contentment that follows feasting, the innocence of the fated men, these elements harmonize with the setting and the encomiastic statements that have characterized the Norman warriors in the historical materials. Godwine's treachery in Guildford, his perversion of the code of hospitality, has been recast into a positive image of royal munificence in the character of Hrothgar.

Further, the subsequent night attack of Grendel's mother is another example of epic transference; her sudden sweep through the hall and surprise attack on the sleeping men are analogous, it seems to me, to the night rush of Harold's men as they penetrated Godwine's hall, caused terror among the troops in the night rest, and snatched Alfred away to his death.

> Cōm þā tō Heorote, ðǣr Hring-Dene
> geond þæt sæld swǣfun. Þā ðǣr sōna wearð
> edhwyrft eorlum, siþðan inne fealh
> Grendles mōdor. Wæs se gryre lǣssa
> efne swā micle, swā bið mægþa cræft,
> wīggryre wīfes be wǣpnedmen,
> þonne heoru bunden, hamere geþrūen,

sweord swāte fāh swīn ofer helme
ecgum dyhtig andweard scireð.
Ðā wæs on healle heardecg togen
sweord ofer setlum, sīdrand manig
hafen handa fæst; helm ne gemunde,
byrnan sīde, þā hine se brōga angeat.
Hēo wæs on ofste, wolde ūt þanon,
fēore beorgan, þā hēo onfunden wæs;
hraðe hēo æþelinga ānne hæfde
fæste befangen, þā hēo tō fenne gang.
Sē wæs Hrōþgāre hæleþa lēofost
on gesīðes hād be sǣm twēonum,
rīce randwiga, þone ðe hēo on ræste ābrēat,
blǣdfæstne beorn. Næs Bēowulf ðǣr.

(*Bwf* 1279–99)

[Then she came to Heorot, where the Ring-Danes slept throughout
the hall. Then immediately, there was reversal for the noblemen,
when Grendel's mother penetrated into [the hall]. The terror, the
war-terror of the woman, was lesser [than Grendel's]—just as great
as is the strength of maidens compared with a weaponed man when
the bound blade, the sword, hammer-forged and shining with gore,
strong in its edges, shears through the opposite boar-image crest-
ing the helm. Then within the hall, the hardened-edge, the sword
was seized from the seat, many a broad shield lifted steady in hand;
no one heeded helm or broad byrnie when the terror seized him.
She was in haste, she wanted out from thence, wanted to save her
life, when she was discovered; quickly she had seized firmly one of
the athelings; then she went out to the fen. He was of heroes in the
rank of champion, the dearest to Hrothgar between the two seas,
a mighty shield-warrior, a man established in his glory, whom she
had cut down in his bed. Beowulf was not there.]

In this passage, Grendel's mother functions as an extension of
Grendel—in a type of teknonymy, her very identity is derived from the

name of her son—and they form a unified force that strives to possess Hrothgar's hall.[64] Both have been characterized variously throughout the poem as murderers and as adversaries of God (e.g., *Godes andsaca, / morðres scyldig, ond his mōdor ēac*, 1682[b]-83), as alien visitants that stalk the borderland wastes and rule the moors (e.g., *þæt hīe gesāwon swylce twēgen / micle mearcstapan mōras healdan / ellorgǣstas*, 1347-49[a]), and both hold a relationship that echoes the Harold-Ælfgifu pairing, with Grendel's paternity questioned. Whatever characterizing attributes and actions the poet has attributed to the son he likewise assigns to the mother. As with Grendel's previous attacks, the royal hall now becomes a battlefield, as the slaughtering battle-figure—whose strength is compared to that of a weaponed man and who later is referred to by use of masculine pronouns—weaves her way among the war troops. The crisis for the warriors intensifies when the *ides āglǣcwīf* (lady, monstrous warrior woman; 1259[a]) snatches up the doomed atheling, their liege lord Æschere—a champion, a mighty shield warrior, established in his glory, and beloved of the king—and escapes to the fen, where she severs his head from his body. Further, the confusion that erupts in Heorot, the Danes' outrage—there was uproar in Heorot (1302[a])—and their mourning of Æschere, that *hæleþa lēofost* (dearest hero, 1296[b]), "that most excellent lifeless thane," an "atheling of exemplary merit" whom Hrothgar lamentingly describes as typifying "whatever a noble should be" (1308-9, 1322-29), are equivalent to the Norman and English chroniclers' lamentations and panegyrical descriptions of that "most noble" Alfred, "unjustly butchered," "worthy of the highest praise for his goodness,

---

64. Mother and son define each other; he is as ironically a *healðegn* (hall thane) as she is a pseudo-*ides* (lady). In addition to having been characterized as murderers and as adversaries of God (1682[b]-83), they are also defined as *feorhgeniðlan* (enemies of life; 969[a], 1540[a]), as *wælgǣst wǣfre* (wandering murderous spirits, 1331[a]), *wælgǣst* "murderous spirits" (1995[a]), as monstrous-like warriors (159ff., 1259), mighty evil foes (712, 737[b], 1339[a]), and alien visitants that stalk the marshes and rule the moors (1347-49[a]); see further Damico, Beowulf's *Wealhtheow and the Valkyrie Tradition*, 113, 226 nn. 23-27.

offspring of a king, descendant of kings," and their aggrievement at his mutilation. Thus, relevant narrative elements produce a set of parallels between the historical and Beowulfian material—the surprise night attack and ensuing execution of the prince; the abandonment of the troops by the host; the resultant mayhem and lamentations that rise up among the troops; the attack by a surrogate of the enemy; and an exemplary hero unjustly executed. These parallels and their sequential ordering, it seems to me, point to a resemblance between the Beowulfian passage and the historical event under consideration here.

The resemblance spills over to the funereal journey to and location of Grendel's abode. The way is difficult; the place, remote and inaccessible. When the men reach the clearing near the shore, they encounter Æschere's bodiless head on the sea-slope—for them, a painful, unexpected sight—and the sea surging with hot gore, presumably his blood.

Oferēode þā æþelinga bearn
stēap stānhliðo, stīge nearwe,
enge ānpaðas, uncūð gelād,
neowle næssas, nicorhūsa fela;
hē fēara sum beforan gengde
wīsra monna wong scēawian,
oþ þæt hē fǣringa fyrgenbēamas
ofer hārne stān hleonian funde,
wynlēasne wudu; wæter under stōd
drēorig ond gedrēfed. Denum eallum wæs,
winum Scyldinga weorce on mōde
tō geþolianne, ðegne monegum,
oncyð earla gehwǣm, syðþan Æscheres
on þām holmclife hafelan mētton.
Flōd blōde wēol—folc tō sǣgon—
hātan heolfre. Horn stundum song
fūslic f(yrd)lēoð. Fēþa eal gesǣt.

(*Bwf* 1408–24)

[Then the son of athelings rode onto high gravelly slopes, along narrow paths, single-file footpaths, a perilous water crossing between precipitous banks of dry ground, many water-monster houses. He, with a few wise ones, rode before to view the plain, until suddenly he came upon gigantic trees, a joyless grove, leaning over a grey rock. For all the Danes, for the friends of the Scyldings, for many a thane, there was pain to suffer in their spirit, grief for each of the nobles, when on the sea-cliff they came upon the head of Æschere. The flood of water surged with blood—the soldiers stared—with hot gore. The horn sang out at times, an eager battle song. The warriors all sat down.]

In general the landscape of the mere has been thought to be imagistic and conceptual, metaphorically creating a horrific space on which the poet stages monstrous happenings. Thus, one parallel to Grendel's realm has been found in Saint Paul's vision of hell in the *Blickling Homilies*.[65] But Grendel's realm also has a kinship with a more realistic space in East Anglia, Guthlac's fenland: a fen of vast size, with "immense marshes" and "dark stagnant pools . . . [with] numerous wooded islands and reeds and tummocks and thickets," a fenland that "extends to the North Sea with manifold wide and lengthy meanderings,"[66] and which in the eighth century had become a frontier,

---

65. *The Blickling Homilies of the Tenth Century, with a Translation, and Index of Words*, ed. R. Morris, Early English Text Society, o.s. 58, 63, 73 (London: N. Trübner, 1874–80), 196–210, esp. 209; see 208 for translation: "*þær ealle wætero niðergewítað, & he þær geseah ofer ðæm wætere sumne hárne stán; & wæron norð of ðæm stáne awexene swiðe hrimige bearwas, & ðær wæron þystrogenipo, & under þæm stáne wæs nicera eardung & wearga. & he geseah þæt on ðæm clife hangodan on ðæm ís gean bearwum manige swearte saula be heora handum gebundne*"; see also n. 25 above, Frank, "'Mere' and 'Sund,'" in *Modes of Interpretation* (157) for additional examples.

66. *Est in meditullaneis Brittanniae partibus inmensae magnitudinis aterrima palus, quae, a Grontae fluminis ripis incipiens, haud procul a castello quem dicunt nomine Gronte nunc stagnis, nunc flactris, interdum nigris fusi vaporis laticibus, necnon et crebris insularum nemorumque intervenientibus flexuosis rivigarum anfractibus, ab austro in aquilonem mare tenus longissimo tractu protenditur* (There is in the midland district of Britain a most dismal fen of immense

a border region, and a refuge for brigands and bandits as well as monks and saints.[67] True, Guthlac's description of the fen marsh is of Crowland, but it captures the variety and range of landscape that marked the East Anglian fenland during the Saxon and medieval periods, an expansive topography of silt and peat brought about by a mixture of salt and fresh watercourses, with peninsulas (described by Gelling as *næssas*) and islands rising above the vast expanse of water, and traversed by treacherous mud trackways or fords.[68] The largest of the British wetlands, the East Anglian fens were the site of important

---

size, which begins at the banks of the river Granta not far from the camp which is called Cambridge, and stretches from the south as far north as the sea. It is a very long tract, now consisting of marshes, now of bogs, sometimes of black waters, overhung by fog, sometimes studded with wooded islands and traversed by the windings of tortuous streams); *Vita Sancti Guthlaci: Felix's Life of Saint Guthlac*, ed. and trans. Bertram Colgrave (Cambridge, UK: Cambridge University Press, 1956), chap. 24, 86–87. See also Michael Swanton's translation in his *Anglo-Saxon Prose* (London: J. M. Dent, 1993), 88–113. Felix's *Life* (dated ca. mid-eighth century) is found in the eleventh-century London, BL Cotton Vespasian D.xxi (ff. 18–40ᵛ), which also contains Ælfrician writings. The edition is Paul Gonser's *Das angelsächsische Prosa-Leben des heiligen Guthlac*, Anglistische Forschungen 27 (Heidelberg: Carl Winter, 1909). Colgrave makes note of the relationship between Guthlac's place of refuge and Grendel's dominion (1 and 182–83), as has Dorothy Whitelock in *The Audience of Beowulf* (Oxford: Clarendon, 1951), 73–76. See Felix's *Life*, xxiv, xxvii, xxxi; for similar descriptions of the topography in the Dragon episode, see chaps. xxviii, xxix, xxxiv. There is always the possibility that the Blickling Homilist used the East Anglian fenlands as his source in his description of Saint Paul's Vision of Hell.

67.   For discussions of the East Anglian fens, see Darby, *Medieval Fenland*, esp. chap. 1; also 2–16; see also his "The Fenland Frontier in Anglo-Saxon England," *Antiquity* 7 (1934): 185; and his *Draining of the Fens*.

68.   Hall, *Fenland Landscapes* and *Fenland Project*. The fenland expanse was composed of silt and clay (the result of saline deposits) and peat (caused by fresh water). See also Darby, *Medieval Fenland*, 93–119; Gelling, above, nn. 28, 31, 32; the discussion of Gelling's and Cronan's readings of *gelād*, as discussed above, 61–63; and P. H. Reaney, *The Place-Names of Cambridgeshire and the Isle of Ely* (Cambridge, UK: University Press, 1943), who notes the term *gelād* as "watercourse," particularly common on the Isle of Ely (335).

religious houses in the Saxon and medieval periods—Peterborough, Thorney, Ramsey, and, of course, Bede's Ely.[69]

The earliest surviving description of Ely is Bede's. In the course of his discussion of Saint Æthelthryth's exhumation and reburial at Ely (a major reason for Ely's fame as a religious center), he describes Ely as being surrounded on all sides by seas and fens:

> Ely (El-ge) is a district of about 60 hides in the kingdom of the East Angles and, as has already been said, resembles an island in that it is surrounded by marshes or by water. It derives its name from the large number of eels which are caught in the marshes.[70]

Though most easily accessible by boat, Ely was not entirely cut off

---

69. Peterborough was established in 655, Thorney in 662, and Ely in 673. After their restoration in the tenth century (Peterborough in 963; Ely in 970; Thorney in 972), the East Anglian monastic foundations were unrivaled in reputation.

70. *Bede's Ecclesiastical History of the English People*, ed. Bertram Colgrave and R. A. B. Mynors (Oxford: Clarendon Press, 1969), book iv.19, 396–97. For a history of Ely, see Keynes, "Ely Abbey 672–1109," in *History of Ely Cathedral*, ed. Meadows and Ramsay, 3–58; Ely, Keynes notes, originally meant "eel-district" (El-ge), but because of the "vast" quantities of eels in the waters and marshes that surrounded it, its name was altered in the eighth or ninth century to El-eg (eel-island), 3. See also his "Ely Abbey," in *Blackwell Encyclopaedia*, ed. Lapidge et al., 166–67; Edward Miller, *The Abbey and Bishopric of Ely* (Cambridge, UK: Cambridge University Press, 1951); R. B. Pugh, *The Victoria County History of Cambridgeshire and the Isle of Ely*, vol. 4 (1953; London: Institute of Historical Research, 1967), 28–89, esp. 28–51, 116–18; and Stubbs, *Historical Memorials*. For discussions of eels as economic assets, see Darby, *Medieval Fenland*, chap. 2; for a discussion of Ely's monastic administration and the education of its young monks at Oxford and Cambridge, see Joan Greatrex, "Rabbits and Eels at High Table: Monks of Ely at the University of Cambridge, c. 1337–1539," in *Monasteries and Society in Medieval Britain, Proceedings of the 1994 Harlaxton Symposium* (Stamford, UK: P. Watkins, 1999), 312–28; and her "Benedictine Observance at Ely: The Intellectual, Liturgical and Spiritual Evidence Considered," in *History of Ely Cathedral*, 80–93. I am grateful to Professor Greatrex for sharing her thoughts on the monks of Ely with me.

from the mainland. When the waters receded in the dry season, on the southern shore of Ely where the fen was narrowest, three mud trackways were operative (reminiscent of Gelling's and Cronan's *gelād*, "water crossing"),[71] two on the western side at Earith and Aldreth, and one on the eastern, connecting the seven-mile island to Soham, a "horseshoe peninsula" of limestone and chalk rock. The trackways and fords gave way to the causeways of the eleventh and twelfth centuries.[72] In his surveys of East Anglian fenlands, David Hall notes that Ely itself comprised a number of "islands," among which were the parishes of Whittlesey, March, and Stuntney (which he translates as "steep island" because of the "striking manner" in which it—like Ely—rose "abruptly out of the Fens"). Stuntney served a crucial function for Ely because "of its strategic position as a major entrance" in the Saxon and medieval period.[73] On Whittlesey (OE *Witlesig*, "Wit(t)el's island"), there remain traces of a complex medieval drainage system, in the form of a "few crooked dykes" that form parts of its boundary, one of which is called Cnut's Dike, while March (OE *mearc*, "boundary"), a type of borderland, was an important site along the land and water routes of the fenlands.[74]

The twelfth-century *Liber Eliensis*[75] expands on Bede's description,

---

71. See above, nn. 31, 32.

72. Darby, *Medieval Fenland*, 106–13, esp. 108, quote at 106.

73. Hall, *Fenland Project*, 30, 40; for names of additional islands composing the Ely complex, see esp. 30.

74. Hall, *Fenland Landscapes*, 12, 46, 56; see also his *Fenland Project*, 124, 130, 165, 171, 174, where he discusses March's positioning in the fenland routings. March (OE *mearc*) was given over to Ely Abbey about 1000. Reaney, *Place-Names of Cambridgeshire*, 253, 258, 339, records the first appearance of *Merc* as "boundary" in 1086. A *mearc* in early Norman topography signified a border town, a type of no-man's-land; see Eleanor Searle's description in her *Predatory Kinship and the Creation of Norman Power, 840-1066* (Berkeley: University of California Press, 1988), 27–29. I find it difficult not to be reminded of *mearcstapa* as an identifying term for Grendel.

75. *LE* ii.105, ed. Blake, 179–81; *LE*, trans. Fairweather, 211–15, esp. 213–14. *LE*, written in the late twelfth century (about 1170) by Thomas (a monk),

when it offers an account of a report on Ely by Deda, a soldier of William the Conquerer, that describes eleventh-century Ely and that has relevance to the Beowulfian landscape. As Bede did, the soldier notes the resemblance of the space to an island "fortified by great waters and broad swamps." Relatively inaccessible and remote, it was most easily reached by boat (fig. 2). It was Ely's inaccessibility that made it a stronghold for later insurrections, as William's army discovered.[76] The soldier describes the copiousness of the vegetation, the abundance of "domesticated animals, the multitude of wild beasts, of deer and hares in groves, of weasels and ermines." The waters, he recounts to William, brim over with "fowl and aquatic swimming things. . . . At the eddies, at a circle of many waters, are innumerable eels, great water wolves [by which he means the voracious pike]," and various other fish that he calls "aquatic serpents."[77]

---

used as its sources the *Liber miraculorum beate virginis* (written by Ælfhelm, a priest of Ely in the mid-tenth century) and the *Libellus Æthelwoldi episcopi*; see Keynes, "Ely Abbey 672–1109," 8.

76. Darby, *Medieval Fenland*, 106–7.

77. *LE* ii.105, ed. Blake, 180–81; *LE*, trans. Fairweather, ii.105, esp. 213–14. The soldier's description is apparently of the summer as he describes the richness of the vegetation; descriptions of winter focus on the fog, sudden winds, and dampness: "Si optatis audire que novi et vidi, cuncta vobis retexam. Intrinsecus insula copiose ditatur, diverso germine repletur et ceteris Anglie locis uberiore gleba prestantior. Agrorum quoque et pascuorum amenitate gratissima, ferarum venatione insignis, pecoribus atque iumentis non mediocriter fertilis, silvis, vineis enim eque laudabilis, aquis magnis et paludibus latis velud muro forti obsita. In qua domesticorum animalium habundantia est et ferarum multitudo, cervorum, dammularum, caperarum et leporum in nemoribus et secus easdem paludes. Insuper luterium, mustelarum, erminarum et putesiarum satis copia est que nunc gravi hieme muscipulis, laqueis vel quolibet capiuntur ingenio. De genere vero piscium volatilium atque natantium, que illic pullulant, quid dicam? Ad gurgites in girum aquarum multarum innumerabiles anguille irretiuntur, grandes lupi aquatici et luceoli, percide, rocee, burbutes et murenas, quas nos serpentes aquaticas vocamus. Aliquando vero isicii simul et regalis piscis rumbus a pluribus capi memoratur. De avibus namque, que ibidem et iuxta mansitant, sicut de ceteris, nisi fastidio sit, exprimemus, anseres

These "aquatic serpents" the soldier was describing belong to a class of ribbon fish (*Anguilla anguilla*), common worldwide as well as along the coast of Britain, to which eels, congers, and morays belong. Eels are sharp-nosed and strongly resemble snakes in appearance, reaching a length of five feet and a weight of twenty or so pounds, with variegated skins. In autumn, some eels become silvery, their snouts sharper, and they travel to the sea to spawn, recalling the *niceras* and *wyrmas* that "often undertake a sorrowful journey on the sail-road."[78] Thus, the Norman soldier's "aquatic serpents" recall the inhabitants of the *fyrgenstrēamas* (vast expanse of waters) in *Beowulf*. The *wyrmcynnes fela* (many of the race of serpent-like aquatic creatures, *Bwf* 1425[b]), *sellice sædracan* (wondrous sea-snakes, *Bwf* 1426[a]), and *sædēor hildetūxum* (sea-beasts with battle-tusks, *Bwf* 1510[b]–11[a]) inhabit that immense expanse of marshland, where, to use Kemp Malone's description, earth and water are mysteriously mingled. It is the *ǣlwihta eard* (land of the eel-creatures, *Bwf* 1500[a]), as Grendel's mother refers to it when she becomes aware of Beowulf's presence in his descent to the bottom of the mere.[79] And it is Grendel's dominion:

---

innumere, fiscedule, felice, merge, corve aquatice, ardei et anetes, quarum copia maxima est, brumali tempore vel cum aves pennas mutant per centum et tres centas captas vidi plus minusve. Non nunquam laqueis et retibus ac glutine capi solent." A comparable difference in describing the same landscape under different conditions can be found in *Beowulf* (837-57, 1408-19), where the journey to the mere is first described in bright light and as being easy, and later as shrouded in mist and fraught with difficulty over a perilous trackway.

78. *oft bewitigað / sorhfulne sīð on seglrāde* (*Bwf* 1428[b]–29).

79. *Sōna þæt onfunde sē ðe flōda begong / heorogīfre behēold hund missēra, / grim ond grǣdig, þæt þǣr gumena sum / ǣlwihta eard ufan cunnode* (As soon as the one who, ravenous for battle, who, grim and greedy, ruled the expanse of the flood for fifty years, discovered that a certain human there from above explored the land of the eel-creatures, 1497–1500). *Ǣlwiht* is a hapax legomenon; following Klaeber, virtually all editors show it with a short æsc and translate it as "foreign" (related to *el-*, "foreign"). However, within the context of the poem, a reading of the word with a long æsc is possible and perhaps more appropriate. Further, in his etymological

on his approach to Heorot, the *mǣre mearcstapa* (notorious boundary stalker) emerges *of mōre under misthleoþum* (from the marsh under the mist-hummocks, *Bwf* 710), and it is to these marshes he flees after his defeat, *under fenhleoðu* (under the fen-hummocks, *Bwf* 820[b]), bits of firm ground that rise above the marsh.[80] Ely, then, provides a reasonable physical parallel to Grendel's mere, to the dominion of the *fēond on helle* (enemy from Hell, *Bwf* 101[b]) as he is first introduced.[81] Given

---

study of "eel" within an Indo-European cultural, mythic, and formulaic context of poetic formulas dealing with heroes doing battle with serpentine creatures (serpent, snake, viper, eel), Joshua T. Katz argues for a reading of *ǣl* (Germ. *Aal*) as "eel" and translates *ǣlwihta eard* as "realm of the eel-wights"; "How to Be a Dragon in Indo-European: Hittite *illuyankaš* and Its Linguistic and Cultural Congeners in Latin, Greek, and Germanic," in *Mir Curad: Studies in Honor of Calvert Watkins*, ed. Jay Jasanoff, H. Craig Melchert, and Lisi Olver (Innsbruck: Universität Innsbruck, 1998), 317–34, esp. 322, 329–30. My thanks to Professor Douglas Simms for referring Professor Katz's article to me. Also notable in the passage is the poet's emphasis on the anonymity of Grendel's mother.

80. Malone, "Grendel and His Abode," 299 n. 3, defines the mist- and fen-hummocks: "A mist-hummock was presumably a bit of firm ground (cp. *fæsten* 104) hidden or ringed by mist. The marsh was said to be under the mist-hummocks because it was at a lower level; in other words, the hummocks rose a bit above the surrounding marsh. A fen-hummock was a hummock thought of in terms of the fen in which it was set rather than in terms of the mist that might or might not be gathered about it."

81. *LE*'s narrator also mentions the swirling waters of the mere as having the force with which to suck a man down to the bottom, and later in his report Deda makes reference to Ely's harmonious monastic community, where the monks sing "praises together so sweetly that you would think the songs were resonating to the Lord in vocal sounds of every variety" (*LE*, trans. Fairweather, 214 and n. 504; *LE*, ed. Blake, 181). The first of these comments brings to mind Beowulf's descent into the mere, and the second recalls the "ellengǣst's" listening to the doxology being sung in Heorot (*Bwf* 86-98). For Virgilian allusions to Grendel's mere, see Andersson, *Early Epic Scenery*, 145–59; Alain Renoir, "The Terror of the Dark Waters: A Note on Virgilian and Beowulfian Techniques," in *The Learned and the Lewed: Studies in Chaucer and Medieval Literature*, ed. Larry D. Benson (Cambridge, MA: Harvard University Press, 1974), 147–60. For the most recent alternative

the poet's tendency toward sound-play, one wonders if a subverbal identification with *insulae haeli* (the isle of Ely) is not operative here.

Additional narrative parallels bolster the similarities between the historical event and (what I argue is) its poetic rendering. Both crimes take place in the dominion of the respective enemy: Alfred dies in the fog and winter mist of the East Anglian marshes, which, being north of the Thames, are under Harold's rule, and Æschere finds his end in Grendel's marshes, "where earth and water are mysteriously mingled." Finally, Alfred's death is a fratricide, ordered by his stepbrother; Grendel and his surrogate, his mother, are allusively aligned, in this first beheading scene and elsewhere, with the brother-killer Cain.

> Grendles mōdor,
> ides āglǣcwīf yrmþe gemunde,
> sē þe wæteregesan wunian scolde,
> cealde strēamas, siþðan Cā*in* wearð
> tō ecgbanan āngan brēþer,
> fæderenmǣge; hē þā fāg gewāt,
> morþre gemearcod mandrēam flêon,
> wēsten warode. Þanon wōc fela
> geōsceaftgāsta; wæs þǣra Grendel sum,
> heorowearh hetelīc.

(Bwf 1258^b–67^a)

[Grendel's mother, monstrous warrior-woman, brooded over her misery, [s]he [one of the masculine pronominal references to Grendel's mother] who dwelt in the dreadful waters, the cold [evil] streams, after Cain had become sword-slayer to his only (beloved) brother, to his father's kinsman; he departed then, stained, marked with murder, fleeing human joys, he inhabited the wilderness.

---

location for Grendel's mere as being on the island of Zealand in Denmark, see the collection of articles in *Beowulf and Lejre*, ed. John D. Niles (Tempe, AZ: ACMRS, 2007), which features an archaeological report by Tom Christensen, director of the 1986-88 Zealand excavation.

Thence sprang many fated spirits; Grendel was one of them, hateful savage outcast.]

As far as I can tell, the historical material reporting the event does not associate Ælfgifu of Northampton or her son Harold Harefoot with Cain, although Harold is alluded to as one of the adversaries of God,[82] epithets used in the poem for Grendel and his mother; yet the action Harold effected against "his father's kinsman" (Alfred was Cnut's stepson) was indisputably in the line of Cain.

One should point out the rhetorical devices used by the poet in his reconstruction of the historical event in his epic, devices commonly used in the making of vernacular epic and, one may add, of historical biography. Displacement and/or separation of narrative units is a case in point. The Beowulfian warrior band is not mutilated and massacred in the epic beheading sequence, for example; rather, the massacres have been displaced and thus treated separately in earlier sequences of the poem (*Bwf* 115–25). Displaced also is the attack upon the prince, his arms, chest, and legs pinned to the ground by his attackers at knifepoint; in the beheading sequence, this image surfaces during Beowulf's struggle with Grendel's mother as she pins him to the ground at knifepoint (*Bwf* 1541–49). Second, Alfred, *se unsceððiga æþeling* (the guiltless atheling), is young, whereas Æschere, the *æþeling ǣrgōd* (atheling of exemplary merit), is portrayed as an inseparable companion in arms to the aged Hrothgar.[83] Third, Æschere is "Yrmenlaf's older brother," whereas Alfred was the younger of the two athelings. These disharmonies of age have been generally accepted as allowable variants in analogic arguments that concern a merging of historical and epic materials. Nonetheless, the twelfth-century historical material presents diverging views as to

---

82. *intimant Dei inimicis*, *EER* iii.4, ed. Campbell, 42–43.

83. *Bwf* 1325-29: [He was] *mīn rūnwita ond mīn rǣdbora, / eaxlgestealla, ðonne wē on orlege / hafelan weredon, þonne hniton fēþan, / eoferas cnysedan* (my confidant and counselor, my comrade in arms when we in the front lines guarded our heads, when the foot soldiers clashed together; *Bwf* 1329). See also *frōdan fyrnwitan* (wise old counselor; *Bwf* 2123ᵃ).

which atheling was older, Edward the Confessor or Alfred atheling.[84] Fourth, although, unlike Alfred atheling, Æschere has not been blinded on the banks of the marshlands, he has been nonetheless unjustly executed by decapitation. The poet here replaced one heinous act by its mythic counterpart. Blindness and beheading are mythic practices meant to humiliate and make the hero (or villain) powerless and a spectacle to his followers.[85] They are punishments for arrogance and excessive pride, sins that have their seat in the head, whether the head belongs to a hero or villain, as, for example, was the blinding and disempowerment of Samson, the erstwhile deliverer of Israel now tied to the mill with slaves. Harold Godwinson's blinding as depicted in the Bayeux Tapestry is a retributive act for his treachery and arrogance in gaining the crown.[86] And, in an analogous manner, Holofernes' payment for his arrogant attempt to seize Bethulia is his decapitated head hung on its ramparts like a trophy for the Assyrians to gaze upon.

One final and pointed rhetorical alteration between the historical and poetic texts is the suppression of the treasonous betrayal of Alfred atheling by Godwine (the chief counselor of Cnut, Harthacnut, and Edward the Confessor) and the transference of the hospitality theme from a betrayer to Hrothgar complete with heroic trappings. Yet one of the most compelling characters in *Beowulf* is

---

84. *HHHA* vi.20; *WMGRA* ii.188.5–6 (336–39); see also *ASC* 2:214n2, for additional sources that refer to Alfred as the firstborn, although this counters the evidence of the charters.

85. Personal communication with David Leeming. My thanks to Professor Leeming for discussing the conventional substitution of these mythic motifs.

86. For a discussion of the blinding of Harold as a symbol, see David J. Bernstein, *The Mystery of the Bayeux Tapestry* (London: Weidenfeld and Nicolson, 1986), 152–58, where he sees Harold's blinding as retribution for the blinding of Alfred; for arguments questioning Harold's death by arrow, see Martin Foys, "Pulling the Arrow Out: The Legend of Harold's Death and the Bayeux Tapestry," in *The Bayeux Tapestry: New Interpretations*, ed. Martin Foys, Karen Overbey, and Dan Terkla (Woodbridge, UK: Boydell Press, 2009), 158–75.

Unferth the *þyle* (counselor, spokesman), whose name denotes discord and who is typified as the "wicked counselor." Described as a man with "a keen eye to personal glory" by Orchard, Unferth is very much a prominent presence in the court. Like the gray eminence that circulated freely within the courts of Cnut, Harold, Harthacnut, and Edward, this eloquent rhetorician sits at the foot of Hrothgar's throne, even though his reputation in the poem connotes treachery, particularly that connected with fratricide (*Bwf* 1165–68).[87] I am tempted to think that the suppression of Godwine's betrayal might have its roots in political considerations at the time of the sequence's adaptation into the poem. Not only was Godwine, father of a future English king and of the future queen of Edward the Confessor, a dominant figure in Cnut's court, but his preeminence was such that he was able to abate Harthacnut's vengeance against those who were responsible for Alfred's death.[88] If, as I tend to believe, the poet were composing his polysemous narrative at a time of political crisis, then rhetorical alterations of displacement, substitution, opposition, and inversion might have been not only desirable but perhaps necessary. He thus cloaked his contemporary plot in fabulous mode that dealt with the desires and deeds of destructive hybrid creatures, primeval monsters in male and female human form, and fused it with the mimetic elements of his literal narrative that concerned the internecine strife and dynastic crises of the ancestral sixth-century Danish court. The effect was a fictionalized distortion of the "factual field,"[89] for the merged mimetic and fabulous narrative is closely unified in time (the poem's present), in

---

87. Orchard, *Companion to Beowulf*, passim, esp. 247–56, quote at 248, and see his n. 35 on 247 for selected references to commentary on Unferth; Klaeber, 3rd ed., 147–50, ll. 499–661.

88. *JWChron* [1040] ii.530–33; see also Keynes, "Cnut's Earls," 43–88, esp. 70–74.

89. The phrase is Hayden White's, "Historicism, History and the Figurative Imagination," in *Tropics of Discourse*, 101–20, esp. 110–12 where he discusses the rhetorical changes effected upon the "factual field" during the process of "historical" representation (at 111).

space (the environs of the court and the mere), and in action (who rules Heorot/England).

The Decapitation of Harold Harefoot

The second historical event under consideration occurred some four years later. Vengeance for Harold Harefoot's murder of Alfred took place after the king's death in 1040 at Oxford, when Harthacnut returned with Queen Emma to England, ascended the throne, and ordered the exhumation and desecration of Harold's corpse. Harthacnut's rule was healing[90] in his benevolent and generous treatment of his men and his half-brother Edward (Alfred's brother and the future ruler of England) and at the same time harsh in his imposition of heavy taxes (the primary reason) and in his treatment of Harold's body.[91] The C- and D-texts of the *Chronicle* are the first to refer to the exhumation and subsequent casting (*sceotan*) of Harold's body into the marsh:

Her swealt Harald cing. Þá sende man æfter Harðacnute to Bricge,

---

90. *HHHA* vi.20 (370n106), for instance, apparently the only witness to Harthacnut's generosity, gives this portrait of the king upon his death in 1042: "Hardecnut rex morte prereptus est, cum regnasset duobus annis, in medio flore iuuentutis sue, apud Lambihithe. Qui clare indolis et benigne iuuentutis fuerat suis. Tante namque largitatis fertur fuisse, ut prandia regalia quatuor in die uicibus omni curie sue faceret apponi, malens a uocatis apposita fercula dimitti, quam a non uocatis apponenda fercula reposci, cum nostri temporis consuetudo sit, causa uel auaricie uel ut ipsi dicunt fastidii, principes semel in die tantum suis escas anteponere." (When he had reigned for two years [1042], King Harthacnut was snatched away by death at Lambeth, in the full flower of his youth. He had been honourable by nature and had the benevolence of youth towards his men. It is said that his generosity was so great that he ordered royal meals to be served four times a day to all his court, preferring rather that they should be invited and leave scraps of what was set before them, than that they should not be invited and beg for scraps to be given to them, since in our time it is the custom among princes, either from avarice or, as they themselves say, from fastidiousness, to serve food to their men only once a day.)
91. See *HHHA* vi.19, where the taxes are enumerated.

wende þæt man wel dyde.] he com ða hider mid lx scipum foran
to middansumera.] astealde þa swiðe strang gyld, þæt man hit
uneaðe aco*m*, *þæt* wæs .viii. marc æt há] him wæs þá unhold eall
þæt this ær gyrnde.] hé ne gefremede éc naht cynelices þa hwile
ðe he ricxode. Hé let dragan up þæne deadan Harald] hine on fen
sceotan. (*ASC* C-text, s.a 1040; *ASC* 1:160)

[In this year king Harold died. Then, they sent for Harthacnut
from Bruges, expecting that they had done well. And before mid-
summer, he arrived here with sixty ships and then levied a severe
tax, of eight marks for every row, which was difficult to comply
with and all who previously had supported him were then dis-
loyal. . . . He did nothing worthy of a king while he governed. He
had the body of the dead Harold dug up and cast into a marsh.]

The historical authorities are the C-, D-, and E-texts of the *Chronicle*,
John of Worcester, and William of Malmesbury, although the event
of the exhumation is noted in other documents as well.[92] There were
apparently two versions. John of Worcester, in the context of criti-
cizing Harthacnut for doing "nothing of royal power," offers the first
version of the treatment of Harold's corpse.

[1040] Nam mox ut regnare cepit, iniuriarum quas uel sibi uel
sue genitrici suus antecessor fecerat rex Haroldus, qui frater
suus putabatur, non immemor, Alfricum Eboracensem archiepiscopum, Goduuinum comitem, Styr maiorem domus, Edricum
dispensatorem, Thrond suum carnificem et alios magne dignita-
tis uiros Lundoniam misit, et ipsius Haroldi corpus effodere et in
gronnam proicere iussit. Quod cum proiectum fuisset, id extra-
here et in flumen Tamense mandauit proicere. Breui autem post

---

92. See *ASC* 2: 218–19, and Freeman, *History of the Norman Conquest*, 1:512,
787–89. The E-text states explicitly that Harold died in Oxford and was
buried at Westminster in London, a disjunction between place of death and
burial that led to John of Worcester's erroneous statement that Harold died
in London. William of Malmesbury and John of Worcester give the death
date as April and the burial place as Westminster.

tempore, a quodam captum est piscatore, et ad Danos allatum sub festinatione, in cimiterio, quod habuerunt Lundonie, sepultum est ab ipsis cum honore. (*JWChron* 530–31)

[[1040] For as soon as he began to rule, remembering the injuries which his predecessor King Harold, who was considered his brother, had perpetrated against both him and his mother, he sent Ælfric, archbishop of York, Earl Godwine, Stor, master of his household, Eadric his steward, Thrond his executioner and other men of great rank to London, and ordered them to dig up Harold's body and throw it into a marsh. When it had been thrown there, he ordered it to be pulled out, and thrown into the River Thames. However, a short time later, it was taken by a certain fisherman, borne in haste to the Danes, and was honourably buried by them in the cemetery they had in London.]

The corpse is dug up and thrown into a marsh, from which it is subsequently dragged out and then thrown into the Thames. On what happened between the moment that Harold's corpse was heaved onto the banks of the marsh and the time it was deposited into its second watery abode, John of Worcester is silent.[93]

In his classic study of the Norman Conquest, E. A. Freeman commented on the status of the dignitaries sent to desecrate Harold's body,[94] and it would be of interest to speculate upon what lay behind Harthacnut's choices. Did Harthacnut, aware of Godwine's involvement in Alfred's death, send the counselor particularly to witness the king's vengeance as a sign of his rage? And was Thrond (Harthacnut's executioner) sent along to execute that vengeance? Although the passage does not describe the reactions of the dignitaries sent to desecrate the body as they dragged out the corpse from the marsh

---

93. Reference to Harthacnut's unworthiness appears first (and only) in *ASC* C- and D-texts, as does the notation of Harthacnut's ordering that Harold's body be hurled into the fen after it had been exhumed.

94. Freeman, *History of the Norman Conquest*, 1:512, 788–89; see also Stafford, *Queen Emma and Queen Edith*, 100.

onto the shore, it is reasonable to surmise that the spectacle must have been unnerving—analogous, perhaps, to the amazed reaction of the martial entourage that accompanied Beowulf to the mere, as it riveted its gaze upon the wondrously strange, giant *wǣgbora* (wave-traveler) that had just been dragged onto the bank (*Bwf* 1432^{b}–41^{a}), after Beowulf had pierced it with his hard *herestrǣl* (war arrow) and his men had showered it with boar-spears and hooked swords.

The desecration of Harold's corpse was Harthacnut's revenge on Harold; in a passage immediately following, John of Worcester tells how the young king exacted wergild for his half-brother's death from Lyfing and Godwine. Godwine's involvement with the fratricide must have been indisputable, for not only did Cnut's former counselor present an outfitted galley to Harthacnut as wergild, complete with eighty seamen clad in byrnies and gilded helmets and carrying Danish axes, but an identical compensation was presented to Edward the Confessor, Alfred's natural brother, upon his accession to the throne.

> Goduuinus autem regi pro sua amicitia dedit trierem fabrefactam, caput uel rostrum deauratum habentem, armamentis optimis instructam, decoris armis electisque octoginta militibus decoratam, quorum unusquisque habebat duas in suis brachiis aureas armillas, sedecim uncias pendentes, loricam trilicem indutam, in capite cassidem ex parte deauratam, gladium deauratis capulis renibus accinctum, Danicam securim auro argentoque redimitam in sinistro humero pendentem, in manu sinistra clipeum cuius umbo clauique erant deaurati, in dextra lanceam que lingua Anglorum ategar appellatur.[95]

> [However, Godwine, to regain his friendship, gave the king a skillfully made galley, with gilded prow or beak, furnished with the best tackle, well equipped with suitable arms and eighty picked soldiers. Each one of them had two golden armlets on his arms, weighing sixteen ounces, was clad in a triple mail corselet, with a part-gilded

---

95. *JWChron* 530–31, (s.a. 1040). The warriors' dress is worthy of comparison with Beowulf's outfit just before he descended into the mere.

helmet on his head, was girt about the loins with a sword with gilded hilts; a Danish axe bound with gold and silver hung from his left shoulder; in his left hand was a shield with gilded boss and studs, in his right a spear called an *ætgar* [javelin, dart, spear] in English.]

William of Malmesbury offers the second version of the exhumation of Harold:

iuuenis qui egregiam pietatem animi in fratrem et sororem ostenderit: germanum enim Eduardum, annosae peregrinationis tedio et spe fraternae necessitudinis natale solum reuisentem, obuiis ut aiunt manibus excipiens indulgentissime retinuit. Veruntamen immaturus in ceteris, per Elfricum Eboracensem episcopum et alios quos nominare piget Haroldi cadauere defosso caput truncari et miserando mortalibus exemplo in Tamensem proici iussit. Id a quodam piscatore exceptum sagena in cimiterio Danorum Lundoniae tumulatur.[96]

[He was a young man who showed an outstandingly affectionate disposition towards his brother and sister; for when his brother Edward was weary of his years of wandering and revisited his native land in hope of a closer relationship with his brother, he received him, as the saying goes, with open arms and kept him as his guest with the greatest kindness. He was, however, immature in other respects, and through the agency of Ælfric archbishop of York and others whom I would rather not name he ordered that Harold's corpse should be exhumed and beheaded, and his head (a pitiable spectacle to men) thrown into the Thames. This was taken in his net by a fisherman, and buried in the Danish cemetery in London.]

Whereas the C-Chronicler expressed antipathy for Harthacnut as king and as avenger of his half-brother, William of Malmesbury presents Harthacnut's court as harmonious and the king as generous to his men and magnanimous to his half-brother Edward the Confessor. Like John of Worcester, he criticizes

---

96. *WMGRA* ii.188.3, at 336–37.

Harthacnut for the savagery of the revenge of his half-brother Alfred's murder and the mutilation of Harold's corpse. Unlike John of Worcester, he pauses to comment on what must have been the grotesque spectacle of a decapitated corpse: "a pitiable example to men." Like Harold's corpse in John of Worcester, Harold's severed head in William of Malmesbury was "thrown into the Thames," then "taken in his net by a fisherman" and brought to the Danes in London,[97] where afterward it was buried in the Danish cemetery.

The Beowulfian Reflex

The relevant passages in *Beowulf* that I suggest may be epic reflexes of the historical events surrounding the decapitation of Harold's corpse are the beheading of Grendel, the retrieval of his head from the mere, its subsequent transport to Hrothgar's court, and its presentation before the king and queen in their court.

In the beheading scene, the passage that began this chapter, Beowulf swims through a maze of ribbon-like fish, sea-beasts, and sea-dragons—traversing the *ǣlwihta eard* (dwelling of the eel creatures, 1500)[98]—to reach Grendel, whom he finds "lifeless" on his resting place:

> wǣpen hafenade
> heard be hiltum Higelāces ðegn
> yrre ond anrǣd, —næs sēo ecg fracod
> hilderince, ac hē hraþe wolde
> Grendle forgyldan gūðrǣsa fela
> ðāra þe hē geworhte tō West-Denum
> oftor micle ðonne on ǣnne sīð,
> þonne hē Hrōðgāres heorðgenēatas
> slōh on sweofote, slǣpende frǣt

---

97. *WMGRA* ii.188.4 [336–37]; *JWChron* 530–31.
98. See n. 79 above; I have altered Klaeber by inserting the macron to the word; it is OE scribal practice to omit long marks over the vowels (although in some instances, long marks do appear).

folces Denigea fȳftȳne men,
ond ōðer swylc ūt offerede,
lāðlicu lāc. Hē him þæs lēan forgeald,
rēþe cempa, tō ðæs þe hē on ræste geseah
gūðwērigne Grendel licgan,
aldorlēasne, swā him ær gescōd
hild æt Heorote. Hrā wīde sprong,
syþðan hē æfter dēaðe drepe þrōwade,
heorosweng heardne, ond hine þā hēafde becearf.
(*Bwf* 1573ᵃ–90)

[Hygelac's thane, angry and resolute, lifted the firm weapon by the hilt; the sword was not worthless to the soldier of battle, for he wanted quickly to repay Grendel in full for many of the attacks of battle he had waged against the West Danes—much more often than on that one occasion when he slaughtered Hrothgar's hearth companions as they slept, consumed fifteen sleeping men of the Danes, and another such number carried away [to the] outside, a loathsome booty. He gave him full reward for that, the fierce champion, now that he saw Grendel lying on his resting place, battle weary [and] lifeless, such had the battle at Heorot harmed him. The corpse split apart, when after [its own] death, it suffered the blow, the hard fierce stroke, and thus he chopped off his head.]

Beowulf's action is one of revenge, to pay Grendel in full (*forgyldan*) not only for the atheling Æschere's mutilation, but now as he gazes on Grendel's corpse, for all the cannibalistic destruction of Hrothgar's hearth companions. *Yrre ond anrǣd* (angry and resolute, 1575ᵃ), *hē him þæs lēan forgeald* (he gave him full reward for that, 1584ᵇ), a phrase that is used elsewhere in the poem only when God "rewards" Cain for his murder of Abel (114ᵇ). Grendel's corpse sprang open when *hē hine þā hēafde becearf* (he thus cut off his head, 1590ᵇ). More graphic than William of Malmesbury's chronicle account of the beheading that shocked the onlookers, the poetic scene alludes to similar elements that caused the historical event—revenge for the fratricide and for all the outrages against the warrior band.

Related to the act of beheading is another parallel to the versions found in John of Worcester and William of Malmesbury; this concerns the fisherman and his catch. The entire beheading scene in *Beowulf* is in an aquatic environment. After he has avenged Æschere and his comrades, Beowulf is characterized as a seaman, as the *lidmanna helm* (protector [or leader] of seamen), the only time the term is used in the poem[99] and the poet has rhetorically elevated the status of his fisherman to harmonize more effectively with his epic poem.

> Cōm þā tō lande lidmanna helm
> swīðmōd swymman; sǣlāce gefeah,
> mægenbyrþenne. (*Bwf* 1623–25[b])

[Then the protector of seamen, strong-minded, came swimming to land; he rejoiced in the sea-booty, in the mighty burden.]

Beowulf swims to land carrying his catch, his sea-booty, a synonym he uses for Grendel's head when he later presents it to Hrothgar to gaze upon (1652–54). Though rhetorically altered, historical fact and epic fiction merge: the catch is a head, and the head is that of a ruler. Further, the poetic figure of Grendel's mighty head being carried on a wæl-stenge (corpse pole or stake) by four men with difficulty (1635–39), calls up the image of a corpse, that of the head of state, being borne on a bier for burial. The chronicles do not specify how the fisherman carried Harold's body (John of Worcester) or head (William of Malmesbury) to London and to the Danish cemetery or church, but most likely it was on a slab of some sort. Nor do the chronicles specify who the Danes might have been to whom the fisherman took Harold's twice-mutilated corpse; nor do they allude to his possibly having received a reward of some kind. It was after all a king's head he had fished up. The epic parallel is less hazy;

---

99. A *hapax legomenon* in Beowulf, one cannot help but be reminded that Cnut was recognized as a leader of the *liðsmanna* at the time of the invasion of England. See R. G. Poole, *Viking Poems on War and Peace: A Study in Skaldic Narrative* (Toronto: University of Toronto Press, 1991), 100–115, for a discussion of Cnut's activities in England in the context of the *Liðsmannaflokkr*.

Beowulf retrieves the head from the mere and lays his sea-booty before the court:

Þā wæs be feaxe on flet boren
Grendles hēafod, þǣr guman druncon,
egeslīc for eorlum ond þǣre idese mid,
wlitesēon wrǣtlīc; weras on sāwon.
(*Bwf* 1647–50)

[Grendel's head was borne by the hair onto the floor where men were drinking, horrible, in front of the nobles, and the lady with them, a wondrous spectacle; men beheld it.]

Having accomplished this act of revenge, having brought the appropriate *wergild* to Hrothgar, the epic hero has earned his heroic identity.

What are the implications, then, of these historical reflexes in *Beowulf*? Certainly, one has to do with the generic nature of the relationship between *Beowulf* and *Grettis saga*, the discussion that opened this chapter. Whereas the Sandhaugar episode resonates with features more consonant with folktale, the cultural milieu of *Beowulf* is closely related to the political events described in the historical documents. The *Beowulf*-poet's adaptation of this popular motif might be better understood as an imaginative means by which he might recast and express contemporary political events in an allusively guarded poetic form. The political theme of dynastic succession; the martial and royal environment; the setting of a vast marshland, with waters peopled with serpent-like aquatic creatures; the structural relationship and setting of the crime and punishment sequence; and any number of topographical details—all are elements found in the historical materials under consideration and in *Beowulf*. It is always possible, of course, that these allusions or patterns, if you will, may be symptomatic and related to historical crimes and punishments of previous centuries (for which, of course, documents do not exist), but even the murder of Edward the Martyr in 978, an assassination attributed to his stepmother Queen Ælfthryth and her son Æthelred the Unready, does not contain the cumulative correspondences under discussion here. These shared features between the historical and poetic texts, I argue, provide a richer and more potent narrative texture to the beheading sequence in *Beowulf* and typify the Anglo-Saxon version of Duggan's description of vernacular epic as "popular historiography" (above Introduction, 17–18).

A further implication has to do with the place of the poem's composition, variously identified as Northumbria, Mercia, Winchester, and East Anglia.[100] If the Beowulfian beheadings were to be taken as reflexes of the historical events under consideration, the place where these events would hold the most significance would be the fenland monastic communities of East Anglia, whose center was Ely. Simon Keynes's study of the history of Ely Abbey demonstrates that despite its location deep in the fens of East Anglia, from its foundation Ely's place in the cultural memory of early England was considerable. Not only did it hold the corpse of Saint Æthelthryth, making it the center of her cult[101] and a major monastic center in the tenth century, but also it was the beneficiary of royal patronage from about the mid-tenth century through the reign of Cnut and Emma,[102] who frequently visited the abbey. Cnut's legendary song, composed in English, marked the occasion of one of their Candlemas visits, celebrating the Purification of the Virgin on 2 February. On one occasion,

---

100. Klaeber, 3rd ed., cxviii–cxix.

101. Keynes, "Ely Abbey 672–1109," 15, 21. Ely was again founded as a male monastic institution in the tenth century. For a recent study of the cult of Æthelthryth, see Virginia Blanton, *Signs of Devotion: The Cult of St. Æthelthryth in Medieval England, 695–1615* (University Park, PA: Pennsylvania State University Press, 2007).

102. Keynes, "Ely Abbey 672–1109," 13–28, 40, 46, discusses Ely's royal patronage under Eadred (946–55), Edgar (959–75), Cnut (1017–35); see also 40: "By whatever criteria it may be judged, Ely Abbey in the late tenth and eleventh centuries was without question one of the most successful foundations of the Benedictine reform movement," holding relics, vast rural estate, economic resources, and treasure; see also T. A. Heslop, "The Production of *de luxe* Manuscripts and the Patronage of King Cnut and Queen Emma," *ASE* 19 (1980): 151–95.

as noted in the *Liber Eliensis* and as Keynes relates, Emma and Cnut were approaching Ely by boat. Nearing the island, the king

> stood up and looked towards the church, which stood out on a hill, for he thought he could hear singing. He soon realised that it was the monks of Ely, singing the divine office, whereupon he urged his men to gather round and sing praise with him. The king was moved by the occasion to compose his own song in English, of which we are given just the beginning:[103]

> Merie sungen ðe muneches binnen Ely
> ða Cnut ching reu ðer by.
> Roweþ cnites noer the lant
> and here we þes muneches sæng.

> [How sweetly sang the monks of Ely
>   when Cnut the king rowed by:
>   "Row, lads, nearer the land,
>   and let us hear the monks' song."]

Unlike Grendel, who, like an anguished Satan gazing upon Paradise, suffers torment upon hearing the scop's clear song of creation as he approaches Heorot, Cnut is filled with joy and marks the moment as creative inspiration by composing a song in praise of the melodious chanting of Ely's monks. It might be considered an astonishing moment considering that a short time previously he had harried and stormed over East Anglia.

---

103. See Keynes, "Ely Abbey 672–1109," 36. Keynes relates another reported visit of Cnut to Ely during deep winter when the king was led by a certain Brihtmær across the frozen marshes; see also *LE* ii.85, ed. Blake, 153–54; *LE,* trans. Fairweather, 181–83; and Stubbs, *Historical Memorials,* 2–10, and his note 2, on 49–52, where he quotes from a letter sent to him by W. W. Skeat, verifying the eleventh century as the date of Cnut's song. On the song's dating and the scene, see also C. E. Wright, *The Cultivation of Saga in Anglo-Saxon England* (Edinburgh: Oliver and Boyd, 1939), 36–38, and R. M. Wilson, *The Lost Literature of Medieval England* (London: Methuen & Co. Ltd., 1952), 159; see also 51–58.

Queen Emma had her own history with Ely as one of the abbey's chief benefactors. As Æthelred's young Norman queen, she began adorning the abbey with gifts, among which were precious, exquisitely embroidered textiles.[104] One of her first visits to Ely may have been when as a young bride (in imitation of Mary's churching) she with Æthelred presented Edward atheling to the monks on Candlemas. Although there is no mention of her having also presented Alfred at the holy altar, it would seem probable that she took Alfred atheling there as well.[105] It would have been an unspeakably nefarious act, worthy of a *fēond on helle* (enemy from Hell), if Harold (whom the *Encomium Emmae Reginae* characterizes as being akin to an antichrist) deposited the helpless atheling into the care of the monks as a grotesque gesture of insult to the young pretender to the throne and to his mother, Emma of Normandy, for Alfred atheling died on 5 February 1037, three days after Candlemas.[106]

The final implication of the foregoing discussion of the beheading sequence in *Beowulf* has to do with the relationship among the historical texts and the poem. One could, of course, entertain the possibility that history imitated art, that an "old," venerated *Beowulf* influenced the historical material (especially that found in the *Anglo-Saxon Chronicle* and in the *Encomium Emmae Reginae*), that the chroniclers knew a version of *Beowulf* and appropriated some of its more colorful features into their reports of Alfred's assassination. But I find it difficult to imagine that type of intertextuality in this instance, for the crime and punishment recorded in the chronicles are of such national

---

104. For Emma's magnanimity, see Stafford, *Queen Emma and Queen Edith*, esp. 143, 149. See also Keynes, "Ely Abbey 672–1109," 35; idem, *EER* [lxxvi–lxxviii]; *LE* ii.79, ed. Blake, at 147–49; iii.50, at 288–94, esp. 293; iii.122, at 371–73; *LE*, trans. Fairweather, 175–77, 357, 461; see also Heslop, "Production of *de luxe* Manuscripts," esp. 157–58, 161, 169, 177, 182–88.

105. Keynes, "Ely Abbey 672–1109," 30; *LE* ii.90, ed. Blake, at 159–61; *LE*, trans. Fairweather, 189–90; Frank Barlow, *Edward the Confessor* (London: Eyre & Spottiswoode, 1970), 32–34.

106. Keynes, *EER* [xxxii] and n. 1; the Bear's Son Tale, of course, is connected with 2 February and Candlemas.

political magnitude and barbarism that the acts themselves extend beyond the need for fictive embellishment. A second possibility suggests the reverse—that the poet made use of the *Chronicle* and the *Encomium*. Although such a claim may at first seem problematic because of the traditional dating of the manuscript at approximately 1000 A.D., now extended to the latter end of the second decade of the eleventh century, it may be useful to remember related arguments by Earl R. Anderson and Andy Orchard on the possible relationship between the *Encomium* and *The Battle of Maldon*, a heroic poem that memorializes the death of Byrhtnoth in 991 (whose bones, by the way, are buried in Ely Cathedral). In his essay, Anderson discusses five parallels that connect the two works and posits that *Maldon* was influenced by the *Encomium*, while Andy Orchard, in an article demonstrating the rhetorical skill of the Encomiast, suggests that the Encomiast borrowed from *Maldon*.[107] Orchard makes a further observation that connects the *Encomium* with the 1036 *Chronicle* poem and directly relates to the discussion at hand: "It may be that in this *Chronicle* poem we hear the authentic echo of the *Encomium*."[108]

Orchard's discussion (like Anderson's) lays a critical foundation for the presentation of the argument expressed in this chapter, which has posited that *Beowulf*, specifically the beheading sequence, may be intricately responsive to the *Encomium* and "The Death of Alfred" mix. For, as discussed earlier, given the possibility of a mid-eleventh-century date range for the more modern Anglo-Carolingian hand of Scribe A, which places his work and the political events that have been examined above within historical proximity, the potential for some manner of intertextuality among the three texts becomes more credible, a proposition that will be examined in the succeeding chapters. One could suppose that, like the Anglo-Saxon chronicler and the monk of Saint-Bertin, the *Beowulf*-poet, struck by the barbarity of

---

107. Earl R. Anderson, "The Battle of Maldon: A Reappraisal of Possible Sources, Date, and Theme," in *Modes of Interpretation in Old English Literature*, ed. Brown et al., 247–72; Andy Orchard, "The Literary Background to the *Encomium Emmae Reginae*," *The Journal of Medieval Latin* 11 (2001): 156–83.
108. Orchard, "The Literary Background to the *EER*," 182.

Alfred's assassination and its tragic effect on the nation, composed a multitiered narrative wherein he obliquely articulated and imaginatively allegorized them as a monster narrative, which he then fused with his mimetic story of the fall of a noble pagan race, the heritage of Cnut's pan-Scandinavian legendary past. But unlike the Anglo-Saxon chronicler and the monk of Saint-Bertin, who directly presented the murder of Alfred as a fratricide by the usurper of the Anglo-Saxon throne, the poet allegorized in fantastic mode that which he found impossible to express as mimetic narrative, either because the events were so profoundly disturbing or because it was politically unwise to do so. He thus created a shadow-world inhabited by the spiritually deformed and joyless, wherein the fratricide Harold Harefoot and his mother emerge as the misshapen and misbegotten Grendel-kin.

Chapters 2 and 3 concern themselves entirely with political forces, events, and personages of a historical past that may have served as inspiration for the imaginative spawning of the Grendel-kin and that were artfully interlaced with the events of the poet's present. I take the cue for the discussion both from the *Beowulf*-poet who continuously calls up the past to shed light on the events of the present and from the singular report of the 1036 C-Chronicler,[109] who despairing of making understandable the present ferocities enacted in Guildford, awakens his memories of a past when men of blood invaded and oppressed England with barbarous slaughters and bestialities, when treachery and avarice were the order of the day in the royal court, and when political assassinations provided the motivation for and set into motion the *fæhðe* (feud) held by the slaughtering *brimwylf* (sea-wolf) and her hateful, bloodthirsty wolf (*heorowearh hetelīc*) of a son. It is to that benighted period, when *Dene comon and her fri∂ namon* (the Danes came, and seized peace here), that I now turn.

---

109. The D-Chronicle's report (except for his treatment of Godwine) stems from the C-Chronicle; see n. 47 above.

CHAPTER TWO

The *Gifstōl* and the Grendel-kin

and fela ungelimpa gelimpð þysse þeode oft and gelome . . . here
and hete on gewelhwilcan ende . . . and Engle nu lange eal sigelease
and to swyþe geyrigde þurh Godes yrre; and flotmen swa strange
þurh Godes þafunge þæt oft on gefeohte an feseð tyne, . . . us eallum to woroldscame, gif we on earnost ænige cuþon ariht under-
standan . . . nis eac nan wundor þeah us mislimpe, forþam we witan
ful georne þæt nu fela geara mænn na ne rohtan foroft hwæt hy
worhtan wordes oððe dæde; ac wearð þes þeodscipe, swa hit þincan
mæg, swyþe forsyngod . . . þurh morðdæda and þurh mándæda,
þurh gitsunga and þurh gifernessa, þurh stala and þurh strudunga,
þurh mannsylena and þurh hæþene unsida, þurh spicdomas and
þurh searacræftas . . . þurh mægræsas and þurh manslyhtas.[1]

[many misfortunes befall this nation again and again . . . devastation
and malice in every province . . . and now the English too long com-
pletely victory-less and too intensely demoralized through God's ire;
and [Danish] sea-forces so strong through God's consent that often
in battle one [Danish ship] puts ten [English vessels] to flight, . . . to
the public shame of us all, if we in earnest were able to understand
any [shame] . . . it is also no wonder [that] it goes wrong with us
because we know full well that for many years now men very often
have by no means cared about what they did in word or deed, but

---

1. *Sermo Lupi ad Anglos*, ed. Dorothy Whitelock, 3rd ed. (London: Methuen
& Co. Ltd., 1963), 59–61, ll. 110-42; for a complete edition of Wulfstan's
homilies, see Dorothy Bethurum, *The Homilies of Wulfstan* (Oxford:
Clarendon Press, 1957); for the *Sermo*, see pp. 266–75.

on the contrary this nation has, as it may seem, greatly transgressed
. . . through murder and evil deeds, through greed and avarice,
through thefts and plunderings, through trafficking and pagan vices,
through treasons and conspiracies . . . through attacks on kinsmen
and manslaughters.]

Wulfstan's *Sermo Lupi ad Anglos*, an eschatological homily on the social and political decadence of a nation battered by external invading forces and internal moral perfidiousness, is a sermon of its time. It portrays a people crushed by the consistent ravaging of the Danish invaders and ruled by a king and counselors who were at once ineffective and incompetent and whose morality had been eroded by megascopic crimes perpetrated against the crown and nobility and egregious treachery toward the people. Written in its final version in 1014 (as its title suggests), possibly after Æthelred's return from exile in Normandy,[2] *Sermo Lupi* is an impassioned plea to all strata of English society to begin again to live righteously and lawfully *on Godes naman* lest all Englishmen—churchmen, nobles, and people—perish together. Unlike the appeal for repentant prayer that distinguished the law-code *VII Æthelred*,[3] the plea fell on deaf

---

2. *Sermo Lupi ad Anglos quando Dani maxime persecuti sunt eos, quod fuit anno millesimo XIIII ab Incarnatione Domini nostri Iesu Christi* is the complete title; Whitelock places the limits of the sermon's date as falling between Æthelred's exile to Normandy during Christmas 1013 and the accession of Cnut in 1016; *Sermo*, 6. It is difficult to imagine its having been composed during the short reign of Sveinn Forkbeard (December 1013-February 1014); see also Bethurum, *Homilies of Wulfstan*, 356. On the developing composition of the *Sermon* (it appears in three versions), see the discussion by Godden, "Apocalypse and Invasion," 142–62, and Simon Keynes, "An Abbot, an Archbishop, and the Viking Raids of 1006–7 and 1009–12," *ASE* 36 (2007): 151–220, esp. 203–13.

3. Two versions of *VII Æthelred* exist, one in Latin, the longer of the two, and in Old English. Keynes surmises that the Latin version is very likely the official document. The date of the code has generally been accepted as being after the 1009 invasion; for a discussion of the code in the context of earlier programs for repentant prayer, see Keynes, "An Abbot, an Archbishop, and the Viking Raids," 179–89. For versions of *VII Æthelred* see *Councils and*

ears, for social anarchy and external depredations continued to mark this benighted historical period, persisting on to Cnut's accession to the throne in 1017.

Wulfstan became archbishop of York in 1002, the year Æthelred and the *witan* turned over twenty-four thousand pounds to buy peace from the Danes; Ealdorman Leofsige, emissary to the Danes on this peace mission, rashly murdered the king's reeve for apparently no cause; Emma of Normandy crossed the sea to become queen of England; and Æthelred ordered the massacre of all the Danes in England on St. Brice's Day,[4] a day of infamy. As archbishop, and soon afterward as legislator,[5] Wulfstan lived to experience the demoralization of a people during the entire length of Æthelred's maturity as king, an anarchical reign that had had its beginnings in the betrayal and assassination of Æthelred's stepbrother, King Edward, at Corfe in 978,[6] perhaps the most profound of the betrayals and treasons that

---

Synods, with Other Documents Related to the English Church: Part I, 871–1066, ed. D. Whitelock, M. Brett, and C. N. L. Brooke (Oxford: Clarendon Press, 1981), 373–82, and A. J. Robertson, ed. and trans., *The Laws of the Kings of England from Edmund to Henry I* (Cambridge, UK: Cambridge University Press, 1925), 108–17 and 336–38nn.

4. See *ASC* 2:182.

5. For a summary of Wulfstan's career, see Whitelock, *Sermo,* 7–17; see also Andy Orchard, "Wulfstan the Homilist," in *Blackwell Encyclopaedia,* ed. Lapidge et al., 494–95.

6. *ASC* A- and C-texts; D, E, F give 979 as the date. On the way to see his stepbrother Æthelred, King Edward was deceptively greeted by members of the household of Ælfthryth, the queen mother, stabbed and hastily buried at Wareham without ceremony, but afterward given ceremonial burial at Shaftesbury in 1001. Though Æthelred was inconsolable at the loss, he apparently punished no one for his stepbrother's murder. For a discussion of the numerous historical texts that record various versions of the political controversies that eventuated in the murder of Edward, see Wright, *Cultivation of Saga in Anglo-Saxon England,* 166–71; Christine E. Fell, *Edward King and Martyr,* Leeds Texts and Monographs, n.s. (Leeds: University of Leeds, 1971), xiv–xx; Simon Keynes, *The Diplomas of King Æthelred "The Unready" : 978–1016: A Study in Their Use as Historical Evidence* (Cambridge, UK: Cambridge University Press, 1980), 163–76; see also

prompted a series of succession crises that dominated eleventh-century court politics from 1005 to 1066 with the fall of the Anglo-Saxon state. Upon his death on 28 May 1023, Archbishop Wulfstan held the position of premier jurist in Cnut's England, legislating and defining functions of state and ecclesiastical authorities, having lived through the transition that marked the end of the Anglo-Saxon kingdom and the establishment and rise of Cnut's Anglo-Danish reign.

Wulfstan's is one voice that condemns the sociopolitical and ecclesiastical anarchy that defined England in those dozen or so years at the beginning of the eleventh century. One could argue that it is the railing voice of an ecclesiastic reformer who has shaped his exhortation to awaken a spiritless, corrupt administration and its citizenry to the imminent dangers of God's impending judgment. Yet other voices bear out Wulfstan's personal impression, though these too offer individual (and one might say arbitrary) interpretations and reconfigurations of the series of complex issues and events that plagued the first two decades of the eleventh century, such as the subtle but critical allegorical voice of Ælfric of Eynsham, as noted in the Introduction (22–24). The import of these events weighed heavily on the mind of every Englishman whether a monastic, historian, annalist, or, as I suggest, vernacular poet. Nor would they be quickly forgotten. The treacherous barbarities associated with the mid-eleventh-century scramble for the throne, for instance, which we have seen the 1036 Chronicler angrily bemoan (65–66, 111–12), are likened to the savagery committed when *Dene comon and her frið namon* (the Danes came and made peace here; *ASC*, s.a. 1036), ranging freely over England earlier in the century's first decade and a half, razing the land and butchering its people, when the struggle for the throne was not only between native political factions, between the Mercians and the West Saxons as in 1036, but between the English and the Danes as well.[7] In 1016, Anglo-Saxon

Sean Miller, "Edward the Martyr," in *Blackwell Encyclopaedia*, ed. Lapidge et al., 163.

7. There are, of course, earlier wholesale attacks for possession of England, which Margaret Ashdown begins at 978 (*English and Norse Documents Relating to the Reign of Ethelred the Unready* [Cambridge, UK: The University Press,

England had become a conquered nation, its internal political weaknesses and moral decline exacerbated by the interminable Danish push to gain England as its own.[8] It is difficult not to sense a note of irony in the Chronicler's phrase *frið namon*, an irony couched in the term itself, especially if one recalls Cnut's methods of dispensing with hostages left in his care as he sailed back to Denmark after Sveinn's death on 2 February 1014:

> And wende þá suðweard oþ he com to Sandwíc, and lét don úp þær ðá gislas þe his fæder gesealde wæron, and cearf of hiora handa and earan and nosa.[9]

1930]), especially the combined attack of Óláfr Tryggvason and Sveinn in 994, which ended in a lasting truce between Óláfr and Æthelred; but it is Sveinn's ravaging of Exeter and Norwich in 1003 that marks the beginning of the end of Anglo-Saxon rule until 1042, with the accession of Edward the Confessor to the throne. The invasion of England came in three waves: Sveinn's 1003 penetration into Exeter and Norwich, followed by Thorkell's to Sandwich (possibly engineered by Sveinn) in 1009, and finally the incursion of Sveinn and Cnut into Gainsborough in 1013.

8. See Simon Keynes, "Re-reading King Æthelred the Unready," in *Writing Medieval Biography 750-1250: Essays in Honour of Professor Frank Barlow*, ed. David Bates, Julia Crick, and Sarah Hamilton (Woodbridge, UK: The Boydell Press, 2006), 77–97, where he offers an objective reassessment of the king's reign in the context of the development of Viking activity, viewing its effect as becoming progressively complex when examined from a variety of vantage points extant in sources from charters to saints' lives. For a ninth-century Frankish response, expressive of a conventional, yet still powerful, mode of perceiving the Viking depredations as God's chastisement of a sinful race, see Simon Coupland, "The Rod of God's Wrath or the People of God's Wrath? The Carolingian Theology of the Viking Invasions," *Journal of Ecclesiastical History* 42 (1991): 535–54. My thanks to Professor Richard Abels for referring me to this work.

9. *ASC* C-text, s.a. 1014. For the annals of 978 to 1017, I follow Margaret Ashdown's edition of the C-text for references and quotations in *English and Norse Documents*, 38–71, 90–106. For a discussion of the C-text's characteristics for the years 976–82 and 983–1022, see O'Brien O'Keeffe, ed., *Anglo-Saxon Chronicle: MS. C*, vol. 5, lxii–lxviii.

[Then he [Cnut] went southward until he came to Sandwich, and there had the hostages who had been given to his father put ashore, and cut off their hands and ears and noses.]

The seeds for the treacherous events of 1036 were found in the past. By retrospectively juxtaposing the barbarities of the deeds carried out by both English and Danes alike when *Dene comon and her frið namon* with the betrayal and mutilation and massacre of Alfred atheling and his troops, the 1036 Chronicler allusively renders Harold Harefoot the living embodiment of those Danes who scalped, disemboweled, and mutilated the English people, as they waged a reign of terror over Æthelred's kingdom.

The following discussion centers on historical and poetic renderings of that turbulent period, the first two decades of the eleventh century, which I suggest spawned the Grendel-kin, in a further example of the *Beowulf*-poet's imaginative transformation of what Hayden White might call actual "fact," to create the fusion of imagination and actuality that, White maintains, infiltrates historical genres as well.[10] The argument dealing with the past is far-ranging and thus more appropriately falls into two parts, the first to be handled in chapter 2 and the second in chapter 3. As in chapter 1, I grapple with the interplay between history and vernacular epic, in particular how it is manifested in the first two-thirds of *Beowulf*. The following pages contain additional illustrations of the inherent polysemous nature of the *Beowulf*-poet's fertile imagination, which I suggest seized major historical events of the early and middle decades of the eleventh century and recast them into a historical allegory in fantastic mode, an intersection of "both mimesis and fantasy."[11]

My argument in chapter 2 begins with Fitt 2 of *Beowulf*, some seventy-four lines that dramatize Grendel's twelve-year onslaught upon Heorot. My historical point of reference will be the Danish attacks

---

10. See Introduction, 18n43.
11. The phrase is Kathryn Hume's, *Fantasy and Mimesis*, esp. 21; see above, Introduction n. 87, for definitions, examples, and uses of fantasy in literature by Tolkien, Rabkin, and Todorov.

on England in the early eleventh century, particularly those between 1003 and 1016, first as treated by twelfth-century Anglo-Norman historians (Henry of Huntingdon, John of Worcester, William of Malmesbury); then by the contemporary Chronicler of the C-text of the *Anglo-Saxon Chronicle*, who himself shows signs of moving from what Cecily Clark has described as a "restrictive" annalistic style to a more rhetorically expansive and syntactically complex literary style;[12] and finally by the Encomiast in relevant units in the *Encomium Emmae Reginae*. For like vernacular poets who selectively reshape historical facts into vernacular epic, historians are subject to principles of unity, causality, and embellishment, principles essential to the very act of composition itself, a point of view central to White's assessment of all historical writings, and Whaley's of Snorri's works, and Tyler's of the Encomiast's as well.[13]

I then turn to what may be characterized as the source of the 1036 struggle for dynastic power between the West Saxon monarchy and the powerful political factions of Mercia—to the question of Cnut's alleged paternity of Harold and the material surrounding Sveinn Álfífuson (OE *Ælfgifu*, ON *Álfífa*), Cnut's illegitimate son with Ælfgifu of Northampton, whom Cnut designated as king of Norway before his death. In great measure, Sveinn and Cnut's victorious campaign in England between 1013 and 1016 resulted from their political alliance with the Mercians (chap. 3, 204–18, passim), those inhabiting the land south of the Humber, the land of the "people of the border,"

---

12. Cecily Clark, "The Narrative Mode of *The Anglo-Saxon Chronicle* before the Conquest," in *England before the Conquest*, ed. Clemoes and Hughes, 215–35, esp. 216–30, quote at 216. See also Ashdown, who sees the development from the early Anglo-Saxon to later Anglo-Norman annalistic writing as reflective of the movement toward the Norse method; *English and Norse Documents*, 18.

13. Diana Whaley's analysis of Snorri Sturluson's historical works, which she calls "imaginative historiography," *Heimskringla*, esp. chaps. 5 and 6, quote at 113; Elizabeth M. Tyler, "Fictions of Family," 149–79, esp. 155–58, 165; see also her "Talking about History," 359–83; see also above, Introduction, 21–22 nn. 44–46.

that is, the *mearcstapan* (the striders of the borderlands),[14] which had served as a natural military zone, important to the political safety of the Anglo-Saxon kingdom from the time of Æthelflæd, Lady of the Mercians.[15] Cnut's personal alliance with Ælfgifu of Northampton, daughter of Ælfhelm, ealdorman of Northampton and, from 993 to 1006, of Northumbria, was the catalytic event that eventually secured the throne for Harold Harefoot as full king in 1037.

In chapter 3, I address Ælfgifu of Northampton and her kin, perhaps the most powerful of the Mercian landed families, and her treatment in contemporary and later English, Scandinavian, and continental texts, ranging from the late eleventh through the thirteenth centuries, in the hope of understanding the source of her treatment in *Beowulf*. Ælfgifu's tyrannical rule as queen mother in Norway (1030–35) is immortalized by the Norwegians as *Álfífu ǫld* (Ælfgifu's time). It is perhaps in line with the Nordic literary tradition of delineating politically powerful women, perceived as dangerous to the political and ecclesiastical structures, as sorceresses, avengers, and predatory animals—the most extreme example in Nordic literature being Þóra/Þorgerðr Hölgabrúðr, wife, beloved, and supernatural protectress of Earl Hákon, the last pagan ruler of Norway, and the most realistic, Gunnhildr *konungamóðir* (mother of kings), wife of King Eiríkr Blóðøx (Bloodaxe)—that one might glimpse Ælfgifu of Northampton as an allegorical rendering of Grendel's mother.

The Fall of Æthelred's England and Imaginative Historiography

The Anglo-Norman Historians and the *Anglo-Saxon Chronicle*

When Henry of Huntingdon begins his account of the military and political events that led to the fall of Æthelred's England in book VI

14. For the definition, see Pauline Stafford, *The East Midlands in the Early Middle Ages* (Leicester, UK: Leicester University Press, 1985), 135.
15. See Stafford, *East Midlands*, passim; see also Peter Hunter Blair, "The Northumbrians and Their Southern Frontier," *Archaeologia Aeliana*, 4th ser., 26 (1948): 105–13.

of his *Historia Anglorum*,[16] he makes free use of rhetorical devices normally associated with literature. Henry's self-conscious disclosure of his compositional trait of compression and authorial selection at the close of book V presents a fitting illustration of the rhetorical principles that come into play both in the commemoration of the "facts" of history and in their "imaginative" representation: "According to my usual practice of giving a simplified explanation, an ordered summary of the abbreviated high points narrated in this book will now be carefully laid before the reader."[17] Henry centers his narration in book VI of the *History* on the events that led to the fall of Æthelred's England to the Danes, which to his mind led to the Norman invasion and takeover of England,[18] and in doing so, he makes free use of compositional devices normally associated with those who "create" literature. He encapsulates, compresses, summarizes, reorders, and finally selects what in his judgment are the "high points" of his historical reportage. Though following closely the C- and E-texts of the *Anglo-Saxon Chronicle*,[19] he readily uses rhetorical figures not found in his sources, more appropriate for poetry rather than history. England "shook like a reed-bed struck by the quivering west wind": this simile with its heightened diction that characterizes the response of the English people to the devastation caused by Sveinn Forkbeard is one such example; Sveinn's military tactics referred to allegorically as his "three companions—plunder, burning, and killing" is another

---

16. *HHHA* vi.1.

17. *HHHA* v.31: "More autem solito, lux apertionis exordinata adbreuiatione genita, perstrictis huius libri summitatibus, lectori diligenter anteponenda est."

18. *HHHA* vi.1, 338–39.

19. On Henry's sources, see Greenway, Introduction, *HHHA* lxxxv–cvii, esp. xci–xcii; see also *ASC* 2:lv, lxxxvi–lxxxvii, and Keynes, "Declining Reputation," 227–53, esp. 238–39; for a discussion of Henry's rhetorical practices and his use of sources, see R. I. Page, *'A Most Vile People': Early English Historians on the Vikings* (London: Viking Society for Northern Research, 1987), esp. 14–20.

(vi.3).[20] Stark antithetical characterization of the leaders is a third: Æthelred *in superbiam elatus et perfidiam polatus* (increases in pride and faithlessness, vi.2) and is shaken *cum mesticia et confusione* (by sorrow and confusion, vi.3) in defeat, while Sveinn rises *fortissimus* (very powerful) and *audacissimus* (very audacious), the man *cui Deus regnum Anglie destinauerat* (for whom God had destined the kingdom of England, vi.3).[21] Likewise, John of Worcester's historical prose depicting the Danish sweep across England may be said to betray devices of fictionality. He freely offers personal assessments of personages: the people mustered for a surprise attack are ineffective or cowardly; Eadric Streona is "crafty and treacherous"; Sveinn, a "tyrant," is called by misnomer a "king," his army sweeping through Wessex with the "bacchanalian fury of wild beasts."[22] These modes of repre-

---

20. *HHHA* 342–43: "quem semper comitabantur tres socie, predatio, combustio, occisio, frenduit omnis Anglia et commota est uelut harundinetum zephiro uibrante collisum."

21. *HHHA* vi.2 and vi.3, 340–45; on Henry's exceptional education in language, rhetoric, and poetic training, see Greenway, Introduction, *HHHA* xxix–xxxix, and her "Henry of Huntingdon as Poet: The *De Herbis* Rediscovered," *Medium Aevum* 74n2 (2005): 329–32; on the interrelationship of Henry's poetic works, see Winston Black, "Henry of Huntingdon's Lapidary Rediscovered and his *Anglicanus Ortus* Reassembled," *Mediaeval Studies* 68 (2006): 43–87, and also most recently, the Introduction to *Henry, Archdeacon of Huntingdon: Anglicanus Ortus: A Verse Herbal of the Twelfth Century*, ed. and trans. Winston Black (Toronto and Oxford: Pontifical Institute of Mediaeval Studies and Bodleian Library, 2012).

22. *JWChron* 2; on John's commentary on the people, 454–55 [1004]: "At illi uel non audebant uel iussa perficere negligebant"; quotes at 456–57 [1006]: "Dolosus et pefidus Edricus Streona"; 474–75 [1013]: "si iure queat rex uocari, qui fere cuncta tirannice faciebat . . . . Suanus tirannus"; 472–73 [1013]: "et rabie ferina debacchantibus." Except for the account of Sveinn in the *Encomium Emmae Reginae*, the Danish king is almost exclusively presented in a negative light, possibly as a result of early assessments of him as an evil and pagan king; for a corrective on Sveinn's life and his achievements as king, see Peter Sawyer, "Swein Forkbeard and the Historians," in *Church and Chronicle in the Middle Ages: Essays Presented to John Taylor*, ed. I. Wood and G. A. Loud (London: Hambledon Press, 1991), 27–40; see also

sentation could be said to be more common to fiction than to fact. But it is William of Malmesbury who seems most literarily ambitious as he interweaves a wide range of sources—oral history, hagiography, prophecy, annals, letters—with creative and expansive abandon in his narration of the Danish takeover of Anglo-Saxon England in the early eleventh century, when the Danish forces were "sprouting out of Denmark like a hydra's head" and Sveinn, the "man of blood," swept through England, while Æthelred "lay yawning."[23]

Some years ago in "The Declining Reputation of Æthelred the Unready," Simon Keynes examined William's singular reinterpretation of the events of Æthelred's reign in the context of the Chronicler's commentary in the C-text of the *Anglo-Saxon Chronicle*. Keynes illustrates the means by which the pro-Norman William refashions the C-Chronicler's criticism of specific events in Æthelred's reign into a more all-inclusive and expansive condemnation of the king's thirty-seven-year rule,[24] in which William ironically describes Æthelred as having occupied rather than ruled the kingdom.[25] In stark contrast to William's unrelenting censure of (and perhaps disgust with) Æthelred, and his vituperative narrative against English stupidity, mismanagement, and mistiming of military offensives, stand the unique style and tone of the C-Chronicler's entries—somewhat more objective than William's in recording the events, yet not without expressions of subdued pity, anger, and frustration at the ineptitude of the king's and of his counselors' leadership.[26] Nor is the Chronicler's annalistic

---

Ian Howard, *Swein Forkbeard's Invasions and the Danish Conquest of England 991–1017* (Woodbridge, UK: The Boydell Press, 2003).

23. *WMGRA* ii.165.5, 272–73: "*nam semper, ut hidrae capitibus, hostibus ex Danemarkia pullulantibus nusquam caueri poterat*"; and ii.2, 300–301: "*Erat Suanus in sanguinem pronus.*" See also under ii.165.7 on Æthelred's inactivity and lack of leadership, which William records throughout.

24. Keynes, "Declining Reputation," 227–53, esp. 236–39. Keynes discusses the period from 978 to 1017, but he focuses on the years 983-1016.

25. *WMGRA* ii.164.1, 268–69.

26. Keynes does not make the comparison, although there is an implied comparison; the difference of voice, tone, and style particular to the two

Chapter Two

commentary covering the years 983–1017 lacking a plethora of poetic devices (assonance, rhyme, alliteration, kenning) and rhetorical figures (antithesis, shifts of perspective), as Keynes elaborately argues and as will be discussed further below. Yet Keynes concluded that as William wrote his account of Æthelred's reign, the "source which exerted the most decisive influence on [him] was undoubtedly his own fertile imagination."[27]

Keynes's examination of the C-text Chronicler's choices in recording events of the Danish incursions into England, especially those between roughly 1003 and 1016, reveals a complex voice of articulate objectivity blended with a distinctive personal involvement.[28] His discussion centers on establishing single authorship, time of composition, and singularity of style for the years 983–1016, placing the Chronicler's composition at about 1017 (although he extends the latter date to 1023), with provenance in London. Although the Chronicler uses exemplars for recording the earlier events in Æthelred's reign (and these, Keynes asserts, are historically accurate), the material dealing with the Danish invasions reflects a more personal contemporary response to acts that culminated in the fall of Anglo-Saxon England to the Danish Cnut, in a narrative style more literary than historical, a characteristic common to the C-, D-, E-, and F- versions of these years.[29] Yet for Keynes it is far from a balanced and dispassionate account of Ælthelred's reign, for it omits information dealing with ecclesiastical, governmental, and dynastic upheavals that likewise occurred during that turbulent period, a selectivity that, in Keynes's view, mars the C-*Chronicle* as an ultimate source,[30]

---

historical accounts is striking.

27. Keynes, "Declining Reputation," 238.

28. In addition to Keynes's discussion of the uniqueness of the C-Chronicler's style and tone, to which I am indebted, see Ashdown, *English and Norse Documents*, 14–18; Clark, "Narrative Mode," 224–30.

29. For variances in the versions, especially those caused by adherence to political affiliations, see Clark, "Narrative Mode," 230–33.

30. Keynes, "Declining Reputation," 236; see also Pauline A. Stafford, "The Reign of Æthelred II: A Study in the Limitations of Royal Policy

though it brings it closer to a historio-literary text. The C-Chronicler, for instance, retains a singular "telescopic" view focused on the regularity of the Danish attacks, which he sharply contrasts with the passivity and ineffectiveness of the English response.[31] The Chronicler's focus on the rapidity of the intruders' attacks in antithesis to the almost paralytic response of the English, Keynes demonstrates, culminates in a depiction of the Danes as striding about the land *swa swa hie wolden* (just as they pleased),[32] while Ælthelred and his counselors continually assemble to draw up ill-chosen strategic responses. In addition, Keynes touches upon the Chronicler's abandonment of the usual "laconic" annalistic style for a more complex phrasal construction and wide-ranging vocabulary and the adaptation of rhetorical devices ("rhyme, alliteration and repetition . . . and antithesis"), vestiges of poetic rather than historical narrative. At times, the Chronicler invests Danish activity with language more common to heroic poetry (his use of kennings, as one instance) than to annalistic prose. He refers to Sveinn's sea-vessels that await him after his sacking of Exeter and Salisbury in 1003 as *yðhengestas* (sea horses): *þær hé wiste his yðhengestas* (where he knew his ships were [waiting]). In 1004, when the English in East Anglia wage heated battle against Sveinn's army, he records that the Danes *hi sylfe sædon þæt hí næfre*

---

and Action," in *Ethelred the Unready*, ed. Hill, 15–46, esp. 16, 29–30, who notes the unofficial nature of the C-version, unlike the chronicles of Alfred and Edward the Elder, as well as a bias toward affairs and personages in eastern England. The blunders and mismanagement of events of the second decade, however, are somewhat supported as noted above by the writings of Wulfstan and Ælfric. Another severe omission in the Chronicler's report deals with the activities in England between 1009 and 1012, and again in 1014, of Óláfr Haraldsson *inn digri* (the stout/ immense), the future saint and king of Norway, whom Cnut ousted from his kingdom in 1030.

31. Keynes, "Declining Reputation," 233.

32. Keynes identifies ten instances of the formula: *swa . . . swa *hi . . . wolde (on)*: 994, 998, 999, 1001, 1006, 1009, 1010 (twice), 1011, 1013 suggestive of the Danish troops' mastery over the land; Keynes, "Declining Reputation," 245n17; see also Ashdown, *English and Norse Documents*, 15n1; and Clark, "Narrative Mode," 229.

wursan handplegan on Angelcynne ne gemitton, þonne Ulfcytel him tobrohte (themselves said that they had never before experienced fiercer *handplegan* [literally "handplay," a kenning for "hand-to-hand fighting," Page's translation of the term]).[33] Finally, giving a slightly different cause for the degradations inflicted on England than Wulfstan, the Chronicler continually represents the ravaging of the land as the "working of evil" rather than as the result of the retributive anger of God. The entry for 1013, for instance, holds the last of nine appearances of the idea of evil as the causative factor in the harrying of England, sometimes expressed by the formula *mæst (*) yfel worhton*; again, it is Sveinn's troops who *worhton þæt mæst yfel ðe æfre æni here gedon meahte* (worked the greatest evil that any army had the power to inflict).[34]

The *Chronicle* entries covering the years 1003–16 understandably were of some political significance, codifying as they did what has been alluded to as the second and third waves of the invasion and subsequent ravaging of Anglo-Saxon England by Sveinn Forkbeard and Thorkell Hávi (the tall) and the incursion and eventual final conquest by Cnut.[35] So trenchant was the memory of the land's devastation that the barbarities of those *Dene* who *comon and her frið namon* remained fresh in the mind of the 1036 Chronicler lamenting the enormities inflicted upon Ælthelred's son. It would not be entirely unreasonable for an epic poet, who might likewise be caught up with the ruthlessness and inhumanity of the Danes' method of making peace, to transform and crystallize Sveinn and his "bacchanalian" troops ranging over England into the monstrous Grendel. For the 1003 Chronicler's complex attitude toward and singular rhetorical presentation of the events of Ælthelred's England during the 1003–16

33. Page, '*A Most Vile People*,' 27; see also Clark, "Narrative Mode," 227, where she associates *handplegan* with Beowulf's wrestling match with Grendel (*Bwf* 718–19ᵃ), although the kenning is not found in the poem.
34. The other eight are at 993, 994 (twice), 997, 1001, 1002, 1009, and 1011; Keynes, "Declining Reputation," 231, 245n16.
35. For a discussion on the Danish invasions of 1003, 1006, 1009, 1011, 1013, see Howard, *Swein Forkbeard's Invasions*, esp. 99–123.

period suggest a rhetorical stance similar to that of the *Beowulf*-poet's engaged yet detached narrative of Grendel's attacks on Heorot. The poet's involved objectivity, punctuated with bursts of frustration in the gnomic passages; his frequent shifts in perspective; his bent toward phrasal, structural, and thematic antithesis; his chronological framing and treatment of events; and his depiction of character are somewhat like the Chronicler's as he, too, retrospectively telescopes the events of a twelve-year period that culminate in the rise of a *feond on helle* (enemy from hell, 101[b]) to the status of a *healðegn* (hall-thane, 142[a]) and half-ruler of Heorot. If one inserts the Beowulfian episode into the poet's contemporary political and cultural milieu, one could be led to suspect that Grendel's reign of terror, his planned nocturnal attacks on Hrothgar's hall, and the *mære* (illustrious) king's continual ineffective responses might be an epic manifestation of the time when—as the 1036 Chronicler recollects and the Chronicler writing between 1016 and 1023 strikingly brings to life—the *Dene comon and her frið namon*.[36]

GRENDEL'S REIGN OF TERROR AND THE *ANGLO-SAXON CHRONICLE*

Grendel's Reign of Terror, Klaeber's title for Fitt 2 of *Beowulf*,[37] the episode that dramatizes Grendel's raids on Heorot, predicates a type of sovereignty, an exertion of royal rule over the Beowulfian Danes, tyrannical and bestial, throughout a lengthy period of time, some twelve years, the poet tells us. Klaeber was seemingly uncomfortable in accepting the raids on Heorot as being fundamentally derived from a folktale narrative, although he admitted their general relation to the fabulous mode.[38] Grendel's raids, he noted, were unlike those of the trolls in folklore, for folktale versions came in doublets

---

36. I follow Keynes's dating of the composition of this section of the C-*Chronicle*, "Declining Reputation," 231.

37. Klaeber, 3rd ed., esp. 132; so Klaeber, 4th ed., 123.

38. Klaeber, 3rd ed., esp. xiv n.1, and passim. There is extensive critical literature on the folkloric elements in the Grendel episodes and extending into their relationship to Icelandic material, in Klaeber, 3rd ed. (xiii–xxix) and in Klaeber, 4th ed., xxxvi–li; see also above chap.1 nn13, 15.

whereas in *Beowulf* there were many in succession,[39] and, one could add, they extend continuously over a dozen years. Moreover, the tonal ambiguity of the poet's judgments, his concentration on the psychology and emotions of the character,[40] and his moral commentary upon and frustration at the unraveling of events distinguish the episode as dynamic and complex in its construction, the antithesis of the elemental linearity of a folktale. Rather, Klaeber suggested, one might look to the historical features of the episode, by which I assume he meant those of legendary history,[41] but which I suggest might be found in the more contemporaneously relevant sociopolitical climate of the poet's culture, as Roberta Frank has often noted,[42] and has more recently been discussed by Leonard Neidorf who argues for the production of the manuscript as being highly relevant to the national turmoil that gripped England during the first two decades of the eleventh century, and who, as part of his argument, associates Grendel's attacks on Heorot with Wulfstan's descriptions of the Viking attacks in *Sermo Lupi*.[43] It was as if, one begins to suspect, the folkloric element was meant to function as a disguise. For what I find remarkable in reading the C-Chronicler's account of the Danish attacks on England between 1003 and 1016 is a certain turn of mind, a parallelism in treatment, tone, and shifting of narrative perspective

---

39. Klaeber, 3rd ed., 133 n.135, and xiv, where he comments upon the difference between the folkloric motif of the dual visits of Yule-trolls as they are used in *Grettissaga* and *Hrólfs saga kraka*, among others, and in *Beowulf*, where the nocturnal visits take place "much oftener"; see, as example, 147ff., 473ff., 646ff.

40. Several essays have dealt with the poet's psychological treatment of Grendel, among which is Michael Lapidge, "*Beowulf* and the Psychology of Terror," in *Heroic Poetry in the Anglo-Saxon Period: Studies in Honor of Jess B. Bessinger, Jr.*, ed. Helen Damico and John Leyerle (Kalamazoo, MI: Medieval Institute Publications, 1993), 373–402.

41. Klaeber, 3rd ed., xivni.

42. See Introduction, 12–17, and passim.

43. Leonard Neidorf, "*VII Æthelred* and the Genesis of the *Beowulf* Manuscript," *Philological Quarterly* 89, nos. 2–3 (2010): 119–39, at 124. My thanks to Mr. Neidorf for drawing my attention to his work.

similar to what we find in the *Beowulf*-poet's depiction of Grendel's Reign of Terror, suggesting that the episode may be the poet's own imaginative version of the Danish forces' sweep through England with the "bacchanalian fury of wild beasts."

The whole of Fitt 2 (115–88) is given over to the narrative of Grendel's *gūðcræft* (war-skill) that terrorizes the Danes. In the scenic organization of the narrative, the action retroactively shifts from the narrator's present to the past, for the attacks constitute a dark episode in the past history of Heorot, predating the introduction of Beowulf and the reestablishment of Heorot in the hands of its rightful ruler. The acts of war perpetrated by the *grimma gǣst* (fierce guest/stranger/ spirit) that the prince comes to avenge are foreshadowed in the passage that functions as a prelude to Grendel's reign:

> Swā ðā drihtguman drēamum lifdon,
> ēadiglīce, oð ðæt ān ongan
> fyrene fre(m)man fēond on helle;
> wæs se grimma gǣst Grendel hāten,
> mǣre mearcstapa, sē þe mōras hēold,
> fen ond fæsten; fīfelcynnes eard
> wonsǣli wer weardode hwīle. (*Bwf* 99–105)

> [Thus the warriors lived in joy,
> blessed-like, until a certain one began
> to perform evils, an enemy from hell;
> That fierce guest/spirit was named Grendel,
> illustrious boundary-stalker who ruled the moors,
> fens, and strongholds; the man of black-joy occupied
> the region of the monsters for a time.]

The antithetical placement of the unsuspecting *drihtguman* (noble warriors) living in blessed joy and the dark joyless man, the *fēond on helle* (enemy from hell), who will wreak *fyrene* (evils) upon them—the antithesis between heroic delight and inexplicable cruelty—serves as an anticipatory summary of the documented deeds graphically depicted in Fitt 2 that culminate in Grendel's nocturnal domination of Heorot. The poet's deliberate depiction of Grendel as *ān . . . fēond*, an unidentified and formless enemy, here and elsewhere,[44] incomprehensible in nature, who had possession of and ranged over large expanses of land, might be said to be an apt description of the amorphous Danish army as it swept at will through every corner of England in the early years of the eleventh century, *ge fyrðon on þá wildan fennas hí ferdon* (marching through and decimating even the wild fens) of East Anglia in 1010, until the land lay wasted and its people slain and mutilated.

Likewise, the poet's condensation of Grendel's attacks upon the Danes is evocative of the C-Chronicler's telescopic rendering of the Danish incursion into England during those dozen years or so at the beginning of the eleventh century:

Swā rīxode ond wið rihte wan,
āna wið eallum, oð þæt īdel stōd
hūsa sēlest. Wæs sēo hwīl micel;
twelf wintra tīd torn geþolode
wine Scyldinga, wēana gehwelcne,
sīdra sorga; forðām [secgum] wearð,
ylda bearnum undyrne cūð
gyddum geōmore, þætte Grendel wan
hwīle wið Hrōþgār, hetenīðas wæg,
fyrene ond fæhðe fela missēra,
singāle sæce; sibbe ne wolde.
(*Bwf* 144–54)

[Thus [Grendel] ruled and fought against rightfulness,
one alone against all, until the best of houses
stood uselessly empty. The time was interminable.
The friendly-lord of the Scyldings endured afflictions,

---

44. This is an attribute readily repeated; see, e.g., lines 101, 143, 164, 439, 725, 748, 984, 1276.

every misery, all conceivable agonies for twelve winters.
Thus, it was patently revealed to men through plaintive song
that Grendel battled against Hrothgar for a time;
waged hostile combat, sinful crime and feud,
continual battle for many a half year. He desired no peace.]

Although Sveinn's harrying of England began at the end of the final decade of the tenth century (Wave I of the conquest), the concerted political effort for the invasion and conquest of England took place from 1003 with the destruction of Exeter to 1016 with the division of England between Cnut in control of Mercia and Edmund Ironside in Wessex.[45] The time span of a dozen years that appears simultaneously in the annals and the poem may, of course, be a happenstance, yet it is remarkable that both Chronicler and poet are deeply and, one might say, emotionally preoccupied with the brutality and devastation inflicted upon a nation by a fierce enemy for a period of approximately a dozen years.

Furthermore, the poet's sensitivity toward Hrothgar—caught in a web of hostile afflictions from which he is unable to extricate himself or his people, misfortunes he has come to accept as the norm—is similar to the Chronicler's rendering of Æthelred, whom he treats, as Keynes points out, with sympathy and respect.[46] Plaintive songs about Hrothgar's afflictions circulated among men (149ᵇ–54ᵃ), lamenting the *hetenīðas* (hostile combat), the *fyrene* (evils), and the *singāle sæce* (continuous battle) that Grendel waged against Hrothgar for *fela missēra* (many a half-year). Hrothgar's afflictions are no less than Æthelred's tribulations on account of the uninterrupted Danish onrush through England during those last twelve years to grasp the kingdom for the Danish king. *Æthelred geheold his rice mid myclum*

---

45. *ASC*, s.a. 994; s.a. 1016. For a discussion of the Danish incursions and the English response, see Ann Williams, *Æthelred the Unready: The Ill-Counselled King* (London: Hambledon Press, 2003), esp. chaps. 3–7; Keynes, "Re-reading Æthelred the Unready," 80–88 and passim; and Howard, *Swein Forkbeard's Invasions*.

46. Keynes, "Declining Reputation," 236.

swince and earfoðnessum þá hwile ðe his líf wæs (Æthelred ruled his kingdom with great toil and many tribulations for the time allotted to his life); he retained the loyalty of his people, who, upon the death of Sveinn, invited him back to England from Normandy, declaring *þæt him nan hlaford leofra nære þonne hiora gecynda hlaford* (that no lord was more beloved to them than the lord of their own race), despite the bungling strategies, despite the ineffectual responses to the Danish attacks.

The preference of subjects for their natural king, faulted or not, above all other princes reported by the Chronicler is likewise a theme alluded to by the poet; it serves as a prelude to the panegyric extemporaneously composed by Hrothgar's scop in praise of Beowulf's defeat of Grendel, a feat that makes the hero *rīces wyrðra* (worthy of a kingdom) and stands in stark contrast to Hrothgar's paralytic actions:

Ðǣr wæs Bēowulfes
mǣrðo mǣned; monig oft gecwæð,
þætte sūð nē norð be sǣm twēonum
ofer eormengrund ōþer nǣnig
under swegles begong sēlra nǣre
rondhæbbendra, rīces wyrðra.–
Nē hīe hūru winedrihten wiht ne lōgon,
glædne Hrōðgār, ac þæt wæs gōd cyning.
(*Bwf* 856b–63)

[Beowulf's glorious deed was chanted there; many said repeatedly
that north or south between the two seas,
throughout the spacious earth, no other
shield-bearer under the expanse of the sky
would ever be more worthy of a kingdom.
Nor did they indeed at all find fault with their friendly lord,
gracious Hrothgar; on the contrary, he was a good king.]

Now this parenthetical intrusion affirming Hrothgar as a *gōd cyning*—after Beowulf has cleansed the hall of the evil—and equating the aged, ineffective king to Beowulf—is gratuitous and cannot be viewed as anything other than ambiguously ironic, for the king's paralysis in ousting the *fyrene* stands in stark contrast to the actions not only of the young hero but of the *gōd cyning* Scyld, the valorous eponymous founder of the Scyldings (*Bwf* 11). Yet despite these deficiencies in Hrothgar's leadership, the nation remains loyal to their *winedrihten*.

Hrothgar's deficiencies as *helm Scyldinga* are pointedly dramatized in the king's reaction to Grendel's first raid, a scene that conflates the twelve-year onslaughts on Heorot. After Grendel's first raid on Heorot, during which he plundered thirty thanes, whose disposition is not revealed until 1579[b]–84[a] (at the exact moment Beowulf avenges the deed by his decapitation of Grendel's corpse), the poet portrays Hrothgar as cowed by the ferocity of the enemy's attack. He is impelled to inactivity and sorrow instead of gathering forces and waging a counterattack:

> Mǣre þēodon,
> æþeling ǣrgōd, unblīðe sæt,
> þolode ðrȳðswȳð, þegnsorge drēah,
> syðþan hīe þæs lāðan lāst scēawedon
> wergan gāstes; wæs þæt gewin tō strang,
> lāð ond longsum! Næs hit lengra fyrst,
> ac ymb āne niht eft gefremede
> morðbeala māre, ond nō mearn fore,
> fǣhðe ond fyrene; wæs tō fæst on þām.
> (*Bwf* 129[b]–37)

[The illustrious king, a prince of eternal goodness, sat in sorrow, the mighty one suffered, he endured distress at the loss of thanes, when they showed him the tracks of the loathsome one, of the accursed spirit/guest; that battle had been too strong, too loathsome and long-lasting. No longer a time passed, but around the following night he [Grendel] again performed

greater slaughters, and, as before, he did not mourn
the feud and evil deeds; he was too resolved on them.]

The mighty king "sat in sorrow," the poet tells us; he "suffered." The inappropriateness of these responses in the *helm Scyldinga* (protector of the Scyldings) is made ironically more striking as they are antithetically juxtaposed with Grendel's failure to mourn or take the time to suffer as he staged his immediate second attack. The poet's portrayal of Hrothgar is at once critical of his grievous betrayal of trust as *helm Scyldinga* and compassionately sympathetic, a complex of reactive responses characteristic of the C-text Chronicler's rendering of the daunted English king. The poet's shift in focus to comment on the intensity, savagery, and length of the attacks—*tō strang, lāð, longsum, tō fæst*—and the regularity of the *fæhðe ond fyrene* is likewise a feature of the C-text Chronicler's depiction of the Danes' interminable incursions on English soil. The Chronicler's continuous description of the Danish attacks as the "working of evil," for instance, is consonant with the poet's depiction of Grendel's acts throughout the poem as *fyrene*.

Still other resemblances between the annalistic narrative of the Danish takeover of England and Grendel's reign of terror suggest that the poet and the annalist may have been engaged with the same historical event. Grendel's relentlessness in executing his campaign of terror is a characteristic of the advancing Danish troops of 1006, which *dydon eal swa hi ær gewuna wæron, heregodon and bærndon and slogon swa swa hi ferdon* (did just as they had been in the habit of doing—they harried and burned and massacred as they carried on), just as the ineffectiveness of the Danes under Hrothgar mirrors the futility of English plans of attack: *Ac hit naht ne beheold þe ma ðe hit oftor ær dide, ac for eallum þissum se here ferde swa he sylf wolde* (but it [the English force] could hold back nothing at all any more than it often previously had done, but on the contrary in spite of all this, the harrying army carried on just as it itself desired).[47] Hrothgar's

---

47. This, from 1006, is one of many examples of the C-Chronicler's comments on English military preparations; see Clark, who sees *heregodon*

warriors make a travesty of their heroic plans of counterattack:

Ful oft gebēotedon bēore druncne
ofer ealowǣge ōretmecgas,
þæt hīe in bēorsele bīdan woldon
Grendles gūþe mid gryrum ecga.
Đonne wæs þēos medoheal on morgentīd,
drihtsele drēorfāh, þonne dæg līxte,
eal bencþelu blōde bestymed,
heall heorudrēore; āhte ic holdra þy lǣs,
dēorre duguðe, þē þā dēað fornam.
 (*Bwf* 480–88)

[Quite often, my champions, emboldened by beer,
would vow over ale cup
that they wanted to remain in the beer hall,
to wait for Grendel's attack with the terror of battle swords.
Then in the morning, when the day lightened,
was this mead hall a hall of warriors shining with gore,
all the floor planks and benches steaming with blood,
a hall stained with the gore of battle. I possessed fewer
beloved daring retainers, whom death then destroyed.]

With a bravado induced by beer, they utter hollow boasts to attack
the enemy with *gryrum ecga*, only to have their encounter with Grendel
turn the mead hall into a "hall of warriors shining with gore." The
emotional space that informs the Beowulfian passage is characterized
by both compassion and irony, for the onerous disgrace that tinges
the warriors' hollow boasts is softened by Hrothgar's disclosure of
them to Beowulf in a type of confession. The use of the term *ōretmecgas*
in this instance, which elsewhere in the poem is used to characterize
Beowulf and his chosen champions (332, 363), is a case in point, for
not only is it suggestive of Hrothgar's inaccurate assessment of his

---

and bærndon and slogon swa swa hi ferdon as key words used to emphasize
the barbarity and "mastery" of the Danes (s.a. 1001, 1003, 1004, 1009, 1010,
1016), "Narrative Mode," 229–30.

men and their own ineffectiveness, but, at the same time, it provides a view of a monarch standing in the midst of a ravaged kingdom.

Nor is the Chronicler's report on the cowardice of the Anglo-Saxons, most strikingly narrated under the years 1003, 1006, 1010, and 1016, where Englishmen fled the field of battle, absent from the Beowulfian poem:

Þā wæs ēaðfynde þē him elles hwǣr
gerūmlīcor ræste [sōhte],
bed æfter būrum, ðā him gebēacnod wæs,
gesægd sōðlīce sweotolan tācne
healðegnes hete; hēold hyne syðþan
fyr and fæstor sē þǣm fēond ætwand.
(*Bwf* 138–43)

[Then (he) was easily found, he who sought
a more spacious resting place elsewhere,
a bed among the [outlying] buildings when it was shown to him,
by a clear sign [that] shone like a beacon,
the hate of the hall-thane. Then he held himself
far and more securely, he who fled the enemy.]

Here, Hrothgar's warriors, those who are to guard Heorot, are subtly and ironically characterized as cowardly, as they choose to find a "more spacious place" of rest far from the hall when warned by signs of impeding battle (literally, beacons, from *gebēacnod*). Like the men of *Maldon* who failed to perform their duty to their lord and country, Hrothgar's warriors fail under the stress of battle, abandoning their lord and duty. Yet, in contrast, one can see the C-Chronicler's depiction of disloyalty and cowardice that runs throughout his account as countering the heroic idealism that finally obtains in *Maldon* despite the 991 defeat, as Jonathan Wilcox has argued.[48] Hrothgar's warriors

48. Jonathan Wilcox, "*The Battle of Maldon* and the *Anglo-Saxon Chronicle*, 979–1016: A Winning Combination," *Proceedings of the Medieval Association of the Midwest* 3 (1996): 31–50. Wilcox's argument centers on reading the C-*Chronicle* as a narrative shaped "through a personal focus" (37) and offers

never recover from the stigma.[49] In Old English vernacular literature, Richard Abels has pointed out, it is not feeling fright that condemns a warrior for cowardice but rather desertion of duty motivated by fear.[50]

This type of controlled irony one sees in *Beowulf* characterizes the Chronicler's entries for 1003–1009, especially that of 1006, as he records the empty boasts and unheroic actions of Englishmen who fled the Danish troops, who, in contrast, always announced themselves by *atendon hiora herebeacen swa hi ferdon* (lighting their war-beacons as they went).[51] The use of *beacen* in both accounts, of course, may be coincidental, yet in both, as noun and verb, it is the *tācen* (sign) of the enemy. Its appearance among the other stylistic similarities is provocative, as is the similarity between the *Beowulf*-poet's continuous characterization of Grendel's onslaughts on Heorot as *fǣhðe ond fyrene* (feud and evils), and the C-Chronicler's characterization of the Danish armies' acts of ravaging as the "workings of evil."[52]

---

narrative patterns from which poem and chronicle are to be read. He does not suggest that the "poet was influenced by the chronicler's narrative" (45).

49. In contrast to Hrothgar's men, Beowulf's warriors on the two occasions when they are attacked by the Grendel-kin, though gripped with terror, do not desert their leader. Nor do they abandon him at the mere, though Hrothgar and his troops forsake the Geats and return to the hall. In the final third of the poem, however, Beowulf's men (save Wiglaf) likewise willfully fail in their duty to their lord.

50. For a study of the depiction of cowardice in Anglo-Saxon literature in the context of the study of the history of emotions, see Richard Abels, "'Cowardice' and Duty in Anglo-Saxon England," *Journal of Medieval Military History* 4 (2006): 29–49, esp. 30–34 (*Elene, Andreas, Beowulf*), 42–46 (*Maldon*, Wulfstan, Cnut II). My thanks to Professor Abels for drawing my attention to his work. See also Dorothy Whitelock for Wulfstan's laws against desertion, in "Archbishop Wulfstan, Homilist and Statesman," *Transactions of the Royal Historical Society*, 4th ser. vol. 24 (1942), 25–45.

51. Keynes, "Declining Reputation," 234.

52. Keynes, "Declining Reputation," 230–31, 245n16.

Finally, the characterization of the annalistic and the Beowulfian *witan* suggests a compositional narrative of the same historical event. The C-Chronicler's portrayal of the ineffectiveness of Æthelred's *witan* in negotiating peace settlements or in planning strategies of attacks or counterattacks appears as a *leitmotiv* in the C-Chronicler's account, as in this example from 1006:

Ágan se cyning þa georne to smeagenne wið his witan hwæt him eallum rædlicust þuhte þæt mon ðissum earde gebeorghan mihte.

[The king then began to deliberate earnestly with his counselors for some plan that seemed most expedient to them, that might effectively defend this land.]

The results of these deliberations were the payment of *gafol* (tribute),[53] which neither in 1006, nor in 1010, nor in other years effected a truce or held the enemy at bay, but rather inflamed it:

Þonne bead man eallan witan to cynge, and man sceolde þonne rædan, hu man þisne eard werian sceolde. Ac þeah mon þonne hwæt rædde, þæt ne stod furðon ænne monað.

[All the counselors were then summoned to the king, and they were obliged to devise a plan how they should defend this land. But on the contrary, although they planned something then, the plan did not continue for even a single month.]

A similar obtuse indecision and futility color the depiction of Hrothgar's counselors, his *witan* of high-ranking nobles, twice touched on with light irony by the *Beowulf*-poet:

> Monig oft gesæt
> rīce tō rūne; ræd eahtedon,
> hwæt swīðferhðum sēlest wære
> wið færgryrum tō gefremmanne. (*Bwf* 171^{b}-74)

---

53. For the payments of *gafol*, beginning at ten thousand pounds in 991 and increasing steadily to the annual contribution of seventy-two thousand pounds in 1017, see Clark, "Narrative Mode," 229.

[Many high-ranking [lords] often sat in council;
  they deliberated about [their] counsel,
  about what might be best done by the brave-hearted ones
  against the terror caused by the sudden onslaughts.]

The deliberations of the "high-ranking ones" were ill-founded, it seems, as the *Beowulf*-poet describes the folly of their expectations of tribute in bargaining for peace with Grendel:

> sibbe ne wolde
> wið manna hwone mægenes Deniga,
> feorhbealo feorran, féa þingian,
> né þǽr nǽnig witena wénan þorfte
> beorhte bóte tó ban*an* folmum;
> (ac se) ǽglǽca éhtende wæs,
> deorc déaþscua, duguþe ond geoguþe,
> seomade ond syrede.
> (*Bwf* 154^b-61^a)

[He [Grendel] desired no peace-pact
  with any man of the Danish military force,
  no termination to the deadly evil; to settle on a tribute;
  none of the counselors there had need to expect
  bright compensation at the hands of the killer;
  but on the contrary, the monster-warrior kept on persecuting,
  the dark death-shadow, ambushing, and devouring
  the troops, young and old.]

The expectation by Hrothgar's *witan* of tribute from the enemy reverses the position of those engaged in bargaining for peace in the *Chronicle* and stands as an ironic exaggeration of the miscalculations by Æthelred's *witan* in negotiating peace settlements by means of tribute, which indeed did not hold back the enemy but rather further induced it to plague and ravage the English people. And one is led to conjecture that the unnamed distress that the zealous spirit/stranger (*ellengǽst, Bwf* 86^a) impatiently suffered for a long time (*earfoðlíce/ þráge geþolode*, 86^b–87^a) may well be the need for satisfaction of a *fæhðe*, and that the deadly evil (*feorhbealo*) he suffered may have been as great as that which incited Sveinn to attack Exeter and Norwich in 1003, as revenge for the murder of his sister Gunnhildr and her husband Pallig, victims of the St. Brice's massacre in April 1002, a barbarous act against the Danes in the Danelaw ordered by Æthelred.[54]

The sympathy of the 1016 Chronicler rests with the defeated house of Æthelred, although he cannot but recognize the king's failed courage and strength in crushing the Danish attacks. The fibre of Æthelred's persona lies in stark contrast to the *Chronicle*'s portrayals of Æthelstan and Edmund in *The Battle of Brunanburh* or Alfred's response to the Great Heathen Army. Nor is the 1016 Chronicler's assessment of Æthelred's diplomacy to be compared with Edgar's as celebrated in Wulfstan's *Chronicle* poems of 959, 973, and 975 D-text.[55] Writing in the 1020s, he cannot avoid acknowledging the rise of the heroic figure of Cnut as the king who must mold out of the rubble what would become a new Anglo-Danish realm, but who, largely until 1016, had been the ravager of England and perpetrator of heinous crimes against its people, in a sense a type of Grendel.

---

54. The St. Brice's Day massacre apparently resulted from Æthelred's having received news of renewed treachery planned by the Danes (among whom was Pallig) to assassinate him and seize the kingdom (*ASC* E-text, s.a. 1002). The previous year, Pallig had betrayed the king by joining the Danish forces at Devon "with all the ships he was able to assemble," despite his pledges of loyalty and his enjoyment of Æthelred's generosity in bestowing upon him lands, gold, and silver (*com Pallig mid þan scipan ðe he gegaderian mihte, forþam þe he asceacen wæs fram Æðelrede cyncge ofer ealle ða ge trywða ðe he him geseald hæfde ón hamon, and on golde and seolfre*); *ASC* A-text, s.a. 1001; *ASC* 1:132, 2:182; Ashdown, *English and Norse Documents*, 96–97, s.a. 1002n11; *WMGRA* ii.177.1–2, 300–301.

55. Bredehoft, *Textual Histories*, 106–10. See more recently Bredehoft's argument on Wulfstan's possible self-imposed anonymity as a means of preventing the poems' being identified as eleventh-century compositions, possibly in response to the sociopolitical climate of the early eleventh century; Thomas A. Bredehoft, *Authors, Audiences, and Old English Verse* (Toronto: Toronto University Press, 2009), esp., 32–38.

Without question, the first two-thirds of *Beowulf* are riveted on the process by which Heorot can shake off Grendel's dark reign over the *sincfāge sel* (jewel-decorated hall, 167[a]) and emerge once again as the best of houses, filled with joy and loud song. With the arrival of Beowulf and his subsequent cleansing of the Grendel-kin from Heorot, the possibility of the restoration of a harmonious kingdom presents itself. The allegorical patterning between figures of historical "fact" and those of "poetry" is self-evident: the night struggle between Beowulf and Grendel within the confines of Heorot, then, may be looked upon as a heroic rendering of the psychomachia topos dramatizing those two facets of Cnut's persona, for from 1016 to his death in 1035 Cnut emerges as (and perhaps may have indeed been) the deliverer of England and the protector of its people. In the reality of history, both the scourge and the savior of England were a single entity; in the epic ahistoricity of the poem, they are sundered into the carnivorous Grendel, the *heorowearh hetelīc* (hateful, bloodthirsty wolf, 1267[a]), who *Heorot eardode, / sincfāge sel sweartum nihtum* (ruled Heorot, the jewel-decorated hall, in the dark night, *Bwf* 166[b]-67), and the *gōda mid Gēata* (good one among the Geats, 195[a]), one who later is judged to be *rīces wyrðra* (worthier of a kingdom, 861[b]) and the *mægenes strengest* (strongest in might, 196[b]) at that day in this life.

Yet not for a moment do I suggest that the *Beowulf*-poet was composing a vernacular epic on the fall of the house of Æthelred, although his compassion for the fallible English king and for his tormented people permeates the first two-thirds of *Beowulf*. The narrative scheme of *Beowulf* seems broader in its historical context, for Cnut's kingdom, as Beowulf's, does in the end fall into foreign hands. The striking combination of narrative elements that we find in the C-Chronicler's "remarkably vivid impression of . . . the incursions and later invasions of the Danes," to quote Keynes,[56] and in the Beowulfian episode of Grendel's Reign of Terror found in Cotton Vitellius A.xv, a cumulative cluster of correspondences that are lacking in earlier chronicles of Danish invasion, such as those suffered by Alfred, the great

---

56. Keynes, "Declining Reputation," 229.

Chapter Two

warrior and king, especially during the years of the Great Heathen Army,[57] does, however, lead me to conclude that Grendel's Reign of Terror could very well represent another account of the struggles of war-torn England in the early eleventh century, as historically cryptic as that account may be. For it is this accumulation of incident, motif, and time, in addition to character and setting, that makes the correspondences between Grendel's Reign of Terror and the historical material compelling. As one would expect, the events recorded in the poem are highly imaginative and betray more poetic embellishment in dramatically demonizing and allegorizing the enemy, in breaking apart principles of chronology, in encoding character identity, and in introducing a fictive figure who embodies the attributes of the greatest of the Scandinavian hero-kings than do the events recorded in the *Chronicle*. Yet both the Chronicler and the poet are gripped by the events and employ similar rhetorical devices and topoi in shaping and creating their historical narratives. And both erase the divide that separates the past from the present. Thus, the events that rocked the political structure of England from 1035 to 1042 might indeed have had their beginning in the first two decades of the eleventh

---

57. See, e.g., Richard Abels, *Alfred the Great: War, Kingship and Culture in Anglo-Saxon England* (London: Longman, 1998), esp. chap. 4; and the recent ethnological discussion that places the poem in a late Alfredian context by Craig R. Davis, "Ethnic Dating of *Beowulf*," 111–29. Nonetheless, the Danish attacks of the ninth century continued before and beyond the confined twelve-year period that characterized those of the first two decades of the eleventh century. Further, it is difficult to imagine timidity or indecision being an attribute of the ninth-century king's character. In private communication, Professor Abels was good enough to offer an alternative ninth-century scenario with Burgraed, the defeated king of Mercia (873–74), to whom Alfred provided assistance, as Hrothgar, and Alfred himself as Beowulf. Yet, there are numerous dissimilarities between Alfred and Beowulf (his leaving no heir, for one) to make the correspondence viable. See also Professor Abels's recent work, "Alfred and His Biographers: Images and Imagination," in *Writing Medieval Biography*, ed. Bates et al., 61–75, where he discusses the complex process of writing biography in addition to offering a critical survey of Alfredian biographies.

century when *Dene comon and her friδ namon.* For may not Cnut's court lamented by the 1036 Chronicler have been as rife with feud and treachery as Æthelred's, or that bemoaned by the Beowulfian messenger, who like the "prophet" of the *Sermo Lupi*, forewarns the nation of its own destruction at the closure of the poem?

One jarring episode in what I hesitantly now venture to call the *Beowulf*-poet's "adaptation" of the scenario of the Danish incursions as Grendel's Reign of Terror is not present in the *Chronicle* or the other historical annals—the *Gifstōl* passage, a scene, however, that is to be found dramatized in the *Encomium*. Books 1 and 2 of the *Encomium* contain the scenario of the Danish conquest of England. Like Henry of Huntingdon, William of Malmesbury, and John of Worcester, the Encomiast encapsulates, compresses, summarizes, reorders, and finally selects the particularities for his version of Sveinn's invasion and conquest of England, a mixture of historical fact and historical license. His treatment understandably is fundamentally different in perspective from that of the other historians, since his task was to laud the founding and continuance of the Anglo-Danish dynasty as one that had brought stability and majesty to the English nation.[58] Composing his history around 1041 for the Anglo-Danish nobility during Harthacnut's reign, he treats both Sveinn and Cnut affirmatively, as would be expected, omitting all the particularized barbarities they inflicted upon the English.[59] He restricts Sveinn's campaigns to the final invasion of 1013, thus suppressing the savage campaign of 1003–05 that laid bare Exeter and that led the C-Chronicler to bewail the Danish king's wasting of Norwich. Even the singularity of the organization of Sveinn's 1013 invasion that eventuated in his takeover of England is truncated: his swift and somewhat effortless voyage from Sandwich to the Humber and

---

58. Keynes proposes that the impetus for the composition of the *Encomium* was to argue for the continuance of the political stability of the nation that had characterized Cnut's reign and that was symbolized by Queen Emma as queen mother; *EER* [lxxi].

59. For a summary of the Encomiast's manipulation of the verifiable historical facts, see *EER* li–lxi [cxxxiii–cxliii], esp. liii–liv.

thence along the Trent to camp at Gainsborough without military resistance from the East Mercians is not even alluded to, an event that would have reminded the mid-eleventh-century Mercian and West Saxon nobility of the role Mercian separatism played in the fall of Æthelred's rule, a role that is underscored in the C-Chronicler's account (see also below 192–94). Rather, for the Encomiast, Sveinn is a king *uirtute armis quoque pollens et consilio Anglicum regnum ui suo subiugauit imperio* (mighty alike in courage and arms and also in counsel; *EER*, Argument, 6/7), a man of peace, whose invasion of England was based on sound political principles that would lead to the peaceful protection of the Danish realm. The resemblance of the panegyric to that of the eponymous founder of the Scyldings, the *gōd cyning* Scyld Scefing, at the opening of *Beowulf* (4–52) is striking, for it stands as a structural parallel to the Encomiast's narrative of Sveinn as deliverer of the Danish nation and founder of the Anglo-Danish dynasty, whose reign functions as a prologue to "the happy reign" of Cnut (*EER* 1.5).

The matter of the Encomiast's book 2, Cnut's 1015 invasion and final conquest of England, is likewise selectively altered to intimate that Cnut's primary motive in invading England was not to subjugate it but rather to regain his inheritance. A man of political talent, purpose, and determination, Cnut is never portrayed battling the English throughout the military operations of 1015–16. It is Thorkell and Eiríkr, on the Danish side, and Edmund Ironside, on the English, who perform extraordinary feats of bravery: Thorkell rages at Sherston; Eiríkr ravages and plunders the countryside; and Edmund, at the Battle of Ashington, exhorts his English subjects to fight for liberty as he himself plunges into the midst of the Danish army, with the fury of a Viking. Cnut remains on the sidelines, untainted by the Danes' bacchanalian fury, prudently conducting the military operations but never participating in them or harming a single English soul, even rejecting Edmund's offer of single combat for London (*EER* 2.8). Thus, the *Encomium*'s depiction of the devastation caused by Danish forces between 1003 and 1016 differs from that found in the other historical sources and in Grendel's Reign of

Terror, the last third of book 2 focusing on the rise of the hero, his marriage to Emma of Normandy, and his development into a dignified and devout Christian king.

Book 3, however, which commences with the political upheaval following Cnut's death in 1035, does contain an episode that is strikingly evocative of the Beowulfian *gifstōl* passage, and it is to this episode that I now turn.

THE GIFSTŌL AND THE SACRO ALTARI

The *Gifstōl* passage is perhaps one of the most controversial narrative units in *Beowulf*:

> Heorot eardode,
> sincfāge sel sweartum nihtum;—
> nō hē þone gifstōl grētan mōste,
> māþðum for Metode, nē his myne wisse.–
> (*Bwf* 166ᵇ–69)

[He dwelt in Heorot, the treasure-decorated hall, in the dark night;
he did not at all have the power to approach the throne,
nor might he know [in the sense of realize or obtain or have a grasp of] his desire (or his intention or delight) for the treasure, because of God (or God's judgment).]

These four and a half lines have been viewed as a vexed passage because of their ambiguity:[60] who (Hrothgar or God) owns the *gifstōl*

---

60. Klaeber's notes to 168–78 (3rd ed., 134–35) and Dobbie's in *ASPR* (4:125–26) reflect a portion of the critical attention the passage has received; see also Chickering's survey of the commentary, *Beowulf: A Dual-Language Edition*, 287–88; also, among others, Betty S. Cox, "The Gifstol and the Ark," in *Cruces of Beowulf* (The Hague: Mouton, 1971), 56–79; Arthur G. Brodeur, *The Art of Beowulf* (Berkeley, CA: University of California Press, 1959), 203–4; W. F. Bolton's introduction in *Beowulf, with the Finnesburg Fragment*, ed. C. L. Wrenn and W. F. Bolton (Exeter, UK: University of Exeter Press, 1996), esp. 188; R. E. Kaske, "The Gifstol Crux in *Beowulf*," *Leeds Studies in English* 16 (1985): 142–51; and Marijane Osborn, "The Great Feud: Scriptural History and Strife in *Beowulf*," *PMLA* 93 (1978): 973–81,

(throne or gift-seat); who (Hrothgar or Grendel) is prohibited from approaching it; and what is it that he (Hrothgar or Grendel) cannot approach—the treasure or the throne or both? It is the general consensus that it is Grendel who is prevented from approaching the throne and attaining the treasure.[61] Despite Grendel's controlling the hall at night, his power to rule Heorot is frustrated, for he cannot attain the *gifstōl* (throne), or, as Klaeber suggests, in loose variation, the *māþðum* (treasure [which here can be dative plural]),[62] because the *Metod* (God or fate or God's representative or judgment) would not permit it. Thus, he cannot obtain his desire, i.e., the throne as the treasure, although here I take "throne" and "treasure" to be two distinct items. In his 1922 edition, outlining its inherent difficulties, Klaeber suspected that the passage might be an interpolation,[63] a view further advanced by Tolkien, who, in arguing for unity of

---

repr. in *Beowulf: Basic Readings*, ed. Baker, 111–25, esp. 116–18. For a word-study on *metode*, see Joseph L. Baird, "'for metode': *Beowulf* 169," *English Studies* 49 (1967): 418–23, who sees the term as referring to an earthly ruler; Robert M. Estrich, "The Throne of Hrothgar *Beowulf*, ll. 168–69," *JEGP* 43 (1944): 384–89, sees the *gifstōl* as referring to Hrothgar's throne; and S. J. Crawford, "*Beowulf*, ll. 168–69," *MLR* 23 (1928): 336, translates *myne wisse* "nor [was he permitted] to work his will upon it [the *gifstōl*]" or "have his pleasure in it." The alternative definitions of *myne wisse* reflect the number of possible readings for the passage in the context of *The Wanderer* (line 27[b]), which has been traditionally compared with *Bwf* 169[b]; see, e.g., *The Wanderer*, ed. T. P. Dunning and A. J. Bliss, Methuen's Old English Library (New York: Appleton-Century-Crofts, 1969), 61–65; *Eight Old English Poems*, ed. R. D. Fulk, 3rd ed. rev., ed. and with commentary and glossary by John C. Pope (New York: W. W. Norton, 2001), 93; *Seven Old English Poems*, ed. John C. Pope (New York: W. W. Norton, 1981), 82–83; see further Klaeber, 4th ed., 126–27.

61. For an understanding of Hrothgar rather than Grendel as the one who could not approach the *gifstōl*, see Margaret Goldsmith, "The Christian Perspective in *Beowulf*," *Comparative Literature* 14 (1962): 71–90; repr. in *Interpretations of Beowulf: A Critical Anthology*, ed. R. D. Fulk (Bloomington, IN: Indiana University Press, 1991), 106n9.

62. See *Bwf* 1048[a], 1898[a], 2103[a], 2788[a].

63. Klaeber, 3rd ed., 134–35.

composition, pointed to the *gifstōl* passage as a "special problem" and described lines 168–69 as "probably a clumsily intruded couplet," including as suspect the apostate passage as well (lines 175–88).[64] One solution was offered by W. F. Bolton in the revised edition of C. L. Wrenn's *Beowulf,* by boldly repositioning lines 168–69 between lines 110–11, to follow the introduction of Cain and his enmity with God.[65] But repositioning seems unnecessary; the passage as it stands serves as a climactic outcome to the narrative summarizing Grendel's nightly ravages over a dozen years. It is also consistent, as Klaeber noted,[66] with the pattern of Grendel's actions as expressed in the passage 644^b–51^a, which explicitly states Grendel's limited rule of Heorot in the dark night.

Book 3 of the *Encomium* opens immediately after Cnut's death in 1035, an event, you will recall, that has thrown the country's political factions into chaos. Harthacnut, Emma and Cnut's son and the rightful heir to the throne, is in Denmark. Emma's other sons—Alfred and Edward by Æthelred—are in Normandy. Only Harold Harefoot, the alleged son of Cnut and Cnut's unofficial consort Ælfgifu of Northampton, is in England. Backed by supporters from Mercia, lands north of the Thames (with a large number of territories owned by Ælfgifu's kin), Harold Harefoot has been permitted half-rule, but only of Mercia, and only until Harthacnut's return to his rightful claim as king. Until then, Wessex is to be ruled by Emma of Normandy. A highly dramatized event in the *Encomium* sheds light on the precariousness of Harold's position as provisional king of half of England and, I suggest, bears strong resemblance to the *gifstōl* passage under discussion. For although he had been supported by a substantial northern faction, Harold still lacked legitimacy as full king. For this he had to be consecrated by the archbishop of Canterbury, Æthelnoth:

---

64. Tolkien, *Monsters and the Critics,* 45–47, 52n34.
65. Wrenn-Bolton, *Beowulf,* 108, translating as follows: "He (Cain) could not draw near to God's throne (as he could have done before his slaying of Abel), that precious thing (bejewelled as in *Ezekiel* or the *Apocalypse*), in the Creator's presence, nor did he feel his love."
66. Klaeber, 3rd ed., 465.

Qui electus metuensque futuri aduocat mox archiepiscopum Aelnotum, uirum omni uirtute et sapientia preditum, imperatque et orat se benedici in regem, sibique tradi cum corona regale suae custodiae commissum sceptrum, et se duci ab eodem, quia ab alio non fas fuerat, in sublime regni solium. Abnegat archiepiscopus, sub iureiurando asserens se neminem alium in regem filiis reg(i)nae Emmae uiuentibus laudare uel benedicere: "Hos meae fidei Cnuto commisit; his fidem debeo, et his fidelitatem seruabo. Sceptrum, coronam sacro altari impono, et hec tibi nec denego nec trado; sed episcopis omnibus, ne quis eorum ea tollat tibiue tradat teue benedicat, apostolica autoritate interdico; tu uero, si presumis, quod Deo mensaeque eius commisi inuadito!" Quid miser ageret, quo se uerteret, ignorabat. Intentabat minas et nihil profecit, spondebat munera et nil lucratus doluit, quoniam uir apostolicus nec ualebat minis deici nec muneribus (flecti). Tandem desperatus abcessit, et episcopalem benedictionem adeo spreuit, ut non solum ipsam odiret benedictionem, uerum etiam uniuersam fugeret Christianitatis religionem. (*EER* 40–41)

[Soon after being chosen, this man, fearing for the future, summoned Archbishop Æthelnoth, a man gifted with high courage and wisdom, and commanded and prayed to be consecrated king, and that the royal sceptre, which was committed to the archbishop's custody, should be given to him together with the crown, and that he should be led by the archbishop, since it was not legal that this should be done by another, to the lofty throne of the kingdom. The archbishop refused, declaring by oath that while the sons of Queen Emma lived he would approve or consecrate no other man as king: "Them Knútr entrusted to my good faith; to them I owe fidelity, and with them I shall maintain faith. I lay the sceptre and crown upon the holy altar, and to you I neither refuse nor give them; but by my apostolic authority, I forbid all bishops that any one of them should remove these things, or give them to you or consecrate you. As for you, if you dare, lay hands upon what I have committed to God and his table." He, wretched man, did not know what to do or whither to turn. He used threats and it did not avail him, he promised gifts and sorrowed to gain nothing, for that apostolic man could not be dislodged by threats or diverted by gifts. At length he departed in despair, and so despised the episcopal benediction, that he hated not only the benediction itself, but indeed even turned from the whole Christian religion.]

The throne and crown of which the combined political forces of Wessex could not deprive him, the archbishop, God's representative, one might say God's symbolic mortal presence, stood in the path of his obtaining.[67]

The scene presents a provocative parallel to the Beowulfian passage. A wretched usurper, seeking legitimacy, enters a sacred place that seems analogous to Heorot wherein the song praising God's creation has been sung; the archbishop, functioning as God's representative and judge, lays an injunction against the usurper's attaining the kingly throne; it is Æthelnoth, the historical surrogate of the *Metod*, who prohibits Harold/Grendel from approaching the *sacro altari* (the sacred *gifstōl*) and grasping the treasures (*māþðum*), which are necessary for the acquisition of the usurper's desire, the throne of England. Though Harold may move about the countryside nominally as king, he has been denied the power, through access to the treasure—the scepter and crown—that will give him the legal right to rule on the throne of England.

---

67. Campbell questions the truth of the story since it is unique to the *Encomium Emmae Reginae*, stating that Harold was crowned after he was elected (*EER* lxiii); nonetheless, as Eric John has pointed out, seeking the archbishop's support and blessing might well be a likely first step (and perhaps necessary) for Harold to take under the fragile political circumstances he found himself in; Eric John, "The *Encomium Emmae Reginae*: A Riddle and a Solution," *Bulletin of the John Rylands University Library of Manchester* 63, no. 2 (1981): 58–94, esp. 82–83; and his *Reassessing Anglo-Saxon England* (Manchester, UK: Manchester University Press, 1996), esp. 165.

Morever, the *Encomium* passage is notable for its Christian sensibility and for the reference to apostasy, motifs that are prominent in the larger context of the *gifstōl* passage, where the Danes, suffering under Grendel's harsh night-rule of Heorot, regress to heathenism:

Hwīlum hīe gehēton æt *h*ærgtrafum
wīgweorþunga, wordum bædon,
þæt him gāstbona gēoce gefremede
wið þēodþrēaum. Swylc wæs þēaw hyra,
hæþenra hyht; helle gemundon
in mōdsefan, Metod hīe ne cūþon,
dæda Dēmend, ne wiston hīe Drihten God,
nē hīe hūru heofona Helm herian ne cūþon,
wuldres Waldend. (*Bwf* 175–83ᵃ)

[At times they performed sacrifices at the heathen temples;
they entreated with words [chants?]
that the soul-slayer might bring relief
from the people's calamity. Such was their custom,
the hope of the heathen; they remembered hell
in their spirit; they had not experienced him who ordained Fate,
the Judge of Deeds; they did not know the Chieftain-God;
nor, indeed, did they know how to praise the Protector of Heavens,
the Ruler of Glory.]

In the *Encomium*, Harold deserts God out of avarice, anger, and pride; in the *gifstōl* passage, the apostates are the Danes who abandon their *Helm* (protector) by performing sacrificial offerings and rituals out of fear and self-interest. These parallels in character, situation, and, in particular, the apostate motif between the historical event and the Beowulfian segment again point to the poet's imaginative energy that can perceive the magnitude of the moral offense inherent in human acts and reconstitute them obliquely into allegorical narrative. Harold Harefoot's persistence in seizing the throne of England in 1036 by any means, occupying himself with nothing that would swerve him from that goal, is an apt comparison with the unrelenting

Danish ravaging of England between 1003 and 1016 that in the end gave Cnut half-rule in Mercia and Edmund half-rule in Wessex. The poet has shattered the constraints of chronology, conflating these two momentous incidences of a divided kingdom in England's history as one, times defined by a human avarice so ferocious and a bestiality so immense that they could be apprehended only within the realm of fantasy. Thus, Harold's avarice, malice, and perverted spirit like that of the Danes—who dismembered, mutilated, and butchered the English in their avarice for England's throne—allusively radiates through Grendel's physically and psychically monstrous form. Both can be comprehended as the carnivorous Grendel, the *heorowearh hetelīc* (hateful, bloodthirsty wolf, 1267[a]), who *Heorot eardode, / sincfāge sel sweartum nihtum* (ruled Heorot, the jewel-decorated hall, in the dark night, *Bwf* 166[b]–67).

The *Encomium* underlies my perception that the bestial Grendel functions as a fantastical allegorization not only of the *Dene* who made peace in England but also of the 1036 inheritor of that reign, Harold Harefoot. These two malevolent forces—one of the past, the other of the present—have been fused by the poet. Several parallels point to that fusion. Both Grendel and Harold rise to dominance in stages. Represented first as an apparition hovering in the darkness about the periphery of Heorot, then as a carnivorous monster deep in his sin, devouring Hrothgar's hearth-companions, Grendel finally gains materiality as the demonic night-ruler of Heorot, one skilled in necromancy, the illustrious *mearcstapa* (strider of the boundary or borderlands) who with his mother rules the waste regions of the borders. A parallel incremental pattern of amassing regal power traces the rise of Harold Harefoot, who appears suddenly as a contender for the throne that he then seizes in stages, first as regent, then as half-ruler of Mercia, the land of the "people of the border," and finally as full king. Second, both Grendel and Harold are associated with fratricide, murder within the kin being the most grievous of all sins—Harold by his order to assassinate his stepbrother Alfred atheling, Grendel, by allusion to Cain, the archetypal brother-killer who, in the context of the poem, brought down a paradisiacal kingdom, treachery of the first order. Finally, like Grendel, whose unsubstantiated paternity forms a topic of concern for the inhabitants of Hrothgar's kingdom (*Bwf* 1335–37ᵃ), Harold carries the stigma of a *hornungr*[68] (bastard son) but with a further complication, for no one knows the sire of either the fictive Grendel or the contender for the throne of England.

THE PATERNITY CONTROVERSY

The paternity controversy and the political issues radiating from it formed the crux of the succession crisis of 1035 and cast the Oxford *witenagemōt* charged with the election of Cnut's successor into turmoil.[69] The C- and D-texts of the *Chronicle* laid the absurdity of the claim on the usurper himself: *Harold þe sæde [þæt] he Cnutes sunu wære [and] þære oðre Ælfgyfe. þeh hit na soð nære* (Harold said that he was Cnut's son by the other Ælfgifu [*ASC* D-text has Ælfgifu of Northampton], though it was not at all true). The E-text (1036) expands the denial but hints at factionalism and fraudulent political backing—*Sume men sædon be Harolde [þæt] he wære Cnutes sunu cynges. [ond] Ælfgiue Ælfhelmes dohtor ealdormannes. ac hit þuhte swiðe ungeleafic manegum mannum* (Some men said of Harold that he was the son of King Cnut, by Ælfgifu, daughter of ealdorman Ælfhelm, but it was

---

68. Joseph Bosworth, *An Anglo-Saxon Dictionary*, ed. and enlarged T. Northcote Toller (London: Oxford University Press, 1898), repr. 1976, s.v. *hornung-sunu*; *An Icelandic-English Dictionary*, ed. Richard Cleasby, enlarged and completed by Gudbrand Vigfusson (Oxford: Clarendon Press, 1874), s.v. *hornungr*; Norse law distinguishes a *hornungr* as a son born of a freeborn woman whose stipulated bride-gift (*mundr*) had not been paid; in Icelandic law, the son born of a freeborn woman and a bondman, hence metaphorically an outcast; see also Margaret Clunies Ross, "Concubinage in Anglo-Saxon England," *Past and Present* 108 (August 1985): 3–34, esp. 16–18.

69. Tryggvi J. Oleson, *The Witenagemot in the Reign of Edward the Confessor: A Study in the Constitutional History of Eleventh-Century England* (Toronto: University of Toronto Press, 1955), esp. chap. 10, "The Witan and the Election and Deposition of Kings," where he discusses the limited power of the *witan* as a group in electing a king (83–86); see also B. A. E. Yorke, "Council, King's," in *Blackwell Encyclopaedia*, ed. Lapidge et al., 124–25; Keynes, *Diplomas*, 126–34.

thought quite unbelievable by many people).[70] The chief negotiators were Leofric for the Mercians and the coalition of the Northumbrians and Londoners, and Godwine for the queen and the West Saxons.

For the West Saxon coalition headed by Queen Emma and Godwine, the issue of Harold's paternity was paramount. It was an especially sensitive issue for Queen Emma, for even though she maintained the palace in Wessex, holding the throne and treasury in trust for Harthacnut, Harold's contention potentially threatened not only Harthacnut's claim but those of Edward and Alfred as well. It was of even greater political import for the Mercian coalition led by Leofric, preeminent of the earls of Mercia and the dominant power in the North. Establishing Harold's right to the throne swiftly was essential if Mercian control were to be retained in the kingdom. For in addition to Harthacnut, Queen Emma's two other sons—Alfred and Edward by Æthelred—might be considered stronger legitimate contenders to the Anglo-Saxon throne, being direct descendants of Cerdic, the founder of the West-Saxon dynastic line, and through Emma they would hold the power of Normandy as surety behind them. Were the princes' claim to succeed by some chance, the political balance of power in England would change drastically, for not only would the power swing solely to Wessex, but the whole country would fall under the influence of Normandy as well.[71] Only the election of Harold Harefoot, who asserted he was the son of Cnut and his unofficial consort, Ælfgifu of Northampton, the niece of Wulfric Spot and a kinswoman of Leofric,[72] would give the Mercians any possibility of retaining their power.

---

70. *ASC* 1:158–61; s.a. 1035 C-, D-text; s.a. 1036 E-text.

71. Stafford, *Unification and Conquest*, 75–77, on the continuing Norman threat to the balance of power in England. See also her inclusion of the heirs of Edmund Ironside as claimants to England's throne (77–78).

72. Stafford, *Unification and Conquest*, 77; Stafford, *Queen Emma and Queen Edith*, 243; Ann Williams, "Leofric" in *Blackwell Encyclopaedia*, ed. Lapidge et al., 282; Keynes, "Cnut's Earls," 74–75, 77–78; for a discussion on the possible kinship between Leofric and the family of Wulfric Spot, Ælfgifu of Northampton's uncle, see Sawyer, *Charters of Burton Abbey*, xliii;

Harold's claim must have been tenuous, as attested by the statements of unbelief recorded in the C-, D-, and E-versions of the *Chronicle* and by the persistent questioning of Harold's legitimacy that emerges in later historical documents. Cnut's alliance with Ælfgifu of Northampton had never been recognized by the Church, since it was in opposition to the Church's teachings; nor did Cnut's own laws support concubinage.[73] A social structure in operation since early Germanic times and not uncommon in early Anglo-Saxon culture, especially in the higher social strata,[74] concubinage presupposes a marital triangle of a male possessing a legitimate spouse and another female partner who was "publicly recognized . . . with customary privileges," but with no legal status, lacking the "formal betrothal and the exchange of gifts between the contracting parties."[75]

---

and J. Hunt, "Piety, Prestige or Politics? The House of Leofric and the Foundation and Patronage of Coventry Priory," in *Coventry's First Cathedral*, ed. G. Demidowicz (Stamford, UK: Paul Watkins, 1994), 97–117; for the most recent and strongest argument for the kinship between Leofric and Ælfgifu of Northampton, see Steven Baxter, *The Earls of Mercia: Lordship and Power in Late Anglo-Saxon England* (Oxford: Oxford University Press, 2007), 35–37, 164–65, appendix 1.

73. See Lawson, *Cnut*, 131–32, where he cites II Cnut 54.1; Stafford, *Queen Emma and Queen Edith*, 233–34, 236–37.

74. For a discussion on the strong probability of its existence in the time of Wilfred (ca. 634-709) in the context of sons' marrying their father's widow, see Eric John, "The Social and Political Problems of the Early English Church," in *Land, Church and People: Essays Presented to H. P. R. Finberg*, ed. Joan Thirsk, Supplement to *Agricultural Historical Review* 18 (1970): 39–63, at 61–2n8; see Clunies Ross who demonstrates its existence as part of the Anglo-Saxon social structure; "Concubinage in Anglo-Saxon England," 3–34: the "specifically Anglo-Saxon traditions may have fallen into decline after the Conquest and the vocabulary of concubinage died with the custom," Clunies Ross, at 18; for changing concepts in legitimate and illegitimate marriages, at 18–32.

75. Clunies Ross, "Concubinage in Anglo-Saxon England," 6–7, 14. For a broader discussion of concubinage as a social structure, encompassing additional levels of society, see Ruth Mazo Karras, "Concubinage and Slavery in the Viking Age," *Scandinavian Studies* 62 (1990): 141–62; see also

Although the alliance was never recognized by the Church, male children born of the match had right of inheritance, this being based on paternal acknowledgment of the child. Thus, though it may have presented a stumbling block, Harold's illegitimacy was not the real obstacle, for under Scandinavian law sons born illegitimately had equal rights of inheritance;[76] it was his identity as Cnut's son that was being questioned. Unlike Harthacnut, who had been recognized as Cnut's heir and was ruling as king of Denmark, or Harold's alleged brother Sveinn, whom Cnut had sent to rule Norway with Ælfgifu of Northampton as regent, Harold had no official endorsement as Cnut's heir. None of the contemporary or later documents—not even those from Scandinavia or the Continent that discuss Cnut's reign—bring forth evidence dated prior to 1035 that would suggest that he was Cnut and Ælfgifu's son, as, for example, they do for Sveinn. Nor does one find the standard portrait of Harold that would normally appear in the Scandinavian materials, as exists for Cnut or Sveinn. Judging by his nickname, Harefoot,[77] which is also not recorded in contemporary documents, he may not have resembled Cnut at all, who is described by *Knýtlinga saga* as

> mestr vexti ok sterkr at afli, manna fríðastr, nema nef hans var þunnt ok eigi lágt ok nǫkkut bjúgt. Hann var ljóslitaðr, fagrhárr ok mjǫk hærðr. Hverjum manni var hann betr eygðr, bæði fagreygðr ok snareygðr. Hann var ǫrr maðr, hermaðr mikill ok

Christine Fell, *Women in Anglo-Saxon England* (Oxford: Basil Blackwell, 1986), esp. chap. 3, "Sex and Marriage."

76. Clunies Ross, "Concubinage in Anglo-Saxon England," esp. 13–18; Stafford, *Queen Emma and Queen Edith*, 73–74; Bibi Sawyer and Peter Sawyer, *Medieval Scandinavia from Conversion to Reformation, c. 800–1500* (Minneapolis, MN: University of Minnesota Press, 1993), 169–71, 173–74; E. Eames, "Mariage et concubinage légal en Norvège à l'époque des Vikings," *Annales de Normandie* 2, no. 3 (1952): 196–208.

77. Harold's nickname, Harefōt, first appears in the thirteenth century, yet nicknames and by-names were constant features of Scandinavian naming patterns. The name is taken to refer to his swiftness of foot, and hence to the rapidity with which he swept across the land and claimed the English throne.

inn vápndjarfasti, sigrsæll, hamingjumaðr mikill um alla hluti, þá
er til ríkdóms heyrði. Ekki var hann stórvitr maðr ok svá Sveinn
konungr með sama hætti ok enn áðr Haraldr ok Gormr, at þeir
váru engir spekingar at viti.[78]

[exceptionally tall and strong, and the handsomest of men except
for his nose which was thin, high-set and rather hooked. He had
a fair complexion and a fine, thick head of hair. His eyes were
better than those of other men, being both more handsome and
keener-sighted. He was a generous man, a great warrior, valiant,
victorious and the happiest of men in style and grandeur. But he
was not a man of great intelligence, and the same could be said
of King Sveinn [Forkbeard] and Harald [Bluetooth] and Gorm
before him, that none of them was notable for wisdom.]

Although the descriptive portrait of a hero is a formula in saga literature, still one senses a note of litotes in the description of the Danish
wígsmíðas (craftsmen of war) who established the Danish kingdom
and conquered Anglo-Saxon England as suffering from a lack of
intelligence.

Sveinn's paternity, on the other hand, is never disputed by contemporary continental chronicles. Rather, ample evidence of Sveinn
as Cnut's son exists in the Scandinavian sources, as for example brief
snapshots of the nascent king, with descriptions of him as "a very
young man, fair in appearance, not fierce in temperament or ambitious" (*mikill æskumaðr, fríðr sjónum, ekki grimmhugaðr né ágjarn, Fsk*
35), as "immature" in "age and counsel" (*bernskr bæði at aldri ok at
ráðum, Hkr, ÓsH* 247) with a hint of lacking talent at speech-making
(*Hkr, Mgóði* 4; *Fsk* 42), and as being subject to domination by his

---

78. *Knýtlinga saga*, in *Danakonunga Sǫgur: Skjǫldunga saga, Knýtlinga
saga, Ágrip af Sǫgu Danakonunga*, Íslenzk Fornrit 35, ed. Bjarni Guðnason
(Reykjavík, 1982), 127; *Knýtlinga saga: The History of the Kings of Denmark*,
trans. Hermann Pálsson and Paul Edwards (Odense: Odense University
Press, 1986), chap. 20, p. 43; for a view of *Knýtlinga saga* (ca. 1240–1259,
attributed to Óláfr Þórðarson) as the last literary descendant of *Heimskringla*,
see Whaley, *Heimskringla*, 46–47.

mother, remarked upon by all the sources. Sveinn's role as one of the heirs to Cnut's kingdom is never questioned, illegitimate though he might be. His function as Cnut's under-king prior to 1035 is clearly documented in *Óláfs saga helga* and *Magnús saga ins góði* in Snorri's thirteenth-century *Heimskringla*, in *Fagrskinna*, and in skaldic poetry.[79] In *Óláfs saga helga* (chap. 239), Sveinn is reported to have been in Wendland (modern-day Poland) with Ælfgifu, sent there by Cnut to rule over Jómsborg. Cnut's mother had been the daughter or sister of Wendland's King Boleslav Chrobry, variously named Gunnhildr or Sígríðr.[80] In the mid- to late 1020s, Wendland was in the thick of a border dispute with Conrad II, Holy Roman Emperor, and Cnut's strategic placement of Sveinn and Ælfgifu in Wendland may have been the Anglo-Danish king's message to Conrad of his military support of the Wendish royal house. In any event, the appearance of Sveinn in Wendland seems to have put an end to the German claim, which would have posed a possible threat to Cnut's northern empire.

Cnut himself had commenced a campaign against Óláfr Haraldsson around 1025 for control of Norway, which lasted until around 1028, placing Norway under Cnut's control.[81] When, in 1030, Óláfr returned to Norway to regain his crown and was killed at the Battle of Stiklestad (near Trondheim) by his own people, Cnut installed Sveinn as ruler.

---

79. *Fagrskinna: Nóregs konunga tal. In Ágrip af Nóregskonunga sǫgum. Fagrskinna–Nóregs konunga tal*, ed. Bjarni Einarsson, Íslenzk Fornrit (ÍF) 29 (Reykjavík, 1985); *Fagrskinna, A Catalogue of the Kings of Norway*, trans. Alison Finlay (Leiden: Brill, 2004); unless otherwise noted, all translations of *Fagrskinna* (*Fsk*) are from the Finlay edition.

80. Lawson, *Cnut*, 23–24, 108–9; Adam of Bremen, *History of the Archbishops of Hamburg-Bremen*, trans. Francis J. Tschan (New York: Columbia University Press, 1959), 78, 81n132; Søren Balle, "Knud (Cnut) the Great," in *Medieval Scandinavia*, ed. Pulsiano et al., 357–59; *Jómsvíkinga saga: The Saga of the Jomsvikings*, trans. N. F. Blake (London: Thomas Nelson and Sons, 1962), vii, chap. 25.

81. *ASC*, C-, D-, E-texts, s.a. 1028; Cnut installed Hákon, son of Eiríkr of Lath, as overseer; see Sighvatr's *Vestrfararvísur* and Thórarin loftunga's (Þórarinn loftunga) *Tøgdrápa*; see Lawson, *Cnut*, 100–101, for a brief summary of the campaign.

While still in Wendland, Sveinn received a message from

Knúts konungs, fǫður hans, at han skyldi fara til Danmarkar, ok þat með, at hann skyldi síðan fara til Nóregs ok taka þar við ríki því til forráða, er í Nóregi var, ok hafa þar með konungsnafn yfir Nóregi. Síðan fór Sveinn til Danmarkar ok hafði þaðan lið mikit. Fór með honum Haraldr jarl ok mart annarra ríkismanna. Þess getr Þórarinn loftunga í kvæði því, er hann orti um Svein Álfífuson, er kallat er *Glælognskviða*:

164. Þat es dullaust,
hvé Danir gerðu
dyggva fǫr
með dǫglingi.
Þar vas jarl fyrst
at upphafi
ok hverr maðr,
es honum fylgði,
annar drengr
ǫðrum betri.
Síðan fór Sveinn í Nóreg ok með honum Álfífa, móðir hans, ok var hann þar til konungs tekinn á hverju lǫgþingi.[82]

[King Knút, his father, that he was to come to Denmark [to muster an invading force]; moreover that then he was to proceed to Norway to rule that land, and that the title of king of Norway was to be conferred upon him. Thereupon Svein proceeded to Denmark with a great force. With him went Earl Harald and many other men of influence. This is mentioned by Thórarin loftunga (praise tongue) in the poem which he composed about Svein,

---

82. *ÓsH* chap. 239 in   Snorri Sturluson, *Heimskringla*, ed. Bjarni Aðalbjarnarson, 3 vols. (Reykjavík: Íslenzk Fornrit, 1979), hereafter *Hkr*; Snorri Sturluson, *Heimskringla: History of the Kings of Norway*, trans. Lee M. Hollander, American-Scandinavian Foundation (1964; Austin, TX: University of Texas Press, 1992), Hollander trans., 514–25. Unless otherwise noted, all translations of Snorri's works are from this translation.

the son of Álfífa, and which is called *Glælognskvitha* (Sea-calm lay):

No one doubts what dapper band
of Danes were with the Dogling [prince]:
first of all came Earl Harald;
after him every man's son
following him more fit than th' other.
Then Svein proceeded to Norway, accompanied by Álfífa, his
mother; and he was accepted as king at every general assembly.]

Þórarinn loftunga was apparently the poet in the courts of Óláfr,
Cnut, and Sveinn, having composed *Hǫfuðlausn* for Óláfr, *Tøgdrápa*
for Cnut, and *Glælognskviða* for Cnut's son around 1031-35.[83] The verse
is perhaps the most reliable witness that Sveinn was Cnut's son,
although every Scandinavian chronicle and skaldic poem that concerns Sveinn Álfífuson refers to him as Cnut's son, and each of them
couples him with his mother, identifying Ælfgifu/Álfífa as the power
behind the throne.

Not so with Harold. Although like Sveinn he is paired with
Ælfgifu of Northampton as her son, unlike Sveinn, for whom ample
documents survive proving his existence prior to 1035 and Cnut's
designation of him as one of the inheritors of his realm, "there is not
a shadow of evidence," to quote E. A. Freeman's response to Saxo's,
Adam of Bremen's, and *Knýtlinga saga*'s analysis of the alleged disposition by Cnut of his realm, "that Harold ever reigned as Under-king
in England."[84] Twelfth- and thirteenth-century documents that note
Harold's accession to the throne and include him in their description
of Cnut's disposition of his realm (for between 1027 and 1030, Cnut
was said to have an "empire" comparable to Conrad's)[85] do so retro-

83. Mary Malcolm, "Þórarinn loftunga," in *Medieval Scandinavia*, ed.
Pulsiano et al., 667.
84. Freeman, *History of the Norman Conquest*, 1: 774–75.
85. Cnut's letter of 1027 to the English in which he claims the title *Canutus,
rex totius Anglie et Denemarcie et Norreganorum et partis Suanorum*; *JWChron*
512 [1031]. For a recent discussion on Cnut's empire-building, see Timothy
Bolton, *The Empire of Cnut the Great: Conquest and the Consolidation of Power*

spectively, from the point of view of arranging and recording a fact, after 1037 when his full accession finally took place or after his death in 1040.[86] Without Cnut's paternal acknowledgment, Harold's identity as Cnut's illegitimate son continued to be questioned throughout his reign, rising to incredulity in later eleventh- and twelfth-century English and Anglo-Norman works, with attacks akin to defamation of character being waged against his mother. Yet despite the skepticism surrounding Harold's paternity that clouded the Oxford *witenagemōt* in 1036, the potency of the coalition of Leofric, the Mercian and Northumbrian nobility, and the Londoners was such that Harold was elected half-king of Mercia and Northumbria, a temporary arrangement (and possibly preplanned) to be sure, for in a little more than a year, after the assassination of Alfred atheling, he became full king of England with Ælfgifu of Northampton as queen mother, even though Harthacnut was still occupied with the Danish-Norwegian conflict.

Thus there were two rulers of England for a time, each with a mother of political might and force determined to possess the *gifstōl*: the consecrated queen Emma of Normandy and the unlawful, Mercian queen rising out of the north fenlands, Ælfgifu of Northampton. It is a situation not unreminiscent of that which is fictionalized in *Beowulf* of two mother-figures, the queen who reigns in the court amid resplendent light and ceremony and supports three princes for Heorot's throne, Hrothulf, Hrethric, and Hrothmund, and the other, the shadow-queen and mother-villain who along with her son rules the *wulfhleoþu*, "slopes belonging to wolves." And like the Beowulfian gallow-minded *brimwylf* (sea-wolf, *Bwf* 1506[a]), Ælfgifu of

---

in Northern Europe in the Early Eleventh Century (The Northern World) (Leiden: Brill Academic Publishers, 2009).

86.   For a discussion of the reliability of genealogical links and pedigrees, and their uses as political propaganda, although not related to the disposition of Cnut's realm, see David N. Dumville, "Kingship, Genealogies and Regnal Lists," in *Early Medieval Kingship*, ed. P. H. Sawyer and Ian N. Wood (Leeds, UK: University of Leeds, School of History, 1977), 72–104, esp. 83–102.

Northampton, too, could lay claim to land belonging to "wolves," for she was the niece of Wulfric Spot and granddaughter of the lady Wulfrun, founder of Wolverhampton, and matriarch of one of the most powerful landed Mercian families in late tenth- and early eleventh-century England whose land-holdings were comparable to a small kingdom.

Chapter 3 concerns itself with Ælfgifu of Northampton and Grendel's mother, the Beowulfian *ides āglǣcwīf* (terrifying noblewoman, *Bwf* 1259[a]). It brings to light Ælfgifu's public image as presented in eleventh- and twelfth-century Anglo-Saxon, Scandinavian, and continental sources and the appropriation and imaginative transformation of this historical personage of wealth and power into the predatory Beowulfian *ides* whose son tyrannized Heorot. In the English historical material she emerges as a dark element in the body politic, a Mercian noblewoman surreptitious in her actions, cunningly duplicitous, sexually promiscuous, and greedily grasping for the throne. Finally, the chapter discusses the political forces and savage events of the late tenth and early eleventh centuries in England that shaped the persona of Cnut's concubine, events that nearly brought about the extinction of Ælfgifu's kin which she was not likely to forgive or forget, but rather harbor and avenge. These forces surfaced at the moment of Cnut's death in 1035, enabling Ælfgifu and the Mercian earls to overcome the political might of Queen Emma and Godwine, and inevitably led to the betrayal of the queen and the assassination of Alfred atheling.

It would not be inconceivable for a poet composing a courtly narrative centered on the dynastic crisis of 1035–36 in the Anglo-Danish court and the assassination of Alfred atheling to allegorize these qualities attributable to a prominent historical figure, whose power was pivotal in the Mercian drive for the English throne, into the heightened fictionalized Beowulfian rapacious being in fantastic mode, Grendel's mother. In this he had precedent, for it is a treatment similar to that lavished on the powerful queen-mother Ælfthryth, alleged murderess of her stepson Edward the Martyr, whose sexuality, rapacity, and shape-changing arts were apparently notorious, but for whom, in contrast to Ælfgifu, two distinctly different types of sources are extant: those that mark Edgar's queen as an offender of the first order, capable of murder, sorcery, and adultery, and those that portray a woman of high intelligence, with compassion for the young, an advocate of female subjects and women religious.[87] In Scandinavian sources, Ælfgifu's transformation is more pronounced. For in the Norse courtly tradition, which the *Beowulf*-poet is appropriating, historical female figures of wealth and power were presented in literary and historical materials in the uncanny mode of witches and sorceresses; in the Icelandic tradition, there are "alternate views, one realistic and the other fantastic."[88]

87. For a positive view of Ælfthryth based on an examination of charters, see Andrew Rabin, "Female Advocacy and Royal Protection in Tenth-Century England: The Legal Career of Queen Ælfthryth," *Speculum* 84 (2009): 261–88; see also the will of Æðelstan atheling, in *Anglo-Saxon Wills*, ed. Dorothy Whitelock (Cambridge, UK: The University Press, 1930), 56–63, at 62. For negative views, see below, chap. 3 n 44.

88. Nora K. Chadwick, "Þorgerðr Hölgabrúðr and the *Trolla Þing*: A Note on Sources," in *The Early Cultures of North-West Europe*, ed. Sir Cyril Fox and Bruce Dickins (Cambridge, UK: The University Press, 1950), 397–417, at 408.

CHAPTER THREE

Álfífa in ríka and the Beowulfian *Konungamóðir*

Unde factum est, ut quidam Anglorum pietatem regis sui iam defuncti obliti mallent regnum suum dedecorare quam ornare, relinquentes nobiles filios insignis reginae Emmae et eligentes sibi in regem quendam Haroldum, quem esse filium falsa aestimatione asseritur cuiusdam eiusdem regis Cnutonis concubinae; plurimorum uero assertio eundem Haroldum perhibet furtim fuisse subreptum parturienti ancillae, inpositum autem camerae languentis co(n)cubinae, quod ueratius credi potest. (*EER* iii.1)[1]

[And so it came to pass that certain Englishmen, forgetting the piety of their lately deceased king, preferred to dishonour their country than to ornament it, and deserted the noble sons of the excellent Queen Emma, choosing as their king one Haraldr, who is declared, owing to a false estimation of the matter, to be the son of a certain concubine of the above-mentioned King Knútr; as a matter of fact, the assertion of very many people has it that the same Haraldr was secretly taken from a servant who was in childbed, and put in the chamber of the concubine, who was indisposed; and this can be believed as the more truthful account.]

---

1. *EER* 38–41, ed. Campbell.

The paternity controversy that spearheaded the 1035 succession crisis did not cease with Harold's accession to the throne. It persisted beyond the confines of the tumultuous Oxford *witenagemōt* that had secured his half-rule of Mercia, and even survived the calamity of Alfred atheling's assassination in 1036. It surfaced in almost every extant document—English, Continental, or Scandinavian from the eleventh through the early fourteenth century—that hinged on rights of succession to the thrones of Cnut's northern kingdom. Pretender or not, Harold had successfully secured the throne of England through the concerted efforts of his politically potent mother Ælfgifu of Northampton and her Mercian kin.

Little is known about Ælfgifu of Northampton from the English documents. Like her Beowulfian counterpart who comes forth from the darkness of the moors into the light of Heorot, Cnut's concubine emerges as a shadow figure from a historical void, wrapped in a malevolent haze with seemingly no past save that she had been irregularly allianced to Cnut sometime around 1013. Except for the official *Chronicle* entry, which at best treats the future queen mother ambivalently, elsewhere without exception she is depicted unsympathetically. As would be expected in discussing the events that occurred at the 1035 *witenagemōt*, the mid-eleventh-century *Encomium Emmae Reginae*, quoted in the epigraph, allusively generalizes the Mercian and Northumbrian coalition as "certain Englishmen," branding them as traitors who preferred to abandon their allegiance to their former king and country and choose a usurper king. Such a description of Leofric must not have sat well with Ælfgifu's Mercian kin who might have had an opportunity to glance at the Latin work. Nor could it have pleased Ælfgifu, who found herself demoted to a nameless concubine, the object of pernicious rumor. For not only was she loosely stigmatized as a traitor, but her status as queen mother was being challenged. By claiming that Harold was the son of a servant, surreptitiously deposited into her chamber, the Encomiast not only emphasizes Harold's unworthiness to rule, being an issue of neither royalty nor nobility, but in addition points offhandedly to Ælfgifu's infertility, her political connivance, and the lengths to which she would go to gain the throne for her son. Yet the Encomiast's rhetorical treatment of the Mercian queen mother pales in comparison to her allegorical depiction as the sluttish Jezebel in the Norman Latin political satire discussed above (28–32) or as the rapacious *brimwylf* (sea-wolf) set on revenge allegorized in *Beowulf* wherein she is likewise the topic of rumor (see below, 181–182).

Ælfgifu's character fared no better in the twelfth century. John of Worcester somewhat hesitantly reports the existence of rumors that circulated about the paternity not only of Harold (as reported in the *Encomium*) but of his brother Sveinn as well:

> [1035] eandem Ælfgiuam ex rege filium habere uoluisse sed nequiuisse, et iccirco recenter natum infantem cuiusdam presbitere sibi afferri iussisse, regemque omnino credulum fecisse, se filium illi ⌊ iam peperisse. . . . Haroldus uero dixit se filium esse Canuti regis et Northamtunensis Alfgiue, licet id uerum esset minime. Dicunt enim nonnulli filium cuiusdam sutoris illum fuisse, sed Alfgiuam eodem modo de illo fecisse quo de Suano fertur egisse. Nos uero, quia res in dubio agitur, de neutrorum genitura quid certi sciuimus definir:[2]

> [that Ælfgifu wanted to have a son by the king, and could not, and therefore ordered the new-born child of some priest's concubine to be brought to her, and made the king fully believe that she had just borne him a son. . . . Harold claimed to be the son of King Cnut by Ælfgifu of Northampton, but that is quite untrue, for some say that he was the son of a certain cobbler, but that Ælfgifu had acted in the same way with him as she is said to have done with Swein. But, because the matter concerned is open to doubt, we have been unable to make a firm statement about the parentage of either.]

One might say that Ælfgifu's rumored infertility had attained a

---

2. *JWChron* [1035], ii.520–21; see also *WMGRA* ii.188.i, 334–35; on Harold, see *VÆdr* i.3, 20; *EER* iii.1, 38–41; and *ASC* 2: 210–11. The latest date of composition of *VÆdr* is ca. 1075; and the text survives in a unique (and mutilated) manuscript of ca. 1100 (Barlow, *VÆdr* xiv and n. 3).

modicum of verity to be included in the annals of the realm. Ælfgifu's reputation had reached its nadir, for John of Worcester's interpretation of the events insinuates that the paternity question hinged on her promiscuity and her trickery.

A rather startling instance depicting Ælfgifu's alleged promiscuity could come from an earlier political document, icon 15 in the *Bayeux Tapestry* (fig. 3). Executed sometime around 1080 at Canterbury, it may be one indication of official attempts to lay the entire blame for the succession struggle on Ælfgifu's clandestine sexual activities. In this version, the serving maid has been eliminated from the script, and it is Ælfgifu of Northampton herself who has become exposed as mother of Sveinn, allegedly fathered by a priest, and of Harold, fathered by a cobbler. The icon is defamatory in that it depicts a cleric fondling the cheek of a certain Ælfgyfa, an action that is humorously, though obscenely, mimicked by a squatting naked male figure in the border below. In a 1980 article, "The Lady Aelfgyva in the *Bayeux Tapestry*," J. Bard McNulty identified the female as Ælfgifu of Northampton, an identification that has been much disputed.[3]

---

3. J. Bard McNulty, "The Lady Aelfgyva in the *Bayeux Tapestry*," *Speculum* 55 (1980): 659–68. Other possible candidates have ranged from Matilda (Duke William's wife); Adeliza (one of his daughters, allegedly betrothed to Harold Godwinsson); Ealdgyth (who actually became Harold Godwinsson's legal wife); Eadgyth (Harold Godwinsson's sister); Abbess Eadgifu (Swegn Godwinsson's concubine, whom he had abducted from a monastery); and finally Emma of Normandy, who had been given the official English name of Ælfgifu when she became Æthelred's queen in 1002; on the latter, see Eric F. Freeman, "The Identity of Aelfgyfa in the Bayeux Tapestry," *Annales de Normandie* 41 (1991): 117–34; Freeman's identification of the figure as Emma of Normandy, though provocative, seems somewhat out of keeping with the situation, for William would hardly be slandering his great-aunt, from whom his rights of succession to the English throne derived. See also Bernstein, *Mystery of the Bayeux Tapestry*, 17, 30, 66; M. W. Campbell, "Aelfgyva: The Mysterious Lady of the Bayeux Tapestry," *Annales de Normandie* 34 (1984): 127–45; Wolfgang Grape, *The Bayeux Tapestry: Monument to a Norman Triumph*, trans. David Britt (Munich and New York: Prestel, 1994); and Lucien Musset (who interprets the caress as a "slap"

McNulty based his conclusion on three fundamental points: (1) that there was only one Ælfgifu of noble rank, living or dead, whose relationship with a cleric involved some kind of sexual notoriety, so well known that only a hint was needed in the tapestry, (2) that she was also reputed to be involved with a workman, and (3) that her indiscretions would be of interest in the discussion of the succession to the English throne, which according to eleventh- and twelfth-century chroniclers was the chief concern of Harold Godwinson's mission to William of Normandy,[4] for Ælfgifu's political alliance with Cnut was considered legal not only by Danes and Norwegians, but by the Normans as well.[5]

The meaning of the iconographic positioning of the figures, McNulty argues, left purposefully ambiguous by the incomplete phrase of the inscription, "Where a cleric and Aelfgyva," is pointedly commented upon by the mimicking naked figures in the lower borders: immediately under the frame is depicted a naked figure mocking the stance of the cleric, and to the frame's left is the figure of a workman, again in a lewd position, whom McNulty identifies as a cobbler.[6] McNulty views the frame as a disjunction in the continuous,

---

and considers her identity a mystery), *The Bayeux Tapestry*, trans. Richard Rex, new edition (Woodbridge, UK: Boydell Press, 2005), 126–28. The definitive work on the tapestry remains Sir David M. Wilson, *The Bayeux Tapestry* (London: Thames and Hudson, 1985); the definitive digital work and essential to any study of the tapestry is Martin K. Foys's *The Bayeux Tapestry, Digital Edition* (Leicester, UK: Scholarly Digital Editions, 2003).

4. McNulty, "Lady Aelfgyva in the *Bayeux Tapestry*," esp. 665–66.

5. Jenny M. Jochens, "The Politics of Reproduction: Medieval Norwegian Kingship," *American Historical Review* 92 (1987): 329–32, esp. 329; Eleanor Searle, "Women and the Legitimization of Succession at the Norman Conquest," *Proceedings of the Battle Conference on Anglo-Norman Studies III* (1980), ed. R. Allen Brown (Woodbridge, UK: Boydell Press, 1981), 159–70, esp. 161–62, 226n8; Eames, "Mariage et concubinage legal," esp. 200–201, 207; Karras, "Concubinage and Slavery," discusses Danish law codes, 149–50; 160n37.

6. See also Bernstein, *Mystery of the Bayeux Tapestry*, 19; *contra* Freeman, "Identity of Aelfgyfa," although part of his argument is based on

documentary narrative of the tapestry and considers it as an iconic representation of the 1035 dynastic crisis, being discussed during a moment of levity between Harold Godwinsson and William of Normandy, prospective claimants to England's throne, as they deride the royal pedigree of Harold Harefoot, the Mercian pretender to the English throne, and debunk dynastic claims by the Norwegians, based in particular on the peace pact between Harthacnut and Magnús góði in the aftermath of Ælfgifu of Northampton and Sveinn Álfífuson's five-year reign in Norway. *Heimskringla* (*Mgóði*, chap. 6) describes a covenant between Magnús and Harthacnut that secured peace in their time and provided for the succession of the kingdoms; if both kings remained childless, the reign of both kingdoms fell to the survivor. Apparently, at Harthacnut's death, Magnús took possession of Denmark and attempted a takeover of England as well.[7]

The question of the paternity of Ælfgifu's sons was therefore of moment to the dynastic succession, not only of England and Normandy, but of eleventh-century Norway as well, where she had

redesigning details on the figure of the cobbler; see also David Hill, "The Bayeux Tapestry and Its Commentators: The Case of Scene 15," *Medieval Life* 11 (Summer 1999): 24–26.

7. For the exchange of letters between Magnús and Edward, see *Fsk*, ed. Einarsson (chaps. 48–49), 216–18; *Fsk*, trans. Finlay, 173–75; *Hkr 3*, ed. Aðalbjarnarson, 65–66 (chaps. 36–37); *Hkr*, trans. Hollander, 575–76; *Morkinskinna*, ed. Finnur Jónsson. SUGNI 53 (Copenhagen: J. Jørgensen, 1932), 52–55 (hereafter *Mks*); *Morkinskinna: The Earliest Icelandic Chronicle of the Norwegian Kings (1030–1157)*, trans. Theodore M. Andersson and Kari Ellen Gade, Islandica 51 (Ithaca, NY: Cornell University Press, 2000), 127–28; unless otherwise noted, all translations of *Morkinskinna* are from the Andersson and Gade edition; see also the *Translatio Sanctae Mildredhae*, where Queen Emma is accused of urging "Magnús of Norway to invade England," and see Campbell's strong skepticism over the tale (*EER* [cxxxi, n. 4]) and Frank Barlow's agreement, "Two Notes: Cnut's Second Pilgrimage and Queen Emma's Disgrace in 1043," *English Historical Review* 73 (1958): 649–55, esp. 652–53, where he sees the 1043 accusation as a parallel to that of 1035; see also Magnús Fjalldal's discussion, *Anglo-Saxon England in Icelandic Medieval Texts* (Toronto: University of Toronto Press, 2005), 54–56.

reigned as regent on behalf of her son Sveinn between 1030 and 1035. Sveinn's rightful claim to rule Norway was strikingly attacked by Tryggvi Óláfsson, alleged son of Óláfr Tryggvason and the English Gyða (*Hkr 1*, *ÓsT*, chap. 32). *Tryggvaflokkr*, attributed to Sighvatr Þórðarson, records the rich supply of blood that was shed when their forces met at the Battle of Sóknar Sound, and *Fagrskinna* (chap. 41) dramatizes Tryggvi's scandalous claim that Sveinn was the son of a priest, unworthy to sit on the Norwegian throne:[8]

> Sveinn Álfífusonr var þá konungr í Nóregi, þá kom vestan af England Tryggvi, sonr Óláfs Tryggvasonar ok Gyðu ensku, ok mæltu sumir, at hann væri prests sonr, en eigi konungs sonr. Hónum kom í mót Sveinn konungr, ok borðusk þeir fyrir norðan Jaðar, þar sem Tungunes heitir. Tryggvi skaut tveim spjotum senn um daginn ok mælti: "Svá kenndi minn faðir mér at messa." Svá hœldisk <hann> því, at hann væri þá líkari Óláfi Tryggvasyni en prestinum. Þar fell Tryggvi; ekki afrek gørði hann meira í Nóregi.[9]

[Sveinn Álfífuson was then king of Norway; then there came east from England Tryggvi, son of Óláfr Tryggvason and the English Gyða, and some said that he was the son of a priest, and not of the king. King Sveinn came against him, and they fought north of Jaðarr, at the place called Tungunes. Tryggvi threw two spears at once that day and said: 'That's how my father taught me to say mass.' With this he was boasting that then he was more like Óláfr

---

8. Both Snorri and *Fagrskinna* refer to a tradition whereby Tryggvi's right of rule in Norway is questioned, likewise revolving around his possibly being the son of a priest; the tradition may have become confused here in the effort to promote Magnús góði as rightful heir to the Norwegian throne, for Tryggvi's birthright is not questioned in Oddr Snorrason's account (*Óláfs saga Tryggvasonar* [ca. 1200], trans. Theodore M. Andersson [Ithaca, NY: Cornell University Press, 2003], chap. 17.

9. *Fsk*, ed. Einarsson, chap. 41, p. 206; *Fsk*, trans. Finlay, 165; and *Tryggvaflokkr* (Skj.BI: 231), quoted by Snorri in *Hkr 2* (*Óláfs saga helga* [hereafter *ÓsH*], chap. 249), who dates the battle at 1033 (*Hkr 2*, 413). See also Oddr Snorrason's *Óláfs saga Tryggvasonar*, trans. Andersson, chap. 17.

Tryggvason than the priest. Tryggvi fell there; he did no more brave deeds in Norway.]

Tryggvi's boastful comment both denigrates Sveinn's warlike capabilities, attributes he would have possessed were he the son of Cnut, and defames his mother's reputation and status as queen mother of Norway. The narrator's tone of approval in relating Sveinn's victory suggests that Sveinn's response to Tryggvi's challenge effectively settled the question of his identity as Cnut's son, as well as his right to reign in Norway.

That there is no such scene endorsing Harold as Cnut's or for that matter as Ælfgifu/Álfífa's son is not surprising, for the national concerns of the Norwegians rested on the legitimacy of Sveinn Álfífuson's foreign rule. What the *Fagrskinna* passage does reveal is that accounts regarding Ælfgifu's alleged promiscuity had voyaged to the northern parts of Cnut's realm.

Elsewhere in the northern sources, Saxo independently lends a note of promiscuity to Ælfgifu's (Alwina's) sexual activities: he identifies her as the mistress of Óláfr Haraldsson, the future *Óláfr helgi*, king of Norway,[10] seduced by Cnut when both he and Óláfr were fighting in England, although obviously on opposite sides. Saxo's source for the allegation is unknown, but if one is to believe that the seduction occurred, it would probably have taken place sometime around 1013–14. Óláfr Haraldsson campaigned in England twice, once as enemy to the English in the company of Thorkell Hávi (1009–12), after which he embarked on harrying expeditions in coastal France and Spain, and again along with Thorkell, serving as a commander in Æthelred's campaign to recapture his kingdom in 1014.[11] Apparently, Cnut did not participate in the incursion of 1009–

---

10. Saxo Grammaticus, *Danorum Regum Heroumque Historia, Books X-XVI: The Text of the First Edition with Translation and Commentary in Three Volumes*, vol. 1, books X, XI, XII, and XIII, ed. and trans. Eric Christiansen (Oxford: BAR, 1980), x. fol. ciiib, 28–29, 34, 188n96.

11. See Campbell's discussion of the chronology of Óláfr's campaigns in England in *EER* 76–80, esp. 77–78.

12, but along with Sveinn Forkbeard invaded England in 1013. If the liaison between Óláfr and Ælfgifu were to have some truth in it, it might be one additional reason for the enmity that existed between Cnut and Óláfr. The *Anglo-Saxon Chronicle* is silent on Óláfr's campaigns in England; yet some verification of his service in England comes from Sighvatr's *Víkingarvísur* (especially stanzas 7-8), which accords with the *Chronicle*'s entries recording Thorkell's battle against Ulfkytel in East Anglia (1010) and his razing of Canterbury (1011). In addition, support for Óláfr's pact with the English king comes from Óttarr svarti's *Óláfsdrápa*, or *Hǫfuðlausn*, which states that the future saint was one of Æthelred's military commanders in the recapture of London and in his campaign against Cnut in Lindsey.[12] It is highly tempting to suspect that Harold Harefoot may have been the son of Óláfr Haraldsson, a descendant of Haraldr *hárfagri* (hair-fair) Hálfdanarson and the son of Haraldr *inn grenski* (Greenlandish), sharing as he did the family name, for it would go a long way toward solving the paternity question. It would also explain the absence of Cnut's paternal acknowledgment of Harold Harefoot as his son. Sadly, except for Saxo, no other northern source remarks upon a clandestine intimacy between Ælfgifu of Northampton and Óláfr Haraldsson, the future Óláfr *inn helgi* (the saint), whom Cnut irreverently referred to as "Stout Legs" (*digri*).[13]

Where, then, do the strands of the paternity narrative lead, except to the conclusion that nearly a millennium after the Oxford meeting of the *witenagemōt* the question of Harold's parentage continues to

---

12. *Víkingarvísur* stanzas 6-9 take place in England; see Christine Fell, "*Víkingarvísur*," in *Speculum Norroenum: Norse Studies in Memory of Gabriel Turville-Petre*, ed. Ursula Dronke et al. (Odense: Odense University Press, 1981), 106–22, esp. 114–18; see also Campbell, *EER* 76–82; see also Campbell's *Skaldic Verse and Anglo-Saxon History*, Dorothea Coke Memorial Lecture (London: Lewis, 1970), 11–12, who quotes Óttarr svarti's verses; Ashdown, *English and Norse Documents*, 156–75, 217–29; on Óttarr svarti, see Russell Poole, "Óttarr svarti," in *Medieval Scandinavia*, ed. Pulsiano et al., 459–60.

13. *Mks*, trans. Andersson and Gade, 101; see Cleasby-Vigfusson, s.v. *digri*.

Chapter Three

perplex? What the strands have unintentionally revealed, however, is that the protagonist of the paternity narrative is not Harold (or Sveinn, for that matter) but rather Harold's mother, who, like her Beowulfian counterpart, is the actual instigator of the action and around whose tenebrious attributes the story revolves. Thus, we find two queens of England for a short period operating independently. For even though she had been exiled to the Norwegian court, leaving the politics of the English court to Queen Emma, these reported fragments of Ælfgifu's character, biased though they be, bear witness to the strength of purpose that enabled her to return to grasp the throne and eventually govern Harold's court, as Frank Stenton surmised, as the "real ruler of England,"[14] much as she had done as *Álfífa in ríka* of Norway. It is to Cnut's irregular Mercian queen mother that I now turn.

Álfífa in ríka and Ælfgifu of Northampton

Some seven non-English historical documents discuss in varying detail Cnut's unofficial "queen," two continental and at least five from twelfth- and thirteenth-century Scandinavia.[15] Except for her portrait by the priest Immo (see below, 173–74), these cannot by their very nature be assessed as contemporary evidence for Ælfgifu of Northampton, since her story underwent narrative transformations in contiguous cultures and languages. But what the texts do capture

---

14. For a discussion of Ælfgifu of Northampton's status as queen mother in the Norwegian and English courts, see F. M. Stenton, *Anglo-Saxon England*, 3rd ed. (Oxford: Clarendon, 1971), 397–98, 405–6, 420–21; quote at 421.

15. *Ágrip af Nóregskonungasǫgum* [ca. 1190], ed. M. J. Driscoll, Viking Society for Northern Research, 10 (London: Viking Society for Northern Research, 1995), chaps. 27, 32, 35; *Fsk* (early 13th century, pre-1225), chaps. 35, 42; *Mks*, ed. Jónsson, 18, 20–22, 33–34, 39–40, 99–100; *Mks*, trans. Andersson and Gade (ca. 1220), 98, 100–101, 111, 115–16, 157–58; *Saxo Grammaticus*, ed. Christiansen (ca. 1220), 28–29, 34, 188n96, where she is mentioned as Óláfr's concubine; Snorri Sturluson's *Hkr 2* (*ÓsH*), (ca.1225–35), chaps. 239, 244, 247; Adam of Bremen, *History of the Archbishops* [ca. 1076], trans. Tschan, book 2, chap. lxxiv (72), mentions her as Cnut's concubine; and a letter written around July or August 1036 by a certain Immo, priest in the court of Conrad II (see below, 173–74).

for the literary historian are the synchronous historical and literary motifs that blend distinctively into a conventional portrait of the treacherous and dangerous politically powerful female, threatening to the male-dominant established political powers, like those commanding female characters that people the Kings' Sagas, the *hetzerin* (goader), Snorri's imaginative expansions of politically powerful historical women, who often function as agents "behind the murders and revenges" of their male kinsmen.[16] The prototype in the Old Norse tradition is the historical Gunnhildr *konungamóðir* (mother of kings), wife of Norwegian king Eiríkr Blóðøx (Bloodaxe), ruler of York (947–48, 952–54) and daughter of King Gormr *gamli* (the aged) of Denmark, Cnut's grandfather.[17]

---

16. Jenny Jochens, "The Female Inciter in the Kings' Sagas," *Arkiv för Nordisk Filologi* 102 (1987): 100–119, at 110–11. The term was coined by Rolf Heller, *Die literarische Darstellung der Frau in den Isländersagas* (Halle: M. Niemeyer, 1958), 98–122, who classified fifty-two cases of the *hetzerin* (goader) type; see also Jochens, "The Medieval Icelandic Heroine: Fact or Fiction?" *Viator* 17 (1986): 35–50; her *Women in Old Norse Society* (Ithaca, NY: Cornell University Press, 1995), 70–75, 173–75; and her *Old Norse Images of Women* (Philadelphia, 1996), 180–82, 281nn17–21; see also Margaret Clunies Ross, "Women and Power in the Scandinavian Sagas," in *Stereotypes of Women in Power: Historical Perspectives and Revisionist Views*, ed. Barbara Garlick, Suzanne Dixon, and Pauline Allen (New York: Greenwood Press, 1992), 105–19, esp. 108–9; R. G. Thomas, "Some Exceptional Women in the Sagas," *Saga-Book of the Viking Society* 13 (1952–53): 307–27; and William Ian Miller, "Choosing the Avenger: Some Aspects of the Bloodfeud in Medieval Iceland and England," *Law and History Review* 1 (1984): 159–204, 181–82n92; on instances of revenge in *Beowulf*, see Miller, 194–203.

17. So identified as the daughter of King Gormr gamli and sister of Haraldr *blátonn* (bluetooth; Sveinn's father and Cnut's grandfather) in *Monumenta Historica Norvegiæ* (ca. 1140 and 1152–54), ed. Gustav Storm (Christiania: A. W. Brøgger, 1880), 105 (uxorem nomine Gunnildam quandam malificam et iniquissimam, Gorms stultissimi Danorum regis filiam ac Thyri mulieris prudentissimae); *A History of Norway and the Passion and Miracles of the Blessed Óláfr*, trans. Deevra Kunin, ed. Carl Phelpstead (London: Viking Society for Northern Research, 2001), 15 ("took to wife a vicious and most iniquitous woman from Denmark named Gunnhildr, the daughter of the notably

Not one source treats Ælfgifu favorably. In *Morkinskinna*, she is presented as the "worst" of Cnut's representatives in Norway, with the "fiercest disposition" and filled with "malice."[18] Álfífa's appearances in *Morkinskinna* are brief, and in these she is depicted as treacherous with touches of sorcery. *Morkinskinna*, for instance, is the sole witness for her having mistakenly poisoned Harthacnut with a drink meant for Magnús at a welcoming banquet for the Norwegian king in Harthacnut's court in Denmark:[19]

Þui næst kemur Alfiua j hollena og fagnade uel Magnuse konungi og kuozt allan soma vilia honum veita. skenker honum sidan og bidr hann drekka. Magnus konungr segir: fyrst skal Hǫrða-Knútr drecka og honum skal fyrst alla þionostu veita. Sidan fær hun Hǫrða-Knúti hornit og drack han af og mællti vid er hann kastade nidr horneno. eigi skyllde. eigi gat hann leingra mællt og æpti sidan til bana. Og syndiz nu þesse suik Alfiuo vid Magnus konung þuiat hun hafdi honum ætlad þenna daudadryck. en hun var þegar ǫll j brut og matte henni þui ecke hegna. Þesse atburdr vard aa setta aare Magnus konungs er Hǫrða-Knútr fieck bana er bædi uar þa ordinn konungr yfir Danmork og Einglandi.[20]

---

foolish Gormr, king of the Danes, and of the notably sagacious woman, Þyri"); for a summation of the discussions on the dating of *Historica Norvegiæ*, see Phelpstead, xi–xvii. In the Icelandic material, however, she is identified as the daughter of Qzurr *lafskegg* (dangling beard) from Hálogaland; see *Egils saga* (94), *Njáls saga* (11), *Fagrskinna* (54), and *Hkr 1* (*Haralds saga ins Hárfagra*, chap. 32, where the father is Qzurr *toti*); see also *Ágrip*, ed. Driscoll, 87–88; and Jochens, "Female Inciter in the Kings' Sagas," esp. 116–19; for a thorough argument in defense of her being the issue of Danish royalty, see Sigurður Nordal, "Gunnhildur konungamóðir," *Samtíð og saga* 1 (1940): 135–55, esp. 141–44.

18. *Mks*, trans. Andersson and Gade, 98 (FJ 17–19).

19. Regarding the manuscript error for Hǫrðaknútr's name, I follow Fjalldal's revision of Jónsson's text of *Morkinskinna* (FJ 34) and his translation; Fjalldal, *Anglo-Saxon England in Icelandic Medieval Texts*, 53, 137nn 32–33; and *Mks* (chap. 5), trans. Andersson and Gade, 111, 422nn4–5.

20. Fjalldal translation, *Anglo-Saxon England in Icelandic Medieval Texts*, 53.

[Then Álfífa entered the hall and welcomed King Magnús warmly, saying that she wished to honor him in every way. She poured for him and asked him to drink. King Magnús said: 'Hǫrða-knútr should drink first and have precedence in every form of service.' Then she gave the horn to Hǫrða-knútr and he drank it off, exclaiming, as he cast the horn aside, 'shouldn't have,' but he got no further and gave his death groan. This demonstrated Álfífa's treachery toward King Magnús because she intended the fatal drink for him. But she vanished instantly so that she could not be punished. This event took place in the sixth year of King Magnús's reign. It was the death of Harthacnut, who had become king of both Denmark and England.]

The scenario is quite unlikely, for the chronology is inaccurate. Neither Álfífa nor Harthacnut would have been in Denmark in the "sixth year" of Magnús's reign. Álfífa would hardly have been in Denmark while her son Harold Harefoot was reigning in England (1037–40), or afterward during Harthacnut's accession as king. But the incident is of interest, first because it is a typical motif for depicting the characteristics of the nefarious sorceress queen that Álfífa shares with Gunnhildr,[21] such as feminine guile (*fagnade uel Magnuse konungi og kuozt allan soma vilia honum veita*) and the slick disappearing act of a magician, and second because on 8 June 1042, Harthacnut did indeed fall dead immediately as he drank a toast to the daughter of Osgood Clapa at her wedding at Lambeth Palace.[22] The scenario piques one's curiosity as to the source of this anecdote and raises suspicions that the king's sudden death at Clapa's wedding celebration for his daughter may not have occurred from natural causes, although there is no report of Ælfgifu's having been in attendance.

---

21. In *Egils saga* 44, Gunnhildr (and Bárðr, Egill's host) offers poisoned ale to Egill, but the situation is quite different; see Fjalldal's comment on the matching characteristics of the two queens (*Anglo-Saxon England in Icelandic Medieval Texts*, 53); noted also by Andersson and Gade, *Mks*, 422n5.
22. *JWChron* ii.532–35 (s.a. 1042); *ASC* E-text, s.a. 1041; *ASC* 2:221.

Ælfgifu's reign as queen mother in Norway is marked by the Norwegians as *Álfífu ǫld* or *ævi* (Ælfgifu's time), a time of oppression, treachery, and cruelty.[23] Sighvatr Þórðarson's verses (ca. 1029–30?), reported in *Ágrip*, are perhaps the earliest of the sources to immortalize its severity:

<E>n þá tók landsfólkit eftir fall konungs fulliga við vesǫld þangat út er Sveinn var ok Álfífa. Ok var þá hǫrmuligt undir því ríki at búa, bæði með ófrelsi ok með óárani, er fólkit lifði meir við búfjár mat en manna, fyr því at aldregi var ár á þeira dǫgum, sem heyra má í vísu þessi er Sigvatr kvað:

3. Álfífu mon ævi
ungr drengr muna lengi
er oxa mat ǫtu
inni skaf sem hafrar;
annat var, þá er Óláfr
ógnbandaðr réð landi,
hverr átti þá hrósa
hjalmar hlǫðnu korni.[24]

[After the death of the king, the people's misery became complete under Sveinn and Ælfgyfu. It was miserable living under their rule, both because of their tyranny and the bad seasons, when the people lived more off cattle fodder than the food of men, because the seasons were never good in their time, as can be heard from this verse by Sighvatr:

3. Ælfgyfu's time
long will the young man remember,
when they at home ate ox's food,
and like the goats, ate rind;
different it was when Óláfr,

---

23. *Álfífu ǫld* in *Heimskringla*; *Álfífu ævi* in *Ágrip* and in Sighvatr's verse.
24. *Ágrip* chap. 32, Driscoll translation.

the warrior, ruled the land,
then everyone could enjoy
stacks of dry corn.]

Even nature, repelled by Ælfgifu's rule, produced bad seasons so
that hunger spread throughout the land. *Óláfs saga helga* (*Hkr 2*, chap.
239) likewise records Álfífa's oppressive, unjust, and discriminatory
laws, much harsher (*sum miklu frekari*) than those of Denmark, which
turned Norwegian freemen into thralls in all aspects of their lives.
From being heavily taxed for the fruits of their labor and outfitting
the king's levies without compensation, to being bound to the confines of their land (as if imprisoned) unless permitted to leave by
royal decree, the Norwegian freemen existed under the legal restraint
"that one Dane should outweigh the worth of ten Norwegians" (*at þá
skyldu danskir menn hafa svá mikinn metnað í Nóregi, at eins þeira vitni
skyldi hrinda tíu Norðmanna vitnum*).

In *Fagrskinna* (chap. 35), greed and oppression defined the double
rule of Sveinn Álfífuson and Álfífa *in ríka*, though in reality it was
Álfífa who, with cruelty and political cunning, was the decisive force
governing the fate of Norway:

> Í þann tíma, er Óláfr konungr var felldr í Þrándheimi, kom sunnan
> Sveinn, sonr Knúts konungs, ok Álfífa, móðir hans, af Danmǫrk
> með miklu liði ok fór þegar norðr í land ok lagði undir sik allt
> ríkit, þat er Óláfr konungr hafði átt. . . . Sveinn konungr var mikill
> œskumaðr, fríðr sjónum, ekki grimmhugaðr né ágjarn. Álfífa móðir
> hans, er kǫlluð var en ríka Álfífa, hón réð mest með konunginum,
> ok mæltu þat allir, at hón spillti í hvern stað ok fór fyrir þá sǫk
> stjórnin illa við landsfólkit, ok svá margt illt stóð af hennar ráðum
> í Noregi, at menn jǫfnuðu þessu ríki við Gunnhildar ǫld, er verst
> hafði verit áðr í Noregi. Um Álfífu ǫld leigðu fiskimenn sjóinn.
> Mǫrg ǫnnur ódœmi váru þá gǫr með mikilli fégirni.[25]

[At the time when King Óláfr had been killed in Þrándheimr,

---

25. *Fks* chap. 35, 161–62.

Sveinn, son of King Knútr, and his mother Álfífa [Ælfgifu] came north from Denmark with a great force, and he went at once to the north of the country and took command of the whole of the kingdom that King Óláfr had ruled. . . . King Sveinn was a very young man, fair in appearance, not fierce in temperament or ambitious. His mother Álfífa, who was called *in ríka* [the Great], decided most things for the king, and everyone said that she did damage in every situation, and for that reason the government was unpopular with the people of the land, and so much ill resulted from her counsels in Norway that people compared this reign with the time of Gunnhildr, which was the worst there had ever been in Norway before that. In the time of Álfífa fishermen paid rent for the sea. Many other outrageous things were done through great greed for money.]

Fagrskinna's comparison of Álfífa *in ríka* with Gunnhildr, the Norse prototype of all "evil and revenging women," encapsulates to a large extent the universal assessment of the character of Cnut's concubine. As with the reports of Ælfgifu's activities, it is with difficulty that one separates historical fact from imaginative fiction in the Gunnhildr narrative.[26] In the *Íslendingasögur* (Sagas of the Icelanders), she appears in varying guises, the most striking being her roles in *Egils saga*, *Njáls saga*, and *Laxdœla saga*;[27] *Egils saga* highlights her tyrannical shrewdness, her skill in magic, and her beauty, whereas *Njála* and *Laxdœla* give priority to her sexuality, though she still retains the stain of sorcery. Even in the politically charged Kings' Sagas, there is a touch of the fantastic about her. Her first appearance in *Heimskringla*, for instance, is couched in a folklorish scenario from which probably

---

26. See Nordal's discussion on fictive treatments of events and characters as a means for authors to reach a deeper historical truth, using the inconsistencies in Gunnhildr's character as a prime example; "Gunnhildur konungamóðir," 149–52; see Heller, *Die literarische Darstellung*, who classifies Gunnhildr as a sorceress-type, 133–36.
27. See also *Gísli saga* (ÍF 6); *Kormáks saga* (ÍF 8); *Hallfreðar saga* (ÍF 8); *Flóamanna saga* (ÍF 14); *Harðar saga* (ÍF 13), and *Þórðar saga hreðu* (ÍF 14).

stem the characteristics of sorcery and sexuality continually attributed to her.[28] Otherwise in the Kings' Sagas, where her consummate
political skills, infamous though they be, are recounted,[29] she is
more realistically portrayed as Eiríkr Blóðøx's wife, who reaches the
height of her political power as a *konungamóðir* (mother of kings)
in the late tenth century after Eiríkr's death. She is remembered for
the successful tactical maneuvers by which her seven sons ascended
to the Norwegian throne and her daughter Ragnhildr, who inherited her mother's taste for murder and deceit, became queen of the
Orkneys (*Orkneyinga saga*, 8–9).[30] Gunnhildr is credited with having
engineered any number of murders of political opponents to secure
the throne for her sons, impressing upon them the danger of rivals,
and is suspected of having prodded Eiríkr to murder his brother.[31]
Jenny Jochens (and to some extent Rolf Heller) see her as a powerful,
and hence dangerous, historical woman who is appropriated by the
authors of both the politically charged Kings' Sagas and the nation-
alistic sagas of the Icelanders and typically transformed into a figure

---

28. *Hkr 1, Haralds saga ins hárfagra*, chap. 32: Gunnhildr has placed herself
under the tutelage of two Finns for instruction as a sorceress. When she
is apprehended alone in the forest by Eiríkr's men, a narrative of rescue
unfolds, revealing her beauty and her cunning sensuality in subduing the
Finns and recounting their subsequent murder by Eiríkr's men which she
arranged and her climactic meeting and alliance with Eiríkr.

29. See Jochens, *Old Norse Images of Women*, 180–82, in her discussion of
Snorri's treatment of Gunnhildr in the Kings' Sagas.

30. The listing of Gunnhildr's sons in *Ágrip* (chaps. 5, 8) is more than
the seven and is at variance with Snorri's count: *Ágrip* includes Gamli,
Guthormr, Haraldr *gráfeldr* (gray-cloak), Ragnfrøðr, Erlingr, Guðrøðr,
Sigurðr *slefa* (drool, or snake), and adds Hálfdan, Eyvindr, and Gormr; see
Driscoll, *Ágrip* 88n15; on the possibility of multiplication of Gunnhildr's
sons, see Nordal, "Gunnhildur konungamóðir," 142.

31. Oddr Snorrason's *The Saga of Olaf Tryggvason*, chaps. 1–5, in *Konunga sögur*
vol. 1; *Óláfs saga Tryggvasonar eftir Odd munk; Helgisaga Óláfs Haraldssonar;
Brot úr Elztu sögu*, ed. Guðni Jónsson (Reykjavík, 1957), 5–19; *Saga of Olaf
Tryggvason*, trans. Andersson, 36–44; *Hkr 1, Óláfs saga Tryggvasonar*, chaps.
2–3, 5, 87; *Hkr 1, Haralds saga Gráfeldar* (*The Saga of Harald Graycloak*), chaps.
3–5, 9, 16.

estranged from society because of her paganism, sorcery, sensuality, and homicidal inclinations, a liminal figure mediating between the social norm and unregulated nature.[32]

In Jochens's view, Álfífa *in ríka* is akin in some measure to the *hetzerin* type, the authoritative, astute, aristocratic woman functioning as antagonist in a male-dominated political court, for her portraits in the Norse compendia, the Kings' Sagas, and skaldic verse follow the *hetzerin* scenario. A powerful woman infringing upon political power invested in and enjoyed by men, contaminating their laws and customs with foreign political aims, would hardly have been welcomed by the independent Norwegian *bœndr* (landed gentry). Ælfgifu/Álfífa had wealth and royal familial connections, and through her alliance to Cnut, her own political influence spread throughout Cnut's northern kingdom. A historical figure who dominates and incites men to political action, she is depicted as infamously evil in her counsel in the Nordic literary tradition, although, as far as is recorded in the historical documents, this may fall short of Gunnhildr's incitements of her husband and sons alike to murder. Ælfgifu/Álfífa's cruelty and oppressive acts toward the Norwegian people in a time of famine betray a character akin to Gunnhildr's "grim" (*greypt*) temperament as described in the Icelandic material (*Egils saga*, chap. 57, as one example).[33] Alleged sexual promiscuity, ambition, paganism, sorcery, and a sharp, manipulative intelligence are attributes that complete the similarities of the *konungamóðir* and Cnut's unofficial consort,[34] attributes that Ælfgifu is not unique in possessing in the English tradition, as will be discussed below. For in times of political and dynastic crises, the *hetzerin* type emerges, as in the domineering

---

32. Heller, *Die literarische Darstellung*, 133–34.
33. Jochens, "Female Inciter in the Kings' Sagas," 116–19. Gunnhildr had a sorrowful end. *Ágrip* (chap. 11) states that she was treacherously deceived while in Denmark and "was taken and sunk in a bog, and, according to many, so ended her days"; but see Driscoll, *Ágrip* 91n39.
34. In addition to Ælfgifu's promiscuity surrounding the births of Sveinn and Harold Harefoot, *Morkinskinna* (chap. 5) reports her having had a daughter who was not Sveinn's sister, by someone other than Cnut.

historical figure of Ælfthryth, Æthelred's mother, and the uncanny Grendel's mother in the ahistorical *Beowulf*.

Óláfs saga helga (*Hkr 2*, chap. 244) brands Álfífa as a pagan, for she is the only person who raises objections to the signs of Óláfr's alleged sanctity and is the prime antagonist to church policy and Norwegian nationalism. Assembled around the newly opened casket holding King Óláfr's uncorrupted body, with hair and nails that have grown as if he has been alive since his martyrdom (*at síðan hafði vaxit hár ok negl, því næst sem þá myndi, ef hann hefði lífs verit hér í heimi alla þá stund, síðan er hann fell* [*ÓsH*, 404]), are Bishop Grímkel, King Sveinn and Álfífa, and all the high-ranking chieftains. The queen mother scoffs at the miraculous event, astutely pointing out that bodies buried in sand do not rot as easily as if they were buried in earth (*Furðu seint fúna menn í sandinum. Ekki myndi svá vera, ef hann hefði í moldu legit*) and then demanding that Óláfr's hair be placed in unhallowed fire to verify his saintliness (*Þá þykki mér hár þat heilagr dómr, ef þat brenn eigi í eldi*). Álfífa's display of arrogance and insolence turns not only the bishop and the chieftains against her but her son King Sveinn as well, for he concurs that Óláfr is indeed a true saint. The concurrence of Church and State on Óláfr's sainthood may not have pleased Álfífa if indeed she had been Óláfr's concubine.

Denial of Óláfr's sainthood was the turning point of *Álfífa ǫld*. From then forward, men took courage to rise up against her unjust rule. At the Niðaróss assembly, as recorded in *Fagrskinna* (chap. 42), for example, Einarr þambarskelfir was able to insult the queen mother openly by alluding to her sexuality, deriding her as a "mare" and Sveinn as her speechless "foal" to the delight of all, without fear of punishment, except for a verbal reprimand from the queen (*Setisk niðr bœndr ok hlýði konungs ørendi, en kurri eigi svá lengr*; Sit down, *bœndr*, and listen to the king's business, and don't grumble like that any longer). Despite the royal command, Einarr inflamed the *bœndr* and broke up the assembly: he

> stóð upp ok mælti, at bœndr skyldu fara heim, "ok hafa menn ill ørendi hingat sótt bæði nú ok fyrr til fundar Álfífu. Megu menn

heldr heima bíða vanréttis, en sœkja allir í einn stað ok hlýða þar einnar konu orðum, þeir <er> þá eigi vildu hlýða konunginum Óláfi, er nú er sannheilagr. Hefir þat verit gǫrt mikit níðingsverk ok hefir nú með illu refzk, er svá margt herfiligt hefir þetta fólk þolat, síðan er þetta ríki kom yfir fólkit. Skyldi þat nú guð vilja, at þat væri skammt ok hefir þó nú verit yfrit langt.[35]

[got up and said that the *bændr* should go home, 'and men have wasted their time coming here for meetings with Álfífa both now and in the past. People might as well wait for injustice at home rather than all come together and listen to the words of one woman there in one place, these men who would not listen before to King Óláfr, who is now truly sainted. It is a most shameful deed that has been done, and it has now been punished heavily, so miserably has this people suffered since this government took power over the people. God must now wish that it will not last long, and yet it has already gone on long enough.']

Einarr's words broke up the assembly; nonetheless, *Álfífa ǫld* continued for a time, for men feared to rise up against Cnut's son.[36]

What the character of the historical Ælfgifu/Álfífa might have been before it was transformed into the powerful and politically dangerous tyrannical "mare" manipulating her "foal" of the Kings' Sagas or into the Beowulfian stalker of the moors one can only surmise, for each national version served a narrative strategy akin to propaganda, revealing more about the political exigencies that prevailed in the different court cultures she lived in than about the queen herself.[37] A statement at the close of chapter 35 in *Fagrskinna* contradicts and makes more complex what has been presented as a treacherous, vicious creature. After detailing Álfífa's "outrageous" deeds done out

---

35. *Fsk* chap. 42, 166.
36. See also *ÓsH* (chap. 247), which summarizes this meeting of the *bændr*.
37. Pauline Stafford, "Writing the Biography of Eleventh-Century Queens," in *Writing Medieval Biography*, ed. Bates et al., 99–109, esp. 103–4, and passim, where she emphasizes the importance of culturally contextualizing a political figure in historical writings.

of "greed," the commentator states: "A peaceful life was given to every man of this country and from abroad, and yet it was almost as if there was no peace for any man's property because of payments and taxes. King Knutr's power brought it about that there was no plundering or killing; but people did not give Álfífa credit for that." What may have been Álfífa's social and political reforms were interpreted as vicious and tyrannical personal acts, the imposition of English constraints over Norwegian personal freedom. As a foreign queen whose charge was to impose Anglo-Danish legal and economic structure on Norway and to forward the best interests of Cnut and of her son as future full king of Norway—actions appropriate to her role as Cnut's regent in Norway—Ælfgifu could not possibly have been perceived by the Norwegian power structure other than as a malevolent tyrannical "mare" manipulating her "foal," even though some benefit may have resulted from her social and political programs. She had dared, as had other historically based women with like personalities, to penetrate the masculine world of power, and like them, she was obliged to undergo defamation. This is not to say that her actions were meant for the good of the Norwegians, for there must have been a kernel of truth in the fictive exaggerations.

In 1034, Óláfr's son, Magnús *góði*, sent for by the men of Þrándheimr, levied troops to win back Óláfr's land (*Fsk* 46; *Hkr 3, Mgóða* 4), and though King Sveinn Álfífuson "had war arrows carried at once in all directions" (*lét hann þegar skera upp herǫr ok senda fjǫgurra vegna frá sér*), few *bœndr* answered the call, and the few who did were untrustworthy.[38] Ælfgifu, Sveinn, and the Danish courtiers fled to Denmark, to King Harthacnut, Cnut and Emma's son, for asylum or perhaps, as the sagas seem to indicate, to muster troops against Magnús. But, as fate would have it, and as *Fagrskinna* (47) reports, "the following summer [1036] Sveinn Álfífuson caught a mortal illness in Denmark,

---

38. *Magnús saga ins góða*, in *Hkr 3*. On Svein and Ælfgifu's flight from Norway, see also Theodoricus Monachus, *Historia de Antiquitate Regum Norwagiensium* (*An Account of the Ancient History of the Norwegian Kings*), trans. and annotated by David McDougall and Ian McDougall (London: Viking Society for Northern Research, 1998), 33.

and that same winter *gamli* Knútr died in England [1035] and was buried at Winchester" (*Næsta sumar eptir fekk Sveinn Álfifusonr banasótt í Danmǫrk, ok þann sama vetr andaðisk gamli Knútr á Englandi, ok var hann jarðaðr í Vinncestr*).[39] With Sveinn's death, Ælfgifu's career as a king's mother seemed to draw to a close; with Cnut's death, any aspirations she may have held to continue as queen of England, unofficial as the position might have been, were dashed.

There is no way of knowing when Ælfgifu returned to England from Denmark. But that she was compelled to do so, if she had any aspirations to be the English *konungamóðir* (mother of kings), which had been Gunnhildr's title in Norway and was to be Emma of Normandy's in 1041 and 1043, is evident from her presence at the fated Oxford meeting of the *witan* of 1035/36, which elected Cnut's successor to the throne. There is a contemporary continental document that may provide a historical basis for and cast a substantial realistic light on what one might otherwise consider as a stereotypical Norwegian view of Álfífa/Ælfgifu's political drive, shrewd machinations, and ambition. A letter sent by a certain Immo, priest in the court of Conrad II, to Azeko, bishop of Worms,[40] quotes messages from England that were brought to Gunnhildr, Harthacnut's sister and Emma and Cnut's daughter, and queen to the future Holy Roman Emperor Henry III. The letter describes Cnut's unofficial queen's networking among, bargaining with, and bribing the members of the Oxford *witan* for the accession of Harold Harefoot:

> Porro autem nec illud vos latere volo, quod legati Anglorum nostrae iuniori domnae, nuper infirmae, nunc autem, Deo gratias!

---

39. On Sveinn's departure, his subsequent death, and the death of Cnut the Great, see further, *Ágrip* chaps. 34–36; *Fsk* chaps. 46–47, *Fsk*, 169–71, trans. Finlay; *Hkr 3* (*Mgóða*) chaps. 4–5; and *Msk* (*Mgóða HHarðr*), trans. Andersson and Gade, 100–102.

40. H. Bresslau, *Jahrbücher des Deutschen Reichs unter Konrad II*, 2 vols. (Leipzig: Duncker & Humbolt, 1879–84), 2: 532, no. 3; W. H. Stevenson reprints an extract of the letter written around July or August 1036, in "An Alleged Son of King Harold Harefoot," *English Historical Review* 28 (1913): 112–17, at 115–16; Keynes, *EER* [xxxii].

valenti, missi sunt; qui vero dixerunt sibi haec: 'infelix ergo,' inquiunt, 'et iniusta noverca vestra, Arduichenut, germano vestro, regnum fraude subripere cupiens, universis primatibus nostris convivia maxima celebravit, et nunc eos prece, nunc pretio corrumpere satagens, iuramentis sibi suoque nato subiugare temptavit; qui vero non solum ei in aliquo huiusmodi non consenserunt, verum etiam nuntios prefato germano vestro, quatenus ad eos cito redeat, unanimes transmiserunt.' Sed illi quidem talia.[41]

[Yet nor do I wish it to escape your notice that envoys of the English were sent to our younger lady (recently unwell, but now, thanks be to God, much better). This is what they told her. 'Your wretched and wicked step-mother, wishing to deprive your brother Harthacnut of the kingdom by fraud, organized a great party for all our leading men, and, eager to corrupt them at times with entreaty and at times with money, tried to subordinate them with oaths to herself and to her son; yet not only did the men not give their consent to her in any such way, but of one accord they despatched messengers to your aforesaid brother, so that he might soon return to them.' But to her indeed [they said] such things.]

On the surface, it would be difficult to interpret Ælfgifu's actions as unfitting in the context of an electoral body politic constituted for the election of a king as reported by Immo; yet in the context of succession politics of Cnut's court between 1035 and 1041, her campaign was politically dangerous, especially to Emma of Normandy.

No less a political being than was her nemesis Emma, as will be discussed in the following chapter, Ælfgifu was unwavering in pushing forward the election of her son as king of England.[42] She may have suffered a diminished status because of the irregularity of

---

41. *EER* [xxxii], Keynes translation.

42. Keynes puts forward further argument from numismatic evidence describing the successful strategy of Ælfgifu and the Mercians in their takeover of the realm—the shift in coinage from minting of the *Jewel Cross* for both Harthacnut and Harold in 1035–36 to the "ubiquitous" coinage in Harold's name in 1036–37; Keynes, *EER* [xxxii–xxxiii].

her alliance to Cnut, lacking the stamp of approval from ecclesiastical and governmental bodies, but her noble birth, the powerful status of her kin, and her having been formally designated as queen mother by Cnut in Norway made her a serious contestant for the throne of England, perhaps more dangerous than her son, sexually fraudulent or not. Some modicum of character assassination was to be expected. For like Gunnhildr, Ælfgifu of Northampton had taken on the role of a *konungsmóðir* whose foremost action was to champion and promote the designation of her son as ruler of a kingdom and to secure for herself a political potency whose center was the court and not the monastery, as Stafford's work has consistently argued.[43] Dominating and steering the political movement of the court to favor her son, Ælfgifu would be subject to charges of, and perhaps indulged in, treachery and murder and the magic arts, as was said of Gunnhildr and of Ælfthryth, Æthelred's mother, the prime historical English model of the *konungsmóðir*.[44] As were Gunnhildr and

---

43. For perhaps the earliest of Stafford's works on this subject, see "Sons and Mothers: Family Politics in the Early Middle Ages," in *Medieval Women: Essays Presented to Professor Rosalind M. T. Hill*, ed. Derek Baker (Oxford: Basil Blackwell, 1978), 79–100, and passim; for continental queens, see 87–90, 94–98; for the contrast between the powerful status of Mercian queens and the lesser prestige of West Saxon female royalty, see 82–86; see also Stafford's "The Portrayal of Royal Women in England, Mid-Tenth to Mid-Twelfth Centuries," in *Medieval Queenship*, ed. John Carmi Parsons (New York: St. Martins Press, 1998), 143–67 and passim; and her *Queens, Concubines, and Dowagers: The Wife in the Early Middle Ages* (Athens, GA: University of Georgia Press, 1983), passim.

44. On Ælfthryth's notorious reputation as alleged murderess of her stepson, Edward the Martyr, her complicity in the murder of her first husband, Ealdorman Æthelwold, by King Edgar, and her shape-changing arts into the appearance of a mare, see generally Stafford, "Sons and Mothers"; Stafford, "Portrayal of Royal Women in England," 149–56; Wright, *Cultivation of Saga in Anglo-Saxon England*, 146–53, 157–71; Fell, *Edward King and Martyr*, esp. xiv–xx; *ASC* E-text, s.a. 979; Byrhtferth's *Vita Oswaldi*, in *Historians of the Church of York and Its Archbishops*, ed. J. Raine, 3 vols., RS 71 (London: Longman, 1879), 1, 399–475, at 449–50; *HHHA* v.27,

Ælfthryth, Ælfgifu must have been a phenomenal personality, who both attracted and repelled the imagination of her contemporaries. Powerful, astute, aristocratic, deceitful, and avaricious in striving for the throne—hers was a personality that incited the imaginations of the Norwegian historians to move into the realm of fiction in their construct of a kaleidoscopic liminal character who strode the path that separates the socially tractable from the untamed natural being. Cnut's irregular queen, as imagined and codified by the Anglo-Saxon, continental, and Scandinavian historians, may be another example of the imaginative transformation that is, as Whaley has argued, at the core of Snorri's "imaginative historiography" in *Heimskringla* and, I venture to suspect, of an Anglo-Danish poet's portrait of an uncanny and rapacious noblewoman in *Beowulf* with the emotional energy and drive of a beast in her thirst for power and revenge. For it may be that only by blending fact and fiction are authors and poets able to reach a deeper historical and poetic truth.[45]

The Beowulfian Konungsmóðir

As in the *Anglo-Saxon Chronicle* and the *Encomium*, the protagonist of the paternity narrative in *Beowulf* is the mother—nameless, dangerous, a social outcast—not Grendel who, having been mortally wounded by Beowulf, has to all intents and purposes disappeared from the narrative. It is Grendel's mother who initiates the action to kill Æschere and carries it to its conclusion. One immediately notices

---

324–25; *JWChron* (s.a. 978), ii.428–31; *WMGR* ii.157, 161, and 162; Gaimar, *L'Estorie des Engleis by Geffrei Gaimar*, ed. A. Bell, Anglo-Norman Texts xiv–xvi (Oxford: B. Blackwell, 1960), 115–31, ll. 3607–4135; Andrew J. Turner and Bernard J. Muir, eds. and trans., "Life of Saint Dunstan," in their *Eadmer of Canterbury: Lives and Miracles of Saints Oda, Dunstan and Oswald* (Oxford: Clarendon, 2006), 59, 144–47; *Liber Eliensis* ii.56, ed. Blake, 127–28; *Book of Ely*, trans. Fairweather, 153–54. For a more positive view of Ælfthryth based on an examination of the charters, see Rabin, "Female Advocacy and Royal Protection in Tenth-Century England," 261–88.

45. As Nordal noted in his discussion of Gunnhildr *konungamóðir*, a woman socially tractable but with an unlimited and overwhelming desire for power; "Gunnhildur konungamóðir," 149–52.

the *Beowulf*-poet's simplification and sharpening of the *konungsmóðir* narrative by his compaction of the two sons into one and consolidation of two realms into a single domain. As in his initial introduction of Grendel, the *Beowulf*-poet's prime intent is to render the mother tantalizingly unrecognizable, if extravagantly dramatic, and like her son she is alien to the court, although she has the status of a courtly figure. Her first identifying epithets are as an avenger (*wrecend*, 1256[b]), a terrifying noblewoman with the strength of a warrior (*ides āglǣcwīf*, 1259[a]), her mind riveted on revenge (*yrmþe gemunde*, 1259[b]), with a nature that is cannibalistic (*ond his mōdor þā gt/ gīfre and galgmōd*, 1276[b]–77[a]). Marked with the sin of Cain (1261[b]–65[a]), she is a *brōga* (terror, 1291[b]), inflicting her *wīggryre* (war-terror, 1284[a]) as she seizes the atheling from his bed (1251–99). The poet is unrelenting in his negative presentation of the avenging, feuding mother, for although the reason usually given for her *sorhfulne sīð* (sorrowful journey) to Heorot to murder Æschere is her despairing state of mind (1276[b]–78) at the loss of her son, the phrase may allude to the bitter course of events that will inevitably lead to the murder of Æschere atheling, an act that throws Hrothgar's kingdom into turmoil.

Some forty-two lines later, a disconsolate Hrothgar, lamenting over Æschere's murder and his now irretrievable personal relationship, erupts into a sharpened, more detailed, and even more rancorous characterization of the atheling's murderer:

> Wearð him on Heorote tō handbanan
> wælgǣst wǣfre; ic ne wāt hwǣder
> atol[46] ǣse wlanc eftsīðas tēah,

---

46. I use *atol* substantively here; in *Helgakviða Hundingsbana I* (38), ON *atall* is used to describe a witch, and in *Helgakviða Hjǫvarðarsonar* (15), it is used as a play on words with the name of Atli: "My name is 'savage.'" See also Klaeber, *The Christian Elements in Beowulf*, trans. Paul Battles, Subsidia 24 (Kalamazoo, MI: Medieval Institute, Western Michigan University, 1996), 10, 22, 23; orig. pub., "Die christlichen Elemente im *Beowulf*," *Anglia* 35 (1911–12). On *wǣfre* to mean "furious," see G. N. Garmonsway, "Anglo-Saxon Heroic Attitudes," in *Franciplegius: Medieval and Linguistic Studies in Honor of Francis Peabody Magoun, Jr.*, ed. Jess B. Bessinger Jr. and Robert P.

fylle gefrēcnod. Hēo þā fǣhðe wræc,
þē þū gystran niht Grendel cwealdest
þurh hǣstne hād heardum clammum,
forþan hē tō lange lēode mīne
wanode ond wyrde. Hē æt wīge gecrang
ealdres scyldig, ond nū ōþer cwōm
mihtig mānscaða, wolde hyre mǣg wrecan,
gē feor hafað fǣhðe gestǣled,
þæs þe þincean mæg þegne monegum,
sē þe æfter sincgyfan on sefan grēoteþ–
hreþerbealo hearde; nū sēo hand ligeþ,
sē þe ēow wēlhwylcra wilna dohte.

(*Bwf* 1330–44)

[A restless slaughtering-visitant became his murderous bane at
Heorot; I do not know where the horror, glorying in the carcass,
took her return journey, emboldened by the fill. [I follow Klaeber,
4th ed., in this emendation; an alternative reading might be: "Or
which of the two [MS *hwæþer*; 198–99] return paths the horror
took, glorying in the carcass, emboldened by the fill."] She has
avenged the feud in which you killed Grendel last night in a vio-
lent manner with your handgrips because he had diminished and
destroyed my people too long; forfeiting his life, he fell in battle.
And now comes the second powerful evil ravager—she wanted to
avenge her kinsman—and greatly fueled the feud [literally, "she
has avenged the feud further, more widely," which calls for retaliation from all of Æschere's men], the heavy-heart sorrow [I follow
Klaeber, 4th ed. here, in accepting *hreþerbealo hearde* as an appositive for *fǣhðe*; 199], as it may seem to many a thane who mourns
after his treasure-giver in his heart. Now the hand lies dead which
dealt with each of your desires.]

The description of Grendel's mother in Fitt 19 as *gīfre and galgmōd*
(greedy and gallows-minded, 1277[a]) is here intensified to evoke a

Creed (New York: New York University Press, 1965), 139–46, at 143.

ravenous beast, exulting in the kill. The terrifying warring noble-woman (*ides āglǣcwīf*, 1259[a]) is escalated into a restless, slaughtering visitant (*wælgǣst wǣfre*), "a horror, glorying in the carcass" (*atol ǣse wlanc*), "emboldened by the fill" (*fylle gefrēcnod*), descriptions of a predatory nature whose rapacity could be said to exceed that of her son, the *heorowearh hetelīc* (hateful, bloodthirsty wolf, 1267[a]), who has devoured Hrothgar's thanes and depleted his hall. His moth-er's cannibalistic inclination is further blatantly asserted in a later scene when the accursed sea-wolf (*brimwylf*, 1506[a]), the powerful sea-woman (*merewīf mihtig*, 1519[a]), struggles with Beowulf in her battle-hall (*nīðsele*, 1513[a]) along the expansive plain of wolves (*grundwyrgen*, 1518[b]; ON *varg-ynja*) at the sea's bottom. The poet elevates the status of this second *mānscaða* to above that of Grendel, calling her *mihtig*;[47] he confounds conceptions of humanity (*wīf, mōdor, ides*) with those found of terrifying monstrosity, a restless cannibalistic creature, a *brimwylf* (sea-wolf, 1599[a]) with *atolan clommum* (savage claws, 1502[a]) and *lāþan fingrum* (loathsome, hostile fingers, 1505[b]).

The stark conflation of the monstrous and the human leads one to consider the possibility that the *Beowulf*-poet might be presenting a historical figure of "wealth and power" in an "uncanny mode," a characterization device, as Nora Chadwick first argued some time ago, often employed by Norse poets and storytellers in their render-ings of historically based females. Chadwick's prime example was the baleful sorceress Þorgerðr Hölgabrúðr, beloved and protectress of Jarl Hákon, last pagan ruler of Norway, and the fantastical doublet of his historical wife of wealth and power, Þóra,[48] whose physical

---

47. Except for the description of the mighty sea beast Beowulf slays in the Breca episode (558[a]) and Grendel's power (as *foremihtig*, 969[b]), in *Beowulf* the adjectival *mihtig* is restricted to descriptions of God (701[a], 1398[a], 1716[a], 1725[a], and 92[a] as the substantive *ælmihtiga*) and Grendel's mother (1339[a], 1519[a]).

48. See Chadwick, "Þorgerðr Hölgabrúðr and the *Trolla Þing*," 397–417, where she examines the numerous narratives dealing with Þorgerðr and Þóra; for the most recent examination of all the sources about Þorgerðr, see John McKinnell, "Þorgerðr Hölgabrúðr and Hyndluljóð," in *Mythological*

traits and qualities she compares with those of Grendel's mother. In a related article exploring the treatment of the monstrous in *Beowulf*, Chadwick arrives at the conclusion that Grendel's mother is probably associated with figures of avenging femininity who are rooted in traditions of historically ruling families long assimilated into the native population.[49] Chadwick's conclusion, unexplored since her observation, touched upon the essence of the Beowulfian characterization. And even though no contemporary scholar has associated the "bloodthirsty" monstrous *ides* with a politically powerful historical figure, language used to describe Grendel's mother fittingly evokes physical traits and qualities of the strong women rendered in uncanny mode in the Norse tradition.[50] For Grendel's mother is not the common insubstantial revenant of folk tradition but rather has materiality, courtly status, and tyrannical character traits that can easily be thought of as heightened metaphors of human actions, traits that we have seen more realistically portrayed in the despotic queen

---

Women: Studies in Memory of Lotte Motz, ed. Rudolf Simek and Wilhelm Heizmann (Vienna: Fassbaender, 2002), 265–90.

49. Nora K. Chadwick, "The Monsters and *Beowulf*," in *The Anglo-Saxons: Studies in Some Aspects of Their History and Culture Presented to Bruce Dickins*, ed. Peter Clemoes (London: Bowes and Bowes, 1959), 171–203, esp. 172–78; for Old Norse mythic parallels for Grendel's mother, see Damico, *Beowulf's Wealhtheow and the Valkyrie Tradition*, 46, 49, 57, 68, 69–70, 102–3, 212n50.

50. Shari Horner, for one, characterizes the monstrosity of Grendel's mother as stemming from the very fact of her being an "illimitable" woman, ungoverned by traditional "institutional enclosure[s]," descriptions that would not be out of place in an Ælfgifu of Northampton delineation; *The Discourse of Enclosure: Representing Women in Old English Literature* (Albany, NY: SUNY Press, 2001), 81–89, 81, 82. Nor would Grendel's mother's inherent sexuality and underlying eroticism first noted by Jane Chance be incompatible with what had been implied or said in contemporary or near-contemporary sources about Ælfgifu of Northampton; Chance, "Structural Unity of *Beowulf*," esp. 253–54; see also her *Woman as Hero in Old English Literature* (Syracuse, NY: Syracuse University Press, 1968), esp. 100–104; nor finally, Dana Oswald's recent discussion of the masculinity and sexual hybridity of Grendel's mother in her *Monsters, Gender, and Sexuality in Medieval Literature* (Cambridge, UK: D. S. Brewer, 2010), 77–83, 91–113.

Chapter Three

Ælfgifu/Álfífa *in ríka*, variously characterized by English documents as promiscuous and by northern historical texts as a terrifying pagan tormentor of the populace, greedy and oppressive, with a dictatorial control over her son.

Immediately following his intense plaint, however, Hrothgar's anguish becomes detached, and the *Beowulf*-poet at last reveals some solid information on the identity of the Grendel-kin. The poet uproots Heorot's menacing assailants, now amplified to two, from the realm of the uncanny and positions them in a more realistic sociopolitical setting among landowners and counselors of the king; at this moment in the narrative, the relationship between history and fiction becomes more plainly manifested (1345–64). The *wælgǣst wǣfre* (restless, slaughtering visitant) and her *heorowearh hetelīc* (hateful, bloodthirsty wolf) of a son, for example, shift from figures of ghoulish fantasy to take on more discernible human forms, though they remain enveloped in a haze of mystery:

"Ic þæt londbūend,[51] lēode mīne,
selerǣdende secgan hȳrde,
þæt hīe gesāwon swylce twēgen

51. Although elsewhere in *Beowulf*, -*būend* (<OE *būan*) carries the general sense of "inhabitants of the land, dwellers," I translate with a more specific signification here as "landowners" to distinguish from *fold-būende*, "earth-dwellers," which may carry the general sense here or have a closer definition of "husbandmen," in either case, a class that most probably would not have been members of Hrothgar's *witan*, taking *selerǣdende* in apposition to *landbūend*. The sense of "landowners" would be related to OE *ge-būan*, "take possession of"; see also ON *bóndi* (m.), *búendr*, *bóendr* (pl.), "owners of lands" (from *búa*). Cleasby-Vigfusson, s.v. *bóndi*, offers a number of examples from Old Icelandic law that distinguishes a *búandi* or *bóndi* as "a man who has land and stock." In ON, the word carries a positive sense to distinguish men of some stature, as, e.g., *Njáll bóndi*, one of several instances of this use. See also its use in *Fagrskinna* (above, 170–71); it may be that the status of the *landbūend* is closer to that of ON *óðalsbóndi*, *óðal* (OE *ēðel*) being a term to describe inherited or patrimonial land; Cleasby-Vigfusson, s.v. *óðal*; on *bóndi* and *óðalsbóndi*; see also P. G. Foote and D. M. Wilson, *The Viking Achievement* (London: Sidgwick & Jackson, 1970), 81–82.

micle mearcstapan mōras healdan,
ellorgǣstas. Ðǣr ōðer wæs
þæs þe hīe gewislīcost gewitan meahton,
idese onlīcnes; ōðer earmsceapen[52]
on weres wæstmum wræclāstas træd,
næfne hē wæs māra þonne ǣnig man ōðer;
þone on gēardagum Grendel nemdon
foldbūende; nō hīe fæder cunnon,
hwæþer him ǣnig wæs ǣr ācenned
dyrna gāsta.
(*Bwf* 1345–57[a]).[53]

[I have heard landowners among my people, counselors in my hall, saying that they have seen two such powerful striders of the borderlands, alien visitants, ruling the moors. According to those who were able to distinguish them with certainty, one of the two was in the likeness of a noble woman; the other, [wretchedly] mis-shapen [according to] the [normal] forms of a man, trod upon the paths of the outcast, except that he was greater [in size; in status] than any other man, whom in times past the dwellers on the land called Grendel. They had no knowledge of a father; whether any of the secret [and, hence, evil] visitants had previously engendered him.]

Hrothgar, it seems, has disengaged himself from his feelings and momentarily put aside his anguish; he volunteers descriptions of his tormentors held by his counselors and landowners, as though he were repeating widely disseminated information. The condemnatory metaphors have shifted away from the uncanny into a type of riddling discourse that one associates with rumor and that is at once

---

52. ON *armr* (OE *earm*), used abusively "wretched, wicked," often of witches; ON *arm-skapaðr* (OE *earmsceapen*), "poor, miserable, mis-shapen"; Cleasby-Vigfusson, s.v. *armr, arm-skapaðr*.

53. Elsewhere in *Beowulf*, *dyrne* carries the connotative value of malevolent treachery, as, e.g., lines 2168 and 2290, where *dyrne cræft* carries the implicit sense of "treacherous or malevolent skill."

Chapter Three

deliberately ambiguous and factual. His tormentors are placed in a wider sociopolitical setting of *londbüende, selerædende,* and *foldbüende*: the mother has been transformed from an *ides āglǣcwīf* into a more realistic being who has the "likeness of a noble woman," with the titillating implication that she is not; the two rulers of the moor no longer are described as *mānscaðan* but are referred to as *micle mearc-stapan* "powerful [or large, great] striders of the borderlands," or more specifically, if one takes the ethnic meaning of *mearcstapan*, a hapax legomenon in *Beowulf*, "striders of the land of Mercia." The son's description is more enigmatic: described as wretchedly misshapen in comparison to the physical forms of men; he trod the paths of the outcast, except that, paradoxically, he was greater than any other man, an allusion we at first associate with his physical frame, but the conjunction *næfne* impels us to consider the possibility that *māra* (the comparative of *micle*) refers to his social status as well: Grendel was not only physically large and powerful, but also of elevated social status. The name Grendel, with the implication that he may now have a different name (*þone on gēardagum Grendel nemdon / foldbüende,* "whom dwellers on the land in times past called Grendel"), is meant to be a solution. It is no solution at all, but rather sets the stage for still another mystifying question: the mystery surrounding the name is compounded by the *micle mearcstapa* son's lacking a father, for the dwellers on the land did not know his father, *hwæþer him ænig wæs ǣr ācenned / dyrna gāsta,* (whether any of the secret visitants had previously engendered him).[54] And one may ask, what is the narrative value of this recognizably human description of the erstwhile ghoulish mother and son pairing? Of what value the insertion of this riddling genealogical information, except to mystify and shock the reader/audience programmed to view Heorot's assailants as nightmarish destructive figures of fantasy?

The passage is purposefully cryptic and, I suggest, functions as a reflex of the contemporaneous paternity issue that plagued England's

---

54. Or "whether any mysterious creature had been engendered before him"; thus in Klaeber, 4th ed., 200 n. to 1355^{b}–57^{a}.

counselors after Cnut's death and surrounded the Ælfgifu-Harold Harefoot pairing. The West Saxon landowners found themselves as perplexed by the mother-and-son pairing as do Hrothgar's *landbuend* (landowners) and *selerǣdende* (counselors in the hall), for they, too, had no knowledge of who Harold's father might have been, except that it was unbelievable to them that it could have been Cnut. One might ask why the *witan* found it unbelievable, for Cnut had had an alliance with Ælfgifu for nearly twenty years; issues of that relationship would have been expected, unless, of course, Harold Harefoot had not resembled the tall, good-looking, thin-faced Cnut in the slightest (above, 145) or his alleged brother Sveinn who is described as being "fair in appearance, not fierce in temperament" (above, 145).

Grendel, fatherless Beowulfian assailant of Heorot, unlike his God-fearing antagonist, is described as a misshapen human (*earmsceapen on weres wæstmum*); allusively associated with pagan necromancy for the second time in the poem, he trod the path of the outcast (*wræclāstas trǣd*), with the associative meaning of following a path of pagan wretchedness, a banishment associated with treason and murder. In *Christ and Satan*, it is a failed insurrection against "heaven's luminary, the Son of God" (*wuldres leoman, bearn healendes*, 85ᵇ–86ᵃ) that forces a *hean and earm* (humiliated and wretched) Satan to be deprived of heaven. Large of limbs (*limwæstmum*) and *fah wið god* (in feud with God), he strides the paths of the outcast (*wadan wræclastas*),[55] much like brother-killer Cain, banished from paradise for his sin against his father's kinsman, and much like Harold after he was refused access to the *sacro altari* (sacred *gifstōl*) and the treasures (*māþðum*). Harold's treacherous command to murder his stepbrother Alfred atheling is no less a crime of treason of the highest order. Moreover, the paradoxical claim that the wretched outcast in *Beowulf* was *māra* than any other man suggests a political and social prominence, akin to that of a king, whose power subsumes his crime, as may have been the case with Æthelred and was with Harold; though a criminal, he retains his status as king.

---

55. *Christ and Satan, ASPR*, ed. Krapp, vol. 1, ll. 81–139.

Figures

Figure 1 (this page and opposite). Godwine embraces Alfred in greeting (above left); Alfred as prisoner before Harold Harefoot (above right); the blinding of Alfred (opposite, right), *La estoire de Seint Aedward Le Rei: The Life*

of St. Edward the Confessor, Cambridge, Cambridge University Library, MS CUL Ee.3.59. Reproduced by kind permission of the Syndics of Cambridge University Library.

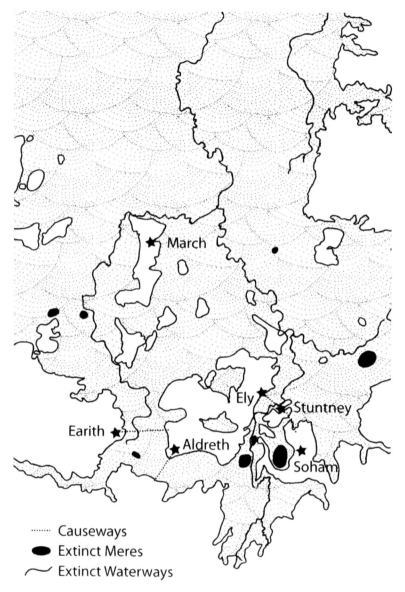

Causeways

Extinct Meres

Extinct Waterways

March

Ely

Stuntney

Earith

Aldreth

Soham

After H.C. Darby, *The Medieval Fenland*

Figure 2. Causeway approach to Ely, adapted from H. C. Darby, *The Medieval Fenland*, 2nd ed. 1974.

Figure 3. Detail of the *Bayeux Tapestry* – 11th Century, Image 15. A Cleric Touches Ælfgyfa's Face. With special permission from the City of Bayeux

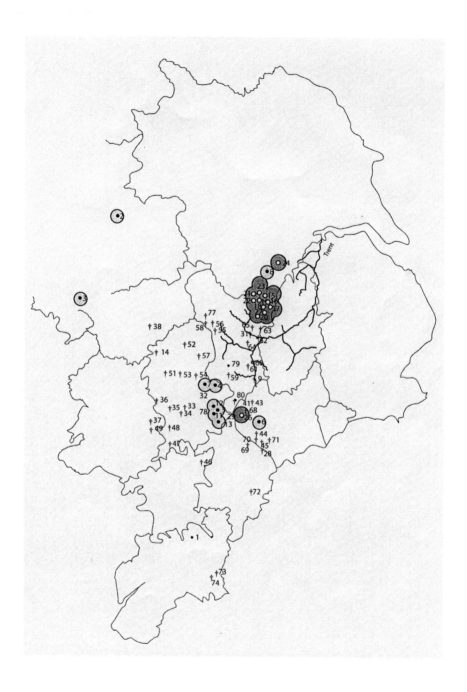

Figure 4 (this page and opposite). Map and legend of the estates in the will of Wilfric Spot, adapted from P. H. Sawyer, *The Charters of Burton Abbey*.

Legend

1. æt Dumeltan (Dumbleton; Archbishop Ælfric)
2. Betux Ribbel & Merse (Between Ribble and Mersey)
3. æt Wirhalum (Wirral; Ælfhelm)
4. Rolfestun (Rolleston; Ælfhelm)
5. Heorlfestun (Harlaston; Ælfhelm)
6. æt Beorelfestune (Barlestone; Wulfheah)
7. æt Mærchamtune (Marchington; Wulfheah)
8. æt Cunugesburh (Conisborough; Ælfhelm)
9. æt Alewaldestune (Wulfheah; [Sawyer does not mark])
10. æt Northtune (Ulfgeat; [Sawyer does not mark])
11. æt Elleforda (Elford; eorman dehter
    [Wulfric's pitiful daughter], with Ælfhelm as protector)
12. æt Acclea (Oakley; eorman dehter
    [Wulfric's pitiful daughter], with Ælfhelm as protector)
13. æt Tamwurthin (Tamworth eorman dehter
    [Wulfric's pitiful daughter], with Ælfhelm as protector)
14. æt Baltrutheleage (Balterley; Wulfgar, retainer)
15. æt Walesho (Wales; Morcar)
16. æt Theogendethorpe (Thorpe Salvin; Morcar)
17. æt Hwitewille (Whitwell; Morcar)
18. æt Clune (Clowne; Morcar)
19. æt Barleburh (Barlborough; Morcar)
20. æt Ducemannestune (Duckmanton; Morcar)
21. æt Moresburh (Mosbrough; Morcar)
22. æt Eccingtune (Eckington; Morcar)
23. æt Bectune (Beighton; Morcar)
24. æt Doneceastre (Doncaster; Morcar)
25. æt Morlingtune (Morcar [Sawyer does not mark])
26. Aldulfestreo (Austery; Morcar's wife Edgyth)
27. æt Paltertune (Palterton; Ælfhelm, kinsman
28. æt Wibbestofte (Wibtoft; Æthelric)
29. æt Twongan (Tonge; Æthelric)
30. Byrtun (Burton upon Trent)
31. Strættun (Stretton)
32. Bromleage (Bromley)
33. Bedintun (Pillaton)
34. Gageleage (Gailey)
35. Witestan (Whiston)
36. Laganford (Longford)
37. Styrcleage (Stirchley)
38. Niwantun æt thære wic (Newton by Middlewich)
39. Wædedun [Sawyer does not mark]
40. Niwantun [Sawyer does not mark]
41. Wineshylle (Winshill)
42. Suttun [Sawyer does not mark]
43. Ticenheale (Ticknall)
44. æt Scenctune (Shenton)
45. æt Wicgestane (Wigston Parva)
46. æt Halen (Halesowen)
47. Hremesleage (Romsley)
48. æt Sciplea (Shipley)
49. æt Suthtune (Sutton Maddock)
50. æt Actune (Sawyer does not mark)
51. Deorlafestun (Darlaston)
52. Rudegeard (Rudyard)
53. Cotewaltune (Cotwalton)
54. Lege (Church Leigh)
55. Acofre (Okeover)
56. Hilum (Ilum)
57. Celfdun (Cauldon)
58. Cætesthyrne (Castern)
59. æt Suthtune (Sutton on the Hill)
60. Morlege (Morley)
61. Brægdeshale (Breadsall)
62. Mortun (Morton)
63. æt Pillesleage (Pilsley)
64. Oggodestun (Ogston)
65. Wynnefeld (North Wingfield)
66. Snodeswic [Sawyer does not mark]
67. æt Tathawyllan (Tathwell, Lincs.
    [Sawyer does not mark]
68. æt Æppebbyg (Appleby Magna)
69. æt Westune (Weston in Arden)
70. Burhtun (Burton Hastings)
71. æt Scearnforda (Sharnford)
72. æt Hereburgebyrig (Harbury)
73. Ealdeswyrthe (Aldsworth)
74. Ælfredingtun (Arlington)
75. Eccleshale [Sawyer does not mark]
76. æt Waddune [Sawyer does not mark]
77. æt Sceon (Sheen)
78. æt Langandune (Longdon;
    community at Tamworth)
79. Bubbandune (Bupton; Bishop/Burton
80. æt Strættune (Stretton; godddaughte
    daughter, Ælfgifu, of Morgar & Eadgut

After Sawyer, *Charters of Burton Abbey*

- ● To Ælfhelm and sons, and to Wulfric's Pitiful Daughter
- ○ To Morcar and his wife, Eadgyth, and their daughter Ælfgifu
- † To Burton Abbey (with Ælfhelm and Archbishop Ælfric as protectors)

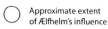
Approximate extent
of Ælfhelm's influence

Approximate extent
of Morcar's influence

Figure 5. Frontispiece, *The Liber Vitae of the New Minster and Hyde Abbey Winchester*, London, British Library, MS Stowe 944, fol. 6r. By permission of the British Library.

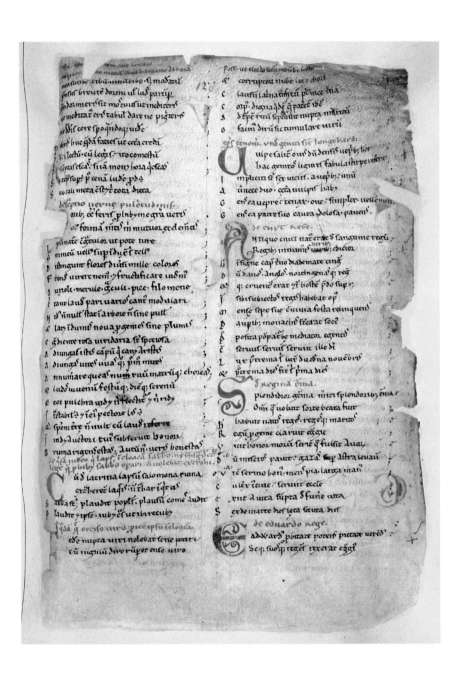

Figure 6. *De regina Emma*, London, British Library, MS Cotton Vitellius A.xii, fol. 131r. By permission of the British Library.

Figure 7. Frontispiece, *Encomium Emmae Reginae*, London, British Library, MS Additional 33241, fol. 1v. By permission of the British Library.

& equitate
Redemptionem misit po
pulo suo. mandauit ine
ternum .testamentum

suum .scm & terribile
nomen eius
Initium sapientiae timor
dni. intellectus bonus

omnibus facientibus ei.
Laudatio eius. manet in
seculum seculi

ALLELVIA REVERSI
BEATVS VIR
quiam & dnm .in
mandatis eius cupit
nimis
Potens in terra erit sem
eius. generatio rectoru
benedicetur
Gloria & diuitiae in domo
eius. & iustitia eius ma
net in seculum seculi
Exortum est intenebris

ONIS AGGEI ET ZACHARIAE ·
lumen rectis corde :
misericors & miserator
& iustus dns
Iocundus homo qui mise
retur & commodat dis
pon & sermones suos in
iudicio. quia in eternu
non commouebitur ;
In memoria eterna erit
iustus. ab auditione ma
la non timebit

· CXI ·
Paratum est cor eius spe
rare in dno . confirmatu
est cor eius non commo
uebitur . donec uideat
inimicos suos | in gla ;
Dispsit dedit pauperibus.
iustitia ei manet in sedm
seculi. cornu eius exaltabit
Peccator uidebit & irascet
dentibus suis fremebit & ta
besc & . desiderii peccatorum p
ibit ;

Figure 8. Psalm 111, *Harley Psalter*, London, British Library, MS Harley 603, fol.
57v. By permission of the British Library.

Figure 9. Beatus Page, *Harley Psalter*, London, British Library, MS Harley 603, fol. 2. By permission of the British Library.

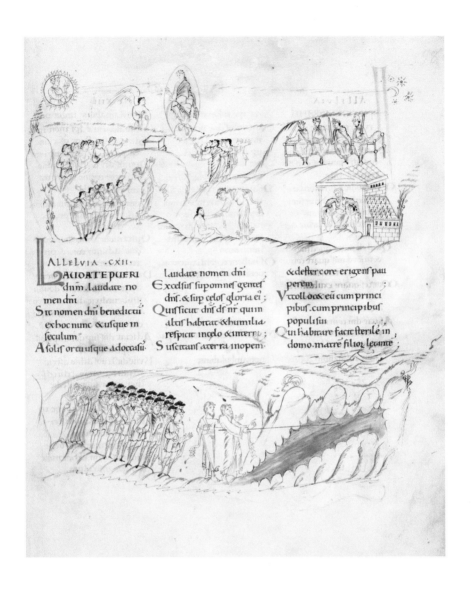

Figure 10. Psalm 112, *Harley Psalter*, London, British Library, MS Harley 603, fol.58r. By permission of the British Library.

Figure 11. Psalm 130, *Harley Psalter*, London, British Library, MS Harley 603, fol. 67v. By permission of the British Library.

CANTICVM. GRADVVM ·CXXXII· in montem fion
ECCE QVAM BO quod defcendit in barba Quo illic mandauit dns
num & quam io barbam aaron benedictionem . & uita
cundum · habitare fratref Quod defcendit in ora ufque in feculum
in unum ueftimenta eiuf · ficut rof
Sicut unguentum in capite · hermon qui defcendit

CANTICVM GRADVVM ·CXXXIII· uraf in fca & benedicite dnm
ECCE NVNC BENE Qui ftatif in domo dni · in a Benedicat te dnf ex ion qui
dicite dnm omnef trif domuf di nri fecit celum & terram
ferui dni In noctibuf extollite man

The Mercian Kin of Ælfgifu

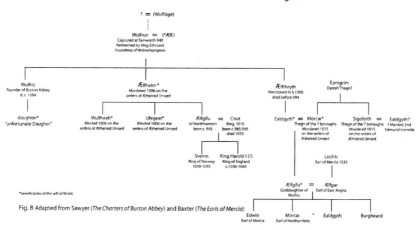

Fig. 8 Adapted from Sawyer (*The Charters of Burton Abbey*) and Baxter (*The Earls of Mercia*)

The Anglo-Danish-Norman Line

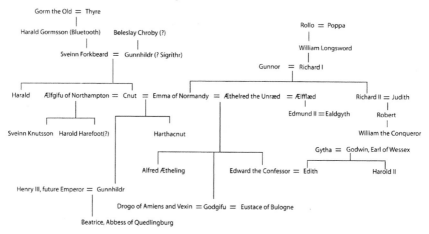

Figure 13 (top). Genealogical diagram: Ælfgifu of Northampton's Mercian kin.
Figure 14 (bottom). Genealogical diagram: the Anglo-Danish-Norman line.

Likewise, the other *micle mearcstapa*, defined as being unlike an *ides*, which in the Beowulfian context denotes a woman of royal rank, holds attributes of Ælfgifu of Northampton. Although Ælfgifu reigned as regent with Sveinn in Norway, she was far from being *sēo hlæfdige* (a term that is used for Cnut's legitimate Norman queen, Emma) in the court, for to an English mind her status was nonetheless that of a counterfeit queen. Like Grendel's mother, who functions as the opposite of the jewel-bedecked and gold-adorned dispenser of treasure reigning in Heorot, not only in structural positioning but in temperament and visage, Ælfgifu of Northampton is portrayed in the historical documents as a mock stereotype of a tyrannical queen. Like Cnut's illegal Mercian consort, who is relegated to holding court in the land of the *Mierce* or, still further from the shores of England, in Wendland and, further north, in Norway, as though she were treading the paths of royal exile, Grendel's mother, in her thirst for revenge, ranges over the wilderness, much as do accursed men cast out of society (OE *wearg*, ON *vargr*). The accursed female sea-wolf (*brimwylf*, 1599[a]) inhabits the sea-plain (*grundwyrgen*, 1518[b]; ON *vargynja*), a term whose connotative value is associated with cannibalism (OE *wearg*, *hearuwearg*; ON *vargr*, "wolf," *vargúlf*, "werewolf"; Goth. *wargiþa*),[56] a character-specific action, reserved only for her and for Grendel, the hateful, bloodthirsty wolf (*heorowearh hetelīc*, 1267[a]) who devours Hondscio hands, feet, and all, drinking his blood and biting his sinews.[57] Grendel's mother, the greedy and gallows-minded (*gīfre*

---

56. Cleasby-Vigfusson, 680; see also Orchard, *Companion to Beowulf*, 155–56.

57. For a discussion of the biblical injunctions against drinking blood known to the Anglo-Saxons from Bede to Ælfric and Wulfstan, see Orchard, *Companion to Beowulf*, 140–41; for the association of blood-drinking with the antediluvian giants in the apocryphal Book of Enoch and its relationship to *Beowulf*, see esp. Robert Kaske, "*Beowulf* and the Book of Enoch," *Speculum* 46 (1971): 421–31, and Ruth Mellinkoff, "Cain's Monstrous Progeny in *Beowulf*: Part I, Noachi tradition," *ASE* 8 (1979): 143–62 , esp. 160. See also Williams, *Cain and Beowulf*, 14–15; Frederick M. Biggs, "I. Enoch," *Sources of Anglo-Saxon Literary Culture: Volume I*, ed. Biggs et al., 25–27.

ond galgmōd, 1277ᵃ) sea-wolf (*brimwylf*, 1599ᵃ), apparently dispatched Æschere in like manner, the motive in both cases being revenge: *Hēo þā fǣhðe wrǣc* (she has avenged the feud, 1333ᵇ). Seven lines later, Hrothgar storms, "*mihtig mānscaða wolde hyre mǣg wrecan, / gē feor hafað fǣhðe gestǣled . . . hreþerbealo hearde*" (the powerful evil-ravager wanted to avenge her kinsman, and greatly fueled the feud . . . the heavy-heart sorrow, 1339-40, 1343ᵃ), he himself calling for retaliation. Mother and son rule over the wolf slopes (*wulfhleoþu*, 1358ᵃ), or hillocks and slopes belonging to the wolves, suggesting that this association may be an identifying attribute. Such are the night-raiders of Heorot, who snatch warriors from their resting places and feast upon them as carrion in their endeavor to gain full dominion over the hall.

"Men driven by avarice," Lady Philosophy explains to Boethius, "are like wolves." She concludes her lesson of sins and their physical manifestation by remarking to the poet that though "wicked men cease to be what they were," they retain the "appearance of their human bodies . . . show[ing] that they once were men."[58] Human bestiality in itself is not a remarkably rare trait but is rather common for those involved in grasping kingdoms in England's history; the accessions to the thrones of England in the tenth and eleventh centuries provide ample narratives of fratricide and assassination, and of revenge, as Keynes, Stafford, and Charles Isley, among others, have illustrated.[59] It is of interest that Ælfgifu of Northampton inhabited lands belonging to the kin of Wulfrun, her grandmother, landed gentry of renown whose alliance Sveinn and Cnut needed if they were to rise as kings of England. It is thus with the Wulfs of Mercia, the owners of the *wulfhleoþu*, where the seeds of revenge that led to

---

58. Boethius, *The Consolation of Philosophy*, trans. Richard Green (New York: Bobbs-Merrill Co., 1962), book 4, prose 3, pp. 82–83; the standard edition is Ludwig Bieler, *Boethii Philosophiae Consolatio* (Turnhout: Brepols, 1957), book 4, prose 3, ll. 15–21, pp. 71–72.

59. Keynes, *Diplomas*, passim; Stafford, "Sons and Mothers," 79–100, as one of several instances in which she addresses the topic; see also Charles Isley, "Politics, Conflict, and Kinship in Early Eleventh-Century Mercia," *Midland History* 26 (2001): 28–42.

Chapter Three

the outrage of the 1036 assassination may lie, that I will conclude this pair of chapters on the early decades of the eleventh century, when *Dene comon ond frið namon*, a past that radiates through the poem's narrative present.

Ælfgifu of Northampton and the Wulfrun kin

It was sometime around 1013, in the midst of Sveinn Forkbeard and Cnut's fateful invasion of England, that Cnut probably allied himself with Ælfgifu of Northampton. Cnut's alliance with Ælfgifu was not without political advantage to the Danish takeover of England, for Ælfgifu was a member of perhaps the most powerful Mercian family. Daughter of Ælfhelm, earl of Northampton and Northumberland, she was the granddaughter of the lady Wulfrun, who had been captured during a raid on Tamworth in 940 by Olaf Guthfrithsson, overlord of York and the Five Boroughs until his death in 941.[60] A person of some value to have been ransomed back by the English,[61] Wulfrun founded Wolverhampton, *æt Hēantūne*, the *hēah tūn* or chief manor of the lady Wulfrun, given to her by Æthelred in 985 a few years after he had become king.[62] She was perhaps the daughter of Wulfsige the Black

---

60. *ASC* D-text, s.a. 943 (for 940); Williams, *Æthelred the Unready*, 33; Dorothy Whitelock, "The Dealings of the Kings of England with Northumbria," in *The Anglo-Saxons*, ed. Clemoes, 80; Phillip Pulsiano, "Norse in England," in *Medieval Scandinavia*, ed. Pulsiano et al., 166–70, at 167. John of Worcester's identification of a Wulfrun as Ælfgifu's mother may have been a confusion for her grandmother, although John is the chief source for the materials on Ælfgifu's kin; *JWChron* [1035] ii.520–21.
61. In his discussion of Wulfrun, Peter Sawyer makes note of the D-Chronicler's tone, intimating that she was a woman of some prominence; Sawyer, *Charters of Burton Abbey*, xl; see also Williams, *Æthelred the Unready*, 33.
62. P. H. Reaney, *The Origin of English Place-Names* (London: Routledge and Paul, 1960), 144–45. The town was originally called *hēahtūne* ("at the high village or estate"), with *Wolver-* added later by Ælfgifu's grandmother, the lady Wulfrun; see also Kenneth Cameron, *English Place-Names* (London: P. T. Batsford, 1996), 144. For a history and description of Wolverhampton in the Anglo-Saxon period, see D. Hooke, "Wolverhampton: The Town

(*maurus, se blaca*), whom Ann Williams characterizes as the "Mercian magnate," for as Williams suggests, his estates, granted to him by King Edmund (ca. 942), spanned Derbyshire and Staffordshire[63] and comprised most of the land with which Wulfrun endowed Wolverhampton minster in the early years of the 990s.[64] Upon her death, Wulfrun's considerable estate passed on to her son Wulfric Spot, Ælfgifu's uncle, founder of the Benedictine house of Burton Abbey, who thus became the head of one of the wealthiest and most influential of landed Mercian families in tenth-century England.[65]

---

and Its Monastery," in D. Hooke and T. R. Slater, *Anglo-Saxon Wolverhampton* (Wolverhampton, UK: Wolverhampton Borough Council, 1986), 5–28, esp. 17–20.

63. Williams proposes that the relationship of Wulfrun to Wulfsige may have been more than that of kinswoman precisely because of the line of inheritance; the lands in Derbyshire and Staffordshire came first to her and then to her son Wulfric Spot; Williams, *Æthelred the Unready*, 33, 58; likewise, Sawyer, *Charters of Burton Abbey*, xxiv, xl, xlii–xlvii, 48, and Burton Charters, nos. 5–7, 27; see also P. H. Sawyer, *Anglo-Saxon Charters: An Annotated List and Bibliography* (London: Royal Historical Society, 1968), nos. 479, 484, 860, 878, 1380, 1606.

64. See Sawyer's summary of Wulfrun's Charter (*Charters of Burton Abbey*, xl), which he places at 994; see also his discussion of the transference of Wulfsige's lands to Wulfrun and Wulfric, inclusive of Bromley and Stretton (xxvii [Doncaster], xxviii [Bromley, Stretton], xliii–xlvii, and nos. 31, 32); Sawyer, *Anglo-Saxon Charters*, 1380 (Wulfrun's foundation charter); see also Hooke, "Wolverhampton," 17–18.

65. On Wulfric and Ælfhelm's prominence as subscribers in the diplomas issued between 980 and 1002 at Æthelred's court, and thereafter that of Ælfhelm, his son Wulfheah, and Wulfgeat, possibly their kin, see Keynes, *Diplomas*, 188–90; see also Sawyer, *Charters of Burton Abbey*, xiii–xliii, esp. xxii, xliii; Whitelock, *Anglo-Saxon Wills*, 46–51, 151–60. Wulfric owned an estate at Tamworth, inherited from his godfather, which he bequeathed to his daughter, who may have been disabled in some way until her death (Sawyer, *Charters of Burton Abbey*, xxii; Whitelock, *Anglo-Saxon Wills*, 46.27–48.5). Wulfric seems to have been closely connected with the community at Tamworth, historically a royal center, bequeathing to them *at Longdon* (Sawyer, *Charters of Burton Abbey*, xix, xxxiv; Whitelock, *Anglo-Saxon Wills*, 50.3).

Wulfric's will bequeaths holdings spanning some ten shires, Cheshire, Derbyshire, Gloucestershire, Leicestershire, Lincolnshire, Shropshire, Staffordshire, Warwickshire, Worcestershire, and Yorkshire,[66] probably comparable in size to a modest kingdom (fig. 4).[67]

Twenty-ninth of thirty-four charters in the Burton repository, the will provides the bulk of the information about the extent of the power and privilege of Wulfrun's immediate kin, identified by the recurrence of personal and dynastic naming patterns of alliteration (*Wulf-/Ælf*).[68] Eleven estates, eight of which lay in Yorkshire and Derbyshire, were bequeathed to Morcar, Wulfric's nephew-in-law and leading thane of the Five Boroughs,[69] one estate to his wife, Ealdgyth

---

66. For a discussion of the estates in Wulfric's will, see Sawyer, *Charters of Burton Abbey*, xxiii–xxxiv, and no. 29; see also Whitelock, *Anglo-Saxon Wills*, 153–59; Williams, *Æthelred the Unready*, 33–37.

67. On the monetary value of the estates, see Sawyer, *Charters of Burton Abbey*, xliv–xlv; as customary, the first bequest of the will was to King Æthelred, which was a combination of a heriot due from an earl and that of a thane (OE *heregeatu*, death-dues, often associated with the return of a gift of weapons, symbolic of the obligations owed the king by nobility); Sawyer, *Charters of Burton Abbey*, xx–xxi; Williams, *Æthelred the Unready*, 33–34; Richard Abels, "Heriot," in *Blackwell Encyclopaedia*, ed. Lapidge et al., 235–36; on lordship, see Baxter, *Earls of Mercia*, 206–17.

68. Wulfrun's charter to Wolverhampton (994), summarized by Sawyer, gives the name of her daughter as Ælfthryth (*Elfthrith*) and that of a kinsman, Wulfgeat, whose "crimes needed expiation," the same Wulfgeat who had been granted lands by King Edgar in 963 (Sawyer, *Charters of Burton Abbey*, xl, 32–33). Sawyer posits the existence of an unnamed husband, whose name, Sawyer suggests, based on the naming patterns given the children, probably began with *Ælf-*; Sawyer, *Charters of Burton Abbey*, xl; Sawyer, *Anglo-Saxon Charters*, 1380; Sawyer proposes that the remaining charters in the repository may have concerned members of the Wulfrun kin (xlviii–xlix); further on Wulfgeat, see Keynes, *Diplomas*, 210–11; Williams, *Æthelred the Unready*, 34–36, 69–70; Whitelock, *Anglo-Saxon Wills*, 164–65.

69. Sawyer, *Charters of Burton Abbey*, xviii–xix; for Morcar's estates, see xxvi–xxvii. The Five Boroughs, at times referred to as the Seven Boroughs, consist of Leicester, Nottingham, Derby, Stamford, and Lincoln; when cited as Seven Boroughs (as in *ASC* C-text, s.a. 1015), they could possibly include

(Wulfric's niece and daughter of his deceased sister, Ælfthryth), and yet another, along with a brooch that belonged to her grandmother, to their daughter, Wulfric's goddaughter, Ælfgifu.[70] Curiously, no provision in the will is made for his other niece, Ælfgifu of Northampton; but, as Peter Sawyer and Ann Williams suggest, she may have already been amply provided for by her father, Ælfhelm.[71] The will also points to a kinship between the families of Leofric, Wulfric, and Ælfhelm, which would have been of some importance to Ælfgifu of Northampton in the turbulent years of 1035 and 1036. Members of Leofric's family held several of the estates belonging to Wulfsige the Black and the Wulfrun kin, among which were Bromley (where Leofric himself died) and Stretton; Elleforda, originally bequeathed to Wulfric's daughter, was one of several held by Ælfgar, Leofric's son.[72] The ties between Leofric's family and the Wulfrun kin were further strengthened when sometime before 1035 Ælfgar married Morcar's daughter Ælfgifu, possibly the namesake of Ælfgifu of

---

either Lindsey and Hatfield, Torksey and York, or York and Bamborough; N. J. Higham, "Five Boroughs," in *Blackwell Encyclopaedia*, ed. Lapidge et al., 186; Williams, *Æthelred the Unready*, 120.

70. There is no definite date of birth for Morcar and Eadgyth's daughter, but it would fall after 994 (the date of Ælfthryth's death), possibly between 1002, when the will might have been drawn up, and 1004, the possible date of Wulfric's death; Sawyer, *Charters of Burton Abbey*, xix–xx. Her name is not recorded in the bequest, but it is generally accepted that she was the Ælfgifu who married Earl Leofric's son Ælfgar; see, e.g., Williams, *Æthelred the Unready*, 132; Sawyer, *Charters of Burton Abbey*, xliii.

71. Sawyer and Williams suggest she may have been too young to be included, but that would make her younger than her namesake, Morcar's daughter, who became the wife of Leofric's son Ælfgar; Sawyer, *Charters of Burton Abbey*, xii; Williams, *Æthelred the Unready*, 120n56.

72. Sawyer, *Charters of Burton Abbey*, xxiv, xxvi, xxix, xxx–xxxi, xliii; for the kin-alliance between Wulfrun's kin and that of Leofric, see particularly Baxter, *Earls of Mercia*, 22, 24–25, 35–37, 59, 139, 144, 165, 180–81, 241; much of their tenurial lands fell in the same shires as those in Wulfric's will (Baxter, 150; see also appendices 2–4).

Northampton, and thus forged a link between a future *konungsmóðir* of England and the house of Leofric.[73]

Wulfric's prominence and the royal favors bestowed upon him and his family by Edmund through Æthelred were part of a policy of national unification followed by the tenth-century kings of Wessex that produced a core of English nobility in Mercia and Northumbria, whose landed wealth and privilege were, as Pauline Stafford notes, "unparalleled" in early England, and whose loyalty was expected to remain entirely with the king.[74] Upon Wulfric's death between 1002 and 1004, the head of the Wulfrun kin became Ælfgifu's father, Ælfhelm, a man of considerable moral stature, with land and means in his own right.[75] Wulfric appointed him protector of his own daughter and of the forty-eight estates he bequeathed to Burton Abbey.[76] Ælfhelm's inheritance from his brother was substantial. Along with his son Wulfheah, he was granted the land between the rivers Ribble and Mersey, which marked the sensitive border between northwest Mercia and Northumbria, and also Wirral, the promontory between the Mersey and the Dee,[77] lands whose inclusion as part of Mercia

---

73. Sawyer, *Charters of Burton Abbey*, xlii–xliii; Ann Williams, *The English and the Norman Conquest* (Woodbridge, UK: Boydell Press, 1995), 54–55nn41, 43; for a summary of the life of Ælfgifu, Morcar's daughter and Ælfgar's wife, see Baxter, *Earls of Mercia*, 299–301.

74. Pauline A. Stafford, "Reign of Æthelred II," 15–46, esp. 17–21, 31–33; Williams, *Æthelred the Unready*, 58; Patrick Wormald, "Engla Lond: The Making of an Allegiance," *Journal of Historical Sociology* 7 (1994): 1–24.

75. He gave Cotingham, Middleton, and Benefield to the Peterborough monastery; *The Chronicle of Hugh Candidus*, ed. W. T. Mellows (London and New York: Oxford University Press, 1949), 69; on his possible ownership of several of the Burton charters, see Sawyer, *Charters of Burton Abbey*, xiii.

76. Sawyer, *Charters of Burton Abbey*, xviii, xix.

77. Separately, Wulfheah also received Barlaston and Marchington in Staffordshire, and Alvaston in Derbyshire; his brother Ufegeat received only Northtune, perhaps because he may have lacked appropriate interest in monastic matters and reform that characterized his uncle and father; Sawyer, *Charters of Burton Abbey*, xviii, xxiv–xxvi.

was apparently due to the military and independent political genius of Æthelflæd, Lady of the Mercians and daughter of King Alfred, whose policies between 902 and 918 toward the Scandinavian and Irish-Norsemen who attacked her borders were largely those of "assimilation rather than expulsion."[78] Ælfhelm also received Rolleston and Harlaston (in Staffordshire, near Burton) and the vast estate of Conisborough (*Cunugesburh*, "the king's stronghold") in Yorkshire, just below the Humber.[79]

At the end of the tenth century and the beginning decade of the eleventh, then, the Wulfrun kin possessed a sizable portion of the northern border that divided Mercia and Northumberland. They were, so to speak, *mearcstapan*, "striders of the land of Mercia," and its borders, accepting both senses of the term. A constant presence in Æthelred's court, they may have been among the strong Mercian voices in support of Æthelred rather than Edward in the succession politics that raged in the court between Edgar's death in 975 and Edward's assassination.[80] They held a place among the king's leading counselors, among whom were the king's mother Ælfthryth and uncle, Æthelweard the Chronicler, and Æthelweard's son Æthelmær, who retired to his monastery Eynsham in 1005 and in 1015, as ealdorman of southwest

---

78. For the political and strategic importance of this region, see M. A. Atkin, "'The Land Between Ribble and Mersey' in the Early Tenth Century," in *Names, Places and People: An Onomastic Miscellany in Memory of John McNeal Dodgson*, ed. Alexander R. Rumble and A. D. Mills (Stamford, UK: Paul Watkins, 1997), 8–18, esp. 10–12, 17–18, quote at 8; according to Sawyer, Wulfric's will establishes that the land was not in royal control in the first years of the eleventh century, but was appropriated by Æthelred after Ælfhelm's murder in 1006 (*Charters of Burton Abbey*, xxiv).

79. Sawyer calculates the area as encompassing ninety OE carucates (a measure of ploughland varying with the lay of the land); Sawyer, *Charters of Burton Abbey*, xxv.

80. Stafford, "Ælfthryth," in *Blackwell Encyclopaedia*, ed. Lapidge et al., 9; Stafford, "Sons and Mothers," 80–81; Sean Miller, "Edward the Martyr," in *Blackwell Encylopaedia*, ed. Lapidge et al., 163; Ann Williams, *Kingship and Government in Pre-Conquest England, c. 500-1066* (New York: St. Martin's Press, 1999), 103.

England, submitted to Sveinn, apparently willingly.[81] In the context of the northward expansion of West Saxon rule, Æthelred's appointment of Ælfhelm as ealdorman of Northumbria in 993 was a politically astute move whereby a loyal Mercian family would have administrative control over an unstable Northumbria,[82] but it may also have been his sign of gratitude for the ealdorman's support.

In 1006, Ælfhelm was duplicitously invited to a feast at Shrewsbury by the king's counselor, Eadric Streona, who posed as his friend and host and then arranged to have him ambushed and murdered while riding in the hunt, apparently on the orders of King Æthelred.[83] In the very same year, Æthelred ordered the blinding of Ælfhelm's sons, Wulfheah and Ufegeat, at the royal estate at Cookham, and stripped Wulfgeat, possibly their kin, of "his possessions and of every dignity" because of his "unjust judgements and arrogant deeds" (*propter iniusta iudicia et superba que gesserat opera, possessionibus omnique honore priuauit*).[84] One might see these fortuitously timed demises

81. Keynes, *Diplomas*, 188–208; Isley, "Politics, Conflict, and Kinship," 30–32; N. J. Higham, *The Death of Anglo-Saxon England* (Phoenix Mill, UK: Sutton Publishing Limited, 1997), 58–59.

82. For the political importance of Ælfhelm's appointment as ealdorman of Northumbria in the context of the expansion of West Saxon rule in the north, see Whitelock, "Dealings," 79–80. As early as 993, Ælfhelm signs as *dux Transhumbranae gentis* in Wulfrun's charter for Wolverhampton.

83. *JWChron* ii.456–59 (s.a. 1006) (there is a slight omission in translation on 459); Sawyer, *Charters of Burton Abbey*, xliii; *ASC* E-text, s.a. 1006, does not record Eadric as being involved in the assassination of Ælfhelm; Whitelock, "Dealings," 80–81; Keynes, *Diplomas*, 211–14; Ann Williams, "Cockles Amongst the Wheat: Danes and English in the West Midlands in the First Half of the Eleventh Century," *Midland History* 11 (1986): 1–22, at 3–5.

84. *JWChron* ii, quote at 456; *ASC* C-, D-, E-text, s.a. 1006; Keynes, *Diplomas*, 210–12; Whitelock, "Dealings," 70–88; Williams, *Æthelred the Unready*, 69–71; on Wulfgeat, see Whitelock, "Dealings," 80–81; Williams, *Æthelred the Unready*, 33–36, 120; Keynes, "Crime and Punishment in the Reign of King Æthelred the Unready," in *People and Places in Northern Europe: Essays in Honour of Peter Hayes Sawyer*, ed. Ian N. Wood and Niels

as Æthelred's intended purge of Ælfgifu's kin,[85] but the complete annihilation was not to occur until 1015. At the *mycel gemōt* (great council) at Oxford summoned by Æthelred, her cousins Morcar and his brother Sigeferth, leading thanes of the Five Boroughs, were assassinated by Eadric Streona, again on the orders of Æthelred,[86] their lands and possessions confiscated by the king, and Sigeferth's wife confined in the monastery at Malmesbury. It is reasonable to conjecture that the treachery and assassinations committed against her family in the early eleventh century would have been impressed on the mind of Ælfgifu of Northampton and may have produced a certain amount of enmity between Cnut's future unofficial consort and the house of Æthelred, an enmity that culminated at last in 1036 with the blinding of Alfred atheling, son of Æthelred and Emma of Normandy, on the orders of Harold Harefoot, Ælfgifu's son. Long-lasting feuds were not out of the ordinary in Anglo-Saxon England, one example being the feud that commenced with the murder of Uhtred (kin of the house of Bamburgh and Ælfhelm's successor) by Thurbrand Hold (on Cnut's orders) in 1016, which lasted until 1073 or 1074.[87] For it is difficult not to notice the broad parallelism in setting, characters, and action between the 1006 Æthelred/Eadric betrayal of Ælfhelm and his sons and the Harold/Godwine betrayal

---

Lund (Woodbridge, UK and Rochester, NY: Boydell Press, 1991), 80–81 and n. 90. See also Isley, "Politics, Conflict, and Kinship," 30–31.

85.   Keynes compares the effect of these murders to that of a "palace revolution"; *Diplomas*, 211.

86.   *ASC* C-text, s.a. 1015 (has Seven Boroughs, see above, n. 69); Whitelock, "Dealings," 80, 87; Williams, *Æthelred the Unready*, 120; *JWChron* ii.478–81 (s.a. 1015). On the geographical centrality of Oxford as the meeting place for major councils involving the conflict of interest between Mercia and Wessex, see John Blair, *Anglo-Saxon Oxfordshire* (Oxford: Sutton Publishing, 1994), 158–59.

87.   See Whitelock, "Dealings," 82–84; see also *Marriage and Murder in Eleventh-Century Northumbria: A Study of "De Obsessione Dunelmi,"* ed. and trans. Christopher Morris (York, UK: University of York, 1992), esp. 2–3, 7, 20–25. *De obsessione Dunelmi* is found in Cambridge, Corpus Christi College MS 139.

of Æthelred's son Alfred atheling in 1036, duplicitously welcomed and invited to a feast, only subsequently to be blinded and abandoned as dead in the wilds of Ely.

The assassination of Ælfhelm and the mutilation of his sons represented what Keynes describes as the "tip of the iceberg" in court politics.[88] Along with the increasing intensity of Danish attacks, a number of events coalesced to bring about a radical change in the power structure of Æthelred's court, beginning with the death of the king's mother, Ælfthryth, around 1001,[89] his second marriage to and consecration of Emma of Normandy in 1002, and the start of a succession crisis caused by the birth of Edward in 1005 that continued beyond Æthelred's death on 23 April 1016. Edward's birth and his claim to the English throne jeopardized the succession rights of the king's sons by his first wife, Æthelstan and his brothers, Edmund and Eadred. Æthelstan's will, confirmed on the day he died (25 June 1014), reveals significant ties between him and several of the king's core advisers, who apparently withdrew voluntarily or were ousted from Æthelred's court between 1005 and 1006, around the year of Edward's birth.[90] More critically, the will discloses strong political bonds between Æthelstan atheling and the northeastern Mercian and East Anglian nobility, among whom were Ælfgifu's cousins, Morcar and Sigeferth, suggesting that the prince's political power base lay in northeastern Mercian territories.[91] The relationship between the

88. Keynes, *Diplomas*, 213.

89. Ælfthryth (died 17 November between 999 and 1001) had been a constant presence at court during the 980s and 990s, and her importance is underlined by the fact that Æthelred's son Æthelstan thanked his grandmother in his will for bringing him up (*and Ælfþryðe minre Ealdemodor þe me afedde*); Whitelock, *Anglo-Saxon Wills*, no. 20, 56–63, quote at 62; see also Isley, "Politics, Conflict, and Kinship," 30–32.

90. Whitelock, *Anglo-Saxon Wills*, 56–63, no. 20; Higham, *Death of Anglo-Saxon England*, 44–47, 56–59; Keynes, *Diplomas*, 267; Keynes, *EER* [xxi n.1]; Keynes, "Æthelstan ætheling," in *Blackwell Encyclopaedia*, ed. Lapidge et al., 17.

91. Whitelock, *Anglo-Saxon Wills*; Stafford, "Reign of Æthelred II," 35–36; Higham, *Death of Anglo-Saxon England*, 42–47; Isley, "Politics, Conflict, and

prince and Morcar, for example, may have been similar in nature to that which exists between a lord and his man, a relationship that may have been more appropriate for the thanes of the Seven Boroughs to have held with King Æthelred himself, and it may be of interest to speculate on what the king's reaction to the will might have been. Æthelstan, for example, bequeathed a coat of mail he had previously given to Morcar (*þære byrnan, þe mid Morkære is*) as part of his heriot to the king.[92] To Morcar's brother Sigeferth, the atheling bequeathed a sword, shield, and horse, and property in Hockliffe, Bedfordshire.[93] It is perhaps their crucial relationship with Æthelstan that secured the brothers' survival during the purge of the Wulfrun kin in 1006, for not only did Morcar continue to be a recipient of the king's favor,[94] but both he and Sigeferth were prominent members of the king's court at Oxford until 1015, at which time they were assassinated, after Æthelstan's death.

Moreover, the king's Northumbrian replacement of Ælfhelm with Uhtred of Bamburgh, who himself could very well have been a member of the Wulfrun kin as Williams suggests,[95] and the further enhancement of Uhtred's status by giving him his daughter Æthelgifu in marriage around 1009, could have been acts of appeasement for Ælfhelm's assassination, although the latter may only have signaled either a shift in Æthelred's expansion policies regarding Northumbria,[96] or his need to retain some shred of loyalty and influence in the Seven Boroughs and Northumbria in order to repel

Kinship," 30–32.

92. Whitelock, *Anglo-Saxon Wills*, no. 20, at 58, l. 16; Sawyer, *Anglo-Saxon Charters*, 1503; Baxter, *Earls of Mercia*, 205–7.

93. Whitelock, *Anglo-Saxon Wills*, no. 20, at 60, ll. 11–13.

94. Williams, *Æthelred the Unready*, 112n10; Sawyer, *Charters of Burton Abbey*, nos. 32 (1009), 34 (1011), 37 (1012) deal with lands given Morcar by Æthelred (Sawyer, *Anglo-Saxon Charters*, nos. 922 [1009], 924 [1011], 928 [1012]).

95. Williams, *Æthelred the Unready*, 74–75, 194n42; see Sawyer, *Charters of Burton Abbey*, xli, 7, 22; nos. 3, 9, 13.

96. Whitelock, "Dealings," 80.

Danish attacks. By the end of 1006, the power structure of Æthelred's court, which had been tilted toward the nobility of northern Mercia and East Anglia, had shifted to Wessex with the support of the West Mercian political faction, headed by Eadric Streona, leader of the Magonsaete, whose domain lay just south of Ribble and Mersey and the Wirral, lands previously held by Ælfhelm. Thus, the main beneficiaries of Ælfhelm's death were Æthelred and his henchman Eadric Streona, whom he appointed ealdorman of all of Mercia (*ealdorman geond Myrcena rice*) and chief adviser to the king,[97] and Emma of Normandy's son Edward atheling. The succession crisis and its accompanying assassination of 1036 may have had its source in the 1006 power clashes between the northeastern Mercia magnates, who endorsed Æthelstan atheling, and Æthelred, who with the coalition of West Saxon and Magonsaete lords championed Emma of Normandy's son, the Anglo-Norman Edward atheling.[98]

By late summer of 1013, the titular head of the Wulfrun kin was Morcar, and most probably it was with him that Sveinn contracted the alliance between Cnut and Ælfgifu.[99] As recorded by the *Anglo-Saxon Chronicle*, on or slightly before August 1013 Sveinn touched on English soil at Sandwich, but instead of following his usual pattern of ravaging the south of England, he sailed around "East Anglia into the mouth of the Humber, and so up along the Trent" to strike camp at Gainsborough,[100] deep in Mercian territory, apparently without

---

97. Keynes, *Diplomas*, 209–14; Stafford, "Reign of Æthelred II," 33–36.

98. See, further, Williams's observation of the similarities between the succession dispute between Edward and Æthelred of 975 and that of 1035, when again the contending parties were the Mercians and the West Saxons; *Kingship and Government*, 103.

99. Higham, *Death of Anglo-Saxon England*, 58–59; Howard, *Swein Forkbeard's Invasions*, 107–8, 116; Lawson, *Cnut*, 47, 60, 131–32; Stafford, "Reign of Æthelred II," 35.

100. *Eastenglum into Humbramuþan, and swa upweard and lang Trentan oð he com to Genesburuh*; Ashdown, *English and Norse Documents*, 60–61; also *JWChron* ii.472–73 [1013]; *ASC* C-, D-, E-texts, s.a. 1013, in *ASC* vol. 1, s.a. 1013.

incurring any opposition from the Mercians, but rather receiving their immediate submission:

sona beah Uhtred eorl *and* ealle Norðhymbre to him, *and* eal þæt folc on Lindesige *and* siððan þæt folc intó Fifburhingu*m*, *and* raðe þæs eall here benorðan Wæclingastræte, *and* him man sealde gislas of ælcere scire.

[Uhtred submitted to him without delay, and all Northumbria with him, and all the people of Lindsey, and then the people belonging to the Five Towns, and soon after that all the Danes that had settled north of Watling Street, and he was given hostages from every shire.][101]

This apparently preplanned alliance between Sveinn and the Mercians and Northumbrians, the "Gainsborough Accord,"[102] possibly brought about by Æthelred's continued distancing himself from Æthelstan atheling and further aggravated by the king's hiring of Thorkell Hávi and Óláfr Haraldsson as mercenaries, made possible Sveinn's victorious sweep through Mercia. Sveinn's subsequent march through the southwest, with the ready submission of Æthelmær, former member of Æthelred's *witan*, brought to a close the retaliation of those who had been either forced to resign or ousted from Æthelred's court during the purge of 1005–6.

Sveinn's victory could not have been achieved without the compliance of the leading Mercian nobility, chief among whom were Ælfgifu's cousins, Morcar and Sigeferth, and their coalition with Uhtred of Northumbria, a coalition that reflects the Mercians' urgent need to recapture political potency in Æthelred's court, lost with Ælfhelm's assassination and the purge of 1006.[103] Cnut's alliance with Ælfgifu thus sealed a political pact that was not without advantage to the northeastern Mercians. Although it was an alliance in *more*

---

101. Ashdown, *English and Norse Documents*, 60–61.
102. The phrase is Higham's; *Death of Anglo-Saxon England*, 56–59.
103. Howard, *Swein Forkbeard's Invasions*, 107–8; for the stages of Sveinn's campaign route, see 111–20; Higham, *Death of Anglo-Saxon England*, 56–59.

Chapter Three

Danico (a handfast match), and not recognized by the Church,[104] it was, nonetheless, essential to Sveinn's Danish takeover of England, for without it, he might not have been able to defeat the Danish-Norwegian coalition of Thorkell Hávi and Óláfr Haraldsson, who had joined ranks with Æthelred's English army, commanded by Eadric Streona.[105] In December 1013, Æthelred sailed to Normandy, joining Queen Emma and her sons, under the protection of Duke Richard II, Emma's brother. Four months after he had struck camp at Gainsborough, Sveinn rose as sole king of England. Such was the political potency of Ælfgifu's Mercian kin.

The first Anglo-Danish reign, however, was brief. On 3 February 1014, Sveinn died, and although Cnut was chosen successor and king by the troops at Gainsborough, before Easter Æthelred was again king of England, his return having been negotiated with the English counselors by Edward, obviously his chosen heir apparent. Æthelred sailed to England on ships provided by Thorkell Hávi. Supported by Thorkell and Óláfr Haraldsson *inn digri* (the stout, immense), the future Óláfr *helgi* (saint) of Norway,[106] Æthelred stormed Lindsey, caught Cnut and the Mercians unprepared, and impelled Cnut to seek haven in Denmark, not to return to England until 1015,[107] and one wonders what role Uhtred might have played in the surprise attack, since Cnut ordered his execution after he became full king of England.

On 25 June 1014, Æthelstan atheling died, leaving a will that, as noted above, associated him with the Mercian leaders Morcar and Sigeferth. When the *mycel gemōt* (great council) convened at Oxford

---

104. Williams, *Kingship and Government*, 198n67; Lawson, *Cnut*, 131–32.
105. Peter Sawyer, "Cnut's Scandinavian Empire," in *Reign of Cnut*, ed. Rumble, 17.
106. Williams, *Kingship and Government*, 99–100; Dorothy Whitelock, *English Historical Documents c. 500-1042* (London: Eyre & Spottiswoode, 1979), hereafter *EHD* vol. 1, no. 13; Sawyer, "Cnut's Scandinavian Empire," 17–18.
107. *ASC* C-text, s.a. 1014; Ashdown, *English and Norse Documents*, 103–4nn25, 27–28.

in August 1015, Æthelred ordered their assassination, confiscated their lands, and incarcerated Sigeferth's wife at the monastery at Malmesbury. In September 1015, in open defiance of his father, and avenging the assassination of his friends, Edmund atheling rode first to Malmesbury where he married Sigeferth's widow, and thence on 8 September to the Seven Boroughs, where he seized Morcar and Sigeferth's lands and *þæt folc eal him tobeah* (all the people submitted to him).[108] Like Æthelstan before him, Edmund was determined to fight for the throne of England in opposition to the sons of Emma of Normandy. Concurrently, Cnut landed at Sandwich to claim his inheritance, and between 1015 and 1016 he battled for England. On 23 April 1016, Æthelred died, and Edmund was chosen king, defending "his kingdom valiantly during his day" (*and hé his rice heardlice werode þá hwile þe hís tima wæs*).[109] After six months of continuous and intense combat, finally at the battle of Ashington (18 October 1016), provisions were made for the partition of the kingdom, Edmund to rule Wessex, and Cnut, Mercia (*feng Eadmund to Westsexan and Cnut to Myrcan*).[110] On 30 November 1016, Edmund died. A few months later, Cnut succeeded to the entire realm, with Ælfgifu of Northampton apparently as his unofficial consort, though the match remained unacceptable to the Church.

In 1017, after his coronation as king of England,[111] in order to secure his political position in England and to avoid a possible succession

---

108. *ASC* C-text, s.a. 1015; *JWChron* [1015], ii.480–81, names Sigeferth's wife as *Aldgyth*, which is the name of Morcar's wife and Wulfric's niece in Wulfric's will. Sigeferth was not among the beneficiaries of Wulfric's will.
109. *ASC* C-text, s.a. 1016.
110. *JWChron* ii.486–93 [1016]; Keynes, *EER* [lvi–lvii]; Williams, *Kingship and Government*, 100–101; *ASC* C-text, s.a. 1016.
111. *ASC*, s.a. 1017; Williams, *Kingship and Government*, 101, 196n28; for Cnut's coronation, see Ralph of Diceto, *The Historical Works of Master Ralph de Diceto*, ed. William Stubbs, RS 68, 2 vols. (London: Longman & Co., 1876), 1: 169–70; see also Pauline Stafford, "The Laws of Cnut and the History of Anglo-Saxon Royal Promises," *ASE* 10 (1982): 173–90, esp. 177–80.

crisis, Cnut married Emma of Normandy, Æthelred's widow, former queen of England, and sister to the reigning duke of Normandy, Richard II.[112] Emma's consecration as queen and co-partner of Cnut's England may have altered but did not dissolve Cnut's relationship with Ælfgifu, although no clear-cut evidence places his Mercian consort within the royal court. Lawson argues her presence as a signatory, after Emma, in the *Liber Vitae* of Thorney Abbey (BL MS Additional 40,000, f.10ʳ) as one of its benefactors along with other members of the royal household on the occasion of a court visit in the 1020s, although there is no critical consensus on this issue. Dorothy Whitelock, for instance, questions the attribution as a copyist's error and identifies the signature (et Ælfgifa) as a gloss on Emma of Normandy, who on the occasion of her marriage to Æthelred in 1002 was given the English name Ælfgifu, which she used on state documents.[113]

Nor did Cnut's marriage to Æthelred's Norman *lāf* (widow) diminish Mercian influence in his court. Leofric's political power increased between Cnut's accession to the throne and his death in 1035, as is evidenced by the increase in his landholdings[114] and the strength of the coalition he led at the Oxford meeting that elected Harold Harefoot as half-ruler of England. Ælfgifu remained a pivotal figure in Cnut's control of the Mercian territories; she was his political foothold in the midlands and his tool with which to forge a united England. For a period, then, there reigned in eleventh-century England two powerful queens in Cnut's court, one Emma of Normandy, the consecrated queen who ruled at court, the other an illegitimate shadow queen who trod the Mercian fenlands,[115] clutching

112. *ASC*, s.a. 1017; Keynes, "Æthelings in Normandy," 173–205; Keynes, *EER* [xxiii–xxiv].

113. Lawson, *Cnut*, 131–32; Dorothy Whitelock, "Scandinavian Personal Names in the *Liber Vitae* of Thorney Abbey," *Saga-Book of the Viking Society for Northern Research* 12 (1937–45), 127–53, esp. 131. See also J. Gerchow, *Die Gedenküberlieferung der Angelsachsen* (Berlin: Walter de Gruyter, 1988), 186–97 (esp. 190), 326–28; Stafford, *Queen Emma and Queen Edith*, 233.

114. Baxter, *Earls of Mercia*, 65, 66 fig. 3.1.

115. In essence, the situation was polygamous and countered Church law,

at the throne for her son. One cannot help but note the similarities with the Beowulfian cluster of characters.

The ménage à trois must have proven to be politically discomfiting for the English nobility and ecclesiastical courts, given the silence of the documents. Nor did it fail to distress the members of the ducal house of Normandy, who were highly apprehensive about the possible loss of their nephews' rights of succession, despite their being the sons of Æthelred and hence the inheritors of Cerdic, for in the face of this untoward marital predicament, the Norman duchy could very well be barred from having access to political influence in England. Yet in the early 1020s, despite their anxieties over the succession of Edward and Alfred, the ducal house of Normandy was able to gather for an evening's entertainment to enjoy the mocking of Cnut's rise to the English throne via his two allegorized queens Jezebel and Semiramis, as the editors and critics of the eponymous poems suggest.[116]

Some nineteen years after Cnut's marriage to Emma of Normandy, however, Ælfgifu of Northampton's prominence as Cnut's consort was still patently evident. Her political influence extended throughout Cnut's northern kingdom, for she had officiated as his queen, first as regent to their son Sveinn in Wendland and then finally in Norway after Óláfr's fall. Although momentarily absent from the royal court, ruling at the periphery of Cnut's northern kingdom, she had nonetheless remained a dangerous rival to the legitimate, consecrated queen, Emma of Normandy, who remained at its center. Their rivalry persisted from the turbulent years of the Danish incursions—when (to recall Wulfstan's apocalyptic vision) injustices ruled (*unrihta to fela ricsode on lande*; *Sermo*, e.g. 11, 13, 61, passim) and disloyalties and betrayals were the order of the day (*þæt lytle getreowþa*

---

which Cnut supported (see II Cnut 54.1); Lawson, *Cnut*, 131; on monogamy, serial monogamy, and polygamy, see Stafford, *Queens, Concubines, and Dowagers*, 71–79, esp. 72, 140; Stafford, "The Reign of Æthelred II," 21; Stafford, "Sons and Mothers," 79–100.

116. See above, Introduction, 25–32, for Dronke's, Ziolkowski's, van Houts's, and Galloway's comments.

wæron mid mannum; Sermo line 10; also lines 61, 72)—to the disordered socio-political climate of the Anglo-Danish England of 1035-37 that allowed for the disregard of the laws governing the royal throne, the assassination of an heir to the throne, the decapitation of the corpse of a pretender king, and the deceit and betrayal of the consecrated queen. Bereft of a husband and mourning an assassinated son, Emma was thrust out of her palace at Winchester "without any pity into the raging winter,"[117] into exile across a rocky Channel to Bruges, where in patience she awaited her revenge.

The exile was brief. In the summer of 1040, accompanied by her son King Harthacnut who (the Encomiast tells us) had come to her aid in Bruges, Emma returned to England to reinstate the Anglo-Danish realm and to reign as its queen mother. It is with this Norman *konungamóðir* and with her poetic transformation as the *bēaghroden* (jewel-bedecked) queen of Heorot that the concluding chapter of this monograph will be concerned, presenting a final argument that the first two-thirds of *Beowulf* may be an innovative epic rendering of national events that were instigated in and fueled throughout the first half of the eleventh century, culminating at last in the mutilation and assassination of Alfred atheling in 1036 and the precipitous fall soon after of the Anglo-Danish reign.

---

117. *ASC* C-text, s.a. 1037, *man draf ðá ut his modor [Harthacnut's] . . . ða cwene. butan ælcere mildheortnesse ongean þone weallendan winter.*

Emma and Wealhtheow: Female Sovereignty and Poetic Discourse

"Hēr is ǣghwylc eorl ōþrum getrȳwe,
mōdes milde, mandrihtne hol[d],
þegnas syndon geþwǣre, þēod ealgearo,
druncne dryhtguman dōð swā ic bidde." (*Bwf* 1228–31)

["Here every noble is to every other true,
with a generous spirit, loyal to the lord;
the thanes are united, the nation is willing,
the warriors, satisfied with drink, do as I bid."]

Queen Wealhtheow's remarks bring a fitting conclusion to the second banquet scene, a scene unparalleled in Old English poetry in its elaborate and expansive depiction of regal munificence within a ceremonial setting. Exalted in style and lavish in its depiction of a heroic society, it has a narrative center that separates it from the first banquet scene, as well as from other feasting scenes in *Beowulf* and in Old English poetry in general and perhaps, as Hugh Magennis has argued in a series of articles, from those in the corpus of Germanic poetry as well.[1]

---

1. Hugh Magennis, "The 'Beowulf' Poet and His '*Druncne Dryhtguman*,'" *Neuphilologische Mitteilungen* 86 (1985): 159–64; see also Magennis, "Saxo Grammaticus and the Heroic Past: Feasting in the *Gesta Danorum*," *Journal*

Expressive more of pomp and ritual than solely of the communal joys and loyalty of the *seledreamas* to which the *Maldon* and *Wanderer* poets nostalgically refer, the scene is heralded by a royal procession led by stout-hearted retainers and followed by King Hrothgar and Queen Wealhtheow, each accompanied by an illustrious retinue, traversing the elevated mead-path to the high hall (*Bwf* 918^b–24). The magisterial gravity of the procession moving toward the *lēoda landgeweorc* (stronghold of nations, *Bwf* 938^a) is further marked by King Hrothgar's ascending the threshold of the hall and addressing the assembly of nobles with a speech of sacral-political content, praising God and offering a *nīwe sibbe* (new kinship, *Bwf* 949^a) to Beowulf, imparting all his worldly goods to the prince (*Bwf* 949^b–950), a preamble to the solemnity of the status-changing event scheduled to take place within the formal setting of a newly decorated Heorot.

Just as unique as the scene's ceremonial setting is the poet's vivid dramatization of female sovereignty in the person of Queen Wealhtheow.[2] At the height of what appears to be the central event

---

of Historical Linguistics and Philology 2 (1985): 2–13; "The Treatment of Feasting in the *Heliand*," *Neophilologus* 69 (1985): 126–33; and "Adaptation of Biblical Detail in the Old English *Judith*: The Feast Scene," *Neuphilologische Mitteilungen* 84 (1983): 331–37.

2.   See Alexandra Hennessey Olsen's summary of the literature on Queen Wealhtheow, in her chapter "Gender Roles," in *Beowulf Handbook*, ed. Bjork and Niles, 311–24, esp. 319–21; see also Orchard, *Companion to Beowulf*, 180–81, 219–20; and Damico, *Beowulf's Wealhtheow and the Valkyrie Tradition*, chaps. 1 and 2, which my present comments on the artistic treatment of Wealhtheow will occasionally draw upon. I have revised my interpretation of some terms in Wealhtheow's speeches in line with Josephine Bloomfield's readings in her "Diminished by Kindness: Frederick Klaeber's Rewriting of Wealhtheow," *JEGP* 93 (1994): 183–203. Bloomfield reinterprets five terms (*milde, glæd, frēondlaþu, līðe, gedēfe*) previously translated by Klaeber and other editors with meanings that highlighted Wealhtheow's domesticated maternity, suppressing the queen's political motivations in the second banquet scene. Wealhtheow appears in seven scenes: two of these in the banqueting hall are major treatments (611–41, 1159^b–1232^a); three are narrative references (664–65^a, closing the first banquet scene; 2016^b–19, recapitulating Wealhtheow's initial appearance; and 2172–76, describing the

of the ceremony proper, the poet brings Queen Wealhtheow into the hall, repeating a rhetorical device used in his introduction of her in the first banquet scene (*Bwf* 611–41). He commands that a singular and sustained focus be placed on the queen, whom he portrays *under gyldnum bēage* (beneath the golden crown, *Bwf* 1163[a]), as he tracks her movements through the assembled court, first addressing Hrothgar, in company with Hrothulf and Unferth on the dais; she then circles toward Beowulf, placed among the gathering of *geogoð ætgædere* (band of young retainers, *Bwf* 1190[a]). Encompassing the scene proper and articulating its political thrust, Wealhtheow's speeches, to be discussed in greater detail below, are those of a female sovereign central to the administrative power of the court, whose authority moves beyond the traditional management of the king's household.[3] Interrelated in their concerns with and clarification of the legalities of inheritance and the orderly disposition of the kingdom, they reveal a character of discriminating political and legal acumen. Her first speech, blatantly political and remarkable for its use of the imperative (*onfōh, spræc, brūc, læf, bēo/wes*), with speed and diplomacy averts a possible dynastic crisis as it lays out the line of succession for the Danish throne and limits the boundaries of Hrothgar's royal promise to Beowulf. Wealhtheow's second speech, again voiced in the imperative, the last four lines of which appear in the epigraph above, further clarifies and systematically lays out the terms of the *nīwe sibbe*, of what may be understood as a royal contract with Beowulf that is meant to bind his future relationship with the queen and, by extension, the Danish people. Bridging the two speeches, the queen bestows jewels of worldly renown and the people's treasure upon Beowulf, her unstinting generosity matching that of Hrothgar. Structurally and thematically, then, the second banquet scene is designed to show

reception of Wealhtheow's *healsbēah* [neck-ring] by Hygd); and two others that appear to be incidental—one outside her separate quarters (923[b]–24) accompanied by her own retinue, and the other in the banqueting hall (1649[b]–50), gazing upon Beowulf's *sǣlāc* (sea-booty, i.e., Grendel's head).

3. For a discussion of the eleventh-century queen's responsibilities in the court, see Stafford, *Queen Emma and Queen Edith*, 97–161.

the interrelatedness of political event and religious ceremony in the magisterial figures of Heorot's sovereigns.[4]

The situational context of Queen Wealhtheow's speeches, performed within a formal, politically potent institutional setting, attests to her singular authority as queen and manifests her power to act in the governance of Heorot. Utterances that command and advise, that promise and praise, they are expressive of a female sovereignty that accords with that apparently possessed by reigning queens of late tenth- and eleventh-century England, a turbulent period in which indeed a royal meddler or two did influence historical events. Pauline Stafford has provided countless examples of powerful queens who affected and redefined the idea of queenship as a political office, an idea that reached its quintessential expression in the figure of Emma of Normandy in the second quarter of the eleventh century,[5] whose

---

4. Yet the import of the queen's speeches has been much contested, the degree and nature of Wealhtheow's authority being the point of contention. Some see her speeches as "ironical" and "pathetic" (Kemp Malone, "Hrethric," *PMLA* 42 [1923]: 268–312, esp. 269–71; see also his, "A Note on *Beowulf* 1231," *Modern Language Notes* 41 [1926]: 466–67); others as misguided and "sorrowing," those of a victim in "tragic isolation" (Irving, *Reading of Beowulf*, 137; and again in *Rereading Beowulf* [Philadelphia: University of Pennsylvania Press, 1989], 27); still others as speech of a "well-honed" political "tool," the "instrument" by which Hrothgar's commands are actualized, with no political substance or autonomous action of her own (Michael J. Enright, "Lady with a Mead Cup: Ritual, Group Cohesion and Hierarchy in the Germanic Warband," *Frühmittelalterliche Studien* 22 [1988]: 170–203; see also his later *Lady with a Mead Cup* [Blackrock, CO. Dublin: Four Courts Press, 1996], where he sees the queen as a cultural figure, in line with the Germanic prophetess Veleda); and, finally, most recently, as attempting "to meddle" in the political game and failing (Orchard, *Companion to Beowulf*, 181, 219–22, at 220). But see Irving's reappraisal in *Rereading Beowulf*, 61, on Wealhtheow's assertiveness in the context of Hrothgar's political ineffectiveness; Damico, *Beowulf's Wealhtheow and the Valkyrie Tradition*, 123–30 and notes; and Bloomfield, "Diminished by Kindness," 183–203.

5. Stafford, *Queen Emma and Queen Edith*; see also her "The King's Wife in Wessex 800–1066," *Past and Present* 91 (1981): 3–27; *Queens, Concubines, and Dowagers*; and "Emma: The Powers of the Queen in the Eleventh

---

sovereign power Stafford has described as a "partnership . . . of the Queen in the king's rule," a partnership that was first expressed in the *ordo* at the consecration of Emma of Normandy as Cnut's queen and that significantly advanced the revised view of Anglo-Saxon queenship. Emma's *ordo* that would have been used for her coronation in 1017, quoting Stafford, "emphasized political rather than nuptial duties," stating that her role was to be "peaceweaver, to bring tranquility in her days, to be an English queen, and to be a consort in royal power," solemn charges of obligations and duties whose political implications significantly advanced the role of Anglo-Saxon queenship.[6] In light of the historical events discussed in the previous chapters and those in the ensuing discussion, the poet's singular dramatization of Queen Wealhtheow clearly foregrounds her potency as co-regent of Heorot, against the background of a sacral-political ceremonial event, the inauguration of a prince.

Unfortunately, no speeches by Queen Emma exist, only summations of them by her biographer in the *Encomium*,[7] the eleventh-

---

Century," in *Queens and Queenship in Medieval Europe*, ed. Anne J. Duggan (Woodbridge, UK, 1997), 3–26.

6. Stafford, *Queen Emma and Queen Edith*, 177–78, quote at 177; see also Keynes, *EER* [xiii–xxxviii], esp. [xxiv–xxvi]. Apparently, the acquisition of institutional power by queens, a by-product of the unification of England into nationhood, had its beginnings in the late tenth century, attested by queens' witnessing of charters and by the *ordo* of Ælfthryth, Emma's mother-in-law, at her coronation with Edgar in 973; Stafford, *Queen Emma and Queen Edith*, 62–64, 163–69; Janet L. Nelson, "Queens," in *Blackwell Encyclopaedia*, ed. Lapidge et al., 383–84, for the development of the institution of queenship in Anglo-Saxon England; on Nelson and the making of queens, see further n. 12 below.

7. This title was given by André Duchesne in the first edition in 1619. The oldest surviving manuscript is not an autograph but the work of two scribes (London, BL, MS Add. 33,241); see Keynes, *EER* [xli–li], for a discussion of the manuscript and transcripts; for the title [xlviin5]. For a discussion of a recension of the *Encomium* copied from another eleventh-century manuscript, composed after the death of Harthacnut during Edward's reign, see Keynes, *EER* [xlix]–[li]; see more recently his discussion and translation of the revised ending of *EER* in what is thought to be the complete Edwardian

century political history in Latin rhyming prose that I have suggested may have a bearing on the composition of *Beowulf*. As related by the Encomiast, Emma's speeches and actions are political, dwelling upon the succession of her sons to the throne and on her office as queen to uphold the solidarity of the kingdom. The first speech, summarized by the Encomiast, deals with a contractual agreement with Cnut for the succession of Emma's offspring; the second relates the welcoming of her son Harthacnut, the soon-to-be king of England, newly arrived from Denmark; and the last serves as the climactic closure to the *Encomium*, celebrating Emma as dowager queen and the reinstatement of a unified and bountiful English court at the start of the new age of King Harthacnut, released from the illegitimate tyrannical reign of Harold Harefoot. Each of these, as I argue below, has its correspondence in theme and in verbal resonance in the speeches of Queen Wealhtheow in *Beowulf*, for it is only in *Beowulf* that we may be hearing the voice of Emma of Normandy.

Noting stylistic and thematic similarities between the *Encomium* and *Beowulf* is not a new idea. Elizabeth M. Tyler was the first, I believe, to notice the remarkably lavish treatment and overriding presence of treasure in the two works.[8] This multivalency of literary and cultural interplay is a signature of the Old English epic, which draws upon biblical, Latin, and Germanic literary traditions. It is especially evident in Wealhtheow's second speech, for in addition to the correspondences it holds with the *Encomium*, the speech contains themes, formulaic phrasing, and syntactical structures connecting it to Old English biblical epic. What I am suggesting here is that,

---

recension found in a 14th-century manuscript known as the "Courtenay Compendium" recently discovered by Timothy Bolton; see Simon Keynes and Rosalind Love, "Earl Godwine's Ship," *ASE* 38 (2009): 185–223, esp. 193–99; see further Timothy Bolton, "A Newly Emergent Mediaeval Manuscript Containing *Encomium Emmae Reginae* with the Only Known Complete Text of the Recension Prepared for King Edward the Confessor," *Mediaeval Scandinavia* 19 (2009): 205–21 (inclusive of two facsimiles of the last two leaves).

8. Tyler, "'Eyes of the Beholder,'" 247–70.

with characteristic virtuosity, the *Beowulf*-poet gave voice to the Encomiast's female sovereign, but with a difference: his queen speaks in a new tongue and in phraseology and meter suited to his Anglo-Saxon epic poem. It is in the context of what Stafford described as the eleventh-century political emergence of female sovereignty in the Anglo-Saxon court that I argue for the *Beowulf*-poet's allusive reconfiguration of Emma of Normandy into his luminous North Germanic female sovereign Wealhtheow.[9]

Emma of Normandy

Without question, Emma of Normandy was a personage to be reckoned with, one who would conceivably capture the imagination of an epic poet. Twice queen, twice queen mother, she maintained a powerful, if at times unsteady, political presence in a man's world for fifty years, from 1002, when she became Æthelred's queen, to her death on 6 March 1052.[10] She reigned during a century that saw the collapse of the Anglo-Saxons, the rise and demise of the Anglo-Danes, and the emergence of the Anglo-Norman state. Entangled in and directing the course of these events were her first husband,

---

9. An interactive resonance between the status and function of historical and literary representations of queens has already been argued by Stafford; she juxtaposes the Carolingian queen in Hincmar's capitulary who controls "revenues and personnel," "organizes the palace," dispenses "gifts," and exemplifies "royal dignity" and "magnificence" and *Beowulf*'s Wealhtheow and the Exeter queen in the *Maxims I*. These literary characters, she argues, are "partial views" of the same queen. What I suggest here is a more specific demonstration of that argument, the poetic refashioning of a contemporary political figure; see Hincmar, *De Ordine Palatii*, ed. A. Boretius, MGH Capitularia Regum Francorum 2 (Hannover: Impensis Bibliopoli Hahnani, 1897), 22 (515–30), ed. and trans. David Herlihy in *The History of Feudalism* (New York: Harper & Row, 1970), 208–27, also cited in Stafford, *Queen Emma and Queen Edith*, 107, 117; Damico, *Beowulf's Wealhtheow and the Valkyrie Tradition*, 21–26, 192–97nn17–27.

10. *ASC*, s.a. 1051; D-text, s.a. 1052; see Keynes, Introduction, [lxxviii, n. 5].

Æthelred the Unready, who though possibly a good king was disempowered and lost a kingdom, and her second, Cnut, who was king of the Anglo-Danish dynasty and ruler of the North (lower Sweden, Denmark, Norway, England) between 1028 and 1030, but who in the end was bereft of progeny to inherit it. Emma's political power seems to have been diffused during her years as Æthelred's queen, which focused more on her procreative function.[11] Although a consecrated queen,[12] she had been "consecrated to the royal bed," a title Stafford describes as "uncommon" and whose first occurrence is in a royal charter of 1004.[13] Emma's political power visibly increased, however, after her consecration as Cnut's consort in 1017, as suggested by the revised *ordo* used at her consecration (see above, 208). Stafford discusses the import of the alterations, especially those found in the series of benedictions over the queen, where she is spoken of as the "glory of the Anglo-Saxons" and a "sharer of rule" over a people, revisions that, for Stafford, bring the queen's consecration in harmony

---

11. Stafford, *Queen Emma and Queen Edith*, 221–24.

12. Emma was not the first consecrated English queen; that place was reserved for Judith, daughter of Charles the Bald, at her marriage to Æthelwulf in 856; see Janet L. Nelson, "Early Medieval Rites of Queen-Making and the Shaping of Medieval Queenship," in *Queens and Queenship in Medieval Europe*, ed. Duggan, 301–15, where she discusses in full the surviving *ordo* used at Judith's coronation and the related documentation. She quotes from a description of the ceremony from the *Annals of St-Bertin*: "and after Bishop Hincmar of Rheims had consecrated her and placed a diadem on her head, he [Æthelwulf] formally conferred on her the title of queen," and points to the significance of the benediction in publicly confirming her as sharer of the throne (306–10, quote at 306). See also her "The Earliest Royal *Ordo*: Some Liturgical and Historical Aspects," in *Politics and Ritual in Early Medieval Europe* (London: Hambledon Press, 1986), 341–60, esp. 343–53.

13. Stafford, *Queen Emma and Queen Edith*, 174, cites charter 909, in Sawyer, *Anglo-Saxon Charters*; see also *EHD* 1: 545–47, no. 127, for translation. See also Stafford's "Emma: The Powers of the Queen," 7 and n. 18, where she cites royal charters in assessing the extent of Emma's powers, and 8, where she identifies Emma as the only "early eleventh-century woman to appear in the witness lists of English royal charters."

with that of the king and are "too dramatic for a liturgical exercise without political content."[14]

A much-discussed image of Emma and Cnut on the frontispiece to the *Liber Vitae of the New Minster and Hyde Abbey* is visually revelatory of the royal partnership (fig. 5). In the center of the portrait are Emma (the inscription identifying her by her assumed political English name, Ælfgifu) and Cnut presenting the golden altar cross. In the upper register directly above the cross sits Christ in majesty with the Virgin Mary to his right and the Apostle Peter to his left, while in the lower register monks observe (and it may be assumed pray over) the presentation ceremony. Catherine E. Karkov analyzed the iconographic significance of this double-ruler portrait, for although the portrait is meant foremost to commemorate Cnut and Emma's donation of the golden altar cross to the New Minster, its composition also points strikingly to the queen's prominence. In the context of double-ruler portraits found in Byzantine and Ottonian art, the New Minster rendering is telling in its departure from the traditional positioning of empresses and queens.[15] The *Liber Vitae* image, which presents Emma wearing a diadem (which in Anglo-Saxon iconographic tradition is associated with divinity),[16] places the queen directly beneath

---

14. Stafford, *Queen Emma and Queen Edith*, 174–78, quotes at 175, 184–85; see also 174n66, where she discusses the *ordo*'s manuscript context and its dating (to ca. 1020 [referring to Dumville]; compared with the Bury psalter, ca. 1025–50 [referring to a personal communication with Michelle Brown]); the revisions are part of the third recension of the Second English *ordo*, found in Cambridge, Corpus Christi College 44; see also Janet L. Nelson, "The Second English *Ordo*," in *Politics and Ritual in Early Medieval Europe*, 361–74 and 380–82, for her discussion of Schramm's thesis.

15. Catherine E. Karkov, *The Ruler Portraits of Anglo-Saxon England*, Anglo-Saxon Studies 3 (Woodbridge, UK: The Boydell Press, 2004), 121–33. Portraits of early English queens were a rarity, and that there are two of Emma tells of her political importance; but, in addition, presenting her as a double donor here is telling of her singular munificence to monastic houses; see Stafford, "Emma: The Powers of the Queen," 3–4; Heslop, "Production of *de luxe* Manuscripts," 151–95, esp. 157.

16. Karkov, *Ruler Portraits*, 130; Nelson, "Earliest Royal *Ordo*," esp. 356–58.

the Virgin and to the right of Christ and the cross, a position traditionally assigned to the king or emperor. For Karkov, this reversal
of positioning reflects Emma's partnership in the reign and indicates
that her queenship was divinely sanctioned by the Virgin, who within
the image functions as Emma's spiritual equivalent.[17] In the context
of Winchester, this connection between Mary's divine queenly status
and the status of earthly queens is a development of one earlier established for Emma's former mother-in-law, Ælfthryth.[18] The double-ruler
portrait in *Liber Vitae* pictorially captures Cnut and Emma's characteristic patronage and largess to churches and abbeys;[19] in her own right,
Emma was liberal in her ecclesiastical donations, for within the *Liber
Vitae*, as Karkov has pointed out, it appears that Emma donated the
"Greek Shrine," listed in the relics donated to the Minster, and she
was especially munificent in her gifts to Ely.[20] But such largess might

---

17. But see Gale Owen-Crocker's discussion of the figure of Emma in the
Liber Vitae illustration, which understands the figure's positioning beneath
the Virgin as validating Emma's second marriage to Cnut, and attributes
its size and its lack of adornment, except for the diadem connecting Emma
to Mary, as being suggestive of her being in subordination to rather than
in partnership with Cnut (Gale R. Owen-Crocker, "Pomp, Piety, and
Keeping the Woman in Her Place: The Dress of Cnut and Ælgifu-Emma,"
in *Medieval Clothing and Textiles*, vol. 1, ed. Robin Netherotn and Gale R.
Owen-Crocker (Woodbridge, UK: Boydell Press, 2006), 41–52, esp. 48,
51–52. Yet the difference of size and ornamentation of the king and queen
may also point to Emma's possessing unquestionable piety in contrast to
Cnut who is positioned beneath a crown that is too large for him, despite
its being brought to him by an angel.

18. Karkov, *Ruler Portraits*, esp. 127, 129, 132; see also Stafford's comments
in her "Emma: The Powers of the Queen," esp. 3–5; and Mary Clayton, *The
Cult of the Virgin Mary in Anglo-Saxon England* (Cambridge, UK: Cambridge
University Press, 1990), 166–67.

19. Heslop, "Production of *de luxe* Manuscripts," 156–62, 179–81, and
appendix II, 182–88.

20. Karkov, *Ruler Portraits*, 124; Heslop, "Production of *de luxe*
Manuscripts," esp. for Emma's donations to New Minster, 187; to Ely, 185;
see also *ASC* F-text, s.a. 1041 (actually 1042), where Emma donates the head
of Saint Valentine to the minster for Harthacnut's soul (*and his moder for*

be expected from a queen whom Stafford judges to have been the richest woman in England until 1043, when she was deprived of her treasures. This double-ruler portrait of the political rulers of England invites comparison with the balanced iconic representation of the sovereigns of Heorot found at the beginning and end of *Beowulf*'s second banquet scene.

A major crisis in Emma's life came in 1035 after the death of Cnut, when the succession dispute dominated and ripped England apart. To review the pool of potential heirs to the throne: Harthacnut, Emma and Cnut's son (who was reigning in Denmark at the time of Cnut's death); Edward and Alfred, Emma's sons by Æthelred (who, at Cnut's accession to the throne in 1016, had been sent to their uncle at the Norman court for safekeeping); and Harold Harefoot, Cnut's alleged son by Ælfgifu of Northampton, Cnut's illegitimate consort, although, as discussed above, the *Anglo-Saxon Chronicle* texts C, D (s.a. 1035), and E (s.a. 1036) as well as later documents disclaim him as Cnut's son. Harthacnut was the legitimate heir, as a result of a possible premarital agreement between Emma and Cnut at the time of their marriage (below, 235), and as indicated by Cnut's appointing him king of Denmark. At Cnut's death, because Harthacnut, embroiled in a war with Norway, was unable to appear before the *witenagemōt* (national council) at Oxford to claim the throne, Harold Harefoot and his mother emerged from the shadows, moved swiftly among the political factions, and succeeded in claiming the throne. A dark period, including exile, ensued for Emma until 1041, when Harthacnut claimed the throne after Harold's death.

It is in the context of these years of national crisis that I explore some attributes of Emma's person that resonate in Wealhtheow's character. In so merging history and poetic epic, the *Beowulf*-poet

---

his sawle gief into niewan mynstre S. Valentines heafod ðas martires); for a full discussion of the thirty-three relics in the Greek *Scrine*, listed as having been donated by Emma to New Minster, see Lynn Jones, "Emma's Greek *Scrine*," in *Early Medieval Studies in Memory of Patrick Wormald*, ed. S. Baxter, C. E. Karkov, J. L. Nelson, and D. Pelteret (Farnham, UK: Ashgate, 2008), 499–508.

broke apart principles of chronology and place; reshaped character relationships; introduced fictive figures; and encoded character identity, time-honored rhetorical alterations by which poets and historical biographers reconstituted history into new works of vernacular epic.[21] These innovative poetic manipulations were patently operative in the *Beowulf*-poet's rendering of the executions of Alfred ætheling and Harold Harefoot (above, chap. 1), in his imaginative transmutation of the Danish incursions into Grendel's Reign of Terror (above, chap. 2), and in his refashioning of *Álfífa in ríka* into the *micle mearcstapa* Grendel's mother (above, chap. 3). The present discussion falls into three parts: first, I point to similarities particular to Wealhtheow and Emma in their singular circumstances as foreign queens and putative captives; I then deal with their function as political peaceweavers and co-rulers of the realm directing its dynastic succession, dramatically brought to life in *Beowulf*; finally, I offer verbal resonances of the *Encomium* in Wealhtheow's speeches that seem less than accidental and that argue that *Beowulf*'s *mǣru cwēn* and the *Encomium*'s *regina famosa* most likely reflect two views of the same queen, Emma of Normandy.

Norman Queen/Norman Captive

In 1017, Cnut succeeded to the realm of England. After Æthelred's sudden death on 23 April 1016 and after the raging battle between Edmund Ironside and Cnut, which resulted in a joint rule that ended with Edmund's death on 30 November 1016, Cnut was chosen king over all England. Sometime before 1 August 1017, *het se cyng feccan him Æþelredes lafe þes oðres cynges him to cwene Ricardes dohtor* (the king commanded that the widow of the late King Æthelred, Richard's daughter, be fetched for him that she might become his queen).[22] The E- and D-versions of the *Anglo-Saxon Chronicle*, with the F-version

---

21. Labeled by J. Duggan as "popular historiography" and cited by Whaley as "imaginative historiography" (see above, 17–18).
22. *ASC*, s.a. 1017.

mentioning the queen's double names—*þæt wæs Ælfgiue (on Englisc.) Ymma (on Frencisc.)*—thus record the beginning of what Simon Keynes has called a "brilliantly contrived double act," a royal partnership that characterized the Anglo-Danish court until Cnut's death on 12 November 1035.[23]

The F-version's tendency to gloss Emma with her two names (also s.a. 1002) is reflected throughout the versions of the *Chronicle*. Although her official name was Ælfgifu, eleventh-century English documents also refer to the queen by her double name, Ælfgifu Imme, or reference one name with the other, while continental, Scandinavian, and later twelfth-century English documents retain her original Norman name.[24] Emma adopted, or was urged by Æthelred to adopt, the English form at her marriage, an action that Stafford notes as being unusual for an early English queen.[25] Æthelred's insistence that his Norman queen bear the English name was meant perhaps to emphasize her "Englishness" and associate her with a line of royal females from Edward the Elder's queen onward to the female royalty that marked his own dynasty.[26] English kings as a rule did not marry foreigners, and Emma was the first foreign queen since Judith, Charles the Bald's daughter, crossed the Channel as Æthelwulf's queen in 856.[27] If indeed Æthelred intended the double naming to minimize Emma's identity as a Norman princess, it did not prove entirely successful. For as the *Chronicle* entry for 1017 as well as later twelfth-century documents suggest, although Emma was *Æþelredes lafe* she

---

23. Keynes, "Cnut," and Stafford, "Emma of Normandy," in *Blackwell Encyclopaedia*, ed. Lapidge et al., 108–9 and 168–69, respectively.

24. On the naming patterns for Emma, see Campbell, *EER*, appendix I, 55–61.

25. Stafford, *Queen Emma and Queen Edith*, 93; Stafford notes that Emma's sisters and her Danish mother, Gunnor, had been given Frankish names but apparently did not use them (213).

26. Stafford, *Queen Emma and Queen Edith*, 172; Karkov, *Ruler Portraits*, 120–21; Barlow, *Edward the Confessor*, 30.

27. *ASC* (A-, B-, C-, E-, and F-texts), s.a. 855; Stafford, *Queen Emma and Queen Edith*, 209.

continued to be *Ricardes dohtor*, and her Norman name, as Alistair Campbell notes, "was widely known, and continued in popular use."[28] Thus, when Cnut commanded that Emma be "fetched" so that she might be his queen, what he was securing was not only his position as king of England—which he blatantly was—but an alliance with Normandy as well.[29]

This was not the first time Emma served as a *friðusibb folca* (peacemaker among nations, or, as V. Grønbech once put it, "peace-power among the disputants"),[30] with primarily a political and diplomatic function. The E-version of the *Chronicle* entry for 1002 notes the arrival of Æthelred's new queen: *And þa on þam ilcan lengtene com seo hlæfdige Ricardes dohtor hider to lande* (And then that same spring, the lady [*sēo hlæfdige*], Richard's daughter, came hither to this land).[31] Some years younger than the mature Æthelred, Richard's daughter was a Norman princess with a double pedigree, born to the Danish noblewoman Gunnor and Richard I, duke of Normandy, grandson of the founder of the Norman dynasty, the Viking chief Rollo (Hrólfr).[32] Her marriage was to serve as a pact of peace, to lessen political tensions caused by Norman incursions along the English

---

28. Campbell, *EER*, appendix I, 56; Keynes, *EER*, xvii and n2.

29. Keynes, *EER,* xxiin3; Searle, *Predatory Kinship Power*, 136–40; Lawson, *Cnut*, 86–87, 92–95.

30. The quote is from Vilhelm Grønbech, *Culture of the Teutons* (orig. *Vor Folkeæt I Oldtiden* [Copenhagen: Jespersen, 1909–12]), trans. William Worster (London: Humphrey Milford, 1931), 1:32–33, 58–61, esp. 59; for the argument that *friðusibb* and *freoðuwebbe* are "poetic metaphors" referring to characters whose function is primarily political and diplomatic, see Damico, *Beowulf's Wealhtheow and the Valkyrie Tradition*, 85.

31. Emma is identified here as Richard's daughter, even though Richard I died on 20 November 996, some five years before Emma's marriage; she continues to be thus identified in later English and Scandinavian documents. See Stafford, *Queen Emma and Queen Edith*, 56–64, for a discussion of *hlæfdige* in the context of terms for queens in OE.

32. Emma was born in the 980s: Stafford, *Queen Emma and Queen Edith*, 210–11; *WJGND* 4.18 (2:128–29, 130–31).

coast and by Norman harboring of Viking raiders.[33] Thus, in 1002, Emma functioned as the "link" that joined two dynasties (despite their less than tranquil political and military relations); but, most important, she extended the influence of the Norman duchy beyond the Continent (and this perhaps was the unstated Norman purpose of the marriage).[34] The stunning consequence of the Norman "link" was made evident not only in 1045, when her son Edward the Confessor— half English, but also half Norman—ascended the throne, ushering in the Anglo-Norman reign, but more strikingly in 1066 when her great-nephew William invaded England and brought to closure the age of the Anglo-Saxons.

Cnut's fetching of Emma resonates in reports found in Norman, Scandinavian, continental, and later twelfth- and thirteenth-century chronicles and in *Semiramis*, the second of the two Norman Latin political satires of the early eleventh century (see Introduction, 25–28). A point of contention centers on Emma's whereabouts between 1014, when, because of Sveinn Forkbeard's invasion, she and her children had fled to Normandy, and 1017 when Cnut commanded she be "fetched" to him. But whatever ambiguity exists is due largely to the narrative of the courtship and prenuptial contract between Emma and Cnut as it appears in the *Encomium Emmae Reginae* (see below, 232–33). Emma is placed in London with Æthelred at the time of his death by the majority of sources, five of which will be discussed here.[35]

---

33. By 991, the political tension between the two countries had escalated to such a pitch that Pope John XV urged Æthelred and Duke Richard I to sign a peace treaty in 991 at Rouen: *Memorials of Saint Dunstan, Archbishop of Canterbury*, ed. William Stubbs, RS 63 (London: Longman & Co., 1874), 37–98, cited in *WJGND* 12n.

34. Stafford, *Unification and Conquest*, 75–76; Searle, *Predatory Kinship*, 136–40.

35. *Die Chronik des Bischofs Thietmar von Merseburg und ihre Korveier Überarbeitung*, ed. Robert Holtzmann, 2nd unabridged ed., vol. 2 (Berlin: Weidmann, 1955), book 7.40 (446–49), trans. Whitelock in *EHD* 1: 347–50, no. 27, is a contemporary and slightly confused source for English

William of Jumièges relates that Queen Emma was in a state of captivity in London, before she was "abducted" and then "bought" by Cnut:

> Rex igitur Chunutus, audita morte regis, suorum consultu fidelium, precauens in futurum, Emmam reginam abstractam ab urbe post aliquot dies sibi iunxit Christiano more, dans pro illa cuncto exercitui in auro et argento penssum illius corporis.[36]

> [When King Cnut heard of the king's death [Æthelred's on 23 April 1016] he consulted members of his council and took steps to safeguard the future. He took Queen Emma from the city [*Emmam reginam abstractam ab urbe*] and married her a few days later according to the Christian rite. In return for her he handed over her weight in gold and silver to the army.]

In an article dealing with political relations between Normandy and England, Elisabeth M. C. van Houts suggests that a more apt translation for *Emmam reginam abstractam ab urbe* would be "[Cnut] kidnapped Queen Emma from the town," placing the event in the context of medieval Scandinavian marital customs, whereby the bride was first seized, then purchased before the marriage was confirmed.[37]

---

affairs. The evidence is discussed by Keynes, "Æthelings in Normandy," 176–77, 182–83; Keynes, *EER* [xx–xxi]; van Houts, "Note on *Jezebel* and *Semiramis*," 18–24; *GND* 5.8–9 (2:18–23); see also van Houts, "The Political Relations between Normandy and England before 1066 according to the *Gesta Normannorum ducum*," in *Les mutations socio-culturelles au tournant des xie–xiie siècles*, ed. R. Foreville and C. Viola (Paris: Centre National de la Recherche Scientifique, 1984), 85–97, esp. 81; Russell Poole's translation of *Liðsmannaflokkr* (vv. 8–10) in *Viking Poems on War and Peace*, 89–90; *Knýtlinga saga*, in *Danakonunga sǫgur*, ed. Guðnason, 107; *Knýtlinga saga: The History of the Kings of Denmark*, trans. Pálsson and Edwards, 31; discussion and text of "Supplement to *Jómsvíkinga saga*," in *EER* 90 and 93; see also *HHHA* 6.15; *WMGRA* ii.180, which follows the *EER* narrative.

36. *GND* 5.9 (2: 20–21); trans. van Houts.

37. Van Houts, "Political Relations between Normandy and England," 87–89; she rightly takes issue with Campbell's argument that Emma was

Once Cnut had abducted the queen, a few days later he married her *Christiano more* and paid for her in gold and silver, legitimating the union. Van Houts's translation "kidnapped" (*abstractam*) is perhaps closer to the point of the scene, for the term corresponds to the Anglo-Saxon *het feccean*, which carries the sense of being carried off by force, in particular when used with women who are "fetched" against their will, as Andy Orchard's field study of the fourteen extant uses of the term reveals.[38]

The closest source in time to the event is Thietmar of Merseburg's (ca. 1017), which places a "grieving" Emma, with her sons and members of her court, in a stronghold at the siege of London and describes the negotiations that supposedly took place between Cnut's command to "fetch" Emma and the marriage *Christiano more* that occurred about a year later. Allegedly, a war-weary Emma sued for peace and "inquire[d] diligently what they required of her":

> [She] at once received the reply from the insatiable enemies, that if the queen would give up her sons to death and redeem herself with fifteen thousand pounds of silver, and the bishops with twelve thousand, and with all the coats-of-mail, of which there was the incredible number of twenty-four thousand, and would give 300 picked hostages as security for these things, she could gain for

---

still in Normandy (94n15) and that Cnut sent word to her brother Richard II for her, arguing that if Cnut had "fetched" Emma from Normandy, William of Jumièges would have said so. Van Houts also observes that the scenes of the siege of London after the death of Æthelred represented in Thietmar of Merseburg, *Knýtlinga saga*, and William of Jumièges are confrontational and call up images not of a request for a bride via diplomacy but rather of a command for surrender.

38. Orchard, "Literary Background to the *EER*," 176: "perhaps most relevantly in this context [are accounts of] the virgin Agatha being fetched for a marriage against her will . . . and . . . in the C-text of the Anglo-Saxon Chronicle for 1046 of how Swein Godwineson . . . *het he feccan him to þa abbedessan on Leomynstre, and hæfde hi þa hwile þe him geliste and let hi syþþan faran ham* (he had the abbess of Leominster fetched, and kept her with him as long as he liked, and then let her go home)."

herself and her companions peace with life; if not, all [the messengers] cried out three times that they should perish by the sword. The venerable queen . . . was extremely agitated at this message and after long deliberation in a vacillating mind replied that she would do this.[39]

Thietmar's report, as often noted, contains inaccuracies, even though it is the source most nearly contemporary to the events themselves; in Dorothy Whitelock's view, it perhaps contains these inaccuracies because it is too close to the events. If, however, the report is taken at face value, it shapes a portrait of Emma as a woman so depraved in her desire for power and survival that she would sacrifice her sons to accomplish her ends.

Knýtlinga saga presents another version of Emma's "fetching," dramatizing Emma's abortive attempt to escape London by ship before being captured by Cnut's men: *váru búnir til hafs . . . fluttu þeir dróttningu á fund Knúts konungs* (just as her retinue was ready to sail . . . they brought [*fluttu þeir*] Queen Emma to King Knut), and it was agreed by the king and his chieftains that he should take Queen Emma as his wife.[40] The three reports largely agree on Emma's having been caught in London in jeopardy of her life, either in captivity or at the point of attempting to escape captivity, and captured by Cnut's men.[41]

The moment in national history when a conquering hero not only subdued England, its army, and its people but captured its queen as well conceivably would have served as a natural inspiration for poetry. And so at the closure of *Liðsmannaflokkr* (which deals with

39. *EHD* 1:348, no. 24. See Whitelock's discussion of the importance of Thietmar's account (138).

40. Trans. Pálsson and Edwards, 31; *Knýtlinga saga*, 107; see the Supplement to *Jómsvíkinga saga*, in *EER* 92–93, where Thorkell captures Emma (93).

41. *Liðsmannaflokkr*, stanzas 8–10, finds Emma ("the pure widow") in a stronghold witnessing the siege of London; see Poole's discussion in *Viking Poems on War and Peace*, 100–115; Stafford, *Queen Emma and Queen Edith*, 22–27; Orchard, "Literary Background to the *EER*," 176–80; see also Van Houts's argument that casts an erotic notoriety over Emma's "fetching," "Note on *Jezebel* and *Semiramis*," 18–24.

Cnut's and Thorkell's campaigns in England), the skald uses the coupling of the king and Æthelred's widow as a metaphor for a peace that was to come after the bloody siege:

Út mun ekkja líta –
opt glóa vǫpn á lopti
of hjalmtǫmum hilmi –
hrein sú's býr í steini
hvé sigrfíkinn sœkir
snarla borgar karla –
dynr á brezkum brynjum
blóðíss–Dana vísi. (stanza 8; Poole translation)[42]

[The pure widow who lives in the stone [stronghold] will look out—often weapons glitter in the air above the king in his helmet—[to see] how valiantly the Danish leader, eager for victory, assails the city's garrison; the sword (*blóðíss*) rings against British mailcoats.]

In the above stanza, the skald inverts the queen's predicament of witnessing the catastrophic siege of London and suggests that the battle of London served as the beginning of the widow's courtship. In stanza 9, the skald continues to depict the daily battle from the lady's point of view, where *Hvern morgin sér horna / Hlǫkk á Tempsar bakka–/ skalat hanga má hungra–/ hjalmskóð roðín blóði* (each morning, on the bank of the Thames, the lady [*horna Hlǫkk*] sees swords stained with blood; the raven must not go hungry). By stanza 10, the skald has sufficiently praised Cnut (and his *liðsmenn*), the enemy is victorious, and the battle for possession of London is over.

Dag vas hvern þat's Hǫgna
hurð rjóðask nam blóði,

---

42. See Poole's discussion of *Liðsmannaflokkr* in his *Viking Poems on War and Peace*, 89–115, stanzas and translations on 89–90; see also Stafford, *Queen Emma and Queen Edith*, 22–27; Orchard, "Literary Background to the *EER*," 176–80.

ár þar's úti vǫrum,
Ilmr, í fǫr með hilmi:
kneigum vér, síz vígum
varð nýlokit hǫrðum,
fyllar dags, í fǫgrum
fit, Lundúnum sitja.
(stanza 10, Poole translation).

[Every day the shield [*Hǫgna hurð*] was stained with blood,
[?lady?], / where we were out [?early?] on our expedition with the
king: / now that these hard battles have been recently concluded,
/ we can settle down, lady [*fyllar dags fit*], in beautiful London.]

The poem moves to a muted (if ironic) closure as the skald addresses
the lady whose nation has been defeated (and before whom the poem
may have been presented), and who herself will be conquered shortly
in a less militant environment.[43]

If the union between Emma and Cnut brought relief to the battle-
weary Danes and English, it did not, as we have seen, have the same
salutary effect on the royal and ecclesiastical courts of Normandy,
who saw it as a threat to the succession rights of the Anglo-Norman
athelings, Edward and Alfred (see Introduction, 24–25). The
Norman Latin political allegory in leonine rhyme, *Semiramis*, composed soon after the union of Emma and Cnut bitingly ridicules
and condemns the yoking of the "whore" of Babylon (Emma) with

---

43. See Frank, "King Cnut in the Verse of His Skalds," 119–22, for another
metaphoric combination of a conquered land and a forced sexual union
in stanza 3 of Hallvarðr's eulogy to Cnut, although Frank does not refer
directly to Emma's "abduction": "the opening image of a broad land (feminine) lying bound, under a (masculine) tree [of gold=Cnut] recalls earlier,
pre-Christian eulogies in which the conquest of a territory is expressed, in
sexual terms, as a forced 'marriage'"; stanza on 120; quote at 122; for Frank's
further discussion of the use of *hieros gamos* motif in skaldic poetry, see "The
Lay of the Land in Skaldic Praise Poetry," in *Myth in Early Northwest Europe*,
ed. Stephen O. Glosecki (Tempe, AZ: ACMRS, 2007), 175–96; for Cnut,
see esp. 182–83.

Jupiter (an allegorized bull, Cnut), as van Houts has argued.[44] Van Houts's argument casts an aura of colorful notoriety over Emma's being fetched by Cnut's men in London and brought to him. The stereotypical charge of unrestrained sexuality we have seen operative in the treatment of powerful and wealthy historical women like Ælfgifu of Northampton, Gunnhildr, and Ælfthryth (above, chapter 3), here, with its classical allusions, has been given a more elegant and aristocratic tone.

Thus, in eleventh-century Anglo-Saxon political history, an illustrious foreign queen reigned over England, a Norman who at a climactic moment in her life found herself in the midst of battle and in captivity, from which she was removed and brought to the conqueror to become his queen. The event would have had national significance to the northern world, affecting as it did the Danish, Anglo-Saxon, and Norman kingdoms. It would not have been quickly forgotten by the Anglo-Saxons that in 1017 Emma of Normandy was the pivotal figure who united the warring factions within the Danish, Anglo-Saxon, and Norman kingdoms.

Beowulf's Norman Captive

Emma's capture by Cnut's men, of course, does not appear in *Beowulf*. Nor can it, for the narrative of lines 86–1686 concerns the struggle for Heorot's throne. Nonetheless, the captivity narrative is indirectly embodied in the poem's plot in the person of Wealhtheow.

I begin with Wealhtheow's name, which first suggested to me that interrelated resonances might obtain between Hrothgar's queen and Emma of Normandy.[45] It is a critical commonplace that the name *Wealhþēow* falls outside the traditional Anglo-Saxon naming patterns (as do *Bēowulf* and *Frēawaru*, for example), and that the poet used

---

44. Van Houts, "Note on *Jezebel* and *Semiramis*," 18–24; see also Introduction, 29–30. Later twelfth-century English sources refer to Emma's union with Cnut in less colorful terms.

45. Damico, *Beowulf's Wealhtheow and the Valkyrie Tradition*, chap. 4.

name-play as a mode of characterization. His onomastic zeal has been demonstrated by critics from Karl Müllenhoff and Axel Olrik to Robert Kaske and Fred Robinson.[46] In *Unferð*, *Mōdþryðo*, *Hygd*, and *Hygelāc*, for instance, Kaske and Robinson find a happy blending of name and character, arguing that Beowulfian names had emblematic functions. Yet in his naming of Wealhtheow, the poet seems to have lost his touch, for the name's most general meaning, "foreign slave," contradicts her status as *cwēn Hrōðgāres*[47] (Hrothgar's queen), *frēolicu folccwēn* (noble queen of the people), *frēolīc wīf* (noble wife or woman), *friðusibb folca* (peace-maker among nations), *ðēodnes dohtor* (prince's daughter), and *mǣru cwēn* (illustrious queen). In her initial presentation, as well as elsewhere in the poem where the poet describes her, the most general meaning of the name jars with her characterization, a disharmony that would have been recognized by an audience.[48] Yet as I have discussed at length elsewhere, the poet's naming of Wealhtheow, rather than pointing to a lapse in his

---

46. Karl Müllenhoff, *Beovulf: Untersuchungen über das angelsächsische Epos und die älteste Geschichte der germanischen Seevölker* (Berlin: Weidmann, 1889), esp. 26; Axel Olrik, *The Heroic Legends of Denmark*, trans. Lee M. Hollander (New York: American-Scandinavian Foundation, 1919), 56–64, examines Unferth and Wealhtheow; Fred C. Robinson, "The Significance of Names in Old English Literature," *Anglia* 86 (1968): 14–59, esp. 43–57 for Wealhtheow, 50–57 for Hygelac; Kemp Malone, "The Daughter of Healfdene," in *Studies in English Philology: A Miscellany in Honor of Frederick Klaeber*, ed. Kemp Malone and Martin B. Ruud (Minneapolis, MN: University of Minnesota Press, 1929), 139–58; R. E. Kaske, "'Hygelac' and 'Hygd,'" in *Studies in Old English Literature in Honor of Arthur G. Brodeur*, ed. Stanley B. Greenfield (Eugene, OR: University of Oregon Books, 1963), 200–206. For Unferth, see also R. D. Fulk, "Unferth and His Name," *Modern Philology* 85 (1987): 113–27; Stanley G. Greenfield, *The Interpretation of Old English Poems* (London: Routledge and K. Paul, 1972), 101–6; the discussion on naming is based largely on Damico, *Beowulf's Wealhtheow and the Valkyrie Tradition*, esp. 62–68, 207–9, esp. nn. 20–22.

47. Six of the ten instances in which *cwēn* (or its compounds) appears in the poem refer to the queen, three occurring in her introductory passage.

48. So Christine Fell, *Women in Anglo-Saxon England*, 66; the name with final *w* appears only in 612[b], at the queen's introduction.

---

creativity, is a further illustration of his onomastic sensibility, for as the studies of E. V. Gordon, Willy Meyer, E. Wessén, and Erik Björkman in particular have noted, the name contains a cluster of meanings that situate Wealhtheow in a literary, mythological, and cultural context.[49] My argument here extends the scope of the poet's onomastic sensibility to include a contemporary political context: through name-play, through the apt naming of Heorot's queen, the poet cryptically makes perceptible the historical Emma.

Both elements of the name have a broad semantic spread; only two of the cluster of meanings are relevant here. Most germane to the present argument is Björkman's examination, which places the queen in a historico-cultural context, associating her with "Romance" territory and seeing her as an abducted noblewoman. Björkman rejected the name's etymological origin in Old English; instead, he posited a derivation from Proto-Norse *WalhaþiwiR (-þiujō), the first element carrying the signification of "Celtic or Romance,"[50] a meaning it retained as it developed into the Old Norse and Old Swedish *val*, referring to those who spoke a foreign tongue in northern France

---

49. E. V. Gordon, "Wealhþeow and Related Names," *Medium Ævum* 4 (1935): 169–75; Erik Björkman, "Zu einigen Namen im *Beowulf*: Breca, Brondingas, Wealhþēo(w)," *Anglia, Beiblatt* 30 (1919): 170–80, esp. 177–80; and E. Wessén, "Nordiska personnamn på -*þiófr*," in *Uppsala Universitets Årsskrift* (Uppsala 1927), 110–18, esp. 110–11, 116. For a discussion of these studies, see Damico, *Beowulf's Wealhtheow and the Valkyrie Tradition*, chap. 4; but see contra, Thomas D. Hill, "'Wealhtheow' as a Foreign Slave: Some Continental Analogues," *Philological Quarterly* 69 (1990): 106–12; see also David A. E. Pelteret, *Slavery in Early Medieval England: From the Reign of Alfred to the Twelfth Century* (Woodbridge, UK: Boydell Press, 1995), 53n15 and 261–334, on OE terminology of freedom and servitude, under *wealh* and *þeow*. For a discussion on popularity of Latin onamastic word-play in the literary milieu of the eleventh century and its relevance to the union between Cnut and Emma, see Galloway, "Word-Play and Political Satire," 195–204.

50. Björkman, "Zu einigen Namen im *Beowulf*," 179–80. *Walha-* had the semantic spread of "Celt, inhabitant of Northern France, Italian, foreign"; see also Pelteret, *Slavery in Early Medieval England*, 319–22, 325–26.

(ON *valir* [OE *Walas* or *Wealas*]; ON *Valland, Valskr* [OE *Wealisc,* Ger *Welsch*]). This specialized ethnic meaning of *wealh* is found in *Wealh-land* (OHG *Walho-lant,* "Gallia"), signifying Normandy in the E-version of the *Anglo-Saxon Chronicle*'s entry for 1040, which documents Edward the Confessor's return to England: *com Eadward Æðelredes sunu cinges hider to lande of Weallande* (Edward, King Æthelred's son, came hither to this country from Normandy).[51] The Old Icelandic *Fagrskinna* (chap. 74) designates *Valland* as an earlier name for Normandy: *Vilhjalmr . . . hann vann þat ríki í Vallandi er síðan var kallat Norðmandi* (William . . . he gained authority in *Valland,* which was afterward called Normandy). And, so, in *Heimskringla*'s *Saga of Óláfr helgi* (chap. 12), "*Aðalráðr*" flees to "*Valland*" after Sveinn Forkbeard's conquest of England.[52] Given the tense interaction between northern Frankish and Scandinavian worlds, the first element of the Beowulfian queen's name could be emblematic of her Norman origin.

Björkman then placed *-þēow* (Proto-Norse *-þiwiR, -þiujo,* m. *-þewaR*) in a cultural context, which even the most conservative critic would argue "need not be interpreted literally."[53] Instead of interpreting *þēow* as "servant" or "slave," he offered the specialized reading of "captive," a semantic spread it held in Proto-Norse, designating a person captured in battle, a reading supported by Wessén's studies on Nordic personal names ending in ON *-þjófr* and their relationship to OE *-þēow.*[54] For Björkman, the ease of communication and trade

---

51. *ASC* 2: 220.
52. *Fsk,* ed. Einarsson; *Hkr* 2, ed. Aðalbjarnason, 13–15.
53. This is in Klaeber, 3rd ed., xxxiii and n. 2; see also his "Proper Names"; see also Klaeber, 4th ed., "Proper Names."
54. Wessén accords with Björkman on the Norse origin for both elements of *Wealhþēow,* offering the masculine *Valþjófr* as evidence ("Nordiska personnamn på *-þiófr,*" 115). His article focuses on the double meaning of *-þjófr* as "servant" and "thief" in Nordic literary and historical names, probably seeing "thief" by extrapolation as someone who has been stolen, and points specifically to Viking raids, which "were aimed, among other things, at obtaining thralls"; he harmonizes the full name etymologically

between the Danes and the Frankish coastal regions, in addition to the frequency of Viking raids along the Frankish coast from the sixth century onward, made it likely that the name *Wealhþēow* designated a Frankish princess captured in battle and brought into the Danish court, but subsequently set free.[55] Björkman's conclusion is striking, for it offers a plausible, though not conclusive, solution for the *Beowulf*-poet's enigmatic and riddling naming of Heorot's queen. It suggests that the poet encoded a nickname by which he could refer allusively to Cnut's captive Norman queen in "guarded" language,[56] for it is a

---

to mean "a servant abducted from a Celtic (Romance) country, prisoner of war" (117). For this connection in OE, see *Đeówdóm* as equivalent to *captivitas*: Bosworth-Toller, s.v. *þeówdóm*; for the prevalence of female abduction as a literary motif in ON and OE literature, see Damico, *Beowulf's Wealhtheow and the Valkyrie Tradition*, chap. 5, esp. 91, a particular example being Melkorka, the captive Irish princess in *Laxdœla saga* (chap. 13); an Anglo-Saxon captive who rose to become queen to Clovis II, queen mother to three Frankish kings, and founder of Chelles and Corbie was Balthild (d. 690); see Pauline A. Stafford, "Powerful Women in the Early Middle Ages: Queens and Abbesses," in *The Medieval World*, ed. Peter Linehan and Janet L. Nelson (London: Routledge, 2001), 398–415.

55. Björkman, "Zu einigen Namen im *Beowulf*," 179–80, esp. 180n1: "In no case did Hrothgar marry a slave. Proto-Norse *-þiwiR* (*-þiujo*) did not necessarily mean bondage any more than did the masculine *-þewaR*. Captives who were of noble birth were often freed quickly" (*Auf keinen Fall hat Hroðgar eine Unfreie geheiratet. Urn. -þiwiR (-þiujo) braucht ebensowenig wie das mask. -þewaR Unfreiheit bedeutet zu haben. Kriegsgefangene edlen Geschlechts wurden öfter bald freigelassen*); and Damico, *Beowulf's Wealhtheow and the Valkyrie Tradition*, 63, 208–9nn21–23. For more on captives, see Michael McCormick, *Origins of the European Economy: Communications and Commerce, A.D. 300–900* (Cambridge, MA; New York: Cambridge University Press, 2001), 733–77, esp. 735–40, 747; and Pelteret, *Slavery in Early Medieval England*, 70, 74–79, 247.

56. Mats Redin, *Studies on Uncompounded Personal Names in Old English* (Uppsala: Akademiska Bokhandeln, 1919), 67, 178–79. Nicknames were apparently used less frequently in Anglo-Saxon England than in Scandinavia, and they were not employed officially to the same extent. However, an increase was seen toward the end of the OE period, presumably due to Scandinavian and Norman influence (178); see Thorvald Forssner,

singular attribute shared by the historical and fictive queens. Once placed in an Anglo-Danish eleventh-century political context, and given the poet's bent toward name-play, *Wealhþēow* could arguably stand as a lexical signature for Emma of Normandy, Cnut's Norman captive, and for what can be viewed as the major event of her life.

The Historical regina famosa

Literary and iconographic images of Emma resonate in the poet's characterization of Wealhtheow. The first of these comes from a late-eleventh-century panegyric. Some years after Emma's death on 6 March 1052, Godfrey, prior of Winchester (1082–1107), composed an internally rhymed epigram, *De regina Emma*, characterizing her as a highly prized ornament well beloved for its perfection: *Splendidior gemma meriti splendoribus Emma* (Emma, a gem more splendid through the splendors of her merits) opens the panegyric to the queen (fig. 6).[57] Godfrey's Emma surpasses the majesty of her

Continental-Germanic Personal Names in England in Old and Middle English Times (Uppsala: K. W. Appelbergs, 1916), esp. 69; Ingrid Hjertstedt, who distinguishes categories of nicknames, *Middle English Nicknames in the Lay Subsidy Rolls for Warwickshire*, Studia Anglistica Upsaliensia 63 (Uppsala: Academiae Upsalien, 1987), 21–23; and J. M. Kemble, "The Names, Surnames, and Nicnames [*sic*] of the Anglo-Saxons," in *Proceedings of the Annual Meeting of the Archaeological Institute at Winchester, 1845* (London, 1846), 92–93, who sees nicknames in the context of personal characteristics.
57. "Splendidior gemma meriti splendoribus Emma, / Omni qua voluit sorte beata fuit. / Hæc habuit natos reges, regesque maritos, / Regum progenie claruit egregie. / Vicit honor morum seriem qua fulsit avorum, / Vicit sermo bonus, mens pia, larga manus. / Dum miseros pavit, gazas super astra levavit, / Cultrix justitiæ serviit ecclesiae. / Exiit avita sumpta de funere vita, / Sex de Marte dies, laeta secuta dies": London, BL, MS Cotton Vitellius A.xii, fol. 131ʳ. *The Anglo-Latin Satirical Poets and Epigrammists of the Twelfth Century*, ed. Thomas Wright, 2 vols. RS 59 (London: Longman, 1872), transcribes the poems. Emma's epigram is found in three manuscripts: London, BL, MS Cotton Vitellius A.xii (which Wright considers the best and from which his transcriptions derive); Oxford, Bodleian Library, MS Digby, No. 65; and Bodleian Library, MS Digby, No. 112.

ancestors, and here he is alluding to Rollo; William I Longsword; Richard I, the fearless, of Normandy; and Gunnor, his extraordinary duchess. Mother of two kings (Harthacnut and Edward),[58] and queen to two others (Æthelred and Cnut), Emma had exemplary characteristics that eclipsed her lineage—noble in mind, excellent in speech, generous, and magnanimous. Naturally open-handed, she dispensed treasures greater than the stars. Although Godfrey's epigram may be dismissed as a typical characterization of a queen, Emma's role as patron to the Church is well attested, as is her connoisseurship in the purchase of relics and her liberality in dispensing them as gifts.[59] But it is Prior Godfrey's rhyme, *gemma/Emma*, that captures the portrait of the queen, resplendent in body as are the treasures "greater than the stars" she offers to others (an image that brings the Beowulfian *bēaghroden cwēn* immediately to mind). The frontispiece to the *Encomium Emmae Reginae* (fig. 7) holds an image of the queen wearing a lily crown that underscores a brilliance of person: the borders of her sleeves and of the closure of her gown contain a string of large oval carbuncles, separated and accentuated by smaller pin-sized jewels. Wearing jewel-studded gowns was not particular to Emma, but the rhyme *gemma/Emma* may have served as an identifying marker, for it is a description—*Emma Normannorum gemma*—appropriated later by Henry of Huntingdon.[60]

The second literary image is found as a cameo-like setpiece in the *Encomium*, a work that is, in Simon Keynes's words, "transparently 'political,'"[61] and its main concern (as Eric John has argued) is to establish the legitimacy of the Danish succession.[62] Commissioned by

---

58. Godfrey omits mention of Emma's daughters: Gunnhild, who became queen of the German king Henry III, son of Conrad II, and future Holy Roman Emperor, and Godgifu, whose second marriage was to Eustace of Boulogne.

59. Heslop, "Production of *de luxe* Manuscripts," esp. 157–58, 161, 169, 177, 182–88.

60. *HHHA* vi.2.

61. Keynes, *EER* [lxviii].

62. John, "*EER*: A Riddle and a Solution," 58–94. John argues for the

Emma, the *Encomium* celebrates the rise of the Anglo-Danish reign of eleventh-century England and Queen Emma as the pivotal monarch in its ascendance.[63] Its Latin rhyming prose reads like a panegyric to the Anglo-Danish reigns of eleventh-century England, beginning with the rise of Sveinn Forkbeard as king of England (1013) and ending with the establishment of Harthacnut, Emma and Cnut's son, as legitimate king of England in 1040, with Edward (Emma's son by Æthelred) as Harthacnut's appointed successor, a codification of a myth of origin of the Anglo-Danish reign, in the tradition of the *Aeneid*, to which the Encomiast refers.[64] The Encomiast—a monk of Saint-Bertin or Saint-Omer—pulls out all his rhetorical stops.[65] In order to highlight Emma's centrality in the Anglo-Danish court, he uses flamboyant alliterative structures, parallelism, balanced structural patterning of phrases and words, and a rhetorical ornateness

---

reliability of the *Encomium* as a historical source in the center of an ongoing political crisis. For views of the *Encomium* as political propaganda, see Körner, *Battle of Hastings*, 47–74, and contra, Miles W. Campbell, "*The Encomium Emmae Reginae*: Personal Panegyric or Political Propaganda?" *Annuale Mediaevale* 19 (1979): 27–45; see also Felice Lipshitz, "*Encomium Emmae Reginae*: A 'Political Pamphlet' of the Eleventh Century?" *Haskins Society Journal* 1 (1989): 39–50, where she argues for the need to read *EER* with an eleventh-century sensibility; and Lawson, *Cnut*, 54–56.

63. *EER*, the introductions by Campbell and Keynes for discussions of Emma; Stafford, *Queen Emma and Queen Edith*; see also Stafford, "Emma: The Powers of the Queen," 3–26; Miles W. Campbell, "Emma, Reine d'Angleterre: Mère dénaturée ou femme vindicative?" *Annale Normandie* (1973): 99–114; his "*Encomium Emmae Reginae*: Personal Panegyric or Political Propaganda?" 27–45; and finally "Queen Emma and Ælfgifu of Northampton: Canute the Great's Women," *Mediaeval Scandinavia* 4 (1971): 66–79; see also Eleanor Searle, "Emma the Conqueror," in *Studies in Medieval History Presented to R. Allen Brown*, ed. C. Harper-Bill et al. (Woodbridge, UK: Boydell Press, 1989), 281–88; Searle, *Predatory Kinship*, esp. 136–40; and Karkov, *Ruler Portraits*, 146–55.

64. See Tyler, "Fictions of Family," 149–79, for a thorough examination of the Encomiast's pointed use of the *Aeneid* particularly in his Prologue and Argument, but also in clusters of allusions within the text proper.

65. Orchard, "Literary Background to the *EER*," 175.

---

similar to that used by the *Beowulf*-poet in his sumptuous rendering of Heorot's queen.

The Encomiast's introduction of Emma is rhetorically embellished, on a par with Dudo's introduction of the Duchess Gunnor:[66]

. . . nil regi defuit absque nobilissima coniuge; quam ubique sibi iussit inquirere, ut inuentam hanc legaliter adquireret, et adeptam imperii sui consortem faceret. Igitur per regna et per urbes discurritur, et regalis sponsa perquiritur; sed longe lateque quaesita, uix tandem digna repperitur. Inuenta est uero haec imperialis sponsa in confinitate Galliae et praecipue in Normandensi regio [ne, stirpe et opibus ditissima, sed tamen pulcritudinis et prudentiae delectamine omnium eius temporum mulierum præstantissima, utpote regina famosa. Propter huiuscemodi insignia multum appetebatur a rege, et pro hoc præcipue quod erat oriunda ex uictrici gente, quæ sibi partem Galliæ uendicauerat inuitis Francigenis et eorum principe. Quid multis immoror? Mittuntur proci ad dominam, mittuntur dona regalia, mittuntur etiam uerba precatoria. Sed abnegat illa, se unquam Cnutonis sponsam fieri, nisi illi iusiurando affirmaret, quod numquam alterius coniugis filium post se regnare faceret nisi eius, si forte illi Deus ex eo filium dedisset. Dicebatur enim ab alia quadam rex filios habuisse; unde illa suis prudenter prouidens sciuit ipsis sagaci animo profutura præordinare. Placuit ergo regi uerbum uirginis,* et iusiurando facto uirgini* placuit uoluntas regis,] et sic Deo gratias domina Emma mulierum nobilissima fit coniunx regis fortis[s]imi Cnutonis. Leta<e>tur Gallia, letatur etiam Anglorum patria, dum tantum decus transuehitur per aequora. Letatur, inquam, Gallia, tantam tanto regi dignam se enixam, Anglorum uero letatur patria, talem se recepisse in oppida. O res millenis milies petita uotis, uixque tandem effecta auspicante gratia Saluatoris. Hoc erat quod utrobique uehementer iam dudum

---

66. Campbell, *EER* cxvii; *Dudo of St Quentin. History of the Normans*, trans. Eric Christiansen (Woodbridge, UK: Boydell Press, 1998), 139, 163–64; and Searle, *Predatory Kinship*, 87–90, 100–107, and "Fact and Pattern in Heroic History: Dudo of Saint-Quentin," *Viator* 15 (1984): 119–38.

desiderauerat exercitus, scilicet ut tanta tanto, digna etiam digno, maritali conuinculata iugo, bellicos sedaret motus (*EER* 2.16).[67]

[. . . the king lacked nothing except a most noble wife; such a one he ordered to be sought everywhere for him, in order to obtain her hand lawfully, when she was found, and to make her the partner of his rule, when she was won. Therefore journeys were undertaken through realms and cities and a royal bride was sought; but it was with difficulty that a worthy one was ultimately found, after being sought far and wide. This imperial bride was, in fact, found within the bounds of Gaul, and to be precise in the Norman area, a lady of the greatest nobility and wealth, but yet the most distinguished of the women of her time for delightful beauty and wisdom, inasmuch as she was a famous queen. In view of her distinguished qualities of this kind, she was much desired by the king, and especially because she derived her origin from a victorious people, who had appropriated for themselves part of Gaul, in despite of the French and their prince. Why should I make a long story of this? Wooers were sent to the lady, royal gifts were sent, furthermore precatory messages were sent. But she refused ever to become the bride of Knútr, unless he would affirm to her by oath, that he would never set up the son of any wife other than herself to rule after him, if it happened that God should give her a son by him. For she had information that the king had had sons by some other woman; so she, wisely providing for her offspring, knew in her wisdom how to make arrangements in advance, which were to be to their advantage. Accordingly the king found what the lady* said acceptable, and when the oath had been taken, the lady* found the will of the king acceptable, and so, thanks be to God, Emma noblest of women, became the wife of the very mighty King

67. *EER*, 32–33, ed. and trans. Campbell. Campbell twice translates *virgo* as "lady" here, downplaying the Marian allusion intimately associated with Emma; see above, the discussion on *Liber Vitae* (above, 212–14) and Catherine E. Karkov, "Emma: Image and Ideology," in *Early Medieval Studies in Memory of Patrick Wormald*, ed. S. Baxter et al., 509–70.

Knútr. Gaul rejoiced, the land of the English rejoiced likewise, when so great an ornament [*decus*] was conveyed over the seas. Gaul, I say, rejoiced to have brought forth so great a lady, and one worthy of so great a king, the country of the English indeed rejoiced to have received such a one into its towns. What an event, sought with a million prayers, and at length barely brought to pass under the Saviour's favouring grace! This was what the army had long eagerly desired on both sides, that is to say that so great a lady, bound by a matrimonial link to so great a man, worthy of her husband as he was worthy of her, should lay the disturbances of war to rest.]

This passage is often cited as contradicting Emma's presence in London during the siege in 1016 (see above, 218–24). If, however, the thrust of the passage is to introduce the themes of shared sovereignty and legitimate accession to the throne, as I believe it is, then the avoidance of the captivity narrative and the insertion here of the Norman realm are appropriate, for the queen, bearer of the future king, is presented as emblematic of royal womanhood in whose person Normandy, Denmark, and England reside.[68] Moreover, by identifying Emma as *regina famosa* at the critical moment she becomes Cnut's consort (*imperialis sponsa*), the Encomiast suggests that she has attained the status of sovereign in her own right.

In his discussion of the *Encomium*'s literary merit in eleventh-century Latin literature, Orchard analyzes the Encomiast's "allusive artfulness" in depicting Emma. For Orchard, the introduction of Emma is a "bombastic set-piece," wherein the Encomiast demonstrates his rhetorical brilliance, using "rhetorical question, alliteration, repetition, and paronomasia in the wooing itself (*Quid multis immoror? Mittuntur proci ad dominam, mittuntur dona regalia, mittuntur etiam uerba precatoria*),

---

68. See, however, Tyler, "Fictions of Family," 153–54, who cites this passage as an example of the Encomiast's "openly" and "deliberately" fictionalizing his political history (154). A portion of the Encomiast's panegyric to Emma is not in London, BL, MS Add. 33, 241; between folios 47 and 48, there is a missing leaf at the end of the gathering.

not to mention the repetition and balanced phrasing" of the depiction of the rejoicing of England and Normandy and the "patterned words" describing the mutual acceptance of the prenuptial dynastic agreement.[69] Although Orchard does not make the connection, perhaps because such extravagant descriptions for queens may have been rhetorical conventions, the Encomiast's rhetorical style is thus similar to the *Beowulf*-poet's elaborately staged entrance for Wealhtheow, his use of balanced chiastic patterning, repetitious alliterative and metrical structures, intricate antithesis and parallelism, and effusive epithets to describe Heorot's queen.[70] It is as if both authors had been schooled in a similar rhetorical tradition, the difference being that the Encomiast writes in Latin prose within the tradition of eleventh-century historiography, while the *Beowulf*-poet, composing in a new tongue within a hybrid form of Germanic and biblical epic, gives public voice to his queen as she executes the tasks of the realm.

The Latin literary images presented above accord with several of the historical queen's attributes, the most fundamental being that she is from Normandy, a part of Gaul that had risen to prominence within the queen's lifetime. For Godfrey, Emma's fame surpasses that of her ancestors, a line that in the year Godfrey composed the epigram included William of Normandy, Emma's grandnephew and the future conqueror of Anglo-Saxon England. The Encomiast, too, emphasizes the centrality of Normandy to Emma's character: politically shrewd in her premarital contract with Cnut, she made certain that a male offspring born to them would be his heir to the throne, as she had previously contracted with Æthelred for Edward, as recorded later in the anonymous *Vita Ædwardi*:

> Antiqui regis Æthelredi regia coniuge utero grauida, in eius partus sobole si masculus prodiret omnis coniurat patria, in eo se dominum expectare et regem, qui regeret uniuersam Anglorum gentem. (*VÆdr* i.1)

---

69. Orchard, "Literary Background to the *EER*," quote at 175.
70. See *Bwf* 612–41, in Damico, *Beowulf's Wealhtheow and the Valkyrie Tradition*, chap. 1.

[When the royal wife of old King Æthelred was pregnant in her womb, all the men of the country took an oath that if a man child should come forth as the fruit of her labour, they would await in him their lord and king who would rule over the whole race of the English]. (Barlow translation)[71]

Armed with lawful promises to her unborn male children, Emma achieved her main objective of securing the succession for her sons, Harthacnut, Edward, and Alfred, and continuing the royal Norman line; as a corollary, she secured her own political office as queen of England.[72] The Encomiast and the prior accord in other descriptions of the *regina famosa*, a queen who had ruled a people (suggested by the Encomiast; a fact for the prior). Emma has wisdom, nobility, wealth, generosity, political acumen, and verbal facility. Described as an ornament (*decus*) by the Encomiast, she is *gemma/Emma* for Godfrey. Finally, the queen functions as a *friðusibb* (peace-maker), effecting the end of hostilities and uniting Normandy and England in her person.

The Beowulfian *mǣru cwēn*

Emma's characteristics resonate in Wealhtheow. Not only may Emma's Norman roots be encoded in the Beowulfian queen's name, but her introduction in the first banquet scene also evokes a begemmed and resplendent *folccwēn*, possessing all the physical and

---

71. *VÆdr*, ed. and trans. Barlow, 7–8, record the court's early acceptance of Edward as heir apparent; see also Elisabeth M. C. van Houts, "Historiography and Hagiography at Saint-Wandrille: The *Inventio et Miracula Sancti Vulfranni*," in Anglo-Norman Studies 12, *Proceedings of the Battle Conference 1989*, ed. Marjorie Chibnall (Woodbridge, UK: Boydell, 1990), 233–51, esp. 247–49; Pauline Stafford, "The Reign of Æthelred II," in *Ethelred the Unready*, ed. Hill, 36–37; and Lawson, *Cnut*, 78–79, 86–88, 113–14.

72. Stafford, "Emma: The Powers of the Queen," in *Queens and Queenship*, ed. Duggan, 16–17, 21–23, discusses the precarious position of English queens, who were still unable to rule independently in eleventh-century England.

mental attributes that characterize Cnut's Emma. Described three times in succession as being begemmed (*goldhroden, bēaghroden, gold-hroden*) and three times as *cwēn*, she at once exhibits tangible wealth and stands as a metaphor for the treasure itself. And like Godfrey's Emma, in line with her status as co-sovereign of Heorot, she dispenses treasure similar to the jewels described by the prior as being "greater [in number] than the stars"—among which is the *healsbēaga mǣst* (greatest of torcs), on a par with Freyja's *Brísinga men*, its beauty and value underscored by the digression narrating its history.

In addition, similarities in action and subtle verbal resonances connect the two queens. In the first banquet scene, Wealhtheow's welcoming of Beowulf in indirect discourse contains verbal and thematic resonances with the Encomiast's description of Emma's welcoming her son Harthacnut. The *Encomium*'s scene is one of homecoming. Emma has longingly awaited Harthacnut's return from Denmark to unseat the usurper Harold Harefoot and assert his rightful claim to the English throne. Harthacnut has just landed, and

> anchoris rudibusque nauibus affixis et nautis qui eas seruarent expeditis recta se uia cum delectis ad hospicium dirigit matris. Qualis ergo meror qualisque letitia in eius aduentu fuerit exorta, nulla tibi umquam explicabit pagina. (*EER* 3.10)[73]

> [having moored his ships with anchors and rods, and having commissioned sailors to look after them, he betook himself directly with chosen companions to the lodging of his mother. What grief and what joy sprang up at his arrival, no page shall ever unfold to you.]

The Encomiast's description of the ships landing, mooring, and being guarded at anchor, of the hero being accompanied by "chosen companions" and subsequently meeting with the Norman queen parallel the Beowulfian sequences describing Beowulf's landing and progress to Heorot (*Bwf* 205–7[a], 258–311, esp. 301–11).[74] Augmenting

---

73. *EER*, 50–51, ed. Campbell.
74. Both passages reflect Virgilian influence, in particular the battle at

the likeness in setting are similarities in the queens' responses on meeting their respective heroes. In the *Encomium*, Emma expresses confidence in God's mercy and regard for her since he has given her the consolation of her son's return:

> item gaudio magno gaudebat, dum superstitem saluum adesse sibi uidebat. Unde uiscera diuinae misericordiae se sciebat respicere, cum nondum tali fru[s]traretur solamine. (*EER* 3.10)[75]

> [likewise she rejoiced with a great joy at seeing the survivor [Harthacnut] safe in her presence. And so she knew that the tender mercy of God had regard for her, since she was still undeprived of such a consolation.]

In the Beowulfian welcoming, in addition to the motifs of joy and fulfillment of a desire for the hero's arrival, Wealhtheow's acknowledgment of and gratitude to God, who has given her consolation for the evils of Grendel, accord with the *Encomium* passage:

> oþ þæt sæl ālamp,
> þæt hīo Bēowulfe, bēaghroden cwēn
> mōde geþungen medoful ætbær;
> grētte Gēata lēod, Gode þancode
> wīsfæst wordum þæs ðe hire se willa gelamp,
> þæt hēo on ænigne eorl gelyfde
> fyrena frōfre. (*Bwf* 623[b]–28[a])

> [until the moment arrived when she, ring-adorned queen, with excellence of mind, bore the mead-cup to Beowulf. She greeted

---

Actium (although in fact the battle of Actium does not appear in the *Aeneid*, but is rather an earlier allegorical interpretation imposed upon the poem). The Encomiast's rendering presents a diffuse and abridged Virgilian parallel, lacking the heroic thrust that characterizes the Beowulfian crossing, even though the Beowulfian version itself is a "reduced" rendering of Virgil's scene; on the Beowulfian crossing, see Andersson, *Early Epic Scenery*, 146–53, at 153; on Harthacnut's crossing, see Tyler, "Fictions of Family," 171–74.

75. *EER*, 50–51, ed. Campbell.

the prince of the Geats, thanked God with words rooted in wisdom because the wished-for thing had come to pass for her, that she might count on a nobleman for consolation for the evils.]

Given the other resemblances between Emma and Wealhtheow, these verbal and thematic correspondences are more than superficial and point to an interrelationship between the poetic dramatization and the Latinate narrative.

A further correspondence deals with the original ending of the *Encomium*, the dedication image of Emma on its frontispiece (see fig. 7), and the iconic dramatization of Wealhtheow in the second banquet scene. The frontispiece presents a tableau of an enthroned Emma in majesty; the figure of the queen commands almost the entire space, with the kneeling author and the queen's sons King Harthacnut and Edward, the heir apparent, at her left, posed in admiration but crowding the edge of the frame. The tableau suggests an idealized triad of a dowager queen with her two reigning sons; but although Harthacnut and Edward wear crowns, they are smaller in size, and it is Emma (rather than Harthacnut) who sits in imperial majesty, wearing the lily crown worn by Anglo-Saxon and Carolingian kings.[76] It is an image, as Catherine E. Karkov suggests, for which there is no real precedent in the Western representation of gendered power.[77]

---

76. Karkov, *Ruler Portraits*, 129, states that, though there are images of Anglo-Saxon queens wearing crowns, no material evidence thus far suggests what such crowns may have looked like.

77. Karkov, *Ruler Portraits*, 152–56; see also Stafford's reading of the image, in which she states that it "may be the earliest representation of an enthroned lay figure in an English associated manuscript," in "Emma: The Powers of the Queen," 5–6, at 5n8. For a discussion of the sources and "the iconography of power" inherent in the sacral-political thrust of the composition (its Marian allusions in the context of female sovereignty and its relationship to presentation portraits of kings, popes, and other important male figures), see also Karkov, "Emma: Image and Ideology," in *Early Medieval Studies*, ed. Baxter et al., 509–20; see also Carol Newman de Vegvar, "A Paean for a Queen," *Old English Newsletter* 26 (1992): 57–58, who discusses the *Encomium* portrait as a fusion of two Carolingian models (the presentation of a book to the donor; the enthroned ruler) and the

Emma emerges after Cnut's death as the Anglo-Danish monarch who was there from the beginning of the dynasty to its heights and, as the Encomiast reports, "embraces absolutely all of what [his] book amounts to,"[78] a book that celebrates the present Anglo-Danish reign (in the figure of Harthacnut), looks forward to the establishment of the Anglo-Norman reign of Edward, and presents Emma as the originator of that dynasty.

Karkov, Orchard, and Stafford find a relationship between the frontispiece and the *Encomium*'s ending:

> Qui fratris iussioni obaudiens Anglicas partes aduehitur, et mater amboque filii regni paratis commodis nulla lite intercedente utuntur. Hic fides habetur regni sotiis, hic inuiolabile uiget faedus materni fraternique amoris. Haec illis omnia prestitit, qui unanimes in domo habitare facit, Iesus Christus,[79] Dominus omnium, cui in Trinitate manenti immarcessibile floret imperium. Amen. (*EER* 3.14)[80]

> [Obeying his brother's [Harthacnut's] command, he [Edward] was conveyed to England, and the mother and both sons, having no disagreement between them, enjoy the ready amenities of the kingdom. Here there *is* loyalty among sharers of rule, here the bond of motherly and brotherly love is of strength indestructible. All these things were granted them by Him, who makes dwellers in a house be of one mind, Jesus Christ, the Lord of all, who, abiding in the Trinity, holds a kingdom which flourishes unfading. Amen.]

The Encomiast's closure mirrors the image of the frontispiece. It captures a victorious Emma in 1041 at the height of an imperial power that matches Cnut's, after having survived the dynastic upheaval that

---

significance of a consecrated, enthroned queen.

78. *EER*, Argument, 7.

79. The phrase *qui unanimes in domo habitare facit, Iesus Christus*, is reminiscent of Psalm 67.7 of the Latin Vulgate and to a lesser extent of Psalm 132.1; see Campbell, *EER* [cxi].

80. *EER*, 52–53, ed. Campbell.

followed Cnut's death, during which her younger son Alfred was bru-
tally murdered and she was driven into exile by the usurper Harold
Harefoot. The Encomiast's benediction and prayer render divine
approval of the new reign.

The gendered power (to use Karkov's phrase) of the image presented in the frontispiece and the Encomiast's closing remarks
underlie the tone and texture of Wealhtheow's appearance in the
second banquet scene, where she, *under gyldnum bēage* (beneath the
golden crown or diadem, *Bwf* 1163[a]), is presented for the first time in
the poem as a queen-mother figure par excellence, an originator of
a heroic race, determining its dynastic succession.[81] The scene dramatizes the regal ceremonial event of the elevation of the hero to a new
sociopolitical status and the election of the future ruler of Heorot at
the start of a new political age, central issues that impact the legitimate continuation of the poem's Danish kingdom. The situation, I
suggest, may be parallel to the dynastic instability that prevailed in
Anglo-Saxon England near the end of the first half of the eleventh
century, reaching a peaceful, if precarious, conclusion for a time with
the investiture of Harthacnut as king in 1041. This is not to imply that
the second banquet scene is an innovative, imaginative dramatization of the Danish king's investiture, for there is no extant evidence
for Harthacnut's coronation.[82] Nonetheless, the lavish presentation

---

81. Whether "diadem" or "crown," the image here may carry Marian
associations, as it does in the *Encomium* and *Liber Vitae* images of Emma
discussed by Karkov; see above, n. 77.

82. George Garnett, "Coronation," in *Blackwell Encyclopaedia*, ed.
Lapidge et al., 122–24, esp. 123; Janet L. Nelson and Peter W. Hammond,
"Coronation," in *Medieval England*, ed. Szarmach et al., 207–9, esp. 208;
but see *JWChron* (s.a. 1040), 528–29 for Harthacnut's being immediately
"raised to the throne of the kingdom." On coronation ceremonies, see P[aul]
L. Ward, "The Coronation Ceremony in Mediaeval England," *Speculum* 14
(1939): 160–78, and his "An Early Version of the Anglo-Saxon Coronation
Ceremony," *English Historical Review* 57, no. 227 (1942): 345–61, where he
speaks of the difficulties in identifying texts used at specific ceremonies;
on this, see also the "Promissio Regis," possibly the coronation oath of
King Æthelred, in *Memorials of Saint Dunstan*, ed. Stubbs, RS 63, 355–57;

of regal weaponry to Beowulf, each item imbued with sacral symbolism and representing the material signs of the duties of kingship,
of defending, judging, and administering a kingdom, with the added
descriptive emphasis on the helmet, which sometime after the ninth
century was replaced by a crown, would suggest that the poet may
have modeled his scene on a type of royal status-changing rite.[83]

Hrothgar's speech to Beowulf at the threshold, which sets into
motion the events that are to unfold within the hall, can be seen as a
prelude to this type of sacral-political ceremony.[84] Hrothgar's speech,
distinguished by its religio-political tone, commences as a praise-song
of thanksgiving to the Almighty for Beowulf's arrival and continues
with a genealogical passage, praising Beowulf's mother in language
that has been generally thought to carry Marian allusions, specifically to the nativity of Christ, the only such allusion in the poem, and
one of its few reverberations of the New Testament.[85] It then immediately articulates the purpose of the ceremonial gathering to take

---

and Robertson, "Promissio Regis," in *Laws of the Kings of England*, 40–43,
311. See also Stafford, "Laws of Cnut," esp. 178–87, who discusses I and II
Cnut as reflecting the possible existence of a Coronation Charter by Cnut,
although no coronation oath is extant.

83. Garnett, "Coronation"; Nelson and Hammond, "Coronation"; see
also Janet L. Nelson, "Inauguration Rituals," in her *Politics and Ritual in
Early Medieval Europe*, 283–307, esp. 290, as well as "Ritual and Reality in
the Early Medieval *Ordines*," in the same volume, 329–39.

84. I begin the status-changing rite celebrating the elevation of Beowulf
onto a more exalted position here at line 925 at the start of Fitt 14 through
Fitt 18, although Klaeber delimits the episode (Royal Entertainment in
Heorot) from 991 to 1250 (Fitt 15–18); Klaeber, 3rd ed., 168; also Klaeber,
4th ed., 176. Both Klaeber 3rd and 4th title ll. 925–90 as "Speech-making
by Hroðgar and Beowulf," 166–68, 172–75, respectively.

85. Klaeber, 3rd ed., 166–67, Luke 11.27; *Bwf* 942ᵇ–46ᵃ: *Hwæt, þæt secgan
mæg / efne swā hwylc mægþa swā ðone magan cende / æfter gumcynnum, gyf hēo
gȳt lyfað, / þæt hyre Ealdmetod ēste wǣre / bearngebyrdo* (Listen, whichever
maiden birthed such a son into the race of mankind, this she has the power
to say, if she still lives, that the time-honored God was gracious to her in her
childbearing); see Karkov, "Emma: Image and Ideology," 509–20.

place within, the elevation of Beowulf to an enhanced sociopolitical status:

> "Nū ic, Bēowulf, þec,
> secg betsta, mē for sunu wylle
> frēogan on ferhþe; heald forð tela
> nīwe sibbe. Ne bið þē [n]ænigre gād
> worolde wilna, þē ic geweald hæbbe.
> Ful oft ic for læssan lēan teohhode,
> hordweorþunge hnāhran rince,
> sæmran æt sæcce. Þū þē self hafast
> dædum gefremed, þæt þīn [dóm] lyfað
> āwa tō aldre. Alwalda þec
> gōde forgylde, swā hē nū gȳt dyde!" (*Bwf* 946^b–56)

[Now, Beowulf, best of warriors,
I want to love you in spirit as [I would] a son.
Henceforth, hold this new kinship rightly.
You will have no lack of the worldly goods over which I have
  power.
Very often I have allotted rewards for less,
honoring with gifts a lesser warrior,
inferior to you in battle. You, by yourself, have
performed deeds so that your fame will live
through all time. The omnipotent Lord
repay you liberally, as he now has done.]

In gratitude for Beowulf's services in ridding Heorot of Grendel's terror, the king expresses his desire for a new relationship with the Geatish prince, but the *nīwe sibbe* Hrothgar proposes, as Klaeber, Bruce Mitchell, Fred C. Robinson, and others have rightly noted,[86]

---

86. Klaeber, 3rd ed., n. 946ff., 167: "The relationship entered into by Hroðgar and Beowulf does not signify adoption in the strict legal sense, but implies fatherly friendship and devoted helpfulness respectively, suggesting at any rate the bonds of loyal retainership." See also *Beowulf: An Edition with Relevant Shorter Texts, including "Archaeology and Beowulf"*

is not to be taken in a literal, legal sense but rather, as the phrase *frēogan on ferhþe* suggests, cosmically and spiritually, describing a relationship based on reciprocal bonds of obligation, loyalty, and grace. Beowulf would seem to understand the relationship in this intangible yet binding sense later as he is about to dive into the mere, reminding Hrothgar, *on fæder stæle* (in the place of a father), to shield and protect his men (*Bwf* 1476–79); and elsewhere in the poem, *frēogan on ferhþe* carries this gnomic understanding, as in line 3176, where the narrator states that one should love his lord in mind and spirit (*ferhðum frēoge*).[87] Moreover, if we are to take into account the word-play suggested by the term *sib*, the bond of kinship being proposed is to serve as a harbinger for a new age of "peace." Hrothgar understands the polysemous nature of that relationship as he bids farewell to Beowulf: *Hafast þū gefēred, þæt þām folcum sceal, / Gēata lēodum ond Gār-Denum / sib gemǣn[e], ond sacu restan, / inwītniþas, þē hīe ǣr drugon, / wesan* (You have brought it about that, for the people, the people of the Geats and the Spear Danes, a mutual peace/kinship is obliged to come to pass and hostilities and malicious acts laid to rest that they previously endured [1855–59ᵃ]). Instead, the *nīwe sibbe* Hrothgar proposes, everlasting and unbounded by time or place, may be rather understood as a kinship akin to those being contracted in Old Testament promissory covenants (to be discussed further below), especially those reported to have taken place between God and Abraham in Genesis 15 and 17, where God rewards Abraham for his past and continuing obedience. Hrothgar's speech, I suggest, sets in motion similar events to those attendant to the elevation of Abraham as patriarch, a situation that may likewise be reflective of the status-changing relationship expressed in the ecclesiastical-political rites of

---

by Leslie Webster, ed. Bruce Mitchell and Fred C. Robinson (Oxford: Blackwell, 1998), esp. 79 ("[*nīwe sibbe*] does not constitute literal adoption but was merely a king's way of affirming a close alliance and firm bond of fealty"). See also Klaeber, 4th ed., n. 946 ff., 173; Chickering, *Beowulf: A Dual-Language Edition*, 319; but see Irving, *Rereading Beowulf*, 55, 61.

87. Throughout *Beowulf*, *ferhþe* carries the meaning of "spirit, mind."

king-making in early England that intangibly and perpetually bound king and people.[88]

At the closure of the *Encomium Emmae Reginae*, the Encomiast makes reference to this type of ceremonial occasion, in summarizing events surrounding Harthacnut's formal civil election and his assumption of royal authority as king of England:

> Igitur principes Anglici parum praemissae fidentes legationi, antequam ab illis transfretaretur, obuii sunt facti optimum factu rati, ut et regi reginaeque satisfacerent, et se deuotos eorum dominationi subderent. His Hardecnuto cum matre certus factus et transmarini littoris tandem portum nactus, a cunctis incolis eiusdem terrae gloriosissime recipitur, sicque diuini muneris gratia regnum sibi debitum redditur. (*EER* 3.13)[89]

> [Under these circumstances the English nobles [the English *witan*], lacking confidence in the legation previously sent, met them [Emma and Harthacnut] before they crossed the sea, deeming that the best course was for them to make amends to the king and queen, and to place themselves devotedly under their dominion. When Hörthaknútr and his mother had been apprised by these men, and when he had at length reached a port on the other side of the sea, he was most gloriously received by all the inhabitants of that country.]

The *Encomium* gives little detail as to what, in all likelihood, were highly charged discussions among members of the *witan* before the

---

88. See Stafford, "Laws of Cnut," 173–90, esp. 173, 177–78. At the prologues of royal codes and grants, a personal statement that serves as an authentication of the code appears; for types and order of inauguration rituals, see Nelson, "Ritual and Reality in the Early Medieval *Ordines*," esp. 335, 337–38; on the indirect connection between Old Testament king-making and royal anointing in early England, see also "National Synods, Kingship and Royal Anointing," in her *Politics and Ritual in Early Medieval Europe*, esp. 248–52.

89. *EER* 52–53, ed. Campbell.

decision was made to establish a *frið and frēondscip* (peace and friend-ship) with and place themselves under the "dominion" of the dow-ager queen, Emma of Normandy, and King Harthacnut, Cnut's son, but such meetings and their attendant celebrations are sure to have taken place.[90]

It is against this type of sacral-political, historically potent back-ground that, I suggest, the *Beowulf*-poet chose to stage the second banquet scene. Beowulf, of course, is not consecrated as king, but his elevation to a new sociopolitical level brings him solidly within the Danish kingdom, tied irrevocably to its future rulers and obliged to promote the solidarity of its court, duties analogous to those that define a relationship of a new king to his people. He is a major player in the ritualistic procedures that take place: the deliberations over the election of Heorot's future king, the status-raising rite that out-lines his responsibilities and obligations, and the ceremonial feast, the three stages in the making of kings in early England.[91] And rather than Hrothgar, as would be expected, the officiator of the ceremonies is Heorot's queen.

Queen Wealhtheow brings to life Stafford's description of female royal power achieved through "verbal politics," displaying her legitimate power as mother of kings and her authority as *friðusibb* in maintaining "order, hierarchy, and coherence" in the reign.[92] In

90. The phrase *frið and frēondscip* appears in Stafford's discussion of a preamble to a possible meeting between Cnut and the *witan* at Oxford in 1018; Stafford, "Laws of Cnut," 173–74.

91. For the paucity of full records detailing the ritual process of royal consecration, see Nelson, "Ritual and Reality in the Early Medieval *Ordines*," esp. 330–33. It is possible, however, to "piece together" informa-tion from various sources that point to three stages inherent in the ritual connected with the making of a tenth-century Anglo-Saxon king (Nelson, 330–36, at 330).

92. Stafford, "Emma: The Powers of the Queen," 10–16, where she discusses the power and authority of eleventh-century queens in general and of Emma in particular, defining power as the "ability to act" and authority as the "right to act" (11, 13); also see her *Queen Emma and Queen*

the presence of the full company of nobles and princes, the queen celebrates victory and solidarity; *Heorot is gefælsod* (Heorot has been purged, *Bwf* 1176[b]) of Grendel's tyrannical hold. *Cynna gemyndig* (mindful of the race [or kin], *Bwf* 613[b]),[93] the queen here emphasizes the race's solidarity based on blood-kinship as an essential to rule and, with sharpness of intellect, directs the orderly disposition of the king's immense treasure, the legalities of which call to mind multi-gift royal wills and charters.[94] Remarkable not only for its use of the imperative but also for the pointed application of pronominal forms in illustrating and clarifying the exactness of their family relationships, the queen's speech is a directive to preserve the orderly transference of the realm within the familial group. She elaborates upon and delimits the stipulations of the king's offer of a *nīwe sibbe* to Beowulf, to whom, admittedly, the Danes are much indebted, but who nonetheless lies outside her blood-kin group. Hrothgar's material goods, the treasure accumulated from the far reaches of the earth that constitutes his worldly dominion, are to go to Beowulf; the kingdom, however, is to go to the kin-group, to Hrothulf, sitting on the dais with Hrothgar (*sib ætgædere*, "[her] kin together" "their peace intact," *Bwf* 1164[b]), as heir apparent, with his brothers Hrethric and Hrothmund, as next in line of succession, seated together with Beowulf among the *giogoð ætgædere* (band of young retainers, *Bwf* 1190[a]). The complementary physical arrangement of the two groups identifies those on the dais

---

Edith, 117, 159.

93. But see Klaeber's glossary, under *cynn*, which he glosses at 613[b] uniquely as "proper proceeding, etiquette, courtesy," whereas elsewhere in the poem the term carries the signification of "race, species" (*Bwf* 98 [species], 702, 712, 735, 810, 914, 1058, 1725 [race]), in effect downplaying Wealhtheow's political status in the poem; Klaeber, 3rd ed., s.a. *cynn*; likewise Klaeber, 4th ed.

94. K. A. Lowe, "Wills," in *Blackwell Encyclopaedia*, ed. Lapidge et al., 478–80, esp. 479; see also Whitelock, ed., *EHD*, for translations of selected royal wills and charters, nos. 130–34; on blood-kinship, inheritance, and right to rule, see Michael D. C. Drout, "Blood and Deeds: The Inheritance Systems in *Beowulf*," *Studies in Philology* 104 (2007): 199–226, esp. 207–12.

as rulers of Heorot for the second time in the poem (*Bwf* 1017ᵃ), as distinct from the group that includes Beowulf, the princes, and the noble *geogoð*, recipients of royal favor, however ambiguous that relationship between the two groups may be.[95]

The queen's grammatical mode of expression and her incisiveness of action in averting a possible dynastic crisis with speed and diplomacy are attributes of a character who holds independent authority to intervene in the political affairs of the realm and who evidently shares equally with Hrothgar the power and dignity of the Danish court, a power and authority that apparently identified female sovereigns of eleventh-century England. The legitimacy of Wealhtheow's actions originates from her rights as queen. No one—not the king, the counselor, or the male courtiers—prevents her from publicly countering the king's wishes (if with diplomacy) and apprising him and the court on dynastic matters. Instead, some twenty-five lines later, after the extended digression relating the history of the great neck-ring, *healsbēaga mǣst*, and Hygelac's ill-fated Frisian raid while bearing the ring (*Bwf* 1201), the court resoundingly acclaims the queen's actions: *Heal swege onfēng* (the hall reverberated with sound, *Bwf* 1214ᵇ).[96] In the context of the present discussion on status-changing rites, the court's acclamation bears a resemblance to the *vivat rex*, the people's shout recognizing their new king.[97] Wealhtheow's bearing and her political acumen are characteristic attributes of the historical Emma

---

95. As noted above (see n. 4), this is a much-contested speech; see also Klaeber, who sees the queen as an advocate for Hrethric as heir apparent (Klaeber, 3rd ed., 179 nn. 1219ᵇ–1220, as one example). These interpretations are the convention, perhaps because of Hrothulf's alleged treachery in the legendary material, but with no textual support in the poem or largely in the legendary materials, as Kenneth Sisam argued long ago (*The Structure of Beowulf* [Oxford: Clarendon Press, 1965], esp. 34–38), an argument as yet not refuted; see also Klaeber, 4th ed., nn. 1017–19, 1169ff., 177, 192.

96. But see Orchard, *Companion to Beowulf*, 221, who judges Wealhtheow's rhetorical talents in her political speeches to be ineffectual because neither Hrothgar nor Beowulf (nor any other prince assembled in the hall) "sees fit to respond."

97. Nelson, "Ritual and Reality in the Early Medieval *Ordines*," 335.

as presented in the historical sources. The narrative cruces that arise stem from, I suggest, the friction caused by the poet's appropriation and consolidation of contemporary "facts" of history and legendary narrative coming into contact with his own imaginative powers.

The royal family described by Queen Wealhtheow, for example, seems akin to Queen Emma's. Wealhtheow's political objective (one might even say demand) to uphold *mīnne . . . glædne Hrōþulf* (my munificent Hrothulf, *Bwf* 1180[b]–81[a]) as the inheritor of the Danish crown is suggestive of a unique familial relationship between the queen and the heir apparent. The queen's distinct relationship to the royal prince on the dais apparently differs from that which she has with Hrethric and Hrothmund.[98] The poet's dense pronominal use marks that distinction, particularly evident in *mīnne . . . glædne Hrōþulf*, a phrase which, in the context of the passage, implies familial exclusivity. The pronoun is further emphasized by its placement as the alliterator, controlling the sound pattern of the line, a disruption of the normal hierarchical pattern of alliteration. No such manipulation of the hierarchical order of alliteration obtains when Wealhtheow speaks of her relationship to Hrethric and Hrothmund, her sons by Hrothgar. The princes are *uncran eaferan* (our two sons), using the dual pronominal form that stresses their joint parentage,

---

98. "'Ic mīnne can / glædne Hrōþulf, þæt hē þā geogoðe wile / ārum healdan, gyf þū ær þonne hē, / wine Scildinga, worold oflætest; / wēne ic þæt hē mid gōde gyldan wille / uncran eaferan, gif hē þæt eal gemon, / hwæt wit tō willan ond tō worðmyndum / umborwesendum ær ārna gefremedon.' / Hwearf þā bī bence, þær hyre byre wæron, / Hrēðric ond Hrōðmund, ond hæleþa bearn, / giogoð ætgædere; þær se gōda sæt, / Bēowulf Gēata be þæm gebrōðrum twæm" (1180–91). ("I know that my munificent [or gracious] Hrothulf will honorably rule the band of young retainers, if you, friend of the Scyldings, relinquish the world before him. I expect that he will wish to requite our sons with goodness, if he bears in mind all that, what honors we two willingly and with glory bestowed on him when he was becoming a child [or in the process of being a child]." She turned then to the bench where their children were, Hrethric and Hrothmund, and the sons of the heroes, the band of young retainers [gathered] together; there the good one, Beowulf of the Geats, sat alongside the two brothers.)

and *hyre byre* (their [or her] sons), when the poet-narrator draws attention to the princes sitting apart from the royal group on the dais. In addition, when Wealhtheow refers to Hrothgar's relationship to Hrothulf, she again signals a select familial relationship, using the second-person pronoun *þīnum*, *þīnum māgum* (your kinsmen or your blood kinsmen, *Bwf* 1178[b]) instead of the plural *ūre* (our) or the dual *uncer* (our two), both of which would have been metrically possible and likewise appropriate, for the semantic spread of *māgum* in the plural dative encompasses a familial range that includes kinsmen (*mǣg>māgum*) and sons (*māga>māgum*). What the poet seems to be conveying here by using the first- and second-person pronouns rather than the dual or plural forms is that Hrothulf's kinship with the king and queen is distinctive: he is *þīnum māgum* to Hrothgar, but *mīnne . . . glædne Hrōþulf* to the queen. This pointed use of pronominal forms for character delineations suggests that the phrase *mīnne . . . glædne Hrōþulf* may very well signal that Hrothulf is the queen's offspring by another marriage. Wealhtheow is thus cryptically presented as the mother of three sons, two sons from one marriage and one from another, which accords with the legendary material[99] and, I suggest, with the "facts" of history. To secure the dynastic succession for her own *māgum* (sons), Hrothulf and the two princes, in the face of an outsider whom Hrothgar would treat as he would a son, is Wealhtheow's driving motive in the scene.

The Beowulfian iconic dramatization of a queen fighting for three legitimate sons' rightful succession to the throne in the face of an outside contender who holds a kinship to the king (however loose) evokes Emma's political maneuvers in the years that followed Cnut's death. Between 1035 and 1041, Emma battled for the succession of her three sons, first for Harthacnut (her son by Cnut) and then

---

99. For the argument suggesting Hrothulf as Wealhtheow's son from another marriage, in the context of the Scylding legendary material (the relationship is reflective of that between the Scylding Hrólfr and Yrsa, the Scylding/Scylfing queen), see Damico, *Beowulf's Wealhtheow and the Valkyrie Tradition*, 123–30; see also Bloomfield, "Diminished by Kindness," who has softened Hrothulf's relationship to Wealhtheow to that of foster son.

Chapter Four

for the two athelings, Edward and Alfred (her sons by Æthelred), who, in a maneuver not unlike the proposed safeguarding of the princes of Heorot (*Bwf* 1836–38), had been sent for safekeeping to the Norman court in 1016, and one of whom was subsequently murdered on the orders of his stepbrother. The fourth contender and outside claimant was Harold Harefoot, Cnut's alleged *mæg* (kinsman, blood relative), his alleged son by his illegal union with Ælfgifu of Northampton. The dynamics of the Beowulfian relationships as they relate to dynastic control seem to me striking, although they do not mechanically duplicate the historical materials.[100] Nor should they; a poet's function in the composition of vernacular epic is not to copy history but rather by allusion and indirection to transform it into an imaginative work of cultural or mythic significance.

Dynastic succession—to secure the English throne for her sons—had been foremost in Emma's mind from the moment she crossed the Channel to become Æthelred's English bride and again later, as Cnut's Anglo-Danish queen; this is signaled by her demands for obligatory oaths from the king and the court (in both marriages) to support her unborn sons as legitimate successors to the English throne. The promise of dynastic inheritance to unborn male princes, the validity of which depended upon Cnut's oath to uphold the prenuptial contractual obligation in the *Encomium* (above, 233–34) and on the pledge of loyalty to the unborn Edward in the anonymous *Vita Ædwardi* (above, 235), may find its place in altered form in Wealhtheow's speech as well, in the use of the term *umborwesende*. When, for example, Wealhtheow asserts that Hrothulf as Heorot's future sole king will be munificent to their two young sons, she assures Hrothgar that the prince will remember the worthy honors (or graces) they bestowed on him when he was still *umborwesendum*,

---

100. In the historical materials, Edward and Alfred (Emma's sons by Æthelred) were older than Harthacnut (Cnut's son). Both the historical Alfred and the legendary Hrethric were murdered on the orders of kin. Sveinn Álfífuson, son of Ælfgifu of Northampton, who died in Denmark prior to Cnut's death and whom Cnut acknowledged, does not appear in the poem.

although the exact nature of these honors is not stated. Klaeber translates *umborwesende*, a term unique to *Beowulf*, as "being a child," giving the impression of the boy Hrothulf growing up in the court. *Umborwesende*, however, carries another, more specialized significadion. Jacob Grimm, many years ago in investigating the term in the context of early Germanic cultures, suggested that *umborwesende* may refer to someone yet "unborn" or still in the womb, in the state of becoming but not yet a child.[101] Such a particularized reading for *umborwesende* in the immediate passage would correspond closely to the promises of succession to Emma's unborn sons in the *Encomium*'s premarital contractual courtship discussed above and referred to in the anonymous *Vita Ædwardi*.

These are subtle correspondences between the historical and the poetic narrative; they reflect the poet's customary polysemous and allusive style and the unnerving discontinuity of his narrative that make demands upon the audience to collect "fragments" of narrative and merge them into a meaningful whole. The immediate discussion thus far has brought forward several "fragments" that compose a point of contact between the historical and the fictive materials. These include a regal setting evocative of ceremonies of investiture; the crucial theme of dynastic unrest in the court caused by the possible claims of three legitimate and one outside contender for the throne; and the related theme of promises made to royal male offspring (perhaps still unborn, if one accepts Grimm's reading). To these one may add the significance of the name *Wealhþēow*, which in its ethnic designation of "Norman captive" may function as a linguistic signature for Queen Emma, as well as the two queens' shared status and bearing as co-sovereigns of realms. Last, if one includes the verbal resonances of the Beowulfian *Gode þancode* passage with the Encomiast's description of the homecoming scene between Emma and Harthacnut, then one could reasonably conclude that the increment of these shared narrative "fragments" suggests that the poet created an epic queen

---

101. Jacob Grimm, *Teutonic Mythology*, trans. James Steven Stallybrass, 4 vols. (London: George Bell & Sons, 1882–88), 1:388–89; see also 1:370.

who, in addition to her other literary, mythological, and legendary associations, may have been meant to evoke the illustrious contemporary political figure Emma of Normandy.

One final detail in Wealhtheow's discourse in the second banquet scene points to the queen's actions as allusively evoking Emma's imperial authority. At the climax of celebratory rites at Heorot, Wealhtheow addresses Beowulf with words that carry incantatory and oracular overtones (*Bwf* 1215–31), the last four lines, quoted in the epigraph that introduced this chapter, attaining the quality of prayer.[102] The third of a series of speeches (indirectly and directly expressed) that concern the binding of a new relationship between Beowulf and the Danes, it complements and is a continuation of Hrothgar's opening address that initiated the ceremony. A speech of benediction, it is structured in two parts, the first of which (1215–27) is remarkable for its ritualistic tone in articulating the prince's elevation to a new status:

> "Brūc ðisses bēages, Bēowulf lēofa,
> hyse, mid hæle, ond þisses hrægles nēot,
> þēo[d]gestrēona, ond geþēoh tela,
> cen þec mid cræfte, ond þyssum cnyhtum wes
> lāra liðe! Ic þē þæs lēan geman.
> Hafast þū gefēred, þæt ðē feor ond nēah
> ealne wīdeferhþ weras ehtigað,
> efne swā sīde swā sæ bebūgeð,
> windgeard, weallas. Wes þenden þū lifige,
> æþeling, ēadig! Ic þē an tela
> sincgestrēona. Bēo þū suna mīnum
> dædum gedēfe, drēamhealdende!"
> (*Bwf* 1216–27)

---

102. Irving, *Reading of Beowulf*, 140–44. Although Irving rightly interprets the religious and ritualistic nature of the queen's speech, his view of her motivation, that she behaves out of premonitory anxiety, has been questioned; see Damico, *Beowulf's Wealhtheow and the Valkyrie Tradition*, 221n32.

["Enjoy [the possession of] this jeweled ring, Beowulf beloved one,

scion of a royal race,[103] with good fortune, and make use of this corselet,

of the people's treasures, and prosper abundantly.

Make yourself known through power, and to these youths be gracious in counsel! I will be mindful to reward you for that.

You have accomplished that which far and near

men will speak of with praise through all ages,

just as wide as the sea surrounds,

the courtyard of the wind, the elevated earthworks. Be, as long as you live,

blessed, prince! I will grant you, as is fitting [or in abundance],

precious treasures. Be you to my sons

fitting [in the sense of judicious] in deeds, joy-blessed one."]

Again using the imperative as her mode of expression and in actions evocative of investiture ceremonies, Queen Wealhtheow presents the jeweled ring to the Geatish prince, exhorting him to prosper and to value life and the treasure won.

As I have argued elsewhere, the presentation of the ring itself has royal and sacral connotations in its connection with Germanic altar or oath rings, the *stallahringr*[104] binding the parties into a new relationship. Thus, one finds such a sacral thrust surrounding the oath-swearing episode in the *Chronicle* entry for 876 recording the ceremony of peace between Guthrum and King Alfred, and in Simeon of

---

103. Though Klaeber defines *hyse* (one of its seven appearances in Old English poetry) as "young man," "scion" is also recorded and would be more appropriate here; see where it appears to have a sacral-monarchal connotative force in *Andreas* (595, 811), referring to Andreas's divine navigator, and in *Elene* (522), to Judas Cyriacus.

104. For a full discussion on the *stallahringr*, see Francis P. Magoun Jr. "On the Old Germanic Altar- or Oath-Ring (*Stallahringr*)," *Acta Philologica Scandinavica* 20 (1949): 277–93; discussed in Damico, *Wealhtheow and the Valkyrie Tradition*, 169–71.

Durham's commemoration of the investiture of Guthred as king of Northumbria, complete with the exchange of oaths and the bestowal of a holy armlet,[105] as well as in late antique art to be discussed below. It is amid the applause of the hall and over the sacral ring that Wealhtheow bestows the people's treasure upon Beowulf and prophesies his future far-reaching renown. She exhorts him to his duty, to counsel the youths well, to treat her sons as is fitting (in the sense of judicious), and pledges in turn to enrich the young scion for those deeds. At last, she utters the blessing: *Wes þenden þū lifige, / æþeling, ēadig* (As long as you live, be blessed, Prince). The degree and nature of Wealhtheow's authority in the court are laid out here. She functions as an oracular figure calling forth spiritual and material blessings and articulating the immutable values that preserve heroic order and that, by extrapolation, she proposes the hero follow. Both her action in presenting the ring and the speech itself evoke principles of commitment, trust, and obligation, irrevocably binding the prince to protect the solidarity of the Danish kingdom and binding her, as representative of that kingdom, to him.

She concludes the ceremony by celebrating the moral and ethical values of the court assembled in the hall as noted in the epigraph—concord, honor, loyalty, magnanimity, community—now that Grendel's tyrannical and unnatural domination has permanently ended:

"Hēr is æghwylc eorl ōðrum getrywe,
mōdes milde, mandrihtne hol[d],
þegnas syndon geþwǣre, þēod ealgearo,
druncne dryhtguman dōð swā ic bidde." (*Bwf* 1228–31)

["Here every noble is to every other true,

---

105. Symeon of Durham, *Historia Ecclesiae Dunelmensis*, in *Symeonis monachi Opera omnia*, ed. T. Arnold, 2 vols., RS 75 (London: Longman, 1882–85), I, 3–135; trans. by Joseph Stevenson, *The Historical Works of Simeon of Durham* (London: Seeley, 1855), 3.2, 621–711, esp. 663–64, chap. 28; repr. Lexington, KY: Ulan Press, 2013. The event was to be accomplished in detail at the command of St. Cuthbert who appeared in a vision to abbot Eadred.

with a generous spirit, loyal to the lord;
the thanes are united, the nation is willing,
the warriors, satisfied with drink, do as I bid."]

This is an appropriate epic closure to a benediction that sanctions and celebrates the elevated status of the hero to a position of regal power. The values expressed—solidarity of the court, loyalty between ruler and ruled, generosity of spirit—are of supreme importance as exemplary directives to the prince at the closure of the status-changing rite that has raised him to the level of protector of Heorot's future rulers. Yet the implication that the queen has received and in the future expects to receive homage from the *druncne dryhtguman* who *dōð swā ic bidde* (do as I bid) has not sat well with most critics: for them, the statement is ironical, an example of Wealhtheow's fragile and ineffectual position in the court, her lack of political acuity in assessing the present or the future, and the inebriated state of the warriors.[106] But there is no textual verification for these views of the queen. No one in the poem disparages her political acuity, as, for example, Hrothgar's political wisdom regarding Freawaru's marriage to Ingeld is questioned by Beowulf (2026–31),[107] or Unferth's blundering by the narrator (1465–71ᵃ). Nor is there a hint that Wealhtheow's act of benediction may be a plea for Beowulf's help in extricating her from the political morass she allegedly finds herself in. *Heorot is gefǣlsod*; the passage celebrates the end of a tyrannical domination and the return to a legitimate reign. The dramatic irony that exists in the scene has to do with the ensuing beheading sequence and attack of Grendel's mother, the other larger-than-life mother-figure in the poem, and little to do with Wealhtheow's lack of political acuity or with the alleged disloyalty of the court or the "unworthiness" of the "drunken" Danes. In this instance, *druncne dryhtguman* is to be taken not as a deprecating phrase but rather, as Magennis has argued, as

---

106. See Klaeber's note to 1219–20 and 1226ᵃ–1227, 3rd ed., 179; Irving, *Reading of Beowulf*, 140–44, and again in *Rereading Beowulf*, 27; Klaeber, 4th ed., nn. to 1219–31.
107. See also Irving, *Rereading Beowulf*, 61, who makes this point.

an expression of the "good life," where communal drinking at a feast is "the essential feature," for the action unifies the loyal court and solidifies heroic values.[108] Magennis points to the poet's final description of the celebratory banquet as *symbla cyst* (choicest of banquets, 1232[b]), where *druncon wīn weras* (the warriors drank wine, 1233[a]). Wealhtheow's allusions to the *druncne dryhtguman* who are *ealgearo* capture the essence of the solidarity and loyalty of a victorious heroic court. In a court where loyalty and generosity of spirit reign among ruler and nobles (*Hēr is æghwylc eorl ōðrum getrywe, / mōdes milde, mandrihtne hol[d]*) and a willing solidarity exists between ruler and ruled, among the thanes and nation (*þegnas syndon geþwǣre, þēod ealgearo*), the warriors indeed can enjoy the fruits of a bountiful court (*druncne dryhtguman*). And, as it is with Emma as portrayed by the Encomiast in Harthacnut's court, it is in the queen's person and regal power that the sum of the court's values and spirit resides.

Moreover, the high seriousness of Wealhtheow's speech is marked by what one may describe as divine sanction that lies behind its ritualistic first part, which contains themes, formulaic phrasing, and syntactical structures that associate it to Old English biblical epic, in particular, to one of God's speeches in *Genesis A*.[109] In his note to 1231[b], Klaeber identifies *dōð swā ic bidde* (do as I bid) as a formula, appearing elsewhere in Old English poetry three times and only in *Genesis A* (*Gen A* 2227[b], 2467[b], and, in variation, 2325[b]).[110] In each

---

108. Magennis, "'Beowulf' Poet and His '*Druncne Dryhtguman*,'" esp. 161; but see his *Images of Community in Old English Poetry* (Cambridge, UK: Cambridge University Press, 1996), chap. 3, esp. 66–69 wherein he suggests the scene as holding an "ironic perspective." See also Fred C. Robinson, *Beowulf and the Appositive Style* (Knoxville, TN: University of Tennessee Press, 1985), 75–77, who sees the crux of the problem as being in modern misinterpretations of drink as essential to ceremonial events, a case of a breach between cultures.

109. I have used George Philip Krapp's edition of *Genesis A* in *The Junius Manuscript*, vol. 1 of *ASPR* (New York: Columbia University Press, 1931) and, where noted, the edition of A. N. Doane, *Genesis A: A New Edition* (Madison, WI: University of Wisconsin Press, 1978).

110. In addition to these three phrasal correspondences between *Genesis*

instance, the phrase is spoken by characters autonomous in behavior and authority (Lot, Sarah, and God).[111] When God himself uses the formula in variation, *dōð swā ic hate* (do as I command), a contextual

---

A and Wealhtheow's speeches noted by Klaeber, there are two more: (1) The queen's greeting of the warriors in the hall upon her first appearance parallels Lot's greeting of the divine guests at the gate of Sodom—both characters are mindful of what is right and fitting (*Gen A*, 2431ᵇ-33; *Bwf* 612ᵇ-14), although in *Beowulf*, there is the additional word-play of *cynn* as "mindful of that which is fitting" and *cynn* as "mindful of the bonds of kinship," a sense that pervades the poem, except where Klaeber defines *cynn* as courtesy, and this only when it refers to Wealhtheow's actions; and (2) Wealhtheow's statement to Hrothgar in her first speech that reminds the king of his death day, *þonne ðū forð scyle, / metodsceaft sēon* (when you will be obliged to go forth to face God's fate, *Bwf* 1179ᵇ-80ᵃ) parallels the *Genesis A*-poet's description of the death of Abraham's father, *þa he forð gewat/ misserum frod metodsceaft seon* (*Gen A*, 1742-43). See further Klaeber, 3rd ed., cx, esp. n. 2; and his "Die ältere *Genesis* und der *Beowulf*," *Englische Studien* 42 (1910): 321-88, esp. 330-31; see also Orchard's discussion of parallels between *Beowulf*, *Genesis A*, and the poems of Junius 11, in *Companion to Beowulf*, 167-68.

111. Lot's exhortation to *doð swa ic eow bidde* is directed to the princes of Sodom, who have come to kill Lot's divine guests. Although the command in context is not parallel to the Beowulfian scene, Lot is presented as a strong, forceful individual sanctioned by God. When the formula *do swa ic þe bidde* is used by Sarah, however, it appears in a passage that touches upon generational issues, in line with the major theme of *Genesis A*, the issue of succession—to whom does God bequeath his created world. The scene depicts Sarah as the dominant figure propelling the narrative line; having given up any expectation that God would keep his promise that she and Abraham will found an ancestral line, she intervenes in God's plan and makes certain that she will be matriarch by proxy (as was her obligation), if necessary. Abraham obeys his wife and takes the handmaid, Hagar, to his bed. Sarah's action is not tainted with God's disapprobation, though their relationship is problematic, for God never speaks to her lovingly and with assurance, as he does to Hagar, for example. Yet it is the thorny Sarah he has chosen to be the great matriarch of the nation (Isaiah 51.2); see Alfred Bammesberger, "The Conclusion of Wealhtheow's Speech (*Beowulf* 1231)," *Neuphilologische Mitteilungen* 91 (1990): 207-8, who suggests a plural imperative reading of *dōð* at 1231.

similarity in theme and image emerges with Wealhtheow's second speech, for the formula in *Genesis A* closes the contractual terms of the covenant of circumcision between God and Abraham.[112]

The second of God's two promissory covenants with Abraham, the covenant of circumcision is expressive of God's "gracious commitment," containing blessings, promises of future favors, and stipulations for reciprocal fulfillment of obligations, differing in emphasis from the legalistic Mosaic covenant with its high proportion of injunctions and mandates.[113] Specific to two individuals who, though unequal in status, share a closeness in spirit and reciprocity in behavior, the

---

112.   Another formulaic phrase Wealhtheow shares with God is *Ic þē þæs lēan geman*, appearing earlier in *Beowulf* when the poet refers to God's retribution on those who fought against him for a long time (*lange þrage; He him þæs lēan forgeald*, "he gave him a reward for that," 114); in *Genesis A*, the phrase refers to God's vengeance on Sodom and Gomorrah because they had displeased the Lord for a *lange þrage*. *Him þæs lēan forgeald* (*Gen A* 2546) and, in variation, to God's rewarding Abraham for having undertaken his journey to Canaan as he had ordered him (*Him þæs lēan forgeald*, *Gen A* 1805). Except for *Gen A* 1805, the phrases have double-l alliteration. The formula is also used by the poet in describing Beowulf's action as he decapitates Grendel (*He him þæs lēan forgeald* [he gave him a reward for that], 1584). Wealhtheow's formulaic phrase *Hafast þū gefēred*, "You have accomplished" (1221), is later spoken by Hrothgar to Beowulf (1855), stating that the prince's actions have brought about peaceful relations between the Geats and Spear-Danes.

113.   Apparently, there are two basic forms of the covenant: the secular (or suzerainty) between two leaders (or king and courtier) and the religious, which in Judaic tradition is then subdivided into the covenant of divine favor (those of Noah, Abraham, and David), which is perpetual, and the Mosaic, which depends upon obedience to the injunctions and rules; quote from *The Oxford Companion to the Bible*, ed. Bruce M. Metzger and Michael D. Coogan (New York and Oxford: Oxford University Press, 1993), s.v. "Covenant"; Rolf Rendtorff, *The Covenant Formula: An Exegetical and Theological Investigation*, trans. Margaret Kohl (Edinburgh: T & T Clark, 1998); for the notion that medieval royal ordinations were indirectly modeled on Old Testament prototypes, see Nelson, "National Synods, Kingship and Royal Anointing," esp. 248–50.

covenant is meant to bind, in this instance, Abraham to his duty.

Þa se ðeoden ymb XIII gear,
ece drihten, wið Abrahame spræc:
"Leofa, swa ic þe lære, læst uncre wel
treowrædenne! Ic þe on tida gehwone
duguðum stepe. Wes þu dædum from
willan mines! Ic þa wære forð
soðe gelæste, þe ic þe sealde geo
frofre to wedde, þæs þin ferhð bemearn.
Þu scealt halgian hired þinne.
Sete sigores tacn soð on gehwilcne
wæpnedcynnes, gif þu wille on me
hlaford habban oððe holdne freond
þinum fromcynne. Ic þæs folces beo
hyrde and healdend, gif ge hyrað me
breostgehygdum and bebodu willað
min fullian. Sceal monn gehwilc
þære cneorisse cildisc wesan
wæpnedcynnes, þæs þe on woruld cymð
ymb seofon niht sigores tacne
geagnod me, oððe of eorðan
þurh freondscipe feor adæled,
adrifen from duguðum. Doð swa ic hate!"
(*Gen A* 2304–37)

["Beloved one, adhere closely to the covenant between us, as I
 will teach thee.
In each season, I will [favor, bring honor to, exult, reward] you
 with prosperity.
Be strong in deeds according to my [will, command, purpose,
 design]!
I will fulfill the covenant faithfully, which I gave you previously
as a pledge for your consolation because your spirit mourned.
You are obliged to sanctify your household.

Chapter Four

Set a true sign of victory on each of your male kin, if you desire
  to have in me
a lord or [faithful, loyal] kinsman for your progeny.
I will be [both] guardian and ruler of your people,
if you [and your household] will obey me with heart and mind,
  and desire
to fulfill my commandments. Each person of your tribe, of the
  male kin,
while still a child, of those who come into the world
after seven nights, will be dedicated [consecrated] to me
by a sign of victory, or be cut off far from earth
with regard to kinship [friendship], driven from prosperity.
You [and your people] do as I command!"]

Although the two speeches have dissimilar situational contexts—
there is no command of circumcision in Wealhtheow's speech, no
expansive depiction of a regal ceremony or assemblage of courtiers as
witnesses surrounding God's—it seems to me, nonetheless, that there
are formal and thematic likenesses, especially in lines 1216–27, which
represent, in essence, a royal contract. Here, the queen gives Beowulf
surety for her future favor, articulating the terms that will bind them
and delineating their individual responsibilities. Like God's address
to Abraham, Wealhtheow's to Beowulf takes the form of a benediction. A ratification of the hero's elevation to a new sociopolitical
status, the speech contains sanctions of blessings, with promises of
prosperity and worldly renown (*Gen A* 2306–8ᵃ; *Bwf* 1220, 1225ᵇ–26ᵃ)
and of continual favor and protection (*Gen A* 2309ᵇ–10ᵃ; *Bwf* 1224–
25). Likewise present are promissory oaths, in exchange for deeds
done, appearing in *Genesis A* 2309–11, *Ic þa wære forð / soðe gelæste* (I
will fulfill our covenant faithfully) and twice in *Beowulf*, *Ic þē þæs lēan
geman* (I will be mindful to reward you for that, 1220ᵇ) and *Ic þē an tela*
(As is fitting, I will grant you treasure, 1225ᵇ)—with the implication
that these oaths are specific to the individuals involved. In that they
are contractual, the oaths are reciprocally obligatory. God offers to
bind himself to Abraham, to strike a new relationship wherein he will

be *hlaford* (lord) to Abraham and a *holdne freond* (faithful kinsman/ friend) to his progeny, but he does so on the condition that Abraham perform his will. God's exhortation *Wes þu dædum from / willan mines!* (Be you strong in deeds according to my will [command, purpose, design], *Gen A* 2308ᵇ–9ᵃ) is paralleled twice in Wealhtheow's speech, once in lines 1219ᵇ–20ᵃ, *cen þec mid cræfte, ond þyssum cnyhtum wes / lāra līðe* (Make yourself known through power, and to these youths be gracious in counsel), and again, more pointedly, in 1226ᵇ–27ᵃ, *Bēo þū suna mīnum / dædum gedēfe* (Be you to my son/sons fitting in deeds),[114] with partial verbatim terminology.

Other parallels exist,[115] as, for example, a similarity in image pattern found in God's first covenant with Abraham:

> Ic þe wære nu
> mago Ebrea, mine selle,
> þæt sceal fromcynne folde þine,
> sidland manig, geseted wurðan,

---

114. *Suna mīnum*, a phrase whose meaning is much contested, and its variation, *suna sīnum*, is spoken, in the first instance, by Beowulf to Hygelac referring to Heorogar's having previously given the *brēost-gewædu* (byrnie), presented to him by Hrothgar, to his "own son" as his inheritance (2160), and again, where he presents Wiglaf with his war-gear, which he would have wished to have bequeathed to his own son (*suna mīnum*, 2729ᵃ); in each case, the term is singular, as it is in 1226ᵇ, although translated by some as plural, as it can be taken here allegorically with reference to Emma's three sons.

115. Noticeably alike, for instance, is the buildup of repetitive clausal structures expressive of commands. These appear five times in *Beowulf*, lines 1216–19, and twice in *Genesis A*, lines 2308ᵇ–9ᵃ and 1213–14ᵃ, and in each instance they are punctuated by a pledge of favor. In addition, the structure of God's repetitive *gif* clauses in the *Genesis A* passage (2314ᵇ–16ᵃ and 1217ᵇ–19ᵃ) also accords with the pattern found in Wealhtheow's first speech (*Bwf* 1182ᵇ–87); see *Genesis A*, ed. Doane, 89–96, for a discussion of syntactical structures in *Genesis A*; see also Klaeber, "Die ältere *Genesis* und der *Beowulf*," 321–88, esp. 331, where he notes the similarity in the clausal structures of Wealhtheow's first speech (1180–87) and that of King Abimelech (*Gen A* 2816–28).

eorðan sceatas oð Eufraten,
and from Egypta eðelmearce
swa mid niðas swa [MS *twa*] Nilus sceadeð
and eft Wendelsæ [MS *wendeð sæ*] wide rice.
Eall þæt sculon agan eaforan þine,
þeodlanda gehwilc, swa þa þreo wæter
steape stanbyrig streamum bewindað,
famige flodas folcmægða byht."
(*Gen A* 2204^b–15)

["Now I give you my pledge, son of the Hebrews,
that the earth, many spacious lands, will be
[carrying a sense of destiny] settled by your progeny,
the surface of the earth from the national boundary
of Egypt to the Euphrates,
as the Nile divides two peoples and the sea [meaning the Medi-
terranean]
again bends around [encloses] the wide dominion.
All that your progeny shall possess [again, carrying a sense of
destiny],
each of the lands of the races, just as the three waters,
the foaming seas, encircle [enclose] with their currents
the lofty stone fortifications, the dwellings of nations."][116]

Here, in a dense simile, God pledges that an unbroken succession
of Abraham and Sarah's progeny will populate the earth's surface
from the national boundary of Egypt to the Euphrates. The architec-
tural imagery, the timelessness of the race's renown, and the expansive circularity of the universe that would mark its boundaries parallel Wealhtheow's prophecy of the timelessness and universality of
Beowulf's future fame (*Bwf* 1221–24a), which will spread "far and
near, just as wide as the courtyard of the wind, the sea, surrounds the
elevated earthworks" inhabited by men (*Hafast þū gefēred, þæt ðē feor*

---

116. Largely following Doane, *Gen A*, 303–4.

ond nēah / ealne wīdeferhþ weras ehtigað, / efne swā side swā sǣ bebūgeð, /
windgeard, weallas). God's covenant with Abraham, like Wealhtheow's
with Beowulf, marks the beginning of a new political age. But it is
not Abraham who will rule God's kingdom; for like Beowulf, who is
exhorted to enjoy and make abundant use of the nation's treasure,
Abraham may inherit the goods of God's creation promised to and
lost by Adam and Eve, but it will be Isaac, Sarah's son, the recipient
of God's joy and bliss, his love and grace (*Gen A* 2333–34), who will
inherit the kingdom.[117]

What, then, are we to make of a speech whose body evokes Old
English biblical poetry and whose ending, a political history in
Latin rhyming prose? Admittedly, except for the formulaic phrase
dōð swā ic bidde, there are no verbatim parallels with the biblical and
secular epic speeches; yet the number of formal and conceptual similarities that do exist between *Genesis A* and *Beowulf* call to mind a
poet who moved freely about a multilingual literary and religious
culture, adapting and transforming forms and themes and incorporating them into a new work. For such a poet, God's speech may have
served as a partial blueprint for Wealhtheow's, despite its different
cultural setting and its lack of pomp and royal court witnesses, for it
stands as the quintessential address suited for his newly consecrated
hero, marking his official entry into the political world of the poem.

If God's speech did serve as the poet's model, why adapt it as
an address for the queen, when it appropriately belonged to King
Hrothgar? It was King Hrothgar who initiated the pledge of a
nīwe sibbe in a speech that functions as a companion to Queen
Wealhtheow's. Structurally, thematically, and dramatically, the benediction at the close of the second banquet scene should have fallen

---

117. See Roberta Frank, who analyzes the dynastic shift imbedded in the
paronomastic structure of the verse line, in "Paronomasia in Old English
Scriptural Verse," *Speculum* 47 (1972): 207–26, esp. 214–15. Frank defines
paronomasia as "referring to the establishing of an etymological or pseudo-
etymological relationship between two or more words, and the *ambiguum*,
referring to the establishment of such a connection between two meanings
contained in one word" (208n7).

to him, if, indeed, he functioned in the poem as the sole monarch of Heorot. Perhaps if the poet had assigned the benediction to Hrothgar, if it had been Hrothgar's male voice that laid out the terms of the contractual agreement with Beowulf, critics might have more easily accepted the political force of the speech and the regal power it represented.[118] But it was to the queen the poet appropriately gave the benediction. For in creating the second banquet scene, it is possible that the *Beowulf*-poet ruminated (as Paul Remley tells us monks were encouraged to do)[119] on the essential political import of God's covenant in its inauguration of a singularly new nation, and in the process of rumination, he may then have associated the biblical passage with the ruling figures of Queen Emma and her son Harthacnut at the reinstatement of Anglo-Danish England's political age at the closure of the *Encomium*, an age whose founding or reinstatement would not have been possible without the strength and endurance of the powerful figure of Emma of Normandy, who, to paraphrase Pauline Stafford, represented the formative model for future female sovereigns of the English nation.[120]

---

118. Male voices resonate in the queen's speeches, as parallel formulaic phrases referred to in the text reveal. If we are meant by these formulaic parallels to discern the queen's character referentially, then the parallels point to a sternness of mind that justly remembers and recompenses betrayal and disobedience and a spirit that values the continuation of bonds of kinship through the distribution of treasure. For a discussion of male anxiety caused by female aggression in *Beowulf* and other OE poems and the quelling of those anxieties when the feminine figures assume male identities, see Klein, *Ruling Women*, esp. 104–7.

119. Paul G. Remley, *Old English Biblical Verse: Studies in Genesis, Exodus and Daniel* (Cambridge, UK: Cambridge University Press, 1996), 40–42. Remley is discussing the Bedean narrative on Caedmon and Aldhelm's praise of the meditative technique *ruminatio* as a method of biblical instruction. For the practice of rumination and memory, see further below 277–78.

120. Stafford, "Emma: The Powers of the Queen," 3–26, esp. 22–23; for Stafford, Emma's consecration "produce[d] the theoretical apotheosis of English Queenship"; *Queen Emma and Queen Edith*, 178.

Some inescapable observations have arisen from the present discussion concerning the interplay between poetry and history, in particular between the *Beowulf*-poet's depth of awareness of contemporary events and his appropriation of those events as recorded in the *Encomium*. The *Beowulf*-poet's unparalleled portrayal of the second banquet scene, for instance, and its dramatization of a united and bountiful court at the start of a reinstated political age may very well be a dramatic elaboration of the Encomiast's description of Harthacnut's court at the close of the *Encomium* after the English nobles have willingly "place[d] themselves devotedly under their [Harthacnut and Emma's] dominion" (*et se deuotos eorum dominationi subderent, EER* ii.22, 36–37). The phrase evokes the enthroned Emma of the *Encomium*'s frontispiece and the pointed association of Emma with Virgil's Octavian in its Argument, although Octavian does not appear in actuality in the *Aeneid*. The Encomiast here is accepting political allegorical interpretations that lie behind Virgil's work,[121] and by his association, Emma emerges as a reinstated singular power, a co-ruler in her son's court as she was in the reign of his father. As in the court of Emma and Cnut, so in that of Emma and Harthacnut, "there is loyalty among sharers of rule" (*Hic fides habetur regni sotiis*), and the bonds between the queen mother and her two sons, King Harthacnut and Edward, the heir apparent, are indestructible. As Cnut "enjoined peace and unanimity among his people" (*pacem et unanimitatem om[n]ibus sjuis indixit, EER* ii.22, 36–7), so all are of a united mind where Harthacnut and Emma rule, and as before, there is full enjoyment of the amenities of the court. The munificence both of Cnut's and of Harthacnut's courts, where food and drink are lavishly provided, is alluded to here,[122] and I suggest idealized and poetically

---

121. See Tyler, "Talking about History," esp. 381–82, and "Fictions of Family," 154, 170, 176, and *passim*, for comments on the pointed parallelism between Emma and Virgil's Octavian effected by the Encomiast, presenting the queen, not in the customary female role of the "power behind the throne," but as the singular powerful force within the court.

122. For views that the *Encomium* may have been written in Harthacnut's court ca. 1041, see Keynes, *EER* lix,lxix; Orchard, "Literary Background

transposed to the hall of Heorot as expressed in the epigraph at the start of this chapter. At the core of both the historical and the epic scenes are the motifs of the willing unification of a people with like purpose; of loyalty and generosity of spirit between sharers of the rule; and of the reigning queen as regulator of the royal dignity of an exemplary court that has been restored to tranquility after great tribulation suffered at the hands of a tyrannical ruler.

One further example of the *Beowulf*-poet's sensitivity to and appropriation of eleventh-century literary, cultural, and sociopolitical events perhaps should be mentioned here, especially with respect to his singular cinematic rendering of the second banquet scene and its associative biblical allusions. I refer to three iconographic interpretations of psalms found in the Harley Psalter (London, British Library, MS Harley 603)—in particular the illustrations of Psalm 111 (fol. 57v) and the "inventive" illustrations of Psalms 130 (fol. 67v) and 132 (fol. 68v) that differ strikingly from those of the Utrecht Psalter.[123] These, I

---

to the *EER*," 157–58. For discussions of the "factionalism" that existed in Harthacnut's court, see Tyler, "Talking about History," esp. 361–62; Keynes, *EER* [lxix–lxxi]. In all sources, Harthacnut's rule is described as being at once tyrannical (because of heavy taxation), merciless toward those who had a hand in the assassination of his half-brother Alfred, and benevolent and generous toward his kin and thanes. For Cnut's munificence as an inherited trait for his sons, see *EER* ii.22, 36–37: *et suis posteris bonum exemplum largitatis totiusque bonitatis reliquit, quod et ipsi adhuc Deo gratias seruuant, optime pollents in regni moderamine et in uirtutum decore* (and left his posterity a good example of munificence and all benevolence, which they also, thanks be to God, still follow, being in a high degree mighty in their management of the kingdom and by the grace of their virtues).

123. The term is Judith E. Duffey's, who identifies seven images as having contemporary reference to ceremonial, monastic, and royal events connected with Cnut and Emma; see "The Inventive Group of Illustrations in the Harley Psalter (British Museum Ms. Harley 603)," Ph.D. diss., University of California, Berkeley, 1977, 160–81, especially 160–62. As does most of Harley 603, the rendering of Psalms 111, 130, and 132 follow the Roman version of the Psalter (although Harley 603 incorporates some Gallican elements as well between Psalms 100 and 105); for black-and-white reproductions of the Harley 603, Paris, and Bury Psalters, see

suggest, may have been part of the *Beowulf*-poet's cultural repertoire and influenced his ornate and spirited dramatization of the second banquet scene. Under production in Christ Church Cathedral Priory, Canterbury, Harley 603 was executed (with some interruptions) from early in the eleventh century to the century's second quarter, with additions and insertions made to the manuscript extending into the twelfth century.[124] The iconographic rendering of Psalm 111, for

---

Thomas H. Ohlgren, ed., *Anglo-Saxon Textual Illustration: Photographs of Sixteen Manuscripts with Descriptions and Index* (Kalamazoo, MI: Medieval Institute Publications, 1992), esp. Psalm 111, pl. 2.74, 220; Psalm 130, pl. 2.90, 236; and Psalm 132, pl. 2.92, 238; for reproductions of the Utrecht Psalter, see E. T. DeWald, ed., *The Illustrations of the Utrecht Psalter* (Princeton, NJ: Princeton University Press, 1933), esp. Psalm CXI, fol. 65v, pl. CIII, faithfully duplicated in Harley 603; Psalm XXX, fol. 74v, pl. CXIV, lower miniature, and Psalm 132, fol. 75v, pl. CXVI, upper miniature, which differ drastically from Harley 603 in composition and iconography of figures; see Duffey, "Inventive Group of Illustrations," 138–44, 150–51. These psalms are not alone in holding contemporary images unique to the Harley; see William Noel, *The Harley Psalter*, Cambridge Studies in Palaeography and Codicology 4 (Cambridge, UK: Cambridge University Press, 1995), for contemporary images unique to Harley and drawn from the illustrator's "own experience," esp. 81–87, quote at 87.

124. The manuscript abruptly ends at f. 73v, possibly because the rest of the leaves were lost, for there is no final folio. On the range of the near half-century dating, see Janet Backhouse, "The Making of the Harley Psalter," *British Library Journal* 10, no. 2 (1984): 97–113, esp. 98, 106, 108. Backhouse bases her examination and reappraisal of Harley 603 on the 1957 rebinding of the manuscript and on T[erence] A. M. Bishop's identification of the Harley's scripts with scribes working at Canterbury, especially the hand of Eadui Basan (Backhouse, 98); see T. A. M. Bishop, "Notes on Cambridge Manuscripts," part 7, "The Early Minuscule of Christ Church, Canterbury," *Transactions of the Cambridge Bibliographical Society* 3 (1963): 413–23, esp. 413, 420; cited also in Backhouse. On the range and variance of dating, see also Noel, *Harley Psalter*, who dates the work of the scribes and illustrators in the early phases of the manuscript to the second decade of the eleventh century at Canterbury (138–39, 140–45). On the range of production of the manuscript and its interruptions during the first two decades of the eleventh, caused by the sacking of Canterbury and the

example, based on its Utrecht exemplar, appears among the group of illustrations developed in the first of the three phases of production, suggesting a date no later than 1020 for the completion of the work on the psalm (so, Backhouse and others), while the illustrations of Psalms 130 and 132, part of the "inventive" group that holds little or no indebtedness to the Utrecht but carries a contemporary orientation, were executed in the second phase of production and have been ascribed by Francis Wormald to the second quarter of the eleventh century, the years covering Cnut's reign.[125]

The first of three recreations of the late ninth-century Utrecht

---

murder of Archbishop Ælfheah (1011–12), its additional interruption by the death of Æthelred, and its resumption after Cnut rose to the throne and Æthelnoth was installed as archbishop of Canterbury, see Rolf Hasler, "Zu zwei Darstellungen aus der ältesten Kopie des Utrecht-Psalters," *Zeitschrift für Kunstgeschichte* 44, no. 4 (1981): 317–39, esp. 321–22 and 338–39; see also Jonathan J. C. Alexander and Claus M. Kaufmann, *English Illuminated Manuscripts 700–1500* (Brussels: Bibliotheque Royale Albert 1er, 1973), 38, cat. no. 15 for the Christ Church assignment and a dating of 1015–25.

125. F[rancis] Wormald, *English Drawings of the Tenth and Eleventh Centuries* (London: Faber and Faber, 1952), 69–70. Backhouse, "Making of the Harley Psalter," 97–98; see also Duffey, "Inventive Group of Illustrations," 161–62, who includes the combined reigns of Harold and Harthacnut within the time range. Following Wormald, Backhouse further groups the illustrations of the three phases of production into four sections, those of the illustrator of Psalm 111 (Hand D) appearing in the third section, while those of the illustrators of Psalms 130 and 131 (Hand F) appear in the fourth section; Backhouse, 98, 105–6, and appendix, 110–11. For a microscopic analysis of the style of the illustrators, see Richard Gameson, "The Anglo-Saxon Artists of the Harley 603 Psalter," *Journal of the British Archaeological Association* 143 (1990): 29–48, esp. 31–33, who discusses illustrator F (the illustrator of 58r–73v), the most digressive from the Utrecht Psalter illustrator, and illustrator D (the illustrator of 57v), the most accurate in image, but with variance in style (34–35); see also Noel, *Harley Psalter*, esp. 59–75, 77–88. For a concise but complete discussion of the manuscript, its provenance, range of dating, scribal divisions, and iconographic groupings, see Elżbieta Temple, *Anglo-Saxon Manuscripts 900–1066* (London: Harvey Miller, 1976), 81–83.

Psalter that had found its way to Canterbury by the end of the tenth century, Harley 603 deftly adapts the style of its source "to reflect the idiom current in its own time," one major contribution being its introduction of color in the drawings, most lavishly demonstrated in the rendering of Psalm 111 on folio 57v by illustrator D, especially in the great variety of red, blue, green, and brown, in this dramatization of unstinting generosity by royal figures (fig. 8).[126] It is this opulence that prompts Backhouse to question the exact purpose for the manuscript's production, for despite its religious content, it is too costly an undertaking and too "sumptuous" in size and decoration for liturgical use; rather, it would be more appropriate for a donor's private meditation. The iconographic renderings of the text, she argues, might be seen as an "aid to the study of and meditation on the psalms."[127] Based on the Christ Church provenance of the text,

------

126. Backhouse, "Making of the Harley Psalter," 97–99, esp. 99; quote at 97. Although color is significantly handled by all the illustrators, Backhouse remarks on illustrator D's use of more color than that represented in other sections of the manuscript, this being reflective of his aim to duplicate the grandeur of the Utrecht prototype. It would seem to me, however, that the intention more directly might have been to surpass it as do all of illustrator D's renderings (ff. 50r–57r), in an effort to draw further attention to the munificence represented. See Noel, who identifies D as D2, arguing that for part of his stint in quire 9 (50r, 51r–54r), D performed double duty as Harley's scribe 2; *Harley Psalter*, 60–68, 73–74, 212; also see Noel's noting of illustrator D's improvements on the Utrecht illustration of Psalm 111 (66–68).

127. Backhouse, "Making of the Harley Psalter," 106–9, quote at 108; on the proposed purpose of Harley 603's being other than liturgical because of its omission of certain essential liturgical parts, its considerable size, and its following the Roman Psalter, see also Hasler, "Zu zwei Darstellungen," 321; Duffey, "Inventive Group of Illustrations," 220–21; and Noel, *Harley Psalter*, who recognizes Harley as a *de luxe* manuscript having been commissioned and meant to be read by a monastic audience (196–202); see also Mary Carruthers' discussion of the psalters (Utrecht and the English psalters inspired by the Utrecht as "study manuscripts") in her *The Book of Memory: A Study of Memory in Medieval Culture*, 2nd ed. Cambridge Studies in Medieval Literature (Cambridge, UK: Cambridge University Press,

and especially on its Beatus green initial (Harley 603, fol. 2) outlined in brown ink, framing two figures, the first being Christ standing within a mandorla against the ascender of the letter B and wearing a bright green-tinted crown, the second being the prostrate figure of an archbishop against a lighter green wash, clearly defined by his pallium, whose face is turned directly to confront the viewer (fig. 9), Backhouse proposes the first owner of Harley 603 as possibly having been Archbishop Æthelnoth of Canterbury. The archbishop may have commissioned it for his own use around the date of his consecration in 1020 by Wulfstan, Archbishop of York.[128] Both Rolf Hasler and Judith E. Duffey, who approach Harley 603's second phase of illustrations as being reflective of a number of contemporary historical interrelationships, likewise argue for Archbishop Æthelnoth's patronage of Harley 603, but not for his own private use. Rather, they posit that the archbishop's intention in commissioning the manuscript was to present it as a gift either for Cnut and Emma, or for Queen Emma alone.[129]

Duffey was the first to make this assertion based on her examination of the "inventive group of illustrations" in Harley 603, which have been significantly altered from their Utrechtian source;[130] Hasler generally agrees, pointing to the significance of several of her findings.[131] One of the most striking changes noted by Duffey (and sup-

---

2008), 282–85, and further below, 321–22.

128. Backhouse, "Making of the Harley Psalter," 108–10, esp. 109. Ohlgren, *Anglo-Saxon Textual Illustration*, pl. 2.3, 149. Backhouse also puts forth, though dismisses, Archbishop Lyfing as a possible patron. Æthelnoth died in October 1038 (109–10), which she connects with the waning interest in completion of the project (110); see also Hasler, "Zu zwei Darstellungen," for other alternative donors, before he, too, settles on Æthelnoth (321–22); see contra, Noel, *Harley Psalter*, esp. 201.

129. Duffey, "Inventive Group of Illustrations," 222–23, cited and discussed by Hasler, "Zu zwei Darstellungen," esp. 317, 322.

130. For Duffey's arguments, see her "Inventive Group of Illustrations," 95–96 (summary of deviations), 150–74 (contemporary references), 222–35 (conclusions).

131. Although Hasler disagrees with some of Duffey's readings, the thrust

ported by Hasler) that points to a contemporary historical significance for Harley 603 is in illustrator F's renderings of Psalm 112, v. 7,
found in the upper-right level of folio 58r, the folio that commences
the second phase of production and the illustrations of Duffey's devi-
ating group (fig. 10). This phase indicates a change of plan away from
the production of a facsimile copy of the Utrecht.[132] Here illustrator F
recasts the scene, shifting from the Utrechtian depiction of four undif-
ferentiated, uncrowned, cowled figures, holding scrolls and books,
in paired conversation and seated on a leaf-decorated square bench,
which Duffey identifies as a stock setting of Utrechtian evangelist

---

of his article is to provide further evidence in support of Duffey's hypothesis of the influence of contemporary historical events and personages on
the second phase of the Harley illustrations. He is mainly concerned with
two illustrations, the first being that of the Holy Trinity (Harley 603, fol.
1r), also an original Harleian illustration (Hasler, 322–30), whose views
on dogma he associates with the work of Ælfric (a friend of Æthelnoth),
and which, he argues, would have been of interest to contemporary artists
and scholars, since those views held a certain currency in the court and in
the monastic community of Christ Church Canterbury (see esp. Hasler,
327–29). The second image Hasler examines is of Psalm 119 (fol. 64r),
in particular the figure of the winged, bearded archer named Ægelmund
(noble protector), which figure he argues (as does Duffey) is associated
with Æthelnoth and might have represented a mythic connection between
Cnut and the first Langobardian king (Hasler, 333–38). Hasler's conclusion differs considerably from that of Duffey, who more directly identifies
the archer with the archbishop (Duffey, "Inventive Group of Illustrations,"
123–25), although both connect the image with Æthelnoth and Cnut.
See also Hasler's concluding remarks on Æthelnoth's friendship with
Ælfric and Cnut and on Cnut's close relationship with the community
at Christ Church Canterbury ("Zu zwei Darstellungen," 337–38); noted
by Backhouse, "Making of the Harley Psalter," 111; but see contra, Noel,
Harley Psalter, 198–99, who argues that the patron could have been any
archbishop.

132. See Gameson on the significance of illustrator F's change of style and
on its pointing, like the division of artistic hands, to a "change of purpose"
in the Harley's production; "Anglo-Saxon Artists," 31; see also above nn.
123, 125.

figures, to an imperial scene of four kings, three with swords held upright, seated on a "pedimented bench with turned columns" used throughout Harley to support royal or heavenly personages.[133] The royal figures are further differentiated by the crowns they wear and the color of their robes, the three in red holding swords turning toward the fourth royal figure in blue. He, in turn, is in animated conversation with the king on his right while holding the interest of all, each figure with its own particularized vibrant facial expression, a scene whose effect is quite different from that of the impressionistic Utrechtian figures. For Duffey, the image is charged with "traditional imperial attributes," symbolic acts evoking the subjection of kings to a king of a higher rank.[134] It is an opportunity, in Hasler's words, "to reflect on the 1017 division of England into four parts by Cnut" on his attainment of the throne.[135]

The arguments for the illustration's contemporaneity proposed by Duffey and Hasler have merit, for Cnut and Æthelnoth held a close friendship begun prior to Cnut's confirmation as king by Æthelnoth; in turn Æthelnoth was indebted to the king for endorsing his own consecration as archbishop,[136] as is suggested by a 1020 letter from Wulfstan sent jointly to Emma and Cnut informing them of Æthelnoth's consecration as archbishop of Canterbury.[137] Moreover, both Emma and Cnut were exceedingly generous to Christ Church

---

133. Ohlgren, *Anglo-Saxon Textual Illustration*, pl. 2.75, 221; DeWald, *Illustrations of the Utrecht Psalter*, pl. CIV, fol. 66r.

134. Duffey, "Inventive Group of Illustrations," 35–36, 108–10, 222.

135. Hasler, "Zu zwei Darstellungen," 315n3. One wonders if the similarity in crowns between the swordless king and the figure on his right, in addition to the conversation between them, might not allude to the closer relationship held between Cnut and Thorkell who was Cnut's second in command for a period and whom Cnut had left in command during his voyage to Denmark in 1019–20. I am uncomfortable with Duffey's interpretation of the adoption icon, immediately positioned on a separate level beneath the image of the four kings; it would not be politically judicious for any queen, let alone Emma, to adopt another woman's children.

136. Lawson, *Cnut*, 148–49.

137. Keynes, *EER* xxvn4.

(and to Canterbury generally, perhaps as a means of nullifying memories of the horrors the city had endured during its sacking), bestowing treasures, relics, and property on the community, with Cnut at one point laying his crown on its altar, which the monks protected and treasured.[138] Cnut's relationship with Christ Church was of such potency that he joined their fraternity and granted Æthelnoth extensive royal authority over his lands and people, noted by Stenton as the "first writ of its kind."[139] Such generosity, Hasler rightly argues, might understandably elicit like magnanimity from the archbishop in the form of the presentation of a *de luxe* psalter, especially a psalter that contained an icon of a royal pair dispensing, unsparingly and benevolently, the fruits of the kingdom to the populace as depicted, for instance, in Harley 603's illustration of Psalm 111 on fol. 57v. It would likewise explain Æthelnoth's depth of loyalty as he heroically protected scepter and crown from the grasp of Harold Harefoot in the dark days of 1036.

The first to discern a relationship between Harley 603 and *Beowulf* was Robert Schichler, who argued that the illustration of Psalm 111 in fol. 57v was a "visual counterpart to Hrothgar's Heorot," an image of a "just man's hall as a building surmounted by a hart's head."[140] Hrothgar's constructing and naming his

---

138. On the laying of the royal crown on the altar of Christ Church, see the Charter of Cnut to Christ Church Canterbury, in A. J. Robertson, ed. and trans., *Anglo-Saxon Charters* (Cambridge, UK, 1956), 158–61, 406–11; Heslop, "Production of *de luxe* Manuscripts," 156–58, 180, and appendix 2, 183, 184. Cnut and Emma's generosity was not restricted to Christ Church or Canterbury generally. As Heslop demonstrates, their patronage and munificence extended throughout the kingdom and the continent. Cnut, for instance, gave his crown to New Minster as well; on Cnut's magnanimity, see also *EER* ii. 34–39.

139. Lawson, *Cnut*, 153–54; Stenton, *Anglo-Saxon England*, 497; also cited in Hasler, "Zu zwei Darstellungen," 338.

140. Robert Lawrence Schichler, "'Glæd Man' at *Heorot: Beowulf* and the *Anglo-Saxon Psalter*," *Leeds Studies in English*, n. s. 27 (1996): 49–68, esp. 49–50; Schichler first lectured on the Beowulfian connection in 1986 (62n6). I am indebted to Professor Schichler for drawing my attention to

hornreced (*Bwf* 704^a) Heorot—to praise God for his munificence and in turn to dispense like bounty to his people (*Bwf* 67^b–82^a)— are the very deeds of the man in verse 9 of Psalm 111,[141] "his horn shall be exalted," which, in Schichler's view, in turn influenced the construction, naming, and societal purpose of Heorot in the poem. In its entirety, Schichler's far-ranging argument centers on the poet's adaptation of the figure of the hart and its incremental use throughout the poem as a depiction of Hrothgar's character. The icon of the horned hart, he argues, is text-specific to *Beowulf*. He further posits a similar symbolic treatment of the image of the hart in several psalms found in Anglo-Saxon Psalter manuscripts, and urges further scholarly examination of the poet's utilization of the psalter in his composition of the poem.[142] My discussion here expands upon Schichler's argument, offering an additional association between the poem and the visual representation of Psalm 111 in Harley 603, 57v, and augments Duffey's interpretation of the "inventive" illustrations of the Harleian Psalms 130 (fol. 67v) and 132 (fol. 68v) by postulating their possible influence on the *Beowulf*-poet's dramatization of the second banquet scene.

If one were to accept the image of the horned hart as representative of the essence of the imperial power, as its appearance on the standard of Sutton Hoo impels us to do, and if one were to embrace the expansive totality of the illustration rather than concentrate on

---

his article.

141. "Dispersit, dedit pauperibus. Iustitia eius manet in saeculum saeculi. Cornu eius exaltabitur in gloria" (He hath distributed, he hath given to the poor: his justice remaineth for ever and ever: his horn shall be exalted in glory), quoted in Schichler, "*Glæd Man*," 50.

142. Schichler examines the Paris Psalter (Paris, Bibliothèque Nationale, MS lat. 8824); the Bury Psalter (Rome, Biblioteca Apostolica Vaticana, MS Reg. lat. 12); on the dating of the Bury Psalter and stylistic comparisons between it and the Harley Psalter, see Schichler, "*Glæd Man*," 61n3; see also, Ohlgren, *Anglo-Saxon Textual Illustration*, esp., 2.74, 220; and DeWald, *Illustrations of the Utrecht Psalter*, esp. pl. C111, 50–51; Schichler, "*Glæd Man*," 49–59, 62nn4, 5.

the development of one of its elements as does Schichler, one would become additionally aware of a thematic relationship between the sociopolitical ceremonial scene portrayed in the Harley illustration and the sacral-political staging of the second banquet scene. As does the Utrechtian icon, the Harley illustration focuses not on the single royal figure of verse 9 but rather on male and female, as their position on a blue-tinted pediment or dais would suggest.[143] In its spatial organization, Harley's opulent royal structure with its expansive, precisely drawn, rounded red-tiled roof and the brightness of the green inks of the clothing and draperies is larger, more solidly defined than the Utrecht, perhaps because illustrator D shifted its positioning or because of his use of vibrant color, or because his clarification of line caused his figures to express a greater feeling of reality.[144] The scene is one of vibrant vitality: the royal pair, equal in size and draped in browns, blues, and greens (the female's green head covering being held up by a tiara), with two young princes between them maintain center focus, each dispensing the fruits of their kingdom to male and female survivors of what apparently has been a period of oppression. In the center foreground reinforcing the action of the royal pair, and in direct contrast to the unredeemable group of soldiers positioned in the immediate left foreground being thrust into Hell's pit by a winged satanic figure, are two cowled figures, one distributing sacks of food to the poor and infirm, the other seated and instructing him. Directly above the royal pair and the princes, on the roof of the palatial structure rises the poised horned hart, his horns in full brown color, a symbol

---

143. There is general agreement that illustrator D is the most accurate adaptor of the Utrecht. See, for example, Gameson's discussion of illustrator D's exceptional draftsmanship, his clarity and precision of line, and his masterful use of color; "Anglo-Saxon Artists," 34–35; likewise, see Noel, *Harley Psalter*, 60–68, who notes D's changes and omissions and who, at one point, is so struck by the illustrator's adaptation that he suspects he may have traced portions of the Utrecht (65); for the additions of illustrator G to the Psalm 111 illustration, see Noel, 112.

144. See Noel's discussion, *Harley Psalter*, 66–68.

of royalty and justice.[145] Finally, at the right, attached to the palatial structure, stands a chapel with a cross and globe on its roof; directly above it, reaching strikingly toward the canopied central dais, God's hand in vibrant red blesses the horned hart, the royal pair, and the unsparing generosity depicted in their action. To a just people thus will be tendered just rewards.

At its core, the illustration of Psalm 111 captures both the imperial generosity attributed by popular sentiment to Cnut and Emma and the munificence of Heorot's royal pair.[146] True, the assemblage of a destitute citizenry in the psalter has been transformed into one of warriors in *Beowulf,* and the gifts proffered are treasures of the state at the investiture of a prince, not sacks of food. But that is the job of poetry; Anglo-Saxon poets did not copy words or images, especially those who may have been bent on emulating Virgil. Rather, they absorbed; they ruminated, using Remley's phrase; they became imbued with that which in their experience had reached out and inspired them. For rumination, as Mary Carruthers' studies of memory and composition have taught us, was an essential activity for monk and poet alike. It produced a state of learning that held as repository all that one had read and heard and appropriated into one's own experience, a compositional activity one sees in operation in authors as various as King

---

145. For the horned hart as a figure of benevolence and justice in other Anglo-Saxon illustrated manuscripts, see Schichler, "*Glaed Man,*" 63nn7, 9; 64n13; See also Thomas H. Ohlgren, *Insular and Anglo-Saxon Illuminated Manuscripts: An Iconographic Catalogue c. A.D. 625 to 1100* (New York: Garland Publishing, Inc., 1986), 361, s.v. "Horn," and 375, s.v. "Moses: horned"; and Ruth Mellinkoff, *The Horned Moses in Medieval Art and Thought* (Berkeley, CA: University of California Press, 1970), esp. chaps. 1–3, on the earliest artistic representations being in Anglo-Saxon England; on the adaptation of the Mosaic horn into bishop's mitre, see Mellinkoff, *Outcasts: Signs of Otherness in Northern Europe of the Late Middle Ages*, 2 vols. (Berkeley, CA: University of California Press, 1993), 1: 83–89, 2: pls. iii.58, iii.62.

146. Among other instances of generosity, note the image of a humbled Cnut's generosity toward the destitute related in the *Encomium* and of Emma's continually relieving the needs of women and children approaching her with hands upraised. *EER* ii.21–22, 36–38; iii.11–12, 50–53.

Alfred in his letter to Bishop Wærferð, Saint Augustine, and Bede's Caedmon, who, Carruthers reminds us, "changed what he learned by hearing in *lectio*, or sermons, into sweetest [vernacular] poetry by recollecting it within himself (*rememorandum rerum*) and ruminating like a clean animal (*quasi mundum animal ruminendo*)."[147] In its essence, the Beowulfian scene, with its sacral and imperial mood, its biblical associations, its ornamented sumptuous setting, and its striking figures of a king and queen ceremoniously displaying their unbounded generosity in distributing the treasures of the nation, captures the spirit of thanksgiving in those who have experienced God's redemptive power and munificence toward the righteous, explicitly expressed in all verses of Psalm 111, which forms the foundation of both the iconic image and the vernacular poetic epic.

Further, two of Duffey's seven "inventive group" reflect a contemporaneity with events and personages in Cnut's reign that likewise may have influenced the unique construction of the second banquet scene—the iconographic rendering of verse 2 in Psalm 130, fol. 67v (fig.11), and that of verse 1 in Psalm 132, fol. 68v (fig.12), both of which Duffey associates with Queen Emma.[148] The work of illustrator F, these, like the image of the four kings on folio 58r, are also uniquely altered from the Utrecht original and may have relevance to the immediate discussion of the Beowulfian poet's composition. Strikingly unlike the Utrechtian rendering of Psalm 130 of a seated mother weaning her child in an undefined, illusionary exterior space, Harley 603 presents the image of a woman of nobility, sharply detailed in dress and expression, seated within and appropriating the entire left

---

147. Essential reading for understanding the importance of the monastic study of memory and its activities of meditation and rumination is Carruthers, *Book of Memory*, esp. chap. 5; on composition and rumination, esp. 206–12; quote at 206. See also the companion volume, *The Craft of Thought: Meditation, Rhetoric, and the Making of Images, 400–1200* (Cambridge, UK: Cambridge University Press, 1998), where she defines memory as a "matrix of a reminiscing cogitation," at 4.

148. Duffey, "Inventive Group of Illustrations," 138–44, 150–51, 168–69.

arch of a "double-arched domed structure," in the act of presenting a large vibrant red ring to a young man, which he accepts. With her left hand, in a gesture of blessing or affection, she touches his forehead. Poised in the entire space of the right arch, he holds a staff, which, in association with the ring, could symbolize another generalized interpretation of the weaning theme of verse 2, a young man's maturation and elevation of status.[149] Yet for Duffey, the breach between the Utrechtian and Harleian is too striking, the Harley's precision of detail in setting, object, character, and action too contrastive, to make such an abstract reading satisfactory. Rather, she interprets the scene as holding royal and sacral implications, especially in the placement of its figures within a double-arched domed structure and in the imposing female figure. Traditionally, in early Christian illustrations, arched or canopied spaces were reserved for the representation of heavenly or earthly royalty, with the figure on the left, as in this instance, larger and enthroned, presenting an unspecified item—but usually not a ring—to the figure or figures on the right.[150] More pointedly, the transference of a ring, or an object in the shape of a ring,

149. Duffey, "Inventive Group of Illustrations," 138, 142–43, wherein she discusses the Augustinian interpretation of the weaning image.

150. See, for example, *The Benedictional of St. Ethelwold* (London, BL MS Add. 49598) for two examples—the illustration of the Presentation in the Temple (f. 34b), where Mary (within the left arch) holds out the baby Jesus to Simeon (within the right), and the illustration of the Dedication of a Church (f.118v), wherein a bishop in deep blue full color (within an arch) stands near an altar and blesses a golden book held by one of six monks in red outline drawing on the right. More closely associated with Harley 603 f.67v in composition is the *Arundel Psalter* (London, BL MS Add. Arundel 155, f. 133r.), which depicts an enthroned Saint Benedict filling the left arch (in deep blue full color), receiving a book from or having given it to a group of monks clustered within the right arch; cited in Duffey, "Inventive Group of Illustrations," 142–43; see Temple, *Anglo-Saxon Manuscripts*, (for *Ethelwold*) 49–53, esp. 50, 51, and Il. 91, and (for the *Arundel Psalter*) 84–85, esp. 84, and Il. 213; Francis Wormald, *The Benedictional of St. Ethelwold* (London: Faber and Faber, 1959), 22, 30, and pls. 4 and 8; and Wormald, *English Drawings*, 43, 66, and pl. 22.

from a superior figure to one of lower status is formulaically depicted in both Roman patrician art and Byzantine representations of coronations, where the figure presenting the ring is sometimes female.[151]

In addition to the ring's symbolic significance in Roman imperial images and Christian images derived therefrom, Duffey does not fail to note the frequency with which the transference of a ring appears in sacral and status-elevation ceremonies in the art and literature of Anglo-Scandinavian culture, noted above in the discussion of the ring-giving ceremony enacted by Wealhtheow and Beowulf. Typified by the *stallahringr*, a temple ring described in medieval Icelandic literature as a *baugr roðinn* (reddened ring), reddened because it had been blessed by sacramental blood, upon which sacred oaths were to be made, these ceremonial oath-rings were used for a variety of purposes from securing legal transactions and peace treaties to transferences or changes of authority and investitures, as occurred, for example, in King Alfred's peace pact with Guthrum over *þam halgan beaga* (the holy ring) or the investiture of Guthred as king of Northumbria by means of the holy armlet.[152] For Duffey, illustrator F intentionally appropriated the ring-giving formula in his unrecognizable modification of the Utrecht image because he had a specific contemporary reference in mind, "some actual or symbolic ceremonial form . . . perhaps of Danish origin, possibly incorporating any or all of the ideas of reward, gift, investiture, oaths of severance or allegiance between a royal mother and son."[153] And although she does not specify what the occasion might have been, she identifies the

---

151. Duffey, "Inventive Group of Illustrations," 142–44, esp. 143.

152. Duffey, "Inventive Group of Illustrations," 139–44; although she does not directly connect the color of the rings, she does point to their identical use, as for example in King Alfred's 876 peace pact with the Vikings (*ASC* 876) and Simeon of Durham's description of Guthred's investiture as king of Northumbria (noted above, 254); see also Magoun, "On the Old Germanic Altar- or Oath-Ring," esp. 279; for another description of the *stallahringr*, see *Eyrbyggja saga*, trans. Hermánn Pálsson and Paul Edwards (London and New York: Penguin, 1973), chap. 4.

153. Duffey, "Inventive Group of Illustrations," 160–61.

figures as representations of Emma and Harthacnut.[154] Because of Harley 603's frequent references to royalty and monastic communities, and to the relationship between its patron Æthelnoth, Christ Church, and the royal court, Duffey's conclusion is not without merit.

Nor is her reading of illustrator F's singular adaptation of Psalm 132, which likewise references the royal court. Delineated on the upper level of Harley fol. 68v, the illustration may, in fact, serve as a visual representation of the congeniality and concord that existed between Emma and Cnut and the brothers at Christ Church, an amicability that may have continued between the brothers and the queen mother Emma after Cnut's death during Harthacnut's brief reign, for it is a singular adaptation of verse 1 rather than verse 2 of the psalm, which references harmony among a monastic community: *quam bonum et quam iucundum est habitare fratres in unum* (How good and how pleasant it is for brothers to dwell together in unity), explicitly delineated in Harley 603 by a group of seven figures clustered in animated conversation under a clearly defined acanthus arbor. Unification of purpose and concord in community drive the theme of the illustration as they do the closure of Queen Wealhtheow's speech of benediction.

Five of the figures are cowled, indicating their fraternity in a monastic community. They differ in size and in dress from the second and third figures from the right, who clearly are not members of the monastic community proper but rather either nobility or royalty. The third figure, young in appearance, holds a goblet or a chalice and leans toward the monk on his right, apparently engrossed in what the cowled figure is saying. The second figure, also in profile but more prominently frontal and enlarged, starkly in contrast to the others, is rendered as a female, wearing a puffed "double-ended headdress" of deep, jeweled blue attached under her chin and a wide-sleeved dress,

---

154. Duffey, "Inventive Group of Illustrations," 144, 167. Duffey makes reference to, but rejects, Harthacnut's appointment to Denmark as its king as a possibility (164–65), and even considers, and rejects, the investiture of Harold Harefoot and Ælfgifu of Northampton, as being highly unlikely in a work whose patron very likely might have been Archbishop Æthelnoth.

whose V-neck collar emphasizes the contours of her breasts and the choker encircling her neck. She, likewise, is held by the words of the animated cowled figure, as is the remainder of the group. The scene depicts a spontaneous vitality and comradeship: two monastic figures (fifth and sixth from the right) seem to be commenting between themselves on the text of the monk's speech addressed to the royal figures, while the final monastic figure (seventh from the right), likewise animated with left hand upraised, bends toward the center. The most startling aspect of this unique Harleian icon is the obvious intentional inclusion of the female figure in the monastic community. For Duffey, the most likely reasonable explanation is that it references either a prominent contemporary abbess, which she finds unlikely since there is no record of a "double monastery or community of women" in Canterbury, or, more likely, "some prominent female," perhaps royal, or a "royal couple" holding a close relationship with a monastic community.[155] During the period when illustrator F was creating his unique adaptations of the Utrechtian illustrations, no other royal figures were as prominently associated with and actively participated in religious houses, especially Christ Church Canterbury, as Cnut and Emma.[156]

The Harley Psalter had currency in both ecclesiastical and royal circles as noted by Backhouse, Hasler, and Duffey and conceivably would have been accessible to and served as inspiration for any eleventh-century learned person in those circles,[157] especially for a poet, whether monk or layman, who was prone to weave together stored images as he did words. Schichler's argument that the illustration of Psalm 111 found on Harley fol. 57v is a "visual counterpart to Hrothgar's Heorot," coupled with Duffey's reading of the

---

155. Duffey, "Inventive Group of Illustrations," 151, 161.
156. Duffey, "Inventive Group of Illustrations," 169–70.
157. That the manuscript was well-used can be seen from the condition of the parchment, which, at times, shows signs of wear, either soiled or worn at the upper or lower edges as, for example, on the folios discussed in this chapter (ff. 2r, 57v, 58r, 67v, 68v), with two tears or cuts on mid-leaf bottom of 57v and some light buckling along the edges on others (ff. 67v, 68v).

Harleian adaptations of Psalms 130 and 132, cannot but bring to mind the sacral-political closure of the second banquet scene, the climax of which foregrounds Queen Wealhtheow, who amid the court's applause, invests Beowulf with enhanced authority and profound responsibility while bestowing upon him a symbol of regal status, the sacred ring, an argument which has been advanced above. The Beowulfian rendering, then, may be understood, not only as a magnification of the ending of the *Encomium* where *fides habetur regni sotiis* (there is loyalty among the sharers of rule) and *inuiolabile uiget faedus materni fraternique amoris* (the bond of motherly and brotherly love is of strength indestructible), but also as a performative manifestation brought forth from the poet's memorial hoard of the Harleian version of the transfer of the sacred ring in Psalm 130 and, in the larger frame of the scene, of Psalm 132's visual representation of a *habitare fratres in unum* (fraternity, or brothers in harmony), joined by male and female royalty in animated conversation, one in the act of bearing a communal goblet. In the Beowulfian adaptation, having invested Beowulf with the sacred ring, Queen Wealhtheow can again proclaim Heorot a community that has reclaimed its joy, content in its desires and needs, loyal to the lord (*mandrihtne hol[d]*—which, in the context of the psalm, one cannot escape a homonymic association with God)— and willingly unified in action (*þegnas syndon geþwǣre, þēod ealgearo*) symbolized by the passing of the communal goblet.

Granted the currency that Harley 603 is said to have enjoyed in the ecclesiastical community and in the royal court, then, it may be worth considering the possibility that the Harleian visual renderings of Psalms 111, 130, and 132, in company with the closure of the *Encomium* and the covenant of circumcision of *Genesis A*, served as part of the Beowulfian poet's cultural repertoire—his repository of sociopolitical *gidda*—upon which he had ruminated. Inspired by what he had read and seen, the *gilphlæden* poet was then moved "to devise new words, artfully joined" (*word oþer fand / sōðe gebunden* [870ᵇ–871ᵃ])—into a unique rendering of the second banquet scene as a climactic dramatization of the investiture of an Anglo-Danish prince, in the line of Virgil, at the start of a new political age. Thus, he brought forth a new creation, the first English vernacular heroic epic, as Cædmon, ruminating upon the Latin songs he had heard, had been moved to compose the first English vernacular praise poem, his doxology to the supreme creator.

Afterword

"History often resembles 'myth,' because they are both ultimately made of the same stuff."[1]

This study began as an examination of notoriously baffling narrative units in *Beowulf*, of which there are more than the eight addressed here. As such, it is by no means an exhaustive discussion even of the first two-thirds of the poem, which represent the work of the eleventh-century hand of Scribe A. Yet these few units examined have brought forth a deeper understanding of the complexity and depth of the poet's compositional process, compelling me to regard the poem extant in Cotton Vitellius A.xv as a double-layered epic narrative, blending legendary, mythical, and religious materials with a metatextual cryptic tale of the civic and martial turmoil taking place in Anglo-Saxon England in the first half of the eleventh century.

As discussed above, the *Beowulf*-poet was not alone in expressing his engagement with the historical events that marked the eventual end of Anglo-Saxon England. In 1014, lamenting the anarchical reign of Æthelred, Wulfstan called passionately for reform and repentant prayer in *Sermo Lupi* and *VII Æthelred*. Similarly, around the close of the first two decades of the century, the C-Chronicler expressed repressed despair at the lassitude of the English and their bungling strategies against the Danes, and at the start of the third decade, the anonymous Norman-Latin satirist of the dialogue poems *Jezebel* and

---

1. Tolkien, "On Fairy-stories," 26–33, quote at 30.

Semiramis allegorized Cnut's accession to the throne of Anglo-Saxon England via his sexual engagements with, to use van Houts's phrase, his powerful "two queens." In 1036, an impassioned and disconsolate C-Chronicler bemoaned the assassination of Alfred atheling, while the anonymous illustrators of Harley 603 codified the restoration of peace in vibrant multicolored images during or after the reign of Cnut and Emma. All these contemporary, at times contrasting, voices compel one to regard the first half of the eleventh century as a time of public and personal anguish.[2] The times weighed heavy on the mind of each individual living in the England of the eleventh century as they did on the *Beowulf*-poet who recorded in elevated style the rise and fall of the last Scandinavian hero-king, crafting in the process the first national secular vernacular epic in Virgilian allegorical mode.

Yet beyond these eight narrative units, still others should exist that point to an integral wholeness for the entire poem. Aspects of the historical narrative of Cnut's reign and that of his sons ought to appear in other perplexing units in the poem, which have not been addressed here, however "oblique and allusive" they might be or however "guarded" the language they would be couched in. For, as often noted, the poet has, one might say intentionally, thematically linked the last third of the poem to the first two-thirds, pointing to unification of narrative line.[3] Surely there must exist a cultural reference for the poet's narration of a bliss-filled Heorot being attacked by a long-brooding *an* (one), the anonymous *feond on helle* (enemy from Hell, or Ely) in Hrothgar's fiftieth year as king and the poet's use of identical language at the start of the last third of the poem in reporting a different creature's aerial onslaught on Beowulf's people in the midst of his fifty-year reign as a *frod cyning, ēþel-weard* (wise king, old guardian of the native land), a structural device Orchard has

---

2. See also Treharne's examination of the cultural angst that existed in England during the final two decades prior to 1066 in *Living Through Conquest*, esp. chaps. 3 and 4.

3. See Rauer, *Beowulf and the Dragon*, esp. 24–31, for one of many discussions on the relationships between the first two-thirds and the last third of the poem.

described as the "poet's stock-in-trade" in effecting unity.[4] It would likewise be difficult not to sense that a historical seed might exist for the contrastive parallelism between Hrothgar's command to construct Heorot for the benefit of the folk (*Bwf* 64–85) and Beowulf's instruction that his men erect his barrow as a solace and an aid to sea travelers. Though Heorot and Beowulf's body, both symbolic of the body politic, are devoured by fire, it is what is within the barrow—the bones of Beowulf and the crafted treasure of kings thought to be of little practical use to men—that transform it into an eternal beacon, as imperishable as the lamenting song of the scop and the piercing keens of the Geatish woman. These images remain unsolved in the context of contemporary events, though they may allude to the timelessness and intrinsic value of art.

Yet even within its limited scope, this discussion has uncovered still another narrative pattern—one that is contemporary and political—for that ever-fluctuating kaleidoscopic poem we know as *Beowulf*. One additional narrative design to the many proposed in the last two hundred years or so of Beowulfian scholarship summarized in Eric Stanley's *In the Foreground: Beowulf*,[5] this monograph has concerned itself primarily with the process of poetic craftsmanship and has thus provided an opportunity to observe the transformations that historical events might undergo at the hands of a poet in the process of composition, how he might break apart the continuities of time, character, and place and refashion the fragments into a literary work engendered by the political angst of a nation. A case in point might be the poet's depiction of the unexpected cowardice of Beowulf's thanes in the last third of the poem. Presented as loyal and tested comrades in every earlier episode in which they appear—from their offering assistance in Beowulf's struggle with Grendel to their waiting poignantly for their lord to rise out of the mere after his

---

4. Orchard, *Companion to Beowulf*, chap. 3 on "Style and Structure," speaking specifically on the effect of double alliteration on passages holding identical language; quote on 64n36.
5. Eric Gerald Stanley, *In the Foreground: Beowulf* (Cambridge, UK: D. S. Brewer, 1994), esp. chaps. 1 and 2.

struggle with Grendel's mother—they stand in contrast to the Danes of Heorot. In the last third of the poem, however, except for Wiglaf, who strongly rebukes his comrades, Beowulf's men shun helping their lord in his fight with the dragon, escaping to a more distant place to save their lives (*Bwf* 2596–99[a]), an action that directly recalls and associates them with the cowardice of Hrothgar's hall thanes, who, during Grendel's repeated attacks, searched for a more spacious location as a resting place (*Bwf* 138–43). In turn, both episodes evoke and would thus be linked to the cowardice and disloyalty of the English during the Danish attacks of 1003–1016 that brought an end to Æthelred's England as lamented by the C-Chronicler and Archbishop Wulfstan. For we may now tentatively concede that the narrative units discussed here conjoin as a historical allegory of the socio-political events during the first half of the eleventh century that brought about the assassination of Alfred atheling and the end of Anglo-Saxon England.

Readers may find it difficult, for instance, to read Grendel's Reign of Terror again without blending *Grendel gongan* (Grendel striding) toward Hrothgar's hall out of the misty slopes (*under misthleopum*) with the Danish troops, the *feond on helle*, ranging through the mist of the East Anglian moors, ravaging the land and mutilating its people, an area that indeed must have been a "hell" in the early decades of the eleventh century as the Blickling homilist relates. For might not St. Paul's image of those "black souls" bound and hanging on a cliff surrounded by icy groves, being clutched at by demons like "ravenous wolves," have its moorings in acts perpetrated against the English by the Danes as they "marched through and decimated even the wild fens" of East Anglia?[6] Such images of life are not easily erased from the collective memory of a country nor of its chroniclers or poets.

---

6. "*[and] he þær geseah ofer ðæm wætere sumne hárne stán; [and] wæron norð of ðæm stáne awexene swiðe hrimige bearwas, [and] ðær wæron þystro-genipo, [and] under þæm stáne wæs nicera eardung & wearga. [and] he geseah þæt on ðæm clife hangodan on ðæm ís gean bearwum manige swearte saula be heora handum gebundne*" (*Blickling Homilies*, ed. Morris, 209); above, chap. 1, n.65.

Nor do I think readers may easily fail to envision the rapacious and cruel *Álfífa in ríka* as presented in the extant historical documents resonating in the figure of the *micle mearcstapa* (great, powerful strider of the borderlands), Grendel's mother, and her mock rule over the Mercian *wulfhleoþu* (slopes belonging to the wolves). Tolkien, of course, was correct to force the attention of the critics on the monsters (although he skirted addressing Grendel's mother) for it is to them that the poet has given over the wheel of control to propel the action of the first 1,650 lines of *Beowulf*.[7] I would venture, however, to adjust slightly Tolkien's extraordinary and densely layered thoughts on *Beowulf*, for it seems to me that what makes the foes in these particular narrative units of the scenario of *Beowulf* "larger and more significant" is not that they are "inhuman"[8] but rather that they are indeed palpably human, ruling over the eleventh-century Mercian *wulfhleoþu* with the avaricious fury of wild beasts.

Tolkien's dragon, with which he expresses displeasure for not being dragon enough, is a figure encircled by any number of mythological and hagiographical allusions and would seem at first to have escaped the taint of historical fact. Although it is commonly associated with the mythological *miðgarðsormr* (world-serpent) destroyed by Þórr, might there not be found in its narrative an additional tier containing reverberations of contemporary, tangible historical actuality? The dragon is described clearly as having a serpentine shape of some fifty feet in length (*sē wæs fiftiges fōtgemearces / lang on legere, Bwf* 3042–43[a]), its physical length recalling the years of reign of Hrothgar, Grendel's mother, and Beowulf. Once defeated—once no longer able to terrorize Beowulf's kingdom nightly with burning flames—it is shoved out onto the sea by Beowulf's men, to be engulfed by the waves— *drācan ēc scufun, / wyrm ofer weall-clif, lēton wēg niman, / flōd fæðmian frætwa hyrde* (moreover, they shoved the dragon, the worm over the

---

7. For a development history of the creation of Tolkien's *Beowulf: The Monsters and the Critics*, see *Beowulf and the Critics by J. R. R. Tolkien*, ed. Michael D. C. Drout (Tempe, AZ: ACMRS, 2002).

8. Tolkien's argument in *Monsters and the Critics*, 35.

elevated shore, they allowed the waves to seize, the surge of the sea to envelop the protector of the treasure, *Bwf* 3131ᵇ–33). Beowulf's men's ejection of the great serpent to the waves stands in parallel to the mourning Danes' release of Scyld's funeral vessel bearing the king's adorned body to the dominion of the sea. Both passages reflect near identical terminology—*Þā gt hīe him āsetton, segen gy(l)denne / hēah ofer hēafod, lēton holm beran, / gēafon on gārsecg* (Then they set a golden standard above him, high above his head, they allowed the waters to bear him away, they released him to the sea, *Bwf* 47–49ᵃ). The golden standard, a metonymic image of the king himself guarding the *frǽtwa* (treasure) that surrounds him in the hold, stands paired with the brilliant golden standard that pours forth light over the entire treasure-floor of the dragon.

In the context of the present argument, it is difficult not to be reminded of Óláfr Tryggvason's gold-ornamented long ship, *Ormr inn langi* (the long serpent), that Sveinn boasted of having captured at the battle of Svǫlð in 1000 or, more to the point, the Encomiast's description of Sveinn's corpse being ferried to Denmark from England.[9] Might not the Beowulfian dragon, then, be an allegorization in a more heightened fantastic mode of Sveinn Forkbeard, who, along with his companions, the Danish *flotmen*[10] (fleet), *dydon eal swa hi ær gewuna wæron, heregodon and bærndon and slogon swa swa hi ferdon* (did just as they had been in the habit of doing–they harried and burned and massacred as they carried on), actions attributed to the Beowulfian *wyrm* and assigned to Grendel in the first two-thirds

---

9. For the *Ormr inn langi* (long serpent), see *Óláfs saga Tryggvasonar*, in *Hkr 1*, ed. Aðalbjarnarson, chap. 101; for the translation of Sveinn's body from England to Denmark, see *EER* ii.3, 18–19. Cnut's *dreki* (dragon), though not the most famous, was not inconsiderable in size, having "sixty rowers' benches" (*Hann sjálfr hafði dreka þann, er svá mikill, at sextøgr var at rúmatali*), *Óláfs saga Helga*, in *Hkr 2*, ed. Aðalbjarnarson, chap. 147; see *EER*, ed. Campbell, appendix V, for a discussion of Norse warships.

10. The term appears as *flothere*, a hapax legomenon in *Beowulf* referring to Hygelac's fleet that landed on the Frisian shore (*Bwf* 2915ᵃ) in the battle against the Hetware.

of the poem? The issue is again that of poetic invention and its relationship to history, an issue addressed over a century ago by Jacob Grimm in a passage cited by Professor Stanley:[11]

The first lesson a sincere mind may learn through the contemplation of ancient fable and legend is that they are based on no vain foundation, no fabulosity, but on truthful *poesis*; if I may . . . so express it; they are based on objective inspiration. However . . . the question has to be asked: In what relationship does narrative truth stand to historical truth; as it were, how does what may be sensed stand in relation to what is palpable and to be grasped? . . . History everywhere emerges from the womb of fable, and neither strives to tear itself loose early from this matrical element, nor is History, however much it might desire it, able to do so later without having to relinquish sometimes a mythical item, sometimes an historical item. . . . This contradiction is to be reconciled and eliminated only by combining both views, that is, neither a purely mythical (divine) truth nor a purely historical (factual) truth is to be ascribed to folk-epic, but by placing the very nature of folk-epic essentially in the permeation of both truths. . . . For in epic, an historical action is required to give to the folk a sense of lively fulfillment, so that divine myth can attach itself to it, each conditioned by the other.

It is a view of imaginative narrative similar to that practiced centuries before by medieval monks and artists based on the mnemonic art of recollection and rumination as reflected in the work of Bede's Caedmon or that of the anonymous poet of the *Vision of the Rood* or in the narratives of Ælfric or in that of the *Beowulf*-poet; and it is the view of creative production also advocated by Tolkien almost a century later in his discussion of the poet's hoard of *gidda*, what he dubbed the "Cauldron of Story" as noted in the epigraph

---

11. Stanley, *In the Foreground: Beowulf*, 7–8; I have condensed the passage considerably here.

introducing this Afterword: "History often resembles 'myth,' because they are both ultimately made of the same stuff." In the modern age, neither Grimm nor Tolkien is alone in finding a fusion of history and poetry in epic; it is a tenet also held by more recent contemporary critics as discussed earlier in this monograph. For it is the assumption underlying Hume's observation that literature is the "product of both mimesis and fantasy" and the remarks of Joseph Duggan and Diana Whaley in their characterization of vernacular epic and Kings' Sagas, respectively, as "popular" and "imaginative" historiography.[12] It would thus seem that it is not the separation of historical fact and poetic design but the artistry of their commingling that elevates the *Beowulf*-poet's narrative design to a sublime epic reality.

The arguments presented in the preceding chapters, nonetheless, are unsettling. Not only do they add still another dimension to the poem's narrative, compelling us to regard the poem, from one perspective, as a social document, a historical allegory of contemporary events and figures that looks ahead to the social and political commentary of Chaucer and Langland,[13] but they solicit a renewed inquiry into the dating issue, an issue that may be unsolvable. In spite of the compelling arguments from a variety of approaches, especially those of Lapidge and Fulk, that argue for an earlier *Beowulf*, my focus of inquiry has centered on the tangible *Beowulf* found in Cotton Vitellius A.xv, an eleventh-century manuscript, a large part of which is written in an eleventh-century hand, including the matter found in the first two-thirds of the poem. Moreover, the poem's eleventh-century context has been significantly advanced by the paleographic and codicological arguments of Dumville and Kiernan to the second decade of the eleventh, although my conclusions would advance Kiernan's thesis of the poem's composition some twenty years. Nonetheless, the foregoing discussion at least

---

12. See J. Duggan, "Medieval Epic as Popular Historiography"; Whaley, *Heimskringla*, and Hume, *Fantasy and Mimesis*. See above, Introduction, 17–19nn42, 44.

13. See Astell, *Political Allegory in Late Medieval England*, and above, Introduction, 20n49.

should provoke further investigation into and reconsideration of the poem's eleventh-century dating, since it points to a possible Beowulfian metatext that fuses contemporary Anglo-Danish politics with the poem's "brilliant North Germanic antiquity" (Frank's phrase), placing the *Beowulf*-poet within cultural and linguistic proximity to the practicing skalds with whom he shares a dictional and compositional tradition. For like the narrative frieze unearthed from the rubble at Winchester and interpreted by Martin Biddle, at the suggestion of Ray Page, as depicting a segment in the northern narrative of Sigmund (the Wælsing of *Beowulf*) and the she-wolf who has come to devour him—a frieze erected to celebrate a shared English and Danish cultural tradition[14]—the poem likewise would function as a document of unification of English and Danish interests, celebrating a shared English and Danish literary tradition. Although the dating of the composition of the poem remains a contestable issue, and perhaps will remain so for many years to come, from what I have encountered here I find it difficult not to argue for the possibility of a composition in the eleventh century.

One could then ask what kind of composition? It is certainly not a composition entirely original, born fully matured like Athena from Zeus's head, without any relations to earlier or contemporary literary traditions. In its formulaic expression and its literary and legendary borrowings alone, the poet reveals his indebtedness to the *Aeneid*[15] and to other indigenous or foreign works, a testament

---

14. Martin Biddle, "Excavations at Winchester 1965: Fourth Interim Report," *The Antiquaries Journal* v. 46, n. 2 (September 1966): 308–32, esp. 329–32, Appendix: A Late Saxon Frieze Sculpture from the Old Minster. Biddle suggests its entire length as possibly being around 80 feet depicting scenes traditionally shared by England and Denmark, with a date of mid-eleventh century and Cnut as its sponsor. The story is found in chapter 5 of the dual language edition of *Vǫlsunga Saga: The Saga of the Volsungs*, ed. and trans. by R. G. Finch (London: Thomas Nelson and Sons, 1965), 6–8.

15. For the *Beowulf*-poet's indebtedness, see esp. above, Introduction, 14–15n36; as a comparison with the use of the *Aeneid* by the Encomiast, see esp. above 19 and n. 46.

to his existence in a syncretic and multilingual courtly society. In such a world, one then conjectures that the poet might have been an inspired reshaper of everything he read and experienced, as were epic poets from Homer to Virgil to Milton to Robert Browning, and not to overlook the eclecticism of Richard Wagner, each contextualizing and reshaping old material into new, into works that might speak to and have relevance for their time. For the untitled Cotton Vitellius A.xv poem to which we have given the name *Beowulf*, taking on the role of authorship to some degree, is a tangible work of the eleventh century; it was copied and in some way transmitted in that turbulent century—facts that point to its having had some cultural relevance to that time—and hence found its way to Laurence Nowell, to Humfrey Wanley, to Grímur Thorkelin, to the present.

The accumulation of parallels between Grendel's Reign of Terror and the narrative of the Danish incursion of England in the C-version of the *Anglo-Saxon Chronicle* is difficult to attribute to mere accident; these parallels point, it seems to me, either to the poet's personal involvement in those events or to his having access to the *C-Chronicle* text itself, which places the poem in the second or third decade of the eleventh century. Further, the parallel action and theme of apostasy between the *Gifstól* passage and the meeting between Harold Harefoot and Archbishop Æthelnoth, a narrative unique to the *Encomium*, extend the possible composition of the poem to nearly mid-century. The poet's dramatization of key scenes in the *Encomium*, such as his rendering of Harthacnut's voyage to Bruges as Beowulf's arrival in Heorot, or the performative representation of *gemma/ Emma* of Normandy as the *béaghroden cwén* (ring- or jewel-adorned queen) Wealhtheow, and his inspired transformation of the assassination and avenging of Alfred atheling into the Beowulfian beheading sequence, moves me to consider that the intertextuality that exists between the Latin historical work and the Anglo-Saxon heroic epic may point to the poet's having had access to the Latin work or to his having been influenced by it in some manner.

This is not an unreasonable conjecture. For one, even in mid-eleventh-century Anglo-Danish England, Latin and Latin literature held primacy in the monastic, political, and literary cultures, as the plethora of prose and poetic works reworked from Latin originals testifies.[16] Second, an intertextuality between the Latin political history and other Old English works has already been noted by Earl Anderson and Orchard,[17] arguments that would lend support to the *Encomium*'s circulation and plausible influence on *Beowulf*, since we lack evidence of the literary influence of *Beowulf* on other works; except for the first and last pages of *Beowulf* in the manuscript that show signs of excessive handling, there is no evidence of its circulation in the mid- to late eleventh century, although it must have circulated in some manner.[18] Third, we know that the *Encomium* was written during a time of political unrest in Harthacnut's reign when the Anglo-Danish reign was losing its popularity and factionalism was again rearing its ugly head, perhaps because of heavy taxation,

---

16. One of many, but still a sound and accessible discussion, is that of Michael Lapidge, "The Anglo-Latin Background," in Stanley B. Greenfield and Daniel G. Calder, *A New Critical History of English Literature, with a Survey of the Anglo-Latin Background by Michael Lapidge* (New York: New York University Press, 1986), 5–37.

17. See above, 100. Anderson argues that a number of parallels between the *Encomium* and *The Battle of Maldon* point to a later date of composition for the OE poem (from ca. A.D. 991 to 1041) [Anderson, "Battle of Maldon," in *Modes of Interpretation*, ed. Brown et al., 247–72]; Orchard finds parallels between the *Anglo-Saxon Chronicle* and the *Encomium* ["Literary Background to the *EER*," 156–83]; see also Tyler (above, 19), for similarities in the treatment of treasure between *Beowulf* and *EER*, "'Eyes of the Beholder,'" 247–70.

18. The circulation of *Beowulf* remains uncertain, an issue that has not been adequately explored. The worn first and last pages of the poem, as reported by Humfrey Wanley (1705), could suggest the poem may have been circulated separately from the Nowell codex itself; see Kiernan, "Legacy of Wiglaf," and above, Introduction, n6. Kiernan does note that *Wonders of the East*, for example, was being read "with some comprehension in Middle English times" (*Beowulf and the Beowulf Manuscript*, 143n53), but to my knowledge, the first evidence of the poem's circulation comes with Nowell's ownership of the codex.

but perhaps also because of the barbarity of Harthacnut's vengeance in beheading Harold's corpse. It was conceived, as Keynes reminds us, as a political document to be circulated among and to exert political influence upon Harthacnut's subjects in order to maintain their loyalty, reminding them of the glory that defined the Anglo-Danish reign and of the treachery that Emma and her sons had endured at the hands of the usurper, in particular the assassination of the martyred prince Alfred atheling.[19] Queen Edith's commission of the *Life of Edward the Confessor* may be looked upon as responding to and vying with Emma's sponsorship of the *Encomium* and her self-representation as the powerful originator of a dynastic line. Lastly, in the tradition of the relationship between Octavian and Virgil, the *Encomium* holds pride of place as a commissioned work by the queen, for the Encomiast reports that she has "enjoined" him to include all the matter contained in his narrative. That matter may, indeed, contain exaggerations; it would hardly contain lies, since the work would then mock rather than praise Emma, who, to quote Keynes, was "the organizing principle of English politics in the first half of the eleventh century: everything that turned touched her, and she turned everything she touched."[20]

To what extent, if any, the historical queen influenced the composition of *Beowulf*, or if she even knew of its existence, we have no evidence, although it would not be at all unfeasible for Emma, given her trilingualism and her acumen in statesmanship, to be sensitive to the multilingualism of the court and its syncretic political composition and to consider it expedient to touch all her subjects, native and foreign alike. She may then have recalled Cnut's letters of 1020 and 1027, which had been addressed not only to leading officials of Church and State but to all free subjects, with promises and assurances of a benevolent and just lordship on all levels, of peace and of an end to their harassments and excessive obligations—his covenant with his people in exchange for their loyalty to himself and

---

19. Keynes, *EER* [lxix–lxx].
20. Keynes, *EER* [lxxviii–lxxix].

obedience to God.[21] It would not be inconceivable that Emma, with her keen awareness of being a foreign queen and her experience of the bitter fragility of fame, might then have deliberated about commissioning her narrative of the glorious rise of the Anglo-Danish monarchy celebrating in epic lamentation England's last hero king to be told in the language of the Anglo-Saxons and expressed in the Germanic poetic form native to all those who had made up Cnut's northern rule.[22] For Beowulf is not only a work of a heightened, associative, and fertile imagination, it is also a "public" poem, a political work concerned with the affairs of state and the persons who run them.

---

21. The 1020 letter survives in Old English in *The York Gospels: A Facsimile with Introductory Essays*, ed. N. Barker (London: Roxburghe Club, 1986); the 1027 letter survives presumably as a Latin translation in *JWChron* 2: 512–19 (s.a. 1031); *WMGRA* 1, ii.183, 324–30; for editions and translations of the letters, see *Councils & Synods, with Other Documents Relating to the English Church*, vol. 1: A.D. 871-1204, ed. D. Whitelock, M. Brett, and C. N. L. Brooke (Oxford: Clarendon Press, 1981), 435–41, 506–13, respectively; see also *EHD*, vol. 1, no. 49 (1019-20), no. 53 (1027); Keynes, *EER* [lxi–lxii]; Patrick Wormald, *The Making of English Law: King Alfred to the Twelfth Century*, vol. 1: *Legislation and Its Limits* (London: Blackwell Publishers, 1999), 347–49; Lawson, *Cnut* 63–64. Finally, see most recently Elaine Treharne's penetrating analysis of Cnut's 1020 and 1027 letters in chap. 2 "The Propaganda of Conquest" in her *Living Through Conquest*, esp. 28–33.

22. For a discussion of Emma's multilingualism in literary and political matters as a resourceful tool to bolster her status as queen, see Elizabeth M. Tyler, "Crossing Conquests: Polyglot Royal Women and Literary Culture in Eleventh-Century England," in her edition, *Conceptualizing Multilingualism in England, c. 800–1250* (Turnhout: Brepols, 2012), esp. 171–183. For a study of thirteenth- and fourteenth-century medieval northern queens (Agnes of Denmark, Euphemia of Norway, and Margareta of Sweden) who commissioned poetic and literary documents as a tool of statecraft (political poems, courtly epics, political poems in rhyming verse, repectively), see William Layher, *Queenship and Voice in Medieval Northern Europe* (New York: Palgrave Macmillan, 2010).

Bibliography

REFERENCE WORKS

Bessinger, J. B., Jr., ed. *A Concordance to The Anglo-Saxon Poetic Records*. Programmed by Philip H. Smith, Jr. Ithaca, NY: Cornell University Press, 1978.

———. *A Concordance to Beowulf*. Programmed by Philip H. Smith, Jr. Ithaca, NY: Cornell University Press, 1969.

Biggs, Frederick M., Thomas D. Hill, Paul E. Szarmach, and E. Gordon Whatley. *Sources of Anglo-Saxon Literary Culture: Volume I*. Kalamazoo, MI: Medieval Institute Publications, 2001.

The Blackwell Encyclopaedia of Anglo-Saxon England. Ed. Michael Lapidge, John Blair, Simon Keynes, and Donald Scragg. Oxford: Blackwell, 2001.

Bosworth, Joseph. *An Anglo-Saxon Dictionary*. Ed. and enlarged T. Northcote Toller. Oxford: Oxford University Press, 1898; repr. 1976. [See also under Toller, T. Northcote.]

Budny, Mildred. *Insular, Anglo-Saxon, and Early Anglo-Norman Manuscript Art at Corpus Christi College, Cambridge: An Illustrated Catalogue*. 2 vols. Kalamazoo, MI: Medieval Institute Publications, 1997.

Cleasby, Richard, ed. *An Icelandic-English Dictionary*. Enlarged and completed by Gudbrand Vigfusson. Oxford: Clarendon Press, 1874.

Dictionary of the Middle Ages. Vol. 4. Ed. Joseph Strayer. New York: Scribner, 1984.

Dictionary of National Biography. Ed. Sir Leslie Stephen and Sir Sidney Lee. Vol. 8. Oxford: Oxford University Press, 1917.

The Dictionary of Old English. Ed. Antoinette diPaolo Healey et al. Toronto: Toronto University Press, 1986–.

Forssner, Thorvald. *Continental-Germanic Personal Names in England in Old and Middle English Times.* Uppsala: K. W. Appelbergs, 1916.

Grimm, Jacob. *Teutonic Mythology.* Trans. James Steven Stallybrass. 4 vols. London: George Bell & Sons, 1882–88.

Hjertstedt, Ingrid. *Middle English Nicknames in the Lay Subsidy Rolls for Warwickshire.* Studia Anglistica Upsaliensia 63. Uppsala: Academiae Upsalien, 1987.

Hofmann, Dietrich. *Nordisch-englische Lehnbeziehungen der Wikingerzeit.* Bibliotheca Arnamagnæana 14. Copenhagen: E. Munksgaard, 1955, 59–101.

Kemble, J. M. "The Names, Surnames, and Nicknames of the Anglo-Saxons." In *Proceedings of the Annual Meeting of the Archaeological Institute at Winchester, 1845.* London, 1846, 92–93.

Medieval England: An Encyclopedia. Ed. Paul E. Szarmach, M. Teresa Tavormina, and Joel T. Rosenthal. New York: Garland Publishing, Inc., 1998.

Medieval Scandinavia: An Encyclopedia. Ed. Phillip Pulsiano, Kirsten Wolf, Paul Acker, Donald K. Fry. New York: Garland Publishing, Inc., 1993.

Ohlgren, Thomas H., comp. and ed. *Insular and Anglo-Saxon Illuminated Manuscripts: An Iconographic Catalogue c. A.D. 625 to 1100.* New York: Garland Publishing, Inc., 1986.

Pugh, R. B. *The Victoria County History of Cambridgeshire and the Isle of Ely.* Vol. 4. 1953; London: The Institute of Historical Research, 1967.

Redin, Mats. *Studies on Uncompounded Personal Names in Old English.* Uppsala: Akademiska Bokhandeln, 1919.

Sawyer, P. H. *Anglo-Saxon Charters: An Annotated List and Bibliography.* London: Royal Historical Society, 1968.

Temple, Elżbieta. *Anglo-Saxon Manuscripts 900–1066.* London: Harvey Miller, 1976.

Toller, T. Northcote. *An Anglo-Saxon Dictionary: Supplement. With rev. and enlarged addenda by Alistair Campbell.* Oxford: Oxford University Press, 1972. [See also under Bosworth, Joseph.]

de Vries, Jan. *Altnordische Literaturgeschichte. Grundriss der germanischen Philologie.* Ed. Hermann Paul. Vol. 15, 1. Berlin: Walter de Gruyter & Co., 1941–42.

Primary Sources

A. Manuscripts and Facsimiles

British Library, MS Add. 33, 241.

British Library, MS Cotton Vespasian D.xxi.

British Library, MS Cotton Vitellius A.xii.

British Library, MS Cotton Vitellius A.xv.

British Library, MS Harley 603.

British Library, MS Stowe 944.

Cambridge University Library, Ee.3.59.

La estoire de Seint Aedward Le Rei: The Life of St. Edward the Confessor, fascimile edition of the unique manuscript (Cambridge University Library Ee.3.59). Introduction by M. R. James. Oxford: University Press, 1920.

The Liber Vitae of the New Minster and Hyde Abbey Winchester, British Library Stowe 944. Ed. Simon Keynes. Early English Manuscript Facsimiles, vol. 26. Copenhagen: Rosenkilde and Bagger, 1996.

The York Gospels: A Facsimile with Introductory Essays by Jonathan Alexander, Patrick McGurk, Simon Keynes, and Bernard Barr. Ed. Nicholas Barker. London: Roxburghe Club, 1986.

Editions and Translations

Adam of Bremen. *History of the Archbishops of Hamburg-Bremen.* Trans. Francis J. Tschan. New York: Columbia University Press, 1959.

Ágrip af Nóregskonungasǫgum. Ed. M. J. Driscoll. Viking Society for Northern Research Text Series 10. London: Viking Society for Northern Research, 1995.

Alexander, Jonathan J. C., and Claus M. Kaufmann. *English Illuminated Manuscripts 700–1500.* Brussels: Bibliotheque Royale Albert 1er, 1973.

The Anglo-Saxon Chronicle: A Collaborative Edition MS. C. Vol. 5. Ed. Katherine O'Brien O'Keeffe. Cambridge, UK: D. S. Brewer, 2001.

The Anglo-Saxon Chronicle: A Collaborative Edition: The Abingdon Chronicle A.D. 956–1066 (MS. C, with Reference to BDE). Vol. 10. Ed. Patrick W. Conner. Cambridge, UK: D. S. Brewer, 1996.

Bibliography

The Anglo-Saxon Chronicle: Two of the Saxon Chronicles Parallel, with Supplementary Extracts from the Others. Ed. Charles Plummer, on the basis of an edition by John Earle. 2 vols. Oxford: Clarendon Press, 1892–99.

The Anglo-Saxon Minor Poems. Ed. E. V. K. Dobbie. *ASPR* 6. New York: Columbia University Press, 1942.

Anglo-Saxon Prose. Ed. and trans. Michael Swanton. London: J. M. Dent, 1993.

The Battle of Maldon AD 991. Ed. Donald Scragg. Oxford: Blackwell, 1991.

The Battle of Maldon. Ed. D. G. Scragg. Manchester: Manchester University Press, 1981.

Bede. *Bede's Ecclesiastical History of the English People*. Ed. Bertram Colgrave and R. A. B. Mynors. Oxford: Clarendon Press, 1969.

Beowulf: A Dual-Language Edition. Trans. Howell D. Chickering. Garden City, NY: Anchor Press/Doubleday, 1977.

Beowulf: An Edition with Relevant Shorter Texts, including "Archaeology and Beowulf," by Leslie Webster. Ed. Bruce Mitchell and Fred C. Robinson. Oxford: Blackwell, 1998.

Beowulf and the Fight at Finnsburg: Third Edition with First and Second Supplements. Ed. Fr. Klaeber. 3rd ed. Lexington, MA: D. C. Heath & Co., 1950. [See also under *Klaeber's Beowulf*.]

Beowulf, with the Finnesburg Fragment. Ed. C. L. Wrenn and W. F. Bolton. 5th Edition. Exeter: University of Exeter Press, 1996.

The Blickling Homilies of the Tenth Century, with a Translation, and Index of Words. Ed. R. Morris. Early English Text Society, o.s. 58, 63, 73. London: N. Trübner, 1874–80.

Boethius. *Boethii Philosophiae Consolatio*. Ed. Ludwig Bieler. Turnhout: Brepols, 1957.

——. *The Consolation of Philosophy*. Trans. Richard Green. New York, Bobbs-Merrill Co., 1962.

Bresslau, H. *Jahrbücher des Deutschen Reichs unter Konrad II*. 2 vols. Leipzig: Duncker & Humbolt, 1879–84.

Byrhtferth. *Vita Oswaldi*. In *Historians of the Church of York and Its Archbishops*, ed. J. Raine. 3 vols. RS 71. London: Longman, 1879.

Das angelsächsische Prosa-Leben des heiligen Guthlac. Ed. Paul Gonser. Anglistische Forschungen 27. Heidelberg: Carl Winter, 1909.

DeWald, E. T., ed. *The Illustrations of the Utrecht Psalter*. Princeton: Princeton University Press, 1933.

Dudo of St Quentin. History of the Normans. Trans. Eric Christiansen. Woodbridge, UK: Boydell Press, 1998.

Eadmer of Canterbury: Lives and Miracles of Saints Oda, Dunstan and Oswald. Ed. and trans. Andrew J. Turner and Bernard J. Muir. Oxford: Clarendon Press, 2006.

Edda: Die Lieder des Codex Regius nebst verwandten Denkmälern. Ed. Gustav Neckel. 4th ed. Rev. Hans Kuhn. Heidelberg: Carl Winter, 1962.

Encomium Emmae Reginae. Ed. and trans. Alistair Campbell, with a supplementary introduction by Simon Keynes. Camden Classical Reprints 4. Cambridge, UK: Cambridge University Press, 1998.

Eyrbyggja Saga. Trans. Hermann Pálsson and Paul Edwards. London and New York: Penguin, 1989.

Fagrskinna: Nóregs konunga tal. In *Ágrip af Nóregskonunga sǫgum. Fagrskinna–Nóregs konunga tal*. Ed. Bjarni Einarsson. Íslenzk Fornrit 29. Reykjavík: Íslenzk Fornrit, 1985.

Fagrskinna, A Catalogue of the Kings of Norway. Trans. Alison Finlay. Leiden: Brill, 2004.

Felix. *Vita Sancti Guthlaci: Felix's Life of Saint Guthlac*. Ed. and trans. Bertram Colgrave. Cambridge: Cambridge University Press, 1956.

Finch, R. G., ed. and trans. *Vǫlsunga Saga: The Saga of the Volsungs*. London: Thomas Nelson and Sons, 1965.

Foys, Martin K. *The Bayeux Tapestry*, Digital Edition. Leicester, UK: Scholarly Digital Editions, 2003.

Fulk, R. D., ed. *Eight Old English Poems. Edited, and with Commentary and Glossary by John C. Pope*. 3rd ed. Revised. New York: W. W. Norton, 2001.

Gaimar. *L'Estorie des Engleis by Geffrei Gaimar*. Ed. A. Bell. Anglo-Norman Texts, xiv–xvi. Oxford: B. Blackwell, 1960.

Genesis A: A New Edition. Ed. A. N. Doane. Madison, WI: University of Wisconsin Press, 1978.

Grettis saga Ásmundarsonar. Ed. Guðni Jónsson. Íslenzk Fornrit 7. Reykjavík: Íslenzk Fornrit, 1936.

Henry, Archdeacon of Huntingdon. *Henry, Archdeacon of Huntingdon: Anglicanus Ortus: A Verse Herbal of the Twelfth Century*. Ed. and trans. Winston Black. Toronto and Oxford: Pontifical Institute of Mediaeval Studies and Bodleian Library, 2012.

Henry, Archdeacon of Huntingdon. *Historia Anglorum: The History of the English Peoples*. Ed. and trans. Diana Greenway. Oxford: Clarendon Press, 1996.

Herlihy, David, ed. and trans. *The History of Feudalism*. New York: Harper & Row, 1970.

Hincmar. *De Ordine Palatii*. Ed. A. Boretius. MGH Capitularia Regum Francorum 2. Hanover: Impensis Bibliopolii Hahnani, 1897. [See also Herlihy, David. *The History of Feudalism*.]

A History of Norway and the Passion and Miracles of the Blessed Óláfr. Trans. Deevra Kunin. Ed. Carl Phelpstead. Viking Society for Northern Research Text Series xiii. London: Viking Society for Northern Research, 2001.

Hugh Candidus. *The Chronicle of Hugh Candidus*. Ed. W. T. Mellows. London and New York: Oxford University Press, 1949.

John of Worcester. *The Chronicle of John of Worcester. Vol. 2: The Annals from 450 to 1066*. Ed. R. R. Darlington and P. McGurk. Trans. Jennifer Bray and P. McGurk. Oxford: Clarendon Press, 1995.

Jómsvíkinga saga: The Saga of the Jomsvikings. Ed. and trans. N. F. Blake. London: Thomas Nelson and Sons, 1962.

The Junius Manuscript. Ed. George Philip Krapp. Vol. 1 of *The Anglo-Saxon Poetic Records*. New York: Columbia University Press, 1931.

Klaeber's Beowulf and the Fight at Finnsburg. Ed. R. D. Fulk, Robert E. Bjork, and John D. Niles, with a Foreword by Helen Damico. 4th ed. Toronto: University of Toronto Press, 2008.

Knýtlinga saga. In *Danakonunga Sgur: Skjǫldunga saga, Knýtlinga saga, Ágrip af Sǫgu Danakonunga*. Ed. Bjarni Guðnason. Íslenzk Fornrit 35. Reykjavík: Íslenzk Fornrit, 1982.

Knýtlinga saga: The History of the Kings of Denmark. Trans. Hermann Pálsson and Paul Edwards. Odense: Odense University Press, 1986.

The Laws of the Kings of England from Edmund to Henry I. Ed. and trans. A. J. Robertson. Cambridge: Cambridge University Press, 1925.

Liber Eliensis. Ed. E. O. Blake. Camden 3rd ser. 92. London: Royal Historical Society, 1962.

Liber Eliensis: A History of the Isle of Ely from the Seventh Century to the Twelfth. Trans. Janet Fairweather. Woodbridge, UK: The Boydell Press, 2005.

Marriage and Murder in Eleventh-Century Northumbria: A Study of "De obsessione Dunelmi." Ed. and trans. Christopher Morris. York, UK: University of York, 1992.

Memorials of Saint Dunstan, Archbishop of Canterbury. Ed. William Stubbs. RS 63. London: Longman & Co., 1874.

Monumenta Historica Norvegiæ. Ed. Gustav Storm. Christiania: A. W. Brøgger, 1880.

Morkinskinna. Ed. Finnur Jónsson. SUGNL. 53. Copenhagen: J. Jørgensen, 1932.

Morkinskinna: The Earliest Icelandic Chronicle of the Norwegian Kings (1030–1157). Trans. Theodore M. Andersson and Kari Ellen Gade. Islandica 51. Ithaca, NY: Cornell University Press, 2000.

Oddr Snorrason. *Óláfs saga Tryggvasonar.* Trans. Theodore M. Andersson. Ithaca, NY: Cornell University Press, 2003.

———. *The Saga of Olaf Tryggvason.* In *Konunga sögur* vol. 1; *Óláfs saga Tryggvasonar eftir Odd munk*; *Helgisaga Óláfs Haraldssonar*; *Brot úr Elztu sögu*, ed. Guðni Jónsson. Reykjavík: Íslendingasagnaútgáfan, 1957.

Ohlgren, Thomas H., ed. *Anglo-Saxon Textual Illustration: Photographs of Sixteen Manuscripts with Descriptions and Index.* Kalamazoo, MI: Medieval Institute Publications, 1992.

The Poetic Edda. Trans. Henry Adams Bellows. New York: American-Scandinavian Foundation, 1923; repr. 1968.

Pope, John C., ed. *Seven Old English Poems.* New York: W. W. Norton & Company, 1981.

Ralph of Diceto. *The Historical Works of Master Ralph de Diceto.* Ed. William Stubbs. RS 68. 2 vols. London: Longman & Co., 1876.

Sawyer, P. H., ed. *The Charters of Burton Abbey.* Anglo-Saxon Charters 2. Oxford: Oxford University Press, 1979.

Saxo Grammaticus. *Danorum Regum Heroumque Historia, Books X–XVI: The Text of the First Edition with Translation and Commentary in Three Volumes.* Vol. 1. Ed. and trans. Eric Christiansen. BAR International Series 84. Oxford: BAR, 1980.

Snorri Sturluson. *Heimskringla.* Ed. Bjarni Aðalbjarnarson. 3 vols. Reykjavík: Íslenzk Fornrit, 1979.

———. *Heimskringla: History of the Kings of Norway.* Trans. Lee M. Hollander. American-Scandinavian Foundation. 1964; Austin, TX: University of Texas Press, 1992.

Symeon of Durham. *Historia Ecclesiae Dunelmensis.* In *Symeonis monachi Opera omnia,* ed. T. Arnold, vol. 1 of 2 vols., RS 75. London: Longman, 1882–85. Trans. Joseph Stevenson as *The Historical Works of Simeon of Durham.* London: Seeley, 1855. Repr. Lexington, KY: Ulan Press, 2013.

Theodoricus Monachus. *Historia de Antiquitate Regum Norwagiensium (An Account of the Ancient History of the Norwegian Kings).* Translated and annotated by David and Ian McDougall. London: Viking Society for Northern Research, 1998.

Thietmar von Merseburg. *Die Chronik des Bischofs Thietmar von Merseburg und ihre Korveier Überarbeitung.* Ed. Robert Holtzmann. Vol. 2. 2nd Unabridged Edition. Berlin: Weidmann, 1955.

Vita Ædwardi Regis. The Life of King Edward Who Rests at Westminster, Attributed to a Monk of Saint-Bertin. Ed. and trans. Frank Barlow. New York: T. Nelson, 1962; repr. New York: AMS Press Inc., 1984.

The Wanderer. Ed. T. P. Dunning and A. J. Bliss. New York: Appleton-Century-Crofts, 1969.

Warner of Rouen. *Moriuht: A Norman Latin Poem from the Early Eleventh Century.* Ed. and trans. Christopher J. McDonough. Studies and Texts 121. Toronto: Pontifical Institute of Mediaeval Studies, 1995.

Whitelock, Dorothy, ed. and trans. *Anglo-Saxon Wills.* Cambridge, UK: The University Press, 1930.

———, ed. *English Historical Documents c. 500–1042.* Vol. 1. London: Eyre & Spottiswoode, 1979.

———, ed. *Sermo Lupi ad Anglos.* 3rd ed. London: Methuen & Co. Ltd., 1963.

———, trans. *The Will of Æthelgifu: A Tenth-Century Anglo-Saxon Manuscript.* Oxford: Oxford University Press, 1968.

Whitelock, Dorothy, M. Brett, and C. N. L. Brooke, eds. *Councils & Synods, with Other Documents Relating to the English Church: Part I, 871-1066. Vol. 1: A.D. 871–1204*. Oxford: Clarendon Press, 1981.

William of Jumièges, Orderic Vitalis, and Robert of Torigni. *The Gesta Normannorum Ducum*. Ed. and trans. Elisabeth M. C. van Houts. 2 vols. Oxford: Clarendon Press, 1992, 1995.

William of Malmesbury. *Gesta Regum Anglorum. The History of the English Kings*. Ed. and trans. R. A. B. Mynors. Completed by R. M. Thomson and M. Winterbottom. 2 vols. Oxford: Clarendon Press, 1998.

William of Poitiers. *The Gesta Guillelmi*. Ed. and trans. R. H. C. Davis and Marjorie Chibnall. Oxford: Clarendon Press, 1998.

Wright, Thomas, ed. *The Anglo-Latin Satirical Poets and Epigrammists of the Twelfth Century*. 2 vols. RS 59. London: Longman, 1872.

Wulfstan. *The Homilies*. Ed. Dorothy Bethurum. Oxford: Clarendon Press, 1957.

Ziolkowski, Jan M., ed. *Jezebel: A Norman Latin Poem of the Early Eleventh Century*. New York: P. Lang, 1989.

SECONDARY SOURCES

Abels, Richard. "Alfred and His Biographers: Images and Imagination." In Bates et al., *Writing Medieval Biography*, 61–75.

——. *Alfred the Great: War, Kingship and Culture in Anglo-Saxon England*. London: Longman, 1998.

——. "'Cowardice' and Duty in Anglo-Saxon England." *The Journal of Medieval Military History* 4 (2006): 29–49.

——. "Heriot." In Lapidge et al., *Blackwell Encyclopaedia*, 235–36.

Amos, Ashley Crandall. *Linguistic Means of Determining the Dates of Old English Literary Texts*. Cambridge, MA: Medieval Academy of America, 1981.

Anderson, Earl R. "The Battle of Maldon: A Reappraisal of Possible Sources, Date, and Theme." In Brown et al., *Modes of Interpretation in Old English Literature*, 247–72.

Andersson, Theodore M. *Early Epic Scenery: Homer, Virgil, and the Medieval Legacy*. Ithaca, NY: Cornell University Press, 1976.

———. "Sources and Analogues." In Bjork and Niles, eds. *A Beowulf Handbook*, 125–48.

Ashdown, Margaret. *English and Norse Documents Relating to the Reign of Ethelred the Unready.* Cambridge, UK: The University Press, 1930.

Astell, Anne W. *Political Allegory in Late Medieval England.* Ithaca, NY: Cornell University Press, 1999.

Atkin, M. A. "'The Land Between Ribble and Mersey' in the Early Tenth Century." In *Names, Places and People: An Onomastic Miscellany in Memory of John McNeal Dodgson,* ed. Alexander R. Rumble and A. D. Mills. Stamford, UK: Paul Watkins, 1997, 8–18.

Backhouse, Janet. "The Making of the Harley Psalter." *British Library Journal* 10, no. 2 (1984): 97–113.

Baird, Joseph L. "'for metode': *Beowulf* 169." *English Studies* 49 (1967): 418–23.

Baker, Peter S., ed. *Beowulf: Basic Readings.* New York: Garland Publishing, Inc., 1995.

Balle, Søren. "Knud (Cnut) the Great." In Pulsiano et al., *Medieval Scandinavia,* 357–59.

Bammesberger, Alfred. "The Conclusion of Wealhtheow's Speech (*Beowulf* 1231)." *Neuphilologische Mitteilungen* 91 (1990): 207–8.

———. "Old English *cuðe folme* in *Beowulf,* Line 1303A." *Neophilologus* 89, no. 4 (2005): 625–27.

Barlow, Frank. *Edward the Confessor.* London: Eyre & Spottiswoode, 1970.

———. "Two Notes: Cnut's Second Pilgrimage and Queen Emma's Disgrace in 1043." *English Historical Review* 73 (1958): 649–55.

Bates, David, Julia Crick, and Sarah Hamilton, eds. *Writing Medieval Biography 750–1250: Essays in Honour of Frank Barlow.* Woodbridge, UK: The Boydell Press, 2006.

Baxter, S., C. E. Karkov, J. L. Nelson, and D. Pelteret. *Early Medieval Studies in Memory of Patrick Wormald.* Farnham, UK: Ashgate, 2008.

Baxter, Steven. *The Earls of Mercia: Lordship and Power in Late Anglo-Saxon England.* Oxford: Oxford University Press, 2007.

Bernstein, David J. *The Mystery of the Bayeux Tapestry.* London: Weidenfeld and Nicolson, 1986.

Biddle, Martin. "Excavations at Winchester 1965: The Fourth Interim Report." *The Antiquaries Journal* 46, no. 2 (September 1966): 308–32.

Biggs, Frederick M. "I. Enoch." In Biggs et al., *Sources of Anglo-Saxon Literary Culture*, 25–27.

Bishop, T[erence]. A. M. "Notes on Cambridge Manscripts." Part VII. "The Early Minuscule of Christ Church, Canterbury." *Transactions of the Cambridge Bibliographical Society* 3 (1963): 413–23.

Bjork, Robert E. "Digressions and Episodes." In Bjork and Niles, eds. *A Beowulf Handbook*, 193–212.

Bjork, Robert E., and John D. Niles, eds. *A Beowulf Handbook*. Lincoln, NE: University of Nebraska Press, 1997.

Bjork, Robert E., and Anita Obermeier. "Date, Provenance, Author, Audiences." In Bjork and Niles, eds. *A Beowulf Handbook*, 13–34.

Björkman, Erik. "Zu einigen Namen im Beowulf: *Breca, Brondingas, Wealhþēo(w)*." *Anglia, Beiblatt* 30 (1919): 170–80.

Blair, John. *Anglo-Saxon Oxfordshire*. Oxford: Oxfordshire Books, 1994.

Blair, Peter Hunter. "The Northumbrians and Their Southern Frontier." *Archaeologia Aeliana*, 4th ser., 26 (1948): 105–13.

Blanton, Virginia. *Signs of Devotion: The Cult of St. Æthelthryth in Medieval England, 695–1615*. University Park, PA: Pennsylvania State University Press, 2007.

Bloomfield, Josephine. "Diminished by Kindness: Frederick Klaeber's Rewriting of Wealhtheow." *JEGP* 93, no. 2 (1994): 183–205.

Bolton, Timothy. *The Empire of Cnut the Great: Conquest and the Consolidation of Power in Northern Europe in the Early Eleventh Century*. Leiden: Brill Academic Publishers, 2009.

——. "A Newly Emergent Mediaeval Manuscript Containing *Encomium Emma Reginae* with the Only Known Complete Text of the Recension Prepared for King Edward the Confessor." *Mediaeval Scandinavia* 19 (2009): 205–21

Bredehoft, Thomas A. *Authors, Audiences, and Old English Verse*. Toronto: University of Toronto Press, 2009.

——. *Textual Histories: Readings in the Anglo-Saxon Chronicle*. Toronto: University of Toronto Press, 2001.

Brodeur, Arthur G. *The Art of Beowulf.* Berkeley, CA: University of California Press, 1959.

Brown, Phyllis Rugg, Georgia Ronan Crampton, and Fred C. Robinson, eds. *Modes of Interpretation in Old English Literature: Essays in Honour of Stanley B. Greenfield.* Toronto: University of Toronto Press, 1986.

Bugge, Sophus. *Helge-Digtene I den Ælder Edda, Deres Hjem og Forbindelser.* Translated into English by W. H. Schofield as *The Home of the Eddic Poems: with especial reference to the Helgi-Lays.* London: D. Nutt, 1899.

Cameron, Angus F., Ashley Crandell Amos, and Gregory Waite et al. "A Reconsideration of the Language of *Beowulf.*" In Chase, ed., *The Dating of Beowulf,* 33–75.

Cameron, Kenneth. *English Place-Names.* 3rd ed. London: B. T. Batsford, 1977.

Campbell, Alastair. *Skaldic Verse and Anglo-Saxon History.* The Dorothea Coke Memorial Lecture. London: Lewis, 1970.

——. "The Use in *Beowulf* of Earlier Heroic Verse." In Clemoes and Hughes, eds, *England before the Conquest,* 283–92.

Campbell, Miles W. "Aelfgyva: The Mysterious Lady of the Bayeux Tapestry." *Annales de Normandie* 34 (1984): 127–45.

——. "Emma, Reine d'Angleterre: Mère dénaturée ou femme vindicative?" *Annale de Normandie* (1973): 99–114.

——. "The *Encomium Emmae Reginae*: Personal Panegyric or Political Propaganda?" *Annuales Mediaevale* 19 (1979): 27–45.

——. "Queen Emma and Ælfgifu of Northampton: Canute the Great's Women." *Mediaeval Scandinavia* 4 (1971): 66–79.

Carruthers, Mary. *The Book of Memory: A Study of Memory in the Medieval Culture,* 2nd ed. Cambridge Studies in Medieval Literature. Cambridge, UK: Cambridge University Press, 2008.

——. *The Craft of Thought: Meditation, Rhetoric, and the Making of Images, 400–1200.* Cambridge, UK: Cambridge University Press, 1998.

Chadwick, Nora K. "The Monsters and *Beowulf.*" In Clemoes, ed., *The Anglo-Saxons,* 171–73.

——. "Þorgerðr Hölgabrúðr and the *Trolla Þing*: A Note on Sources." In *The Early Cultures of North-West Europe,* ed. Cyril Fox and Bruce Dickins. Cambridge, UK: The University Press, 1950, 397–417.

Chambers, R. W. *Beowulf: An Introduction to the Study of the Poem with a Discussion of the Stories of Offa and Finn.* 3rd ed. Supplement by C. L. Wrenn. Cambridge, UK: The University Press, 1967.

——. "Beowulf's Fight with Grendel and Its Scandinavian Parallels." *English Studies* 11 (1929): 81–100.

Chance, Jane. "The Structural Unity in *Beowulf*: The Problem of Grendel's Mother." *Texas Studies in Language and Literature* 22 (1980): 287–303. Repr. in Damico and Olsen, ed., *New Readings on Women in Old English*, 248–61.

——. *Woman as Hero in Old English Literature.* Syracuse, NY: Syracuse University Press, 1986.

Chase, Colin, ed. *The Dating of Beowulf.* Toronto, 1981; 2nd ed. Toronto: University of Toronto Press, 1997.

Clark, Cecily. "The Narrative Mode of *The Anglo-Saxon Chronicle* before the Conquest." In Clemoes and Hughes, eds., *England before the Conquest*, 215-35.

Clayton, Mary. "Ælfric's Esther: A *Speculum Reginae*?" In *Text and Gloss: Studies in Insular Language and Literature*, ed. Helen Conrad-O'Brian, Anne-Marie D'Arcy, and John Scattergood. Blackrock, UK: Four Courts Press, 1999, 89–101.

——. *The Cult of the Virgin Mary in Anglo-Saxon England.* Cambridge, UK: Cambridge University Press, 1990.

Clemoes, Peter A. M., ed. *The Anglo-Saxons: Studies in Some Aspects of Their History and Culture Presented to Bruce Dickins.* London: Bowes and Bowes, 1959.

——. "The Chronology of Ælfric's Works." In Clemoes, ed., *The Anglo-Saxons*, 212–47.

Clemoes, Peter, and Kathleen Hughes, ed. *England before the Conquest: Studies in Primary Sources Presented to Dorothy Whitelock.* Cambridge, UK: The University Press, 1971.

Coupland, Simon. "The Rod of God's Wrath or the People of God's Wrath? The Carolingian Theology of the Viking Invasions." *Journal of Ecclesiastical History* 42 (1991): 535–54.

Cox, Betty S. *Cruces of Beowulf.* The Hague: Mouton, 1971.

Crawford, S. J. "*Beowulf*, ll. 168–69." *Modern Language Review* 23 (1928): 336.

Cronan, Dennis. "Old English *gelād* 'Passage across Water.'" *Neophilologus* 71 (1987): 316–19.

Damico, Helen. *Beowulf's Wealhtheow and the Valkyrie Tradition*. Madison, WI: University of Wisconsin Press, 1984.

———."*Sörlaþáttr* and the Hama Episode in *Beowulf*." *Scandinavian Studies* 55 (1983): 222–35.

———. "*Þrymskviða* and the Second Fight in *Beowulf*: The Dressing of the Hero in Parody." *Scandinavian Studies* 58, no. 4 (1986): 407–28.

Damico, Helen, and Alexandra Hennessey Olsen, eds. *New Readings on Women in Old English*. Bloomington, IN: Indiana University Press, 1990.

Darby, H. C. *The Draining of the Fens*. Cambridge, UK: University Press, 1940.

———. "The Fenland Frontier in Anglo-Saxon England." *Antiquity* 7 (1934): 185.

———. *The Medieval Fenland*. 2nd ed. Newton Abbot, UK: David & Charles, 1974.

Davis, Craig R. "An Ethnic Dating of *Beowulf*." *ASE* 35 (2006): 111–29.

Dronke, Peter. *Poetic Individuality in the Middle Ages: New Departures in Poetry, 1000–1150*. 2nd ed. London: University of London, 1986.

Drout, Michael D. C., ed. *Beowulf and the Critics by J. R. R. Tolkien*. Tempe, AZ: ACMRS, 2002.

———. "Blood and Deeds: The Inheritance Systems in *Beowulf*." *Studies in Philology* 104 (2007): 199–226.

Duffey, Judith E. "The Inventive Group of Illustrations in the Harley Psalter (British Museum Ms. Harley 603)," PhD diss. University of California, Berkeley, CA, 1977.

Duggan, Anne J., ed. *Queens and Queenship in Medieval Europe*. Woodbridge, UK: Boydell Press, 1997.

Duggan, Joseph. "Medieval Epic as Popular Historiography: Appropriation of Historical Knowledge in the Vernacular Epic." In *La Littérature historiographique des origines à 1500. Grundriss der romanischen Literaturen des Mittelalters*, ed. Hans Ulrich Gumbrecht et al. Vol. 11.1. Heidelberg: C. Winter, 1986, 285–311.

Dumville, David N. "*Beowulf* Come Lately: Some Notes on the Paleography of the Nowell Codex." *Archiv für das Studium der neueren Sprachen und Literaturen* 225 (1988): 49–63. Repr. as chap. 7 in his *Britons and Anglo-Saxons in the Early Middle Ages*.

———. "The *Beowulf*-Manuscript and How Not to Date It." *Medieval English Studies Newsletter* 39 (December 1998): 21–27.

———. *Britons and Anglo-Saxons in the Early Middle Ages*. Brookfield, VT: Variorum, 1992.

———. "Kingship, Genealogies and Regnal Lists." In *Early Medieval Kingship*, ed. P. H. Sawyer and Ian N. Wood. Leeds, UK: University of Leeds, School of History, 1977, 72–104.

Eames, E. "Mariage et concubinage légal en Norvège à l'époque des Vikings." *Annales de Normandie* 2, no. 3 (1952): 196–208.

Enright, Michael J. *Lady with a Mead Cup*. Blackrock, Co. Dublin: Four Courts Press, 1996.

———. "Lady with a Mead Cup: Ritual, Group Cohesion and Hierarchy in the Germanic Warband." *Frühmittelalterliche Studien* 22 (1988): 170–203.

Estrich, Robert M. "The Throne of Hrothgar—*Beowulf*, ll. 168–69." *JEGP* 43 (1944): 384–89.

Fell, Christine E. *Edward King and Martyr*. Leeds Texts and Monographs, n.s. Leeds, UK: University of Leeds, 1971.

———. "*Víkingarvísur*." In *Speculum Norroenum: Norse Studies in Memory of Gabriel Turville-Petre*, ed. Ursula Dronke et al. Odense: Odense University Press, 1981, 106–22.

———. *Women in Anglo-Saxon England*. Oxford: Basil Blackwell, 1986.

Fjalldal, Magnús. *Anglo-Saxon England in Icelandic Medieval Texts*. Toronto: University of Toronto Press, 2005.

———. *The Long Arm of Coincidence: The Frustrated Connection between Beowulf and Grettis Saga*. Toronto: University of Toronto Press, 1998.

Fleischman, Suzanne. "On the Representation of History and Fiction in the Middle Ages." *History and Theory* 23 (1983): 278–310.

Fletcher, Angus. *Allegory: The Theory of a Symbolic Mode.* Ithaca, NY: Cornell University Press, 1964.

Foote, P. G., and D. M. Wilson. *The Viking Achievement.* London: Sidgwick & Jackson, 1970.

Foys, Martin "Pulling the Arrow Out: The Legend of Harold's Death and the Bayeux Tapestry." In *The Bayeux Tapestry: New Interpretations*, ed. Martin Foys, Karen Overbey, and Dan Terkla. Woodbridge, UK: Boydell Press, 2009, 158–75.

Frank, Roberta. "The *Beowulf* Poet's Sense of History." In *The Wisdom of Poetry: Essays in Early English Literature in Honor of Morton W. Bloomfield*, ed. Larry D. Benson and Siegfried Wenzel. Kalamazoo, MI: Medieval Institute Publications, 1982, 53–65.

———. "King Cnut in the Verse of His Skalds." In Rumble, ed., *Reign of Cnut*, 106–24.

———. "The Lay of the Land in Skaldic Praise Poetry." In *Myth in Early Northwest Europe*, ed. Stephen O. Glosecki. Tempe, AZ: ACMRS, 2007: 175–96.

———. "'Mere' and 'Sund': Two Sea-Changes in *Beowulf*." In Brown et al., *Modes of Interpretation in Old English Literature*, 153–72.

———. "Old Norse Memorial Eulogies and the Ending of *Beowulf*." *The Early Middle Ages, Acta* 6 (1982): 1–19.

———. "Paronomasia in Old English Scriptural Verse." *Speculum* 47 (1972): 207–26.

———. "A Scandal in Toronto: The Dating of '*Beowulf*' a Quarter Century On." *Speculum* 82 (October 2007): 843–64.

———. "Skaldic Verse and the Date of *Beowulf*." In Chase, ed., *The Dating of Beowulf*, 123–39.

———. "Terminally Hip and Incredibly Cool: Carol, Vikings, and Anglo-Scandinavian England." In *Remakes: A Symposium in Honor of Carol J. Clover, Representations* 100 (Fall 2007): 23–33.

Freeman, Edward A. *The History of the Norman Conquest of England: Its Causes and Its Results, Vol. 1: The Preliminary History of the Election of Edward the Confessor.* 3rd ed. rev. Oxford: Clarendon Press, 1867.

Freeman, Eric F. "The Identity of Aelfgyfa in the Bayeux Tapestry." *Annales de Normandie* 41 (1991): 117–34.

Fulk, R. D. "Contraction as a Criterion for Dating Old English Verse." *JEGP* 89 (1990): 1–16.

——. "Dating *Beowulf* to the Viking Age." *Philological Quarterly* 16 (1982): 354–55.

——. *A History of Old English Meter*. Philadelphia: University of Pennsylvania Press, 1992.

——. "On Argumentation in Old English Philology, with Particular Reference to the Editing and Dating of *Beowulf.*" *ASE* 32 (2003): 1–26.

——. "Unferth and His Name." *Modern Philology* 85 (1987): 113–27.

Galloway, Andrew. "Word-Play and Political Satire: Solving the Riddle of the Text of *Jezebel.*" *Medium Ævum* 68, no. 2 (1999): 189–208.

Gameson, Richard. "The Anglo-Saxon Artists of the Harley 603 Psalter." *Journal of the British Archaeological Association* 143 (1990): 29–48.

Gardner, John. *Grendel*. New York: Knopf, 1979.

Garmonsway, G. N. "Anglo-Saxon Heroic Attitudes." In *Franciplegius: Medieval and Linguistic Studies in Honor of Francis Peabody Magoun, Jr.*, ed. Jess B. Bessinger, Jr. and Robert P. Creed. New York: New York University Press, 1965, 139–46.

Garmonsway, G. N., and Jacqueline Simpson. *Beowulf and Its Analogues, including Archaeology and Beowulf by Hilda Ellis Davidson*. New York: E. P. Dutton & Co., Inc., 1971.

Garnett, George. "Coronation." In Lapidge et al., *Blackwell Encyclopaedia*, 122–24.

Gelling, Margaret. "The Landscape of *Beowulf.*" *ASE* 31 (2002): 7–11.

——. *Place-Names in the Landscape*. London: J. M. Dent & Sons, 1984.

Gelling, Margaret, and Ann Cole. *The Landscape of Place-Names*. Stamford, UK: Shaun Tyas, 2000.

Gerchow, J. *Die Gedenküberlieferung der Angelsachsen*. Berlin: Walter de Gruyter, 1988.

Ginzberg, Louis. *The Legends of the Jews*. Trans. Henrietta Szold. Philadelphia: Jewish Publication Society of America, 1937–1966.

Godden, Malcolm. "Apocalypse and Invasion in Late Anglo-Saxon England." In *From Anglo-Saxon to Early Middle English: Studies Presented to E.*

G. *Stanley*, ed. Malcolm Godden, Douglas Gray, and Terry Hoad. Oxford: Oxford University Press, 1994, 130–62.

———. "Biblical Literature: The Old Testament." In Godden and Lapidge, eds., *Cambridge Companion to Old English Literature*, 206–26.

Godden, Malcolm, and Michael Lapidge, ed. *The Cambridge Companion to Old English Literature*. Cambridge: Cambridge University Press, 1991.

Goldsmith, Margaret E. "The Christian Perspective in *Beowulf*." *Comparative Literature* 14 (1962): 71–90. Repr. in *Interpretations of Beowulf: A Critical Anthology*, ed. R. D. Fulk. Bloomington, IN: Indiana University Press, 1991, 103–19.

———. *The Mode and Meaning of 'Beowulf.'* London: Athlone Press, 1970.

Gordon, E. V. "Wealhþeow and Related Names." *Medium Ævum* 4 (1935): 169–75.

Grape, Wolfgang. *The Bayeux Tapestry: Movement to a Norman Triumph.* Trans. David Britt. Munich and New York: Prestel, 1994.

Greatrex, Joan. "Benedictine Observance at Ely: The Intellectual, Liturgical and Spiritual Evidence Considered." In Meadows and Ramsay, eds., *History of Ely Cathedral*, 80–93.

———. "Rabbits and Eels at High Table: Monks of Ely at the University of Cambridge, c. 1337–1539." In *Monasteries and Society in Medieval Britain, Proceedings of the 1994 Harlaxton Symposium*. Stamford, UK: P. Watkins, 1999, 312–28.

Greenfield, Stanley B. "The Extremities of the Beowulfian Body Politic." In *Saints, Scholars, and Heroes: The Anglo-Saxon Heritage*, ed. Margot H. King and Wesley M. Stevens. Vol. 1. Collegeville, MN: Hill Monastic Manuscript Library, St. John's University, 1979, 1–14.

———. *The Interpretation of Old English Poems*. London: Routledge and K. Paul, 1972.

———. "Three Beowulf Notes: Lines 736b ff., 1331b ff., 1341–44." In *Medieval Studies in Honor of Lillian Herlands Hornstein*, ed. Jess B. Bessinger, Jr. and Robert Raymo. New York: New York University Press, 1976, 169–72.

Greenway, Diana. "Henry of Huntingdon as Poet: The *De Herbis* Rediscovered." *Medium Aevum* 74, no. 2 (2005): 329–332;

Grønbech, Vilhelm. *Culture of the Teutons* (orig. *Vor Folkeæt I Oldtiden* [Copenhagen, 1909–12]). Trans. William Worster. London: Humphrey Milford, 1931.

Haber, Tom Burns. *A Comparative Study of the Beowulf and the Aeneid.* 1931; New York: Phaeton Press, 1968.

Hall, David. *Fenland Landscapes and Settlement between Peterborough and March.* East Anglian Archaeology Report no. 35. Cambridge, UK: Fenland Project Committee, Cambridgeshire Archaeological Committee, 1987.

———. *The Fenland Project, no. 10: Cambridgeshire Survey, the Isle of Ely and Wisbech.* East Anglian Archaeology Report no. 79. Cambridge, UK: Fenland Project Committee, Cambridgeshire Archaeological Committee, 1996.

Harris, Joseph C. "Eddic Poetry." In *Dictionary of the Middle Ages.* Vol. 4, ed. Joseph Strayer. New York: Scribner, 1984, 385–92.

———. "Eddic Poetry." In *Old Norse-Icelandic Literature: A Critical Guide,* ed. Carol J. Clover and John Lindow. Islandica 45. Ithaca, NY: Cornell University Press, 1985, 68–156.

———. "Eddic Poetry as Oral Poetry: The Evidence of Parallel Passages in the Helgi Poems for Questions of Composition and Performance." In *Edda: A Collection of Essays,* ed. Robert J. Glendinning and Haraldur Bessason. Icelandic Studies 4. Winnipeg: University of Manitoba Press, 1983, 210–42.

———. "A Nativist Approach to *Beowulf*: The Case of Germanic Elegy." In *Companion to Old English Poetry,* ed. Henk Aertson and Rolf H. Bremmer Jr. Amsterdam: VU University Press, 1994, 45–62.

Harris, Richard L. "The Deaths of Grettir and Grendel: A New Parallel." *Scripta Islandica* 24 (1973): 25–53.

Hasler, Rolf. "Zu zwei Darstellungen aus der ältesten Kopie des Utrecht-Psalters." *Zeitschrift für Kunstgeschichte* 44, no. 4 (1981): 317–39.

Heller, Rolf. *Die literarische Darstellung der Frau in den Isländersagas.* Halle: M. Niemeyer, 1958.

Heslop, T. A. "The Production of *de luxe* Manuscripts and the Patronage of King Cnut and Queen Emma." *ASE* 19 (1980): 151–95.

Higham, N. J. *The Death of Anglo-Saxon England.* Phoenix Mill, UK: Sutton Publishing Limited, 1997.

———. "Five Boroughs." In Lapidge et al., *Blackwell Encyclopaedia*, 186.

Hill, David. "The Bayeux Tapestry and Its Commentators: The Case of Scene 15." *Medieval Life* 11 (Summer 1999): 24–26.

———, ed. *Ethelred the Unready: Papers from the Millenary Conference*. British Archaeological Reports, British Series 59. Oxford: BAR, 1978.

Hill, Thomas D. Introduction. In Biggs et al., *Sources of Anglo-Saxon Literary Culture*, 1:xvi–xviii.

———. "'Wealhtheow' as a Foreign Slave: Some Continental Analogues." *Philological Quarterly* 69 (1990): 106–12.

Hooke, D. "Wolverhampton: The Town and Its Monastery." In D. Hooke and T. R. Slater, *Anglo-Saxon Wolverhampton*. Wolverhampton, UK: Wolverhampton Borough Council, 1986, 5–28.

Howard, Ian. *Swein Forkbeard's Invasions and the Danish Conquest of England 991–1017*. Woodbridge, UK: The Boydell Press, 2003.

Howe, Nicholas. *Migration and Mythmaking in Anglo-Saxon England*. New Haven, CT: Yale University Press, 1989.

Hume, Kathryn. *Fantasy and Mimesis: Responses to Reality in Western Literature*. New York: Methuen, 1984.

Hunt, J. "Piety, Prestige or Politics? The House of Leofric and the Foundation and Patronage of Coventry Priory." In *Coventry's First Cathedral*, ed. G. Demidowicz. Stamford, UK: Paul Watkins, 1994, 97–117.

Hutcheson, B. R. "Kaluza's Law, the Dating of *Beowulf*, and the Old English Poetic Tradition." *JEGP* 103 (2004): 297–322.

———. *Old English Poetic Metre*. Woodbridge, UK: D. S. Brewer, 1995.

Irvine, Martin. "Cynewulf's Use of Psychomachia Allegory: The Latin Sources of Some 'Interpolated' Passages." In *Allegory, Myth, and Symbol*, ed. Morton W. Bloomfield. Harvard English Studies 9. Cambridge, MA: Harvard University Press, 1981, 39–62.

Irving, Edward B. *A Reading of Beowulf*. New Haven, CT: Yale University Press, 1969.

———. *Rereading Beowulf*. Philadelphia: University of Pennsylvania Press, 1989.

Isley, Charles. "Politics, Conflict, and Kinship in Early Eleventh-Century Mercia." *Midland History* 26 (2001): 28–42.

Jochens, Jenny M. "The Female Inciter in the Kings' Sagas." *Arkiv för Nordisk Filologi* 102 (1987): 100–119.

———. "The Medieval Icelandic Heroine: Fact or Fiction?" *Viator* 17 (1986): 35–50.

———. *Old Norse Images of Women*. Philadelphia: University of Pennsylvania Press, 1996.

———. "The Politics of Reproduction: Medieval Norwegian Kingship." *American Historical Review* 92 (1987): 329–32.

———. *Women in Old Norse Society*. Ithaca, NY: Cornell University Press, 1995.

John, Eric. "*The Encomium Emmae Reginae*: A Riddle and a Solution." *Bulletin of the John Rylands University Library of Manchester* 63, no. 2 (1981): 58–94.

———. *Reassessing Anglo-Saxon England*. Manchester, UK: Manchester University Press, 1996.

———. "The Social and Political Problems of the Early English Church." In *Land, Church and People: Essays Presented to H. P. R. Finberg*, ed. Joan Thirsk. Supplement to *Agricultural Historical Review* 18 (1970): 39–63.

Jones, Lynn. "Emma's Greek *Scrine*." In *Early Medieval Studies in Memory of Patrick Wormald*, ed. S. Baxter et al., 499–508.

Jorgensen, Peter A. "The Two-Troll Variant of the Bear's Son Folktale in *Hálfdanar saga Brönufóstra* and *Gríms saga loðinkinna*." *Arv* 31 (1975): 35–43.

Karkov, Catherine E. "Emma: Image and Ideology." In *Early Medieval Studies in Memory of Patrick Wormald*, ed. S. Baxter et al., 509–70.

———. *The Ruler Portraits of Anglo-Saxon England*. Anglo-Saxon Studies 3. Woodbridge, UK: The Boydell Press, 2004.

Karras, Ruth Mazo. "Concubinage and Slavery in the Viking Age." *Scandinavian Studies* 62 (1990): 141–62.

Kaske, Robert E. "*Beowulf* and the Book of Enoch." *Speculum* 46 (1971): 421–31.

———. "The Gifstol Crux in *Beowulf*." *Leeds Studies in English* 16 (1985): 142–51.

———. "'Hygelac' and 'Hygd.'" In *Studies in Old English Literature in Honor of*

Arthur G. Brodeur, ed. Stanley B. Greenfield. Eugene, OR: University of Oregon Books, 1963, 200–206.

Katz, Joshua T. "How to Be a Dragon in Indo-European: Hittite *illuyankaš* and Its Linguistic and Cultural Congeners in Latin, Greek, and Germanic." In *Mir Curad: Studies in Honor of Calvert Watkins*, ed. Jay Jasanoff, H. Craig Melchert, and Lisi Olver. Innsbruck: Institut für Sprachwissenshaft der Universität Innsbruck, 1998, 317–34.

Keynes, Simon. "An Abbot, an Archbishop, and the Viking Raids of 1006–7 and 1009–12." *ASE* 36 (2007): 151–220.

———. "The Æthelings in Normandy." *Anglo-Norman Studies* 13 (1991): 173–205.

———. "Æthelstan ætheling." In Lapidge et al., *Blackwell Encyclopaedia*, 17.

———. "Cnut's Earls." In Rumble, ed., *Reign of Cnut*, 43–88.

———. "Crime and Punishment in the Reign of King Æthelred the Unready." In *People and Places in Northern Europe: Essays in Honour of Peter Hayes Sawyer*, ed. Ian N. Wood and Niels Lund. Woodbridge, UK and Rochester, NY: Boydell Press, 1991.

———. "The Declining Reputation of King Æthelred the Unready." In Hill, ed., *Ethelred the Unready*, 227–53.

———. *The Diplomas of King Æthelred "The Unready" : 978–1016: A Study in Their Use as Historical Evidence.* Cambridge, UK: Cambridge University Press, 1980.

———. "Ely Abbey." In Lapidge et al., *Blackwell Encyclopaedia*, 166–67.

———. "Ely Abbey 672–1109." In Meadows and Ramsay, ed. *History of Ely Cathedral*, 3–58.

———. "Queen Emma and *The Encomium Emmae Reginae*." Introduction to the 1998 Reprint. *Encomium Emmae Reginae*, ed. Campbell, [xiii-lxxx].

———. "Re-reading King Æthelred the Unready." In Bates et al., *Writing Medieval Biography*, 77–97.

Kiernan, Kevin S. *Beowulf and the Beowulf Manuscript*. New Brunswick, NJ: Rutgers University Press, 1981; rev. ed., Ann Arbor: University of Michigan Press, 1996.

———. "The Eleventh-Century Origin of *Beowulf* and the *Beowulf* Manuscript." In Chase, ed., *The Dating of Beowulf*, 9–21. Repr. in *Anglo-Saxon*

Manuscripts: Basic Readings, ed. Mary P. Richards. New York: Garland Publishing Inc., 1994, 277–99.

———. "The Legacy of Wiglaf: Saving a Wounded *Beowulf*." In Baker, ed. *Beowulf: Basic Readings*, 195–218.

Klaeber, Frederick. "*Aeneis* und *Beowulf*." *Archiv* 126 (1911): 40–48, 339–59.

———. "Die ältere *Genesis* und der *Beowulf*." *Englische Studien* 42 (1910): 321–88.

———. "Die christlichen Elemente im *Beowulf*." *Anglia* 35 (1911–12). Translated by Paul Battles as *The Christian Elements in Beowulf*. Subsidia 24. Kalamazoo, MI: Medieval Institute Publication, 1996.

Klein, Stacy S. *Ruling Women: Queenship and Gender in Anglo-Saxon Literature*. South Bend, IN: University of Notre Dame Press, 2006.

Körner, Sten. *The Battle of Hastings: England and Europe 1035–1066*. Lund: C. W. K. Gleerup, 1964.

Lapidge, Michael. "The Anglo-Latin Background." In Stanley B. Greenfield and Daniel G. Calder, *A New Critical History of English Literature, With a Survey of the Anglo-Latin Background by Michael Lapidge*. New York: New York University Press, 1986, 5–37.

———. "The Archetype of *Beowulf*." *ASE* 29 (2000): 5–41.

———. "*Beowulf* and the Psychology of Terror." In *Heroic Poetry in the Anglo-Saxon Period: Studies in Honor of Jess B. Bessinger, Jr.*, ed. Helen Damico and John Leyerle. Kalamazoo, MI: Medieval Institute Publications, 1993, 373–402.

———. "Three Latin Poems from Æthelwold's School in Winchester." *ASE* 1 (1972): 85-137.

Lawrence, William Witherle. *Beowulf and Epic Tradition*. 1928; repr. New York: Hafner Publishing, 1963.

———. "*Beowulf* and the Saga of Samson the Fair." In Malone and Ruud, eds., *Studies in English Philology*, 172–81.

———. "Grendel's Lair." *JEGP* 38 (1939): 477–80.

———. "The Haunted Mere in *Beowulf*." *PMLA* 27 (1912): 208–45.

Lawson, M. K. *Cnut: The Danes in England in the Early Eleventh Century*. London and New York: Longman, 1993.

Layher, William. *Queenship and Voice in Medieval Northern Europe*. New York: Palgrave Macmillan, 2010.

Lee, Alvin A. "Symbolism and Allegory." In Bjork and Niles, eds., *A Beowulf Handbook*, 233–54.

Liberman, Anatoly. "Beowulf-Grettir." In *Germanic Dialects: Linguistic and Philological Investigations*, ed. Bela Brogyanyi and Thomas Krömmelbein. Amsterdam: J. Benjamins, 1986, 353–401.

Lipshitz, Felice. "*Encomium Emmae Reginae*: A 'Political Pamphlet' of the Eleventh Century?" *Haskins Society Journal* 1 (1989): 39–50.

Liuzza, Roy Michael. "On the Dating of *Beowulf*." In Baker, ed., *Beowulf: Basic Readings*, 281–302.

Mackie, W. S. "The Demons' Home in *Beowulf*." *JEGP* 37 (1938): 455–61.

Magennis, Hugh. "Adaptation of Biblical Details in the Old English *Judith*: The Feast Scene." *Neuphilologische Mitteilungen* 84 (1983): 331–37.

———. "The '*Beowulf*' Poet and His '*Druncne Dryhtguman*.'" *Neuphilologische Mitteilungen* 86 (1985): 159–64.

———. *Images of Community in Old English Poetry*. Cambridge, UK: Cambridge University Press, 1996.

———. "Saxo Grammaticus and the Heroic Past: Feasting in the *Gesta Danorum*." *Journal of Historical Linguistics and Philology* 2 (1985): 2–13.

———. "The Treatment of Feasting in the *Heliand*." *Neophilologus* 69 (1985): 126–33.

Magoun, Francis P., Jr. "Danes, North, South, East, and West, in *Beowulf*." In *Philologica: The Malone Anniversary Studies*, ed. Thomas A. Kirby and Henry Bosley Woolf. Baltimore, MD: Johns Hopkins Press, 1949, 20–24.

———. "On the Old Germanic Altar- or Oath-Ring (*Stallahringr*)." *Acta Philologica Scandinavica* 20 (1949): 277–93.

Malone, Kemp. "The Daughter of Healfdene." In Malone and Ruud, eds., *Studies in English Philology*, 139–58.

———. "Grendel and His Abode." In *Studia Philologica et Litteraturia in Honorem L. Spitzer*, ed. A. G. Hatcher and K. L. Selig. Bern: Francke, 1958, 297–308.

———. "Hrethric." *PMLA* 42 (1923): 268–312.

————. "A Note on *Beowulf* 1231." *Modern Language Notes* 41 (1926): 466–67.

————. "Review of *Beowulf: An Introduction to the Study of the Poem with a Discussion of the Stories of Offa and Finn* by R. W. Chambers." *English Studies* 14 (1932): 190–93.

Malone, Kemp, and Martin B. Ruud, ed. *Studies in English Philology: A Miscellany in Honor of Frederick Klaeber.* Minneapolis, MN: University of Minnesota Press, 1929.

McConchie, R. W. "Grettir Ásmundarson's Fight with Kárr the Old: A Neglected *Beowulf* Analogue." *English Studies* 63 (1982): 481–86.

McCormick, Michael. *Origins of the European Economy: Communications and Commerce, A.D. 300–900.* Cambridge, UK; New York: Cambridge University Press, 2001.

McKee, Helen. "Script, Anglo-Saxon." In Lapidge et al., *Blackwell Encyclopaedia,* 409–10.

McKinnell, John. "Þorgerðr Hölgabrúðr and Hyndluljóð." In *Mythological Women: Studies in Memory of Lotte Motz,* ed. Rudolf Simek and Wilhelm Heizmann. Vienna: Fassbaender, 2002, 265–90.

McNulty, J. Bard. "The Lady Aelfgyva in the *Bayeux Tapestry.*" *Speculum* 55 (1980): 659–68.

Meadows, Peter, and Nigel Ramsay, eds. *A History of Ely Cathedral.* Woodbridge, UK: The Boydell Press, 2003.

Mellinkoff, Ruth. "Cain's Monstrous Progeny in *Beowulf*: Part I, Noachi Tradition." *ASE* 8 (1979): 143–62.

————. *The Horned Moses in Medieval Art and Thought.* Berkeley: University of California Press, 1970.

————. *Outcasts: Signs of Otherness in Northern Europe of the Late Middle Ages,* 2 vols. Berkeley: University of California Press, 1993.

Metzger, Bruce M., and Michael D. Coogan, eds. *The Oxford Companion to the Bible.* New York, Oxford: Oxford University Press, 1993.

Miller, Edward. *The Abbey and Bishopric of Ely.* Cambridge, UK: Cambridge University Press, 1951.

Miller, Sean. "Edward the Martyr." In Lapidge et al., *Blackwell Encyclopaedia,* 163.

Miller, William Ian. "Choosing the Avenger: Some Aspects of the Blood-feud in Medieval Iceland and England." *Law and History Review* 1 (1984): 159–204.

Mortensen, Lars Boje. "Stylistic Choice in a Reborn Genre: The National Histories of Widukind of Corvey and Dudo of St. Quentin." In *Dudone di San Quintino*, ed. Paolo Gatti. Trento: Università degli studi di Trento, 1995, 77–102.

Müllenhoff, Karl. *Beovulf: Untersuchungen über das angelsächsische Epos und die älteste Geschichte der germanischen Seevölker*. Berlin: Weidmann, 1889.

Musset, Lucien. *The Bayeux Tapestry*, trans. Richard Rex. New edition. Woodbridge, UK: Boydell Press, 2005.

———. "Rouen et l'Angleterre vers l'an mil: du nouveau sur le satiriste Garnier et l'école littéraire de Rouen au temps de Richard II." *Annales de Normandie* 24 (1974): 287–90.

Neidorf, Leonard. "VII Æthelred and the Genesis of the *Beowulf* Manuscript." *Philological Quarterly* 89, nos. 2–3 (2010): 119–39.

Nelson, Janet L. "The Earliest English *Ordo*: Some Liturgical and Historical Aspects." In Nelson, *Politics and Ritual in Early Medieval Europe*.

———. "Early Medieval Rites of Queen-Making and the Shaping of Medieval Queenship." In Duggan, ed., *Queens and Queenship in Medieval Europe*, 301–15.

———. "Inauguration Rituals." In Nelson, *Politics and Ritual in Early Medieval Europe*.

———. "National Synods, Kingship and Royal Anointing." In Nelson, *Politics and Ritual in Early Medieval Europe*.

———. *Politics and Ritual in Early Medieval Europe*. London: Hambledon, 1986.

———. "Queens." In Lapidge et al., *Blackwell Encyclopaedia*, 383–84.

———. "Ritual and Reality in the Early Medieval *Ordines*." In Nelson, *Politics and Ritual in Early Medieval Europe*.

———. "The Second English *Ordo*." In Nelson, *Politics and Ritual in Early Medieval Europe*.

Nelson, Janet L., and Peter W. Hammond. "Coronation." In Szarmach et al., *Medieval England*, 207–9.

Newman de Vegar, Carol. "A Paean for a Queen." *Old English Newsletter* 26 (1992): 57–58.

Niles, John D. *Beowulf: The Poem and Its Tradition.* Cambridge, MA: Harvard University Press, 1983.

———, ed. *Beowulf and Lejre.* Tempe, AZ: ACMRS, 2007.

———. "Myth and History." In Bjork and Niles, ed., *A Beowulf Handbook*, 213–32.

Noel, William. *The Harley Psalter.* Cambridge Studies in Palaeography and Codicology, 4. Cambridge, UK: Cambridge University Press, 1995.

Nordal, Sigurður. "Gunnhildur konungamóðir." *Samtíð og saga* 1 (1940): 135–55.

O'Keeffe, Katherine O'Brien. "Body and Law in Late Anglo-Saxon England." *ASE* 27 (1998): 209–32.

———. "Source, Method, Theory, Practice: Reading Two Old English Verse Texts." *Bulletin of the John Rylands University Library of Manchester* 76 (1994): 51–73.

Oleson, Tryggvi J. *The Witenagemot in the Reign of Edward the Confessor: A Study in the Constitutional History of Eleventh-Century England.* Toronto: University of Toronto Press, 1955.

Olrik, Axel. *The Heroic Legends of Denmark.* Trans. Lee M. Hollander. New York: American-Scandinavian Foundation, 1919.

Olsen, Alexandra Hennessey. "Gender Roles." In Bjork and Niles, eds., *A Beowulf Handbook*, 311–24.

Orchard, Andy. *A Critical Companion to Beowulf.* Cambridge, UK: D. S. Brewer, 2003.

———. "The Literary Background to the *Encomium Emmae Reginae*." *The Journal of Medieval Latin: A Publication of the North American Association of Medieval Latin* 11 (2001): 156–83.

———. *Pride and Prodigies: Studies in the Monsters of the Beowulf Manuscript.* Toronto: University of Toronto Press, 1995.

———. "Wulfstan the Homilist." In Lapidge et al., *Blackwell Encyclopaedia*, 494–95.

Osborn, Marijane. "The Great Feud: Scriptural History and Strife in

Beowulf." *PMLA* 93 (1978): 973–81. Repr. in Baker, *Beowulf: Basic Readings*, 111–25.

Oswald, Dana. *Monsters, Gender, and Sexuality in Medieval Literature*. Cambridge, UK: D. S. Brewer, 2010.

Otis, Brooks. "The Odyssean *Aeneid* and the Illiadic *Aeneid*." In *Virgil: A Collection of Critical Essays*, ed. Steele Commager. Englewood Cliffs, N.J.: Prentice-Hall, 1966, 89–106.

Owen-Crocker, Gale R. "Pomp, Piety, and Keeping the Woman in Her Place: The Dress of Cnut and Ælfgifu-Emma." In *Medieval Clothing and Textiles*, vol. 1, ed. Robin Netherton and Gale R. Owen-Crocker. Woodbridge, UK: Boydell Press, 2006, 41–52.

Page, R. I. *'A Most Vile People': Early English Historians on the Vikings*. London: Viking Society for Northern Research, 1987.

Panzer, Friedrich. *Studien zur germanischen Sagengeschichte, vol. 1: Beowulf*. Munich: C. H. Beck, 1910.

Pelteret, David A. E. *Slavery in Early Medieval England: From the Reign of Alfred to the Twelfth Century*. Woodbridge, UK: Boydell Press, 1995.

Poole, R. G. "Óttarr svarti." In Pulsiano et al., *Medieval Scandinavia*, 459–60.

———. "Sighvatr Þórðarson." In Pulsiano et al., *Medieval Scandinavia*, 580–81.

———. *Viking Poems on War and Peace: A Study in Skaldic Narrative*. Toronto: University of Toronto Press, 1991.

Pulsiano, Phillip. "Norse in England." In Pulsiano et al., *Medieval Scandinavia*, 166–70.

Rabin, Andrew. "Female Advocacy and Royal Protection in Tenth-Century England: The Legal Career of Queen Ælfthryth." *Speculum* 84 (2009), 261–88.

Rabkin, Eric S. *The Fantastic in Literature*. Princeton, NJ: Princeton University Press, 1976.

Rauer, Christine. *Beowulf and the Dragon: Parallels and Analogues*. Cambridge, UK: D. S. Brewer, 2000.

Reaney, P. H. *The Origin of English Place-Names*. London: Routledge and Paul, 1960.

———.*The Place-Names of Cambridgeshire and the Isle of Ely.* Cambridge, UK: The University Press, 1943.

Remley, Paul G. *Old English Biblical Verse: Studies in Genesis, Exodus and Daniel.* Cambridge, UK: Cambridge University Press. 1996.

Rendtorff, Rolf. *The Covenant Formula: An Exegetical and Theological Investigation.* Trans. Margaret Kohl. Edinburgh: T & T Clark, 1998.

Renoir, Alain. "The Terror of the Dark Waters: A Note on Virgilian and Beowulfian Techniques." In *The Learned and the Lewed: Studies in Chaucer and Medieval Literature*, ed. Larry D. Benson. Cambridge, MA: Harvard University Press, 1974, 147–60.

Robinson, Fred C. *Beowulf and the Appositive Style.* Knoxville: University of Tennessee Press, 1985.

———. "The Significance of Names in Old English Literature." *Anglia* 86 (1968): 14–59.

Rosier, James L. "*Heafod* and *Helm*: Contextual Composition in *Beowulf*." *Medium Ævum* 37 (1968): 137–41.

———. "The Uses of Association of Hands and Feasts in *Beowulf*." *PMLA* 78 (1963): 8–14.

Ross, Margaret Clunies. "Concubinage in Anglo-Saxon England." *Past and Present* 108 (August 1985): 3–34.

———. "Women and Power in the Scandinavian Sagas." In *Stereotypes of Women in Power: Historical Perspectives and Revisionist Views*, ed. Barbara Garlick, Suzanne Dixon, and Pauline Allen. New York: Greenwood Press, 1992, 105–19.

Rumble, Alexander R., ed. *The Reign of Cnut: King of England, Denmark and Norway.* Studies in the Early History of Britain. London & New York: Leicester University Press, 1994.

Samuel, Irene. "Semiramis in the Middle Ages: The History of a Legend." *Mediaevalia et Humanistica* 2 (1944): 32–44.

Sawyer, Bibi, and Peter Sawyer. *Medieval Scandinavia from Conversion to Reformation, c. 800–1500.* Minneapolis: University of Minnesota Press, 1993.

Sawyer, Peter. "Cnut's Scandinavian Empire." In Rumble, ed., *Reign of Cnut*, 10–22.

———. "Swein Forkbeard and the Historians." In *Church and Chronicle in the*

Middle Ages: Essays Presented to John Taylor, ed. I. Wood and G. A. Loud. London: Hambledon Press, 1991, 27–40.

Searle, Eleanor. "Emma the Conqueror." In *Studies in Medieval History Presented to R. Allen Brown*, ed. C. Harper-Bill et al. Woodbridge, UK: Boydell Press, 1989, 281–88.

———. "Fact and Pattern in Heroic History: Dudo of Saint-Quentin." *Viator* 15 (1984): 119–38.

———. *Predatory Kinship and the Creation of Norman Power, 840–1066*. Berkeley: University of California Press, 1988.

———. "Women and the Legitimization of Succession at the Norman Conquest." *Proceedings of the Battle Conference on Anglo-Norman Studies III* (1980), ed. R. Allen Brown. Woodbridge, UK: Boydell Press, 1981, 161–62.

Shippey, Thomas A. "The Fairy-Tale Structure of *Beowulf*." *Notes and Queries*, n.s. 16, no. 1 (January 1969): 2–11.

Sisam, Kenneth. *The Structure of Beowulf*. Oxford: Clarendon Press, 1965.

Stafford, Pauline. "Ælfthryth." In Lapidge et al., *Blackwell Encyclopaedia*, 9.

———. *The East Midlands in the Early Middle Ages*. Leicester, UK: Leicester University Press, 1985.

———. "Emma: The Powers of the Queen in the Eleventh Century." In Duggan, ed., *Queens and Queenship in Medieval Europe*, 3–26.

———. "Emma of Normandy." In Lapidge et al. *Blackwell Encyclopaedia*, 168–69.

———. "The King's Wife in Wessex 800–1066." *Past and Present* 91 (1981): 3–27.

———. "The Laws of Cnut and the History of Anglo-Saxon Royal Promises." *ASE* 10 (1982): 173–90.

———. "The Portrayal of Royal Women in England, Mid-Tenth to Mid-Twelfth Centuries." In *Medieval Queenship*, ed. John Carmi Parsons. New York: St. Martins Press, 1998, 143–67.

———. "Powerful Women in the Early Middle Ages: Queens and Abbesses." In *The Medieval World*, ed. Peter Linehan and Janet L. Nelson. London: Routledge, 2001, 398–415.

———. *Queen Emma and Queen Edith: Queenship and Women's Power in Eleventh-Century England.* Oxford: Blackwell, 1997.

———. *Queens, Concubines, and Dowagers: The Wife in the Early Middle Ages.* Athens, GA: University of Georgia Press, 1983.

———. "The Reign of Æthelred II: A Study in the Limitations of Royal Policy and Action." In Hill, ed., *Ethelred the Unready,* 15–46.

———. "Sons and Mothers: Family Politics in the Early Middle Ages." In *Medieval Women: Essays Presented to Professor Rosalind M. T. Hill,* ed. Derek Baker. Oxford: Basil Blackwell, 1978, 79–100.

———. *Unification and Conquest: A Political and Social History of England in the Tenth and Eleventh Centuries.* London: Hodder Arnold, 1989.

———. "Writing the Biography of Eleventh-Century Queens." In Bates et al., *Writing Medieval Biography,* 99–109.

Stanley, Eric Gerald. *In the Foreground: Beowulf.* Cambridge, UK: D. S. Brewer, 1994.

———. "Paleographical and Textual Deep Waters: <a> for <u> and <u> for <a>, <d> for <ð> and <ð> for <d> in Old English." *ANQ* 15, no. 2 (Spring 2002): 64–72.

Stenton, F. M. *Anglo-Saxon England.* 3rd ed. Oxford: Clarendon Press, 1971.

Stevenson, W. H. "An Alleged Son of King Harold Harefoot." *English Historical Review* 28 (1913): 112–17.

Stitt, J. Michael. *Beowulf and the Bear's Son: Epic, Saga, and Fairytale in Northern Germanic Tradition.* New York: Garland Publishing, Inc., 1992.

Stubbs, Charles William. *Historical Memorials of Ely Cathedral.* New York: Charles Scribner's Son; London: J. M. Dent & Co., 1897.

Thomas, R. G. "Some Exceptional Women in the Sagas." *Saga-Book of the Viking Society* 13 (1952–53): 307–27.

Thormann, Janet. "The *Anglo-Saxon Chronicle* Poems and the Making of the English Nation." In *Anglo-Saxonism and the Construction of Social Identity,* ed. Allen J. Frantzen and John D. Niles. Gainesville: University of Florida Press, 1997, 60–85.

Todorov, Tzvetan. *The Fantastic: A Structural Approach to a Literary Genre.* Trans. Richard Howard. Cleveland, OH: Press of Western Reserve University, 1973.

Tolkien, J. R. R.. *Beowulf: The Monsters and the Critics*. Repr. of 1936 *Proceedings of the British Academy*. Oxford, 1958.

———. "On Fairy-stories." In *The Tolkien Reader*. New York: Ballantine Books, 1966, 3–84.

Townend, Matthew. "Contextualizing the *Knútsdrápur*: Skaldic Praise-Poetry at the Court of Cnut." *ASE* 30 (2001): 145–79.

———. "Viking Age England as a Bilingual Society." In *Cultures in Contact: Scandinavian Settlement in England in the Ninth and Tenth Centuries*, ed. D. M. Hadley and J. D. Richards. Studies in the Early Middle Ages 2. Turnhout: Brepols, 2000, 89–105.

Treharne, Elaine. *Living Through Conquest: The Politics of Early England, 1020–1220*. Oxford: Oxford University Press, 2012.

Twomey, Michael W. "Allegory and Related Symbolism." In Szarmach et al., *Medieval England*, 22–26.

Tyler, Elizabeth M. "Crossing Conquests: Polyglot Royal Women and Literary Culture in Eleventh-Century England." *Conceptualizing Multilingualism in England, c. 800–1250*, ed. Elizabeth M. Tyler. Turnhout: Brepols, 2012, 171–96.

———. "'The Eyes of the Beholder Were Dazzled': Treasure and Artifice in the *Encomium Emmae Reginae*." *Early Medieval Europe* 8 (1999): 247–70.

———. "Fictions of Family: The *Encomium Emmae Reginae* and Virgil's *Aeneid*." *Viator* 36 (2005): 149–79.

———. "Talking about History in Eleventh-Century England: The *Encomium Emmae Reginae* and the Court of Harthacnut." *Early Medieval History* 13 (2005): 359–83.

van Houts, Elisabeth M. C. "Historiography and Hagiography at Saint-Wandrille: The *Inventio et Miracula Sancti Vulfranni*." In *Anglo-Norman Studies* 12, *Proceedings of the Battle Conference 1989*, ed. Marjorie Chibnall. Woodbridge, UK: Boydell, 1990, 233–51.

———. "A Note on *Jezebel* and *Semiramis*, Two Latin Norman Poems from the Early Eleventh Century." *The Journal of Medieval Latin* 2 (1992): 18–24.

———. "The Political Relations between Normandy and England before 1066 according to the *Gesta Normannorum ducum*." In *Les mutations socio-culturelles au tournant des xie–xiie siècles*, ed. R. Foreville and C. Viola. Paris: Centre National de la Recherche Scientifique, 1984, 85–97.

———. "A Review of *Jezebel. A Norman Latin Poem of the Early Eleventh Century*, ed. Jan M. Ziolkowski." *Journal of Medieval Latin* 1 (1991), 204–6.

von Sydow, Carl W. "Beowulf och Bjarke." *Studier i nordisk filologi* 14:3. *Skrifter utgivna av svenska litteratursällskapet in Finland* 170 (1923): 1–46.

Ward, P. L. "The Coronation Ceremony in Mediaeval England." *Speculum* 14 (1939): 160–78.

———. "An Early Version of the Anglo-Saxon Coronation Ceremony." *English Historical Review* 57, no. 227 (1942): 345–61.

Wessén, E. "Nordiska personnamn på –*þiófr*." In *Uppsala Universitets Årsskrift*. Uppsala, 1927, 110–18.

Whaley, Diana. *Heimskringla: An Introduction*. Viking Society for Northern Research, 8. London: University College, 1991.

Whitbread, L. "The Hand of Æschere: A Note on *Beowulf* 1343." *Review of English Studies* 25 (1949): 339–42.

White, Hayden. Introduction, "The Poetics of History." *Metahistory: The Historical Imagination in Nineteenth-Century Europe*. Baltimore, MD: Johns Hopkins University Press, 1973.

———. *Tropics of Discourse: Essays in Cultural Criticism*. Baltimore, MD: Johns Hopkins University Press, 1978.

Whitelock, Dorothy. "Archbishop Wulfstan, Homilist and Statesman." *Transactions of the Royal Historical Society* 4th ser. 24 (1942): 25–45.

———. *The Audience of Beowulf*. Oxford: Clarendon Press, 1951.

———. "The Dealings of the Kings of England with Northumbria." In Clemoes, ed., *The Anglo-Saxons*, 70–88.

———. "Scandinavian Personal Names in the *Liber Vitae* of Thorney Abbey." *Saga-Book of the Viking Society for Northern Research* 12 (1937–45): 127–53.

Whitman, Jon. *Allegory: The Dynamics of an Ancient and Medieval Technique*. Oxford: Clarendon Press, 1987.

Wilcox, Jonathan. "The *Battle of Maldon* and the *Anglo-Saxon Chronicle*, 979–1016: A Winning Combination." *Proceedings of the Medieval Association of the Midwest* 3 (1996): 34.

Williams, Ann. *Æthelred the Unready: The Ill-Counselled King*. London: Hambledon and London, 2003.

———. "Cockles Amongst the Wheat: Danes and English in the West Midlands in the First Half of the Eleventh Century." *Midland History* 11 (1986): 1–22.

———. *The English and the Norman Conquest*. Woodbridge, UK: Boydell Press, 1995.

———. *Kingship and Government in Pre-Conquest England, c. 500–1066*. New York: St. Martin's Press, 1999.

———. "Leofric." In Lapidge et al., *Blackwell Encyclopaedia*, 282.

Williams, David. *Cain and Beowulf: A Study in Secular Allegory*. Toronto: University of Toronto Press, 1982.

Wilson, David M. *The Bayeux Tapestry*. London: Thames and Hudson, 1985.

Wilson, R. M. *The Lost Literature of Medieval England*. London: Methuen & Co. Ltd, 1952.

Wormald, F[rancis]. *The Benedictional of St. Ethelwold*. London: Faber and Faber, 1959.

———. *English Drawings of the Tenth and Eleventh Centuries*. London: Faber and Faber, 1952.

Wormald, Patrick. "Engla Lond: The Making of an Allegiance." *Journal of Historical Sociology* 7 (1994): 1–24.

———. *The Making of English Law: King Alfred to the Twelfth Century*, vol. 1: *Legislation and Its Limits*. London: Blackwell Publishers, 1999.

Wright, C. E. *The Cultivation of Saga in Anglo-Saxon England*. Edinburgh and London: Oliver and Boyd, 1939.

Yorke, B. A. E. "Council, King's." In Lapidge et al., *Blackwell Encyclopaedia*, 124–25.

Index

Abels, Richard, 126, 131n57

Aeneid, 14, 18–19

Ailred of Rievaulx, 61

Ælfgar, estate of, 190

Ælfgifu (Emma's English name at marriage to Æthelred), 216

Ælfgifu (Morcar's daughter), 190

Ælfgifu of Northampton: accused of accidently poisoning Harthcnut, 163–64; accused of sorcery, 163–64; accused of treachery, 171–72; aspiration to be konungamóðir (mother of kings), 153, 161, 173–76; Cnut's alliance with, 143–44, 156, 175; Cnut's sons with, 25, 108; as Cnut's unofficial queen, 29, 39, 109, 161, 187, 197–98, 200–202; compared to Gunnhildr, 167, 169; Emma and, 149–50, 161, 185; Grendel's mother compared to, 150–51, 180–81, 185; Harold Harefoot and, 38–39, 75, 101, 136, 141, 148–49, 152–55, 159, 161, 173–74; Jezebel as allegory of, 25n62, 31; Óláfr Haraldsson and, 159–60, 170; powerful Mercian family of, 39, 109, 136, 149–50, 175, 186–90, 194, 199; promiscuity of, 159–60, 169, 180–81; as queen mother, 149, 161, 165–67; queen of Heorot compared to, 149–50; reign in Norway, 109, 157–59, 165–67,

170–72, 288; sons of, 58–59, 148, 153–55, 157–59; Sveinn and, 108, 146, 148, 157–59, 170–72; unsympathetic portrayals of, 153–56, 163, 175; various accounts of, 161–62

Ælfhelm, 109, 187, 190–97

Álfífa. See Ælfgifu of Northampton

Álfífa in ríka (Álfífa the powerful). See Ælfgifu of Northampton

Alfred, King, 10n23; Great Heathen Army vs., 129, 131n57; peace pact with Guthrum, 254, 280

Alfred atheling, 99, 131n57; Æschere as parallel to, 75–76, 85–86; Beowulf's parallels to murder of, 71, 84; betrayal of, 194, 295; documentation of murder of, 38–39, 56–58, 61, 66–71; Emma trying to assure as Cnut's successor, 235–36; Godwine's betrayal of, 67–69, 86–87, 91–92; murder of men under, 67–69; murder ordered by Harold, 64, 140, 149; mutilation of, 69–70, 76, 194; as possible successor to throne, 58, 66, 137, 142, 202, 214; revenge for murder of, 88–93

Ælfric of Eynsham, 22–24, 105, 271n131

Ælfthryth: influence in Æthelred's court, 170, 192, 195n89; as ko-

The Battle of Maldon, 14, 100, 125, 125n48

Bayeux Tapestry, Ælfgifu's portrayal in, 155–57

beaghroden cwēn (ring-adorned queen), 39. *See also* Wealhtheow

"Bear's Son Tale," 47–48, 49n16

Bede, 79–80, 291

beheading: of Æschere, 75–76; of Grendel, 93–94; of Harold's corpse, 39, 92–93, 294–296

beheading sequence, in Beowulf, 34, 41, 43, 46, 55; changing interpretations of, 37–38; possible influence of historical texts, 99–101; as refashioning of folklore, 44–45, 50; relation to political events, 45–46, 56–57, 85–87

Beowulf: acknowledged as future ruler, 241–44, 246; character of, 33–34, 55–56; Danes and, 252–53, 255; descent into mere, 82, 83n81, 93; effects of killing Grendel, 121–22, 243; fight with Grendel's mother, 44, 47n11, 179; Hrothgar and, 205–6, 243–44; not to inherit kingdom, 263; presenting Grendel's head to Hrothgar, 41, 95–96; as protector of Wealhtheow's sons, 254, 260–61; rewards for killing Grendel, 243, 247, 254–55, 263; warriors under, 126n49, 286–87; Wealhtheow giving ring to, 255, 282; Wealhtheow's speech to, 237–38

Beowulf-poet: balancing roles, 51–52; and Genesis A, 258–64; influences on, 56, 267–73, 282–83, 292–94; making history fictional, 214–15, 265-267; rhetorical devices used by, 176–77; rhetorical stance of, 115–16, 130; style of, 84, 224–26, 234–35; use of history by, 284

Bible, 244, 259n113; allusions to, 242; psalms in Harley Psalter, 267–83; reconstructed materials in Cotton Vitellius A.xv, 36–37; style of, 257–64; use in allegorical poetry, 21–24

Biddle, Martin, 293

Bishop, Terence A. M., 268n124

Björkman, Erik, 226–28

Blickling Homilies, 77

Bloomfield, Josephine, 205n2, 250n99

Boethius, on avarice, 186

Bolton, Timothy, 209n7

Bolton, W. F., 136

Bredehoft, Thomas, 66, 129n55

Burton Abbey, 188, 189, 191

Cain: allusions to, 37–38, 84–85, 94; Harold and Grendel linked to, 33-34, 71, 84–85, 140, 184

Campbell, Alastair, 14n36, 138n67, 217, 219n37

Carolingian script, 7n12

Carruthers, Mary, 277

Chadwick, Nora, 179–80

Chambers, R. W., 49, 55–56

Chance, Jane, 180n50

Christ and Satan, 184

Christ Church, 270–74, 280–82

Clark, Cecily, 108

classics, reconstructed materials from, 36–37

Clayton, Mary, 23–24

Cnut: accession to English throne, 199–201, 285

compositional methods, 23; compression of 2, 110, 116, 119–120; history made into poetry by,

286; of narrative lines, 18, 36; reconstructed materials in, 17–18, 36–37; role of rumination in, 277; substitution, 2, 16–17. *See also* style

concubinage, not recognized by Church, 143

Conrad II, Holy Roman Emperor, 146

Cotton Vitellius A.xv, 4, 36; dating of, 5–6; as eleventh-century manuscript, 8, 292

"Courtenay Compendium," 209n7

Cronan, Dennis, 54

culture, Anglo-Danish, 8, 10–11, 15–16, 293–95

Danelaw, 10n23, 24, 129

Danes, 104, 119, 157, 289; atrocities in England by, 65, 105, 110–15, 139, 287; attacks on England by, 102–3, 117, 123, 128–34, 195, 202; all of Æthelred's England to, 109–12, 198–99; Grendel's Reign of Terror equated to attacks by, 107–8, 119, 121–23, 126, 130, 287, 293; Harold Harefoot linked to destructiveness of, 66, 107, 140; Harold's burial by, 90, 93, 95; incompetence of English against, 284, 287; Norway vs., 149, 214; St. Brice's Day massacre of, 104, 129; Sveinn and, 172, 198–99, 289

Danes, in Beowulf, 256, 288; Grendel and, 118, 139

dating, of Beowulf, 4–5, 10n23, 11n26, 45, 100, 131n57; eleventh-century culture and, 8, 16; evidence for eleventh-century composition, 39–40, 131, 291–92; scribal hands in, 7–8, 46; skaldic verse in, 9–11

dating, of skaldic verse, 8n17

Davis, Craig R., 10n23, 131n57

De regina Emma (Godfrey), 229–30

"The Death of Alfred," 66, 100

The Death of Edward the Martyr, 66n57

decapitation. See beheading

Deda, on Ely, 81

democracy, after Cnut's death, 214

demons, Grendel symbolizing, 33–34

Denmark, 199, 234; Harthacnut ruling, 58–59, 136, 144, 149, 214, 280n154

dragon, symbolism of, 288–89

Dronke, Peter, 25–28

Duchesne, André, 208n7

Dudo, compositional methods of, 10n24

Duffey, Judith E., 267n123, 271–73; on Harley Psalter, 275, 278–79, 281–82

Duggan, Joseph, 17

Dumville, David N., 6, 7, 291

dynastic crises, 3, 66, 104–5, 197, 200; after Cnut's death, 35-36 58–59, 134, 136; Ælfgifu's manipulations in, 173–74; Æthelred and sons in, 195; effects of Cnut's two queens on, 202, 223; emergence of hetzerin in, 169–70; in history vs. in Beowulf, 250–51; mothers and sons in, 39, 174–75; paternity controversy and, 141–49, 153, 157–59

Eadred, claim to English throne, 195

Eadric Streona, 111, 193, 194, 199; Ælfhelm's murder and, 193, 197; supporting power shift to Wessex, 196–97

Eadgyth, inheritance of, 189–90

Earl Harald, 147–48

East Anglia, 38, 77–83, 84, 97, 119

Edgar, King, 175n44, 192

Edith, Queen, 295

Edmund Ironside, King, 129, 133, 188, 195; half-rule of Wessex, 120, 139, 200, 215; seizing lands of Sigeferth and Morcar, 199–200

Edward, King (the Confessor), 60, 99, 197; age relative to brother, 85–86; as Æthelred's heir apparent, 199, 223, 235, 251; claim to English throne, 142, 195; effects of mother's marriage on rights of succession, 25, 29, 223; Godwine's reparations to, 91–92; as Harthacnut's successor, 231, 235–36, 266; Harthacnut's treatment of, 88, 92; as possible successor after Cnut's death, 58, 202, 214; reign of, 4, 218, 240

Edward, King (the Martyr), 96–97, 104, 150–51, 175n44, 192

Einarr þambarskelfir, 170–71

Eiríkr Blóðøx (Bloodaxe), 162, 168

Ely, Isle of, 64–65, 78n68, 97; Alfred taken to, 70–71; eels and other fish around, 79n70, 81–82; inaccessibility of, 79–81; monastery on, 79, 83n81, 97, 213; as parallel to Grendel's mere, 83; royal patronage for abbey at, 97–99

embellishment, in creation of narrative, 18

Emma of Normandy, Queen, 155n3, 173, 214, 229n58, 266; Ælfgifu and, 150, 185, 201–2; allegorical treatments of, 24–25; ancestors of, 217, 229–30, 235; as Æthelred's queen, 99, 104, 195, 217–18; Christ Church and, 280–81; Cnut and, 30, 39,

212–13, 219–21; Cnut's fetching of, 218–19, 223–24; Cnut's marriage contract with, 218, 233, 234; Cnut's marriage to, 29, 37, 200, 215–17, 223, 224; as Cnut's queen, 201–02, 208, 211–12; as co-ruler with Cnut, 211–12, 266; as co-ruler with Harthacnut, 266; De regina Emma about, 229–30; and dynastic inheritance, 24–25, 29

Encomium Emmae Reginae, 3, 18–19, 111n22, 153, 209n7; Alfred's murder in, 61–62, 66–71; circulation of, 294–95; on Cnut, 218, 251–52, 277; commissioned by Emma, 295; on conquest of England, 132–33; on Danish attacks on England, 30, 108, 133–34; on Emma, 39, 231, 234, 266n121; ending of, 240–41, 282–83; frontispiece image in, 230, 239–40; on Harold, 99, 136–41, 139, 293; on Harthacnut, 237–38, 245; impetus for, 132n58, 230–31; influence on Beowulf, 265, 294; influences on, 99–101, 237n74; introduction of Emma in, 231–34; style of, 100, 209–10, 234–35

England, 24n61, 157; Æthelred's defense of, 104, 127–9, 287; atrocities against Danes in, 104, 107; Beowulf's Heorot as, 35; as center of Anglo-Danish kingdom, 15, 45–46; Cnut changing from ravager to king of, 129–30, 133–34; Cnut's accession to throne of, 32–33, 37; Danes' atrocities in, 65–66, 110–11, 140, 287; Danes' attacks on, 117, 123, 130–31, 131n57, 139, 195, 202; Danes' invasions of, 22, 30, 102–03, 105n7, 109–15, 133, 159–60; Danes taking over, 108–9, 198–99, 221–23, 287; divided into half-rules, 120, 138–39, 149, 200, 273; Grendel's Reign of Terror equated to Danes' attacks on, 107–8, 121–23, 126, 130, 287, 293; Harold Harefoot's reign over, 136–41, 149, 161; Norman invasions of, 110, 217–18; Normandy's relations with, 28, 142, 217–19, 236; place-names of, 52–54; poetry traditions in, 27–28, 33; political chaos in, 38, 102–5, 117, 285; succession crises in, 35–36, 58–59, 104–5, 157–58; Sveinn's conquest of, 108–9, 132–33, 198–99; topography of, 52–55, 54n30, 77n66, 78–79; unification of, 201, 209, 215, 234; waves of conquests of, 120

epics, 5n7, 5n9, 36, 50, 85; Old English, 209–10

epics, vernacular, 251, 291; heroic, 10, 34, 283; history reconstructed into, 17–18, 97, 107–8, 214–15; secular, 2, 14, 285

Eustace, count of Boulogne, 60n44

Exodus, as allegorical, 22–23

Fagrskinna, on Sveinn and Ælfgifu's reign in Norway, 158–59, 166–67, 170–72

fantasy, literary uses of, 35

feud narratives, 41–42, 45

Five Boroughs, 189, 194

Fjalldal, Magnús, 48n13, 49n16, 50

folklore, 50; elements in Beowulf, 48–49, 55–56; Grettis saga Ásmundarsonar as, 46, 49n16, 96; Icelandic, 46, 55–56, 116n38, 167–68; influence on Beowulf, 44–45, 47n11, 50; narratives of Grendel's Reign of Terror compared to, 116–17; stories of Gunnhildr in, 167–68

Frank, Roberta, 8, 12n28, 51, 117, 223n43, 263n117; in dating of Beowulf, 10–13; on skaldic verse, 8–10

Freeman, E. A., 90, 148

Freeman, Eric F., 155n3

Fulk, Robert D., 5

Gainsborough Accord, 198

Galloway, Andrew, on queens poems, 25–27, 31–32

Gameson, Richard, 276n143

Gardner, John, 35n87

Geats, 10n23, 11n25, 15, 126n49; Beowulf as prince of, 249m98, 258n112

gelād, 78n68, 80

Gelling, Margaret, 52–54

Gesta Normanorum Ducum (William of Jumièges), 61

Gifstōl passage, 2, 38, 132, 134–41, 293

God, 135–36, 138–39, 184, 265; Abraham and, 258–59, 262–63; speeches in Genesis, 257–64

Godden, Malcolm, 21–22

Godfrey, De regina Emma by, 229–30, 235

Godgifu (Emma's daughter), 60n44, 230n58

Godwine, 59, 142, 150; Alfred's murder by, 65, 67–69, 86–87, 91–92; defecting to Harold Harefoot, 60–61, 65; at exhumation and desecration of Harold's corpse, 90–91; Hrothgar as parallel to, 71–74

Godwinson, Harold, 156

Goldsmith, Margaret E., 33–34

Gormr gamli, King, 162

Graham, Timothy C., 46n10

Great Heathen Army, 129, 130–31

Greenfield, Stanley B., 43

Grendel, in Beowulf, 98, 185; attacks on Heorot by, 2, 45, 107–8, 115–16, 122–24; beheading of, 37–38, 41, 43–45, 93–94; Beowulf's fight with, 44; Beowulf's rewards for killing, 243, 247; characterizations of, 33–34, 75, 118–19; compared Icelandic folklore, 116n38; Danes vs., 94, 118; head of, 95–96; interpretations of realm of, 51–52, 54–55; mother as extension of, 74–75, 84, 183–84; mother's search for vengeance for, 42, 177–78; night-rule by, 38, 129–30, 139–40; as parallel to invading Danes, 107–8, 115, 140; paternity of, 2, 38, 75, 140–41, 183–84; realm of, 76–83, 82–83; tribute expected in peace negotiations with, 127–28

Grendel's mother, 2, 38, 170; Ælfgifu compared to, 109, 150–51, 180–81, 185, 288; Æschere killed by, 75, 176; attack by, 41, 44, 71–75, 256; Beowulf's fight with, 44, 47n11, 179; descriptions of, 75, 176–80, 182–83; as extension of Grendel, 74–75, 84; as konungamóðir, 176–87; seeking vengeance, 42, 185–86; as uncanny depiction of powerful women, 179–80, 182

Grettis saga Ásmundarsonar, 46, 49n16, 50–51, 54–56, 96

Grímkel, Bishop, 170

Grimm, Jacob, 252, 290–91

Grønbech, V., 217

Gunnhild (Harthacnut's sister, Emma and Cnut's daughter), 173–74, 230n58

Gunnhildr (or Sígríðr), possibly Cnut's mother, 146

Gunnhildr, sister of Sveinn, avenged for murder on St. Brice's Day, 128

Gunnhildr konungamóðir (mother of kings), 162, 164, 173, 175–76; stories of, 167–69

Gunnor, Emma's mother, 27, 217

Guthlac's fenland, descriptions of, 77–78

Guthred, king of Northumbria, 254, 280n152

Guthrum, 254, 280

Gyða, mother of Tryggvi Óláfsson, 158

Hall, David, 80

Haraldr blátonn (bluetooth), 162n17

Haraldr hárfagri Hálfdanarson, 160

Haraldr inn grenski, 160

Harley Psalter Illustrations: compared to Utrecht's, 267–73, 275–78, 280-283; potential influence on Beowulf, 274–78, 282–83

Harold Harefoot, King: accession to throne, 109, 149, 174n42, 209; Ælfgifu helping secure throne for, 173–74; Alfred sent to, 60, 64, 73; beheading of corpse of, 39, 57, 88–93, 294–95; death of, 214; as embodiment of brutal earlier Danes, 66, 107, 140; Godwine defecting to, 60–61; Grendel as allegory of, 140; as half-king of Mercia, 149, 201; head of, 92–93; lineage disparaged, 152–54; not resembling Cnut, 144–45, 184; paternity of, 141–49, 152–55, 159–60, 214; persistence in seizing throne, 136, 139–40

Harris, Richard L., 49n16

hart, symbolism of, 274–75, 276n145

Harthacnut, King, 157, 172, 280;

Álfífa accidently poisoning of, 163–64; death of, 164; Edward as appointed successor to, 231, 266; Emma and, 39, 203, 235-236, 239–40, 266; Godwine and, 87, 91–92; orders beheading of Harold's corpse, 57, 89–93, 294–95; reign of, 88–89, 92, 241, 265–66, 294–95; reigning in Denmark, 58–59, 149, 280n154; return to England, 88, 209, 237–38

Hasler, Rolf, 270–74

Heaney, Seamus, 54n31

heathenism, Danes regressing to, 139

Heimskringla, 18, 157, 176

Helgi poems, 11–12, 11n26, 12n28

Heller, Rolf, 168

Henry of Huntingdon, 108–10

Heorot, 3, 149, 274, 283, 287; attackers of, 181–82; Beowulf and, 13, 241–42, 246, 255; as England, 35; Grendel's attacks on, 45n7, 107–8, 116–28, 285; Grendel's stranglehold on, 38, 129–30, 140; Hrothgar's reign in, 122–23, 247–49; Wealhtheow in, 206–08

hetzerin (goader) type, 162, 169–70

Hincmar, Bishop, 210n9, 211n12

Historia Anglorum (Henry of Huntingdon), 109–10

historiography: imaginative, 18, 176, 291; interrelationships of poetry and history, 18–19; rhetoric of, 108, 110–12

history: Beowulf-poet's use of, 36, 214–15, 286; poetry and, 18–19, 265, 286, 289–91; reconstructed in vernacular epics, 17–18, 107–8

Homer, 14n36

Homily on Esther (Ælfric), 23–24

Hondscio, Grendel consuming, 185

Horner, Shari, 180n50

Howe, Nicholas, 22

Hrethric, in Beowulf, 149, 247, 249–50

Hrothgar, 34, 45, 94, 120, 131n57, 182, 274; on Æschere's murder, 42, 177–78; in banquet scenes, 205, 253, 264; Beowulf and, 95–96, 205–6, 242–44; in Gifstōl passage, 135–36; ineffectiveness of, 122–24, 127–28; scop of, 19–20; successors to, 247–51; warriors' loyalty to, 121–22; witan of, 127–28, 181n51, 182

Hrothmund, in Beowulf, 149, 247, 249–50

Hrothulf, in Beowulf, 149, 247–51

Hume, Kathryn, 35n87

Immo, 161, 173–74

Ingeld, 256

Irving, Edward, 38, 253n102

Jarl Hákon, 179–80

Jezebel, 25–33, 202, 285–86; as allegory of Ælfgifu, 25n62, 31

Jochens, Jenny, 162, 168–69

John, Eric, 138n67, 230

John of Worcester, 108, 111, 187n60; on Harold's corpse, 89–93; on Harold's paternity, 154–55

John XV, Pope, 218n33

Judith. See Æthelwulf

Jupiter, Cnut compared to, 30

Karkov, Catherine E., 212–13, 239

Kaske, Robert, 225

Katz, Joshua T., 82n79

Ker, Neil, 6n11, 7

Keynes, Simon, 28, 58, 103n3, 174n42; on Æthelred, 106n8, 112–14; on Ely, 79n70, 97–98; on Emma, 216, 295; on Encomium Emmae Reginae, 132n58, 230, 295

Kiernan, Kevin S., 6, 45, 291

Klaeber, Frederick, 82n79, 247n95, 253n102; on Gifst^l passage, 135–36; on Grendel's Reign of Terror, 116–17; on umborwesendum, 251–52; on Wealhtheow's speeches, 257, 262n115

Knútsdrápur, as political poem, 8–9

Lady Philosophy. See Boethius

landowners: in Beowulf, 181n51, 182

landscapes: English topography related to Beowulf's, 52–55; Grendel's realm, 76–77; Grettis saga's Sandhaugar terrain linked to Beowulf, 50–51, 54–55

Lapidge, Michael, 5, 27–28, 33

Latin literature, in Anglo-Danish culture, 294–95

Lawrence, W. W., 48–50, 50–52, 54–55

Lawson, M. K., 201

Leofric, 59, 142, 149, 190, 201

Liber Eliensis, on Ely, 80–81

Liber Vitae of the New Minster and Hyde Abbey, 212–13

Liberman, Anatoly, 50

Life of Edward the Confessor, 296

Life of St. Edward the Confessor (Ailred of Rievaulx), 61

linguistics, in dating of Cotton Vitellius A.xv, 6–7

Liðsmannaflokkr, 221–23

London, 234; siege of, 220–22, 234; skaldic verse centered in, 8–9

Lot, exhortation to princes, 258n111

Mackie, W. S., 51–52

Magennis, Hugh, 204, 256–57

Magnús góði, 157, 158n8, 163–64, 172

Malone, Kemp, 51–52, 54–55

marriage, Christian vs. pagan customs of, 28

Maxims I, 210n9

McNulty, J. Bard, 155–57

mearc, 80n74

mere, 51, 77; Beowulf's descent into, 82, 83n81, 93, 126n49; East Anglian setting for, 38, 83; as Grendel's realm, 82–83

metaphors, 43, 56

metrics, in dating poems, 5n9

The "Missal" of St. Augustine's Abbey, 46n10

monsters, in Beowulf, 35–36, 289–90

Morcar, 189, 190n70, 194–99

Moriuht, queens poems compared to, 27, 31

Morkinskinna, on Ælfgifu, 163

narrative: compositional principles in creation of, 18; discontinuity of, 252; Germanic, 47–48; layers of, 49; multiple lines of, 36; parallel, 21–23; reconstruction of history, legend, myth, 13–14, 17, 36–37; shared, 20

Neidorf, Leonard, 117

Noel, William, 268n124

Nordal, Sigurður, 176n45

Normandy: Æthelred's sons in, 58, 136, 218; ducal house of, 28, 202; Emma and, 24–25, 217–18, 234–36; relations with England, 142,

Rouen, 28, 32–33
rumination, 277

Sarah in Genesis A, 258n111, 263
Satan, as outcast, 184
satires, 27, 30–33
Sawyer, Peter, 189n68, 190, 192n78
Saxo, 159–60
Saxon period, East-Anglian fenlands in, 78–79
Saxons, invasion by, 66n57
Scaldingi, Dane and Anglo-Saxon ancestral line, 10
Scandinavia, nicknames in, 228n56
Schichler, Robert, 274–75, 282
Scribe A, of Beowulf, 7–8, 16, 40, 46, 100
Scribe B, of Beowulf, 7, 46n10
scriptorium, lesser, 7
Scyld Scefing, 122, 133
Scylding kings, 11, 17
Scyldings, 1–3, 11n25, 14, 122–23
sea-wolf, Grendel's mother described as, 35, 101, 154, 179, 185
Semiramis, 25–33, 284–85; on Cnut and Emma, 30, 202, 218, 223
Sermo Lupi ad Anglos (Wulfstan), 102–4, 117, 285
sexuality, 180n50; Ælfgifu accused of promiscuity, 154–57, 159–60, 169–71, 180–81; attributed to powerful women, 28, 167, 224; in queens poems, 26n66, 27–8
Sigeferth, 194, 196, 198–99
Sigemund, 20
Sighvatr Þórðarson, 13, 158, 160, 165
Simeon of Durham, 254
Sisam, Kenneth, 247n95
skaldic verse, 8n17; Beowulf com-

pared to, 12n28, 15; in dating of Beowulf, 9–11; in Old Norse, 12–13
skalds, and Beowulf-poet, 293
Snorri Sturluson, 18, 108n13, 158n8, 162, 176
sorcery, 163–64, 168n28, 184
sovereignty, female, 2, 39, 205–7, 210, 239n77, 265
St. Brice's Day massacre, of Danes, 104, 129
Stafford, Pauline, 175, 191; on Emma, 211, 214, 265; on female sovereignty, 207–8, 210, 246, 265
Stanley, Eric, 287, 291
Stenton, Frank, 161
style, 108n12, 126, 131, 285; in analysis of literary parallels, 16–17, 20; of Anglo-Saxon Chronicle, 108, 112–14, 126; biblical, 258n112, 262n115; disparate elements woven into, 49–50; of Encomium, 209–210, 231, 234–235; of epics, 2, 85, 209–210; of histories, 108, 110–12, 214–215; of Jezebel and Semiramis, 25, 26n66; of Nordic and Anglo-Saxon poetry, 11, 277; popularity of word-play, 31–32, 225n49; of queens poems, 27; use of rhetorical devices in, 85, 87–88, 110–12. See also compositional methods
style, of Beowulf, 10n24, 34, 126; compared to biblical, 258n112, 264; Helgi poems compared to, 11–12; influences on, 237n74, 264; irony in, 127, 256; of narratives of Grendel's Reign of Terror, 115–17; rhetorical devices in, 43, 85, 131, 176–77, 252; similarity to Encomium's, 209–210, 234–235; skaldic verse compared to, 10–11, 15; sound-play in, 84, 224–26; use of pronouns in, 248–50
Sveinn Álfífuson: Ælfgifu and, 146,

148, 165–67, 170–72; claim to Cnut's throne, 145–46; death of, 172–76; paternity of, 145, 148, 154, 158–59; reign in Norway, 108, 144, 146–48, 157–59, 161, 165–67, 170–72

symbolism: of dragon, 289–90; of ring transferred, 278–79

Thietmar of Merseburg, 220–21

Thorkell Hávi, 133, 198–99, 273n135; in invasions of England, 115, 159–60

Thrond, at exhumation of Harold's corpse, 90

throne, English, 66, 103, 138, 139, 200, 218, 247; Cnut's accession of, 200; Grendel's desire for, 135, 140; Harthacnut claiming, 214, 245; mothers and sons in quest for, 153, 214, 251; violence and treachery in struggle for, 186, 202–3. *See also* dynastic crises

Tolkien, J. R. R., 34, 44, 135–36, 289, 292

Townend, Matthew, 8–9

treasure, 138, 290; for Beowulf, 254–55; Emma and, 209, 214; prominence in Beowulf, 135, 209, 236–37, 247

Treharne, Elaine, 297n21

tribute: Æthelred's payment of, 127–29; in peace negotiations with Grendel, 127–28

Tryggvaflokkr, 158

Tryggvi Óláffson, 158–59

Tungunes, battle at, 158–59

Tyler, Elizabeth M., 18–19, 209

Ufegeat, 191n77, 193

Uhtred of Bamburgh, 196, 198–99

Unferth, 87, 256

Utrecht Psalter: Harley and, 278, 282; illustrations of, 267–73, 275–76

van Houts, Elisabeth M. C.: on Cnut's marriage to Emma, 223–24; on Normandy's relations with England, 219–20; on queens poems, 25–31

Vestrfararvísur (Western Journeys, Sighvatr), 13

Vikingarvísur, 160

Vikings, 117, 217, 228. *See also* Danes

Virgil, 14, 266; epics and, 36, 286; influence of, 237n74, 277

Vita Ædwardi, 235, 251–52

Vita Ædwardi Regis, 61

Wanley, Humfrey, 3n6

Warner of Rouen, 27, 31

Wealhtheow, Queen, in Beowulf, 2; in banquet scenes, 204–7, 241, 252–55, 256–64; benediction by, 264–65, 281; compared to Emma, 224, 228–29, 234–38, 248, 252, 293; description of, 234–35, 236; female sovereignty of, 205–8; presents ring to Beowulf, 279, 283; power of, 246, 255–56; significance of name, 224–29, 236, 252; sons of, 249–51, 255, 260; speeches of, 206, 207n4, 248, 256–64

Wendland, Ælfgifu regent in, 202

Wessén, E., 228

Wessex, 191; Edmund's half-rule of, 139, 200; Emma holding throne in, 136, 142

West Mercians, royal supporting power shifts to Wessex, 196–97

West Saxon court, 4, 10n23, 14, 66, 66n57, 142; northward expansion of, 192–93, 196

Whaley, Diana, 18, 108, 176

White, Hayden, 107

Whitelock, Dorothy, 103n2, 201, 221

Widukind, compositional methods of, 10n24

Wilcox, Jonathan, 125–26

William of Jumièges, 61, 219

William of Malmesbury, 108; on desecration of Harold's corpse, 89, 92–93; on fall of Æthelred's England, 112–13

William the Conqueror, 81, 156, 218

Williams, Ann, 188, 190, 197n98

Williams, David, 33–34

Winchester, 9, 27

witan (councilors), 58–59, 184, 245; Æthelred's, 126–29, 198; election of Cnut's successor by, 141, 173; Hrothgar's, 127–28, 181n51, 182

wolves: Grendel described as, 101, 179, 185; land of, 150, 186

women, 108, 264n118; image included with monastic brotherhood, 281–282; as konungamóðir (mother of kings), 173, 174–75, 175–76; portrayals of powerful, 151, 162, 164, 167–69, 171–72, 179–80, 182, 239; sexuality attributed to powerful, 28, 167, 224; sovereignty of, 207–208, 246

Wormald, Francis, 269

Wrenn, C. L., 136

Wulfgeat, 189n68, 193

Wulfheah, 191, 193

Wulfric Spot, 142–43, 150, 188, 190–91

Wulfrun, 150, 186–89

Wulfrun kin, 188–92, 197–98

Wulfs of Mercia, 186

Wulfsige, 188n64

Wulfsige the Black, 190

Wulfstan, 115, 117, 129, 271, 285; as archbishop of York, 104–5; Sermo Lupi ad Anglos by, 102–4; use of allegory, 22–23

Ziolkowski, Jan M., 26–31

Þóra; as Þorgerðr Hölgabrúðr, 179–80

Þórarinn loftunga, as court poet, 148

About the Author

———

HELEN DAMICO is Professor Emerita of English Medieval Language and Literature at the University of New Mexico, where she was twice selected as Outstanding Teacher and honored as UNM Presidential Teaching Fellow. She is a founder of its Institute for Medieval Studies, a recipient of the New Mexico Humanities Award for Lifetime Contributions to the Humanities, and a member of The Medieval Academy of America and recipient of its CARA Award for Outstanding Service to Medieval Studies. She is also an Honorary Member of the International Society of Anglo-Saxonists. She edited the three volumes of *Medieval Scholarship: Biographical Essays in the Formation of a Discipline* and is the author of *Beowulf's Wealhtheow and the Valkyrie Tradition*.